Monographs in Theoretical Computer Science
An EATCS Series

Editors: W. Brauer G. Rozenberg A. Salomaa

On behalf of the European Association
for Theoretical Computer Science (EATCS)

Advisory Board: G. Ausiello M. Broy C. S. Calude
S. Even J. Hartmanis J. Hromkovič N. Jones
T. Leighton M. Nivat C. Papadimitriou D. Scott

T0142070

Springer
Berlin
Heidelberg
New York
Hong Kong
London
Milan
Paris
Tokyo

Zhou Chaochen
Michael R. Hansen

Duration Calculus
A Formal Approach to Real-Time Systems

With 20 Figures

 Springer

Authors

Prof. Zhou Chaochen
Chinese Academy of Sciences
Institute of Software
South Fourth Street 4
Zhong Guan Cun
100080 Beijing
China
zcc@ios.ac.cn

Assoc. Prof. Dr. Michael R. Hansen
Informatics and Mathematical Modelling
Technical University Denmark
Building 321
2800 Lyngby
Denmark
mrh@imm.dtu.dk

Series Editors

Prof. Dr. Wilfried Brauer
Institut für Informatik der TUM
Boltzmannstr. 3, 85748 Garching, Germany
Brauer@informatik.tu-muenchen.de

Prof. Dr. Grzegorz Rozenberg
Leiden Institute of Advanced Computer Science
University of Leiden
Niels Bohrweg 1, 2333 CA Leiden, The Netherlands
rozenber@liacs.nl

Prof. Dr. Arto Salomaa
Turku Centre for Computer Science
Lemminkäisenkatu 14 A, 20520 Turku, Finland
asalomaa@utu.fi

Library of Congress Cataloging-in-Publication Data

Zhou Chaochen, 1937–
Duration calculus: a formal approach to real-time systems / Zhou Chaochen, M. R. Hansen.
p. cm. – (EATCS monographs on theoretical computer science)
Includes bibliographical references and index.

1. Real-time data processing. 2. Formal methods (Computer science) 3. Mathematics–Data processing.
I. Hansen, Michael R., 1956– II. Title. III. Series.
QA76.54.H37 2004 005.2'73–dc22 2003066406

ACM Computing Classification (1998): D.2.1, D.2.4, D.3.1, F.3.1, F.4.3

ISBN 978-3-642-07404-2

This work is subject to copyright. All rights are reserved, whether the whole or part of the material is concerned, specifically the rights of translation, reprinting, reuse of illustrations, recitation, broadcasting, reproduction on microfilm or in any other way, and storage in data banks. Duplication of this publication or parts thereof is permitted only under the provisions of the German Copyright Law of September 9, 1965, in its current version, and permission for use must always be obtained from Springer-Verlag. Violations are liable for prosecution under the German Copyright Law.

Springer-Verlag is a part of Springer Science+Business Media

springeronline.com

© Springer-Verlag Berlin Heidelberg 2010
Printed in Germany

The use of general descriptive names, trademarks, etc. in this publication does not imply, even in the absence of a specific statement, that such names are exempt from the relevant protective laws and therefore free for general use.

Cover Design: KünkelLopka, Heidelberg

Printed on acid-free paper   45/3142/GF - 5 4 3 2 1 0

Preface

Duration calculus (abbreviated to DC) represents a logical approach to the formal design of real-time systems. In DC, real numbers are used to model *time*, and Boolean-valued (i.e. $\{0,1\}$-valued) functions over time are used to model *states* of real-time systems. The *duration* of a state in a time interval is the accumulated presence time of the state in the interval. DC extends *interval logic* to a calculus that can be used to specify and reason about properties of state durations.

Research on DC began during the ProCoS project (ESPRIT BRA 3104), when the project was investigating formal techniques for designing safety-critical real-time systems. In a project case study of a gas burner system, it was realized that state duration was useful for specifying the real-time behavior of computing systems. A research program on state duration was therefore initiated by the project in 1990. The first paper on DC was published in 1991. Since then, research on DC has covered the development of logical calculi, their applications and mechanical support tools. The success of DC has also stimulated similar research on other formal approaches.

The aim of this book is to present DC in a systematic and coherent way.

1. The book emphasizes the Boolean state model of real-time systems and its formalization in DC. The model comprises Boolean states, state transitions and events, and superdense transitions. The formalization is carried out in DC with both contracting and expanding interval modalities, so that not only safety properties but also liveness and fairness properties of real-time systems can be handled. In order to analyze the dependability of real-time systems, a probabilistic duration calculus is introduced.

2. The book explains how DC can be applied to formal specification and verification of real-time systems through selected case studies, which include software systems, e.g. a real-time scheduler, and software-embedded systems (also called hybrid systems), e.g. a gas burner.

3. The book provides readers with theoretical results on the completeness, decidability and a model-checking algorithm of DC. These results are fundamental to the mechanical support tools for DC, but the tools themselves are not elaborated on in the book.

Acknowledgments

The authors express their sincere thanks to C.A.R. Hoare and A.P. Ravn, the coauthors of the first publication on DC, to the other site leaders of the ProCoS project, i.e. D. Bjørner, H. Langmark and E.-R. Olderog, and to other colleagues who have contributed to the study of DC. We hope that all of their names and publications have been included in the references. Otherwise, we apologize for any mistake that we may have made.

The authors thank the following institutions and projects which have supported the authors in the preparation of this book: the Computer Science Laboratory, Institute of Software, Chinese Academy of Science; Informatics and Mathematical Modelling, Technical University of Denmark; the International Institute for Software Technology, United Nations University; and the Chinese Natural Science Foundation project 60273022.

October 2003,

Beijing   *Zhou Chaochen*
Lyngby   *Michael R. Hansen*

Contents

1. Introduction

1.1 Real-Time Systems

A real-time system is a computing system with real-time requirements. Let us consider the following two examples of real-time systems.

1.1.1 Two Examples

Deadline-Driven Scheduler

Consider a finite number of processes, say $p_1, p_2, \ldots, p_m$, which share a single processor. Each process p_i has a periodic behavior. In a period of length T_i, process p_i requests a constant amount of processor time C_i, where $C_i < T_i$.

We assume that the request periods for process p_i start at times $k \cdot T_i$, for $k = 0, 1, 2, 3, \ldots$.

The purpose of the scheduler is to grant processor time to the processes, i.e. to schedule the processes, so that process p_i runs on the processor for C_i time units in every period, for $i = 0, 1, \ldots, m$.

Figure 1.1 shows a schedule for first two periods of process p_i. In the first period, from time 0 to time T_i, three pieces of processor time, with durations C_{i_1}, C_{i_2} and C_{i_3} are scheduled for p_i. The requirement of p_i is fulfilled in the first period, since $C_i = C_{i_1} + C_{i_2} + C_{i_3}$. In the second period, from time T_i to time $2 \cdot T_i$, two pieces of processor time are scheduled for p_i. However, the requirement of p_i is not satisfied in the second period, as $C_i > C'_{i_1} + C'_{i_2}$.

$$
\begin{array}{cccccc}
C_{i_1} & C_{i_2} & C_{i_3} & & C'_{i_1} & C'_{i_2}
\end{array}
$$

p_i:

$$\qquad 0 \qquad\qquad\qquad\qquad\qquad T_i \qquad\qquad\qquad\qquad 2 \cdot T_i$$

$$C_i = C_{i_1} + C_{i_2} + C_{i_3}$$
$$C_i > C'_{i_1} + C'_{i_2}$$

Fig. 1.1. Schedules for p_i in the first two periods

The requirement for the scheduler is to fulfill all requests of the processes. This is a real-time requirement, as any request of a process must be fulfilled before its expiration.

The deadline-driven scheduling algorithm was proposed in [85]. It satisfies this requirement, under the assumptions that the scheduler overhead is negligible and

$$\sum_{i=1}^{m} \frac{C_i}{T_i} \leq 1 \, .$$

In this algorithm, the expiration time of a request is called the *deadline* of the request. The algorithm *dynamically* assigns priority to each process according to the urgency, i.e. the deadline, of its current request. A process will be assigned the highest priority if it is the most urgent, i.e. the deadline of its current request is the nearest, and will be assigned the lowest priority if it is the least urgent, i.e. its deadline is the furthest. At any instant, only one of the processes, with the highest priority and an unfulfilled request, can be selected to *occupy* or even *preempt* the processor.

The correctness of the algorithm is not obvious. Reference [85] has provided an informal proof of it.   □

Gas Burner

This example was first investigated in [145]. A gas burner is either heating when the flame is burning or idling when the flame is not burning, and it alternates indefinitely between heating and idling. Usually, no gas is flowing while it is idling. However, when it changes from idling to heating, gas must be flowing for a little time before it can be ignited, and when a flame failure occurs, gas will be flowing before the failure is detected and the gas valve is closed. Hence, there may be a time interval in which gas is flowing and the flame is not burning, i.e. where gas is *leaking*. A design of a safe gas burner must ensure that the time intervals where gas is leaking do not become too long.

Let us assume that the ventilation required for normal combustion would prevent a dangerous accumulation of gas provided that the proportion of leak time is not more than one-twentieth of the elapsed time for any time interval at least one minute long – otherwise the requirement would be violated immediately on the start of a leak. This is also a real-time requirement.

Turning next to the task of design, certain decisions must be taken about how the real-time requirement is to be met. For example, it could be decided that for any period where the requirement is guaranteed, any leak in this period should be detectable and stoppable within one second; and to prevent frequent leaks, it is acceptable that after any leak in this period, the gas burner rejects the switching on of gas for thirty seconds. The conjunction of these two decisions implies the original requirement, a fact which must be proved before implementation proceeds.

After justification of the design decisions, a computer program can be designed accordingly, and hosted in the gas burner. This program interacts with a flame sensor to detect flame failures, and controls the opening and closing of the gas valve, so that the design decisions, and hence the requirement, can be satisfied.   □

Both the deadline-driven scheduler and the gas burner are real-time systems, although the first one is a software system, and the second is a software-embedded system, also called a hybrid system.

Duration calculus (abbreviated to DC) is a logical approach to designing real-time systems. Real numbers are used to model time, and functions from time to Boolean values are used to model the behavior of real-time systems. On the basis of interval logic, DC provides a formal notation to specify properties of real-time systems and a calculus to formally prove those properties, such as the satisfaction of the requirements for the deadline-driven scheduling algorithm and for the design decisions of the gas burner.

1.1.2 Real Time

At the level of requirements, real time is often understood popularly as continuous time. However, at the level of implementation, a piece of software is implemented in a computer where time progresses discretely according to the machine cycle of the computer.

For example, the gas burner, a software-embedded system, is used in an environment where time progresses continuously. However, the embedded software of the gas burner may run in a computer with a certain machine cycle, and interacts with other physical components via *sensors* and *actuators* which operate discretely.

Although the deadline-driven scheduler, a software system, is hosted in a computer where time progresses discretely, the correctness of the deadline-driven scheduling algorithm is expected to be independent of the specific host computer, i.e. the algorithm can be better understood in terms of continuous time.

Therefore, the interface between continuous time and discrete time has become an important research topic in designing real-time systems.

For DC, we have adopted *continuous* time and chosen real numbers to model this continuous time. Discrete time, as a countable subset of the real numbers, can be defined in DC. It is definitely true that not every requirement satisfiable in continuous time can be implemented by a computer. For example, no computer can send out two signals separated by a distance less than its machine cycle, although, because of the density of continuous time, one can always find two time instants with an arbitrarily small distance between them.

In [32], a subset of DC formulas is identified, from which discrete implementations called digital controllers can be synthesized. References [19, 20, 25, 137, 138, 156] introduce discrete states to approximate continuous states, and provide rules to refine continuous specifications expressed as DC formulas into discrete implementations.

1.1.3 State Models

In DC, *states* and *events* are used to model the behavior of real-time systems. However, the book concentrates on state models until Chap. 9, where state models are extended with the addition of events. A *Boolean state model* of a real-time system is a set $P_1, P_2, \ldots, P_i, \ldots$ of Boolean-valued (i.e. $\{0,1\}$-valued) functions over time, i.e.

$$P_i : \text{Time} \rightarrow \{0,1\},$$

where Time is the set of the real numbers.

Each Boolean-valued function, also called a *Boolean state* (or simply a *state*) of the system, is a *characteristic* function of a specific aspect of the system behavior, and the whole set of Boolean-valued functions characterizes all of the relevant aspects of the behavior.

Deadline-Driven Scheduler

In order to prove the correctness of the deadline-driven scheduler, we introduce the following states to model the behavior of the scheduler:

$$\text{Run}_i : \text{Time} \rightarrow \{0,1\}$$
$$\text{Std}_i : \text{Time} \rightarrow \{0,1\}$$
$$\text{Urg}_{ij} : \text{Time} \rightarrow \{0,1\},$$

for $i, j = 1, 2, \ldots, m$.

The states Run_i $(i = 1, 2, \ldots, m)$ are used to characterize the processor occupation. $\text{Run}_i(t) = 1$ means that p_i is running in the processor at time t, while $\text{Run}_i(t) = 0$ means that p_i is not running at t.

The states Std_i $(i = 1, 2, \ldots, m)$ characterize the standing of the request. $\text{Std}_i(t) = 1$ means that at time t the current request of p_i is still standing. Namely, the current request of p_i is yet to be fulfilled at time t. $\text{Std}_i(t) = 0$ means that at t the current request of p_i is not standing anymore. In other words, the current request of p_i has been fulfilled by time t.

For a pair of processes p_i and p_j $(i \neq j)$, the state Urg_{ij} describes which of the processes is more urgent, where urgency is defined in terms of the distance to the start of the next request period. Thus, $\text{Urg}_{ij}(t) = 1$, for $i, j = 1, 2, \ldots, m$ and $i \neq j$, means that p_i is more urgent than p_j at time t, and $\text{Urg}_{ij}(t) = 0$ means that p_i is less urgent than or as urgent as p_j at time t.

It is obvious that any set of the above functions which characterizes a possible behavior of the deadline-driven scheduler must satisfy certain properties. For example, at any time t, if $\mathrm{Run}_i(t) = 1$, then $\mathrm{Run}_j(t) = 0$ for $j \neq i$, as the processes share a *single* processor. The properties which capture the scheduling algorithm are more complicated.

DC provides a formal notation to specify the real-time properties of the scheduling algorithm in terms of states Run_i, Std_i and Urg_{ij}. Furthermore, the real-time requirement of the scheduler can also be expressed in DC through these states, and the correctness of the scheduling algorithm can then be verified using DC. □

A Boolean state model of a system represents an abstraction of the behavior of the system, and may be refined to more primitive states during the design and the implementation of the system. In particular, for designing a software-embedded system, a Boolean-valued state may be finally refined to real-valued functions which model the behavior of physical components of the system, as in control theory. We call the real-valued functions a *real state model* of the system. Consider the example of the gas burner.

Gas Burner

The gas burner is a software-embedded system. To verify the design decisions against the requirement, one may start with a single Boolean state to model the critical aspect of the system

$\qquad$ Leak : Time $\rightarrow \{0, 1\}$,

where $\mathrm{Leak}(t) = 1$ means that gas is leaking at time t, and $\mathrm{Leak}(t) = 0$ means that gas is not leaking at t.

However, at a later stage of the design one may have to specify the phases of burning and idling of the gas burner, and introduce more primitive Boolean states of the system such as Gas and Flame to characterize the flowing and burning of gas. Then Leak can be pointwise defined as a Boolean expression containing Gas and Flame:

$\qquad$ $\mathrm{Leak}(t) \ \widehat{=} \ \mathrm{Gas}(t) \wedge \neg \mathrm{Flame}(t)$,

for any $t \in$ Time.

Boolean operators (e.g. $\neg$ and $\wedge$) for states are therefore included in DC, so that a composite state of a real-time system can be refined to primitive states of the system.

However, the flow of gas is actually a real-valued function of time, and can be determined by the degree of opening of a gas valve. To describe the valve, a function

$\qquad$ Valve : Time $\rightarrow [0, \Theta]$

is introduced, where $\text{Valve}(t) = \theta$ means that the valve is opened to a degree θ $(0 \leq \theta \leq \Theta)$ at time t.

The Boolean state Gas can be regarded as an abstraction of the real-valued function Valve. For example, one may define this state such that gas is present at t when $\text{Valve}(t)$ is above some threshold θ_0 $(0 < \theta_0 < \Theta)$:

$$\text{Gas}(t) = \begin{cases} 1, & \text{if } \text{Valve}(t) \geq \theta_0 \\ 0, & \text{otherwise} \end{cases}.$$

In other words, Gas becomes the characteristic function of a property of the real-valued function Valve.

Furthermore, the opening and the closing of the valve are controlled by a piece of software embedded in the gas burner, which governs the application of a force to open or close the valve. This applied force can be expressed as another real-valued function:

$$\text{Force} : \text{Time} \rightarrow [-\Omega, \Omega],$$

where Ω stands for the greatest strength of the applied force. The real-valued functions Force and Valve are called *real states* of the gas burner, and join with other functions to form a *real state model* of the system. The relation between Force and Valve may be defined by a differential equation obtained from mechanics. □

As a design calculus for software-embedded systems, research on DC has explored possibilities to capture parts of real analysis (see [165, 170]), and hence to specify real state models of software-embedded systems. However, this book will not present a real state model.

1.1.4 State Durations

The notion of state *duration* is used to specify the behavior of real-time systems. The duration of a Boolean state over a time interval is the accumulated presence time of the state in the interval.

Let P be a Boolean state (i.e. $P : \text{Time} \rightarrow \{0, 1\}$), and $[b, e]$ an interval (i.e. $b, e \in \text{Time}$ and $e \geq b$). The duration of state P over $[b, e]$ equals the integral

$$\int_b^e P(t)\, dt.$$

Let us use the two examples described above to illustrate the importance of state durations in specifying real-time behavior.

Deadline-Driven Scheduler

The real-time requirement of the scheduler is to fulfill all the process requests before their expiration. This requirement can be expressed in terms of durations of the states Run_i, for $i = 1, 2, \ldots, m$.

Let us assume that all the processes raise their first request at time 0. Thus, every nth request of p_i is raised at time $(n-1)T_i$ and expires at time nT_i, where $n = 1, 2, \ldots$. Therefore, the scheduler fulfills the nth request of p_i iff the accumulated run time of p_i in the interval $[(n-1)T_i, nT_i]$ equals the requested time C_i. Namely, the duration of state Run_i over the interval $[(n-1)T_i, nT_i]$ is equal to C_i:

$$\int_{(n-1)T_i}^{nT_i} \mathrm{Run}_i(t)\, dt = C_i.$$

Hence, the requirement is satisfied by the scheduler iff the duration of Run_i over the interval $[(n-1)T_i, nT_i]$ is equal to C_i, for all $i = 1, 2, \ldots, m$ and $n = 1, 2, \ldots$.   □

Gas Burner

The real-time requirement of the gas burner is that the proportion of leak time in an interval is not more than one-twentieth of the interval, if the interval is at least one minute long. This requirement can be expressed in terms of the durations of Leak as follows:

$$(e-b) \geq 60\,\mathrm{s} \;\Rightarrow\; 20\int_b^e \mathrm{Leak}(t)\, dt \leq (e-b),$$

for any interval $[b, e]$.   □

A mathematical formulation of these two requirements can hardly leave out state durations. Since the processor may be preempted *dynamically*, the duration of Run_i extracts the accumulated running time of p_i from the dynamic occupation of the processor. Also, since gas leaks occur owing to *random* flame failures, the duration of Leak extracts the accumulated leak time of gas from the random flame failures. Therefore, state durations are adopted in DC to specify the behavior of real-time systems.

The *distance* between states (or events) is another important measurement of real-time systems. This was studied extensively before the development of DC, for example, by the use of timed automata [5], real-time logic [69], metric temporal logic [72] and explicit clock temporal logic [54].

However, state durations are more expressive than distances between states in the sense that the latter can be expressed in terms of the former, but not vice versa. With state durations, one can first express the *lasting period* of a state. That a presence of state P lasts for a period $[c, d]$ (for $d > c$), written $P[c, d]$, can be expressed as follows:

$$\int_c^d P(t)\, dt = (d-c) > 0,$$

if we do not care about instantaneous absences of P. This expression is read in real analysis as

"P appears almost everywhere in $[c, d]$" .

Thus, real-time constraints on the lasting periods of states can be expressed in terms of state durations.

Gas Burner

Consider the first design decision in the case of the gas burner. Let $[b, e]$ be an interval where we want to guarantee the requirement of the gas burner. The first design decision is that any leak in $[b, e]$ should not last for a period longer than one second. This can be expressed as

$$\forall c, d : b \leq c < d \leq e.(\text{Leak}[c, d] \ \Rightarrow \ (d - c) \leq 1\,\text{s})\,.$$

Real-time constraints on distances between states can be expressed in terms of state durations similarly. Consider the second design decision in the case of the gas burner. The second design decision is that the distance between any two consecutive leaks in the guarantee period $[b, e]$ must be at least thirty seconds long:

$$\forall c, d, r, s : b \leq c < r < s < d \leq e.$$
$$(\text{Leak}[c, r] \wedge \text{NonLeak}[r, s] \wedge \text{Leak}[s, d]) \ \Rightarrow \ (s - r) \geq 30\,\text{s}\,,$$

where NonLeak is a state defined from Leak using the negation ($\neg$):

$$\text{NonLeak}(t) \ \hat{=} \ \neg\text{Leak}(t)\,,$$

for any $t \in \text{Time}$.

The above formulation of the second design decision for the gas burner can be changed to a syntactically weaker but semantically equivalent one:

$$\forall c, d, r, s : b \leq c < r < s < d \leq e.$$
$$(\text{Leak}[c, r] \wedge \text{NonLeak}[r, s] \wedge \text{Leak}[s, d]) \ \Rightarrow \ (d - c) \geq 30\,\text{s}\,.$$

The equivalence of these two formulas can be proved as follows. It is obvious that the first formula implies the second one. In order to prove the other implication, we assume that there are

$$c' < r < s < d' \text{ in } [b, e]$$

such that

$$\text{Leak}[c', r], \text{NonLeak}[r, s], \text{Leak}[s, d'] \text{ and } (s - r) < 30\,.$$

Under this assumption, we let

$$\eta = (30 - (s - r)) > 0$$
$$c = \max\{c', (r - (\eta/3))\}$$
$$d = \min\{d', (s + (\eta/3))\}\,.$$

Then, it is easy to prove that

$c < r < s < d$ in $[b, e]$

and

Leak$[c, r]$, NonLeak$[r, s]$, Leak$[s, d]$ and $(d - c) < 30$.

So, by the contraposition law of propositional logic, we complete the proof of the equivalence of the two formulations of the second design decision.   □

However, the equivalence of these two formulas holds only for continuous time. In the rest of this book, when we are concerned with a continuous time domain, we shall adopt the second formulation, since it corresponds to a simpler formalization of the second design decision for the gas burner in DC. In Chap. 12 we shall deal with a discrete time domain and shall formalize the second design decision differently.

By axiomatizing integrals of Boolean-valued functions, DC provides a possible way to introduce notions of real analysis into formal techniques for designing software-embedded real-time systems. Notions of *integral* and/or *differential* have also been adopted in studies of automata [4, 99], statecharts [92], temporal logic of actions (TLA) [76] and communicating sequential processes (CSP) [55], when considering software-embedded systems.

State durations, as integrals of Boolean-valued functions, are functions from time intervals to real numbers. The state durations of DC have been axiomatized on the basis of the interval logics proposed in [1, 27, 43], which can be regarded as logics for functions of time intervals.

1.2 Interval Logic

By interval logic we mean logics in the sense of [1, 27, 43], for example. We view these logics as logics for time intervals. Let Intv be the set of time intervals, i.e.

Intv $\hat{=}$ $\{ [b, e] \mid b, e \in$ Time $\wedge b \leq e \}$.

1.2.1 Interval Variables

In these logics, we can express properties of functions of time intervals, called *interval variables*.

Let v_i (for $i = 1, 2, 3, 4$) be interval variables, i.e.

v_i : Intv $\rightarrow$ $\mathbb{R}$,

where $\mathbb{R}$ denotes the set of real numbers.

A formula such as $v_1 \leq (v_2 + v_3 \cdot v_4)$ is interpreted in interval logic as a function from $\mathbb{I}\text{ntv}$ to the truth values $\{tt,ff\}$:

$$v_1 \leq (v_2 + v_3 \cdot v_4) \; : \; \mathbb{I}\text{ntv} \; \rightarrow \; \{tt,ff\} \, .$$

An interval $[b, e]$ satisfies the formula iff the value of v_1 of $[b, e]$ is less than or equal to the sum of the value v_2 of $[b, e]$ and the product of the values of v_3 and v_4 of $[b, e]$.

Therefore, interval logic provides a *functional* calculus for specifying and reasoning about properties of functions of intervals in a succinct way, such that the arguments of the functions (i.e. the intervals) are not referred to explicitly.

The interval *length* is a specific interval variable denoted ℓ, i.e.

$$\ell \; : \; \mathbb{I}\text{ntv} \; \rightarrow \; \mathbb{R} \, .$$

For an arbitrarily given interval $[b, e]$, ℓ delivers the value $(e - b)$, i.e. the length of $[b, e]$.

The duration of the state P (written $\int P$) is another interval variable,

$$\int P \; : \; \mathbb{I}\text{ntv} \; \rightarrow \; \mathbb{R} \, .$$

For an arbitrarily given interval $[b, e]$, the value of the interval variable $\int P$ is the duration of P in $[b, e]$, i.e. the value

$$\int_b^e P(t) \, dt \, .$$

Gas Burner

The requirement of the gas burner can be expressed in terms of the state duration $\int\text{Leak}$ as

$$GbReq \; \hat{=} \; \ell \geq 60 \; \Rightarrow \; 20\int\text{Leak} \leq \ell \, ,$$

where 60 stands for 60 seconds. (Henceforth we choose the *second* as the time unit in the example of the gas burner.)   □

1.2.2 Interval Modalities

The set of intervals $\mathbb{I}\text{ntv}$ is the semantic domain of interval logic. In interval logic, *modalities* are used to define structures among intervals, such as one interval is a subinterval of another interval, or an interval is made of two adjacent subintervals. Those structures are present in the descriptions of the two design decisions for the gas burner. For example, the first design decision expresses a real-time property of a subinterval in which leaking occurs. The second design decision expresses a real-time requirement for three adjacent subintervals.

In the literature of mathematical logic, logics of modalities are called *modal* logics [15, 66]. The semantics domain of a modal logic is usually called a *frame* and it consists of a set of *worlds* and a *reachability relation* of the worlds. Thus, an interval logic is a modal logic which takes intervals as worlds.

In [1, 43, 147], twelve unary modalities and three binary modalities are suggested for defining various interval reachabilities. We list here four of the modalities, which are used later in this chapter.

The Subinterval Modality ◇

The subinterval modality ◇ (Fig. 1.2) is a unary modality. For any formula ϕ, $\Diamond\phi$ is a new formula which holds for an interval iff ϕ holds for some *subinterval*.

Mathematically, an arbitrary interval $[b, e]$ satisfies $\Diamond\phi$ iff there exist c, d such that $b \leq c \leq d \leq e$ and the interval $[c, d]$ satisfies ϕ. Thus, from the interval $[b, e]$ one can reach its subintervals with $\Diamond\phi$.

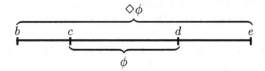

Fig. 1.2. The modality ◇

The dual of ◇ is □, which is defined as

$$\Box\phi \,\hat{=}\, \neg\Diamond\neg\phi.$$

Hence, $[b, e]$ satisfies $\Box\phi$ iff any subinterval of $[b, e]$ satisfies ϕ.

With □, one can formulate the first design decision for the gas burner, that any leak in the guarantee period of the gas burner must be stoppable within one second.

First, the mathematical definition of $P[c, d]$ (i.e. P takes the value 1 almost everywhere in a nonpoint interval $[c, d]$) can be expressed as a formula without mentioning the interval explicitly:

$$\lceil P \rceil \,\hat{=}\, \int P = \ell \,\wedge\, \ell > 0.$$

Then, the following formula is a formalization of the first design decision:

$$Des_1 \,\hat{=}\, \Box(\lceil \text{Leak} \rceil \,\Rightarrow\, \ell \leq 1).$$

□

The Chop Modality $\frown$

The chop modality $\frown$ (Fig. 1.3) is a binary modality introduced into interval logic by [43]. For formulas ϕ and ψ, the new formula $\phi \frown \psi$ is satisfied by an interval iff the interval can be chopped into two adjacent subintervals such that the first subinterval satisfies ϕ and the second one satisfies ψ.

In other words, the interval $[b, e]$ satisfies the formula $\phi \frown \psi$ iff there exists m $(b \leq m \leq e)$ such that $[b, m]$ satisfies ϕ and $[m, e]$ satisfies ψ.

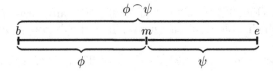

Fig. 1.3. The modality $\frown$

The reachability relation defined by $\frown$ is a ternary one. It provides access to adjacent subintervals of an interval, and hence defines a temporal *order* among subintervals of an interval.

With $\frown$ and $\square$, one can formalize the second formulation of the second design decision for the gas burner given in Sect. 1.1.4:

$$Des_2 \ \widehat{=} \ \square((\lceil \text{Leak} \rceil \frown \lceil \neg\text{Leak} \rceil \frown \lceil \text{Leak} \rceil) \ \Rightarrow \ \ell \geq 30) \,.$$

To prove the correctness of the two design decisions is therefore to prove the validity of the formula

$$(Des_1 \wedge Des_2) \ \Rightarrow \ GbReq \,.$$

In fact, the subinterval modality $\diamondsuit$ can be derived from the chop modality, since

$$\diamondsuit\phi \ \Leftrightarrow \ (\text{true} \frown (\phi \frown \text{true})) \,,$$

where "true" stands for a formula which is satisfied by any interval. Therefore, the second design decision (as well as the first one) for the gas burner can be expressed in an interval logic of state durations with $\frown$ as the only modality.
□

A modality is called *contracting* if the modality provides access only to *inside* parts of a given interval, i.e. subintervals of the interval. $\diamondsuit$ and $\frown$ are two examples of contracting modalities. With the contracting modality $\frown$, we have expressed the two design decisions for the gas burner which can guarantee the *safety*-critical requirement of the gas burner.

However, contracting modalities cannot express *unbounded liveness* and *fairness* properties of computing systems, since these properties are about properties *outside* any given time interval. Modalities which provide access to the region outside a given interval are called *expanding* modalities. In the following we give two examples of expanding modalities.

The Right Neighborhood Modality $\Diamond_r$

The modality $\Diamond_r$ (Fig. 1.4) is a unary modality. An interval satisfies $\Diamond_r \phi$ iff a *right neighborhood* of the *ending* point of the interval satisfies ϕ.

Mathematically, $[b, e]$ satisfies $\Diamond_r \phi$ iff there exists $d \geq e$ such that interval $[e, d]$ satisfies ϕ.

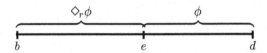

Fig. 1.4. The modality $\Diamond_r$

Thus, $\Diamond_r$ provides access to right neighborhoods of e from $[b, e]$. Since right neighborhoods of e are outside $[b, e]$, $\Diamond_r$ is an expanding modality.

The modality $\Box_r$ is the dual of $\Diamond_r$ and is defined as

$$\Box_r \phi \;\;\hat{=}\;\; \neg \Diamond_r \neg \phi .$$

That is, an interval satisfies $\Box_r \phi$ iff any right neighborhood of the ending point of the interval satisfies ϕ.

With $\Diamond_r$, one can specify properties related to future time, such as liveness and fairness properties of computing systems. Consider the example of the gas burner. Let HeatReq be a state to characterize a request for heat from the gas burner. The formula

$$\lceil\text{HeatReq}\rceil \;\;\Rightarrow\;\; \Diamond_r(\textstyle\int \text{Flame} > 0)$$

expresses the condition that if one raises a heat request, then there will exist a presence of Flame in the future. This formula can represent an additional requirement for the gas burner, to reject a safe but *dead* gas burner.

The Left Neighborhood Modality $\Diamond_l$

The modality $\Diamond_l$ (Fig. 1.5) is a unary modality. An interval satisfies $\Diamond_l \phi$ iff a *left neighborhood* of the *beginning* point of the interval satisfies ϕ.

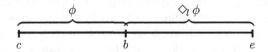

Fig. 1.5. The modality $\Diamond_l$

Mathematically, $[b, e]$ satisfies $\Diamond_l \phi$ iff there exists $c \leq b$ such that interval $[c, b]$ satisfies ϕ.

Thus, the modality $\Diamond_l$ provides access to the past time of a given interval. It is also an expanding modality.

The dual of $\Diamond_l$ is designated by $\Box_l$. An interval $[b, e]$ satisfies $\Box_l \phi$ iff any left neighborhood of b satisfies ϕ:

$$\Box_l \phi \,\,\hat{=}\,\, \neg \Diamond_l \neg \phi \,.$$

$\Box$

In Chap. 11 of this book, it is proved that all twelve unary modalities and three binary modalities of interval logic can be derived from $\Diamond_r$ and $\Diamond_l$ in a first-order logic with interval length ℓ. However, this book will use $\frown$ as the only modality, except in Chap. 11, where the liveness and fairness properties of computing systems are discussed.

1.3 Duration Calculus

Research on DC was initiated by the case study [145] in connection with the ProCoS project (ESPRIT BRA 3104 and 7071). Several real-time formalisms were investigated in order to specify requirements and design decisions for a gas burner system; but they all failed in this case study. Two main observations of this case study were that the notion of a time interval was useful and that the notion of a state duration was convenient. This led to the first publication on DC [168] in 1991. Since then, research on DC has considered different models of real-time systems, applications of DC and mechanical support tools for DC.

In [161], there is a brief overview of early research on DC, and in [51], there is a detailed account of the logical foundations of DC.

1.3.1 Models

Different models are used by designers of real-time systems at different design stages. In order to accommodate all necessary models, sets of functions over time, called *states*, are used to model real-time systems in DC. In the state

models, real-valued functions are called *real states* of systems, and characteristic functions of properties of underlying real states are called *Boolean states*.
Boolean states are assumed *stable*, i.e. any presence (or absence) of a Boolean
state must last for some period, and are represented by Boolean-valued *step*
functions. *Events* are taken to be transitions of Boolean states.

First, a basic calculus – the calculus for durations of Boolean states – was
developed, and then other models were introduced by adding to the basic
calculus extra axioms, which formalize the models and also their interrelations
with the Boolean state model.

Boolean State Model

The basic calculus of DC [168] axiomatizes state durations for the Boolean
state model, i.e. integrals of Boolean-valued functions, under an assumption
of *finite variability* (also called the *non-Zeno phenomenon*) of states. The
assumption of finite variability stipulates that any state can only change its
presence and absence finitely many times in any bounded time period. That
is, only finitely many state transitions can take place in any bounded time
period. The interval modality used in the basic calculus is the chop modality
⌢. This calculus can be used to specify and verify state-based safety properties of real-time systems. Formalizations of other models are *conservative*
extensions of this calculus.

Boolean State and Event Model

The Boolean state and event model was studied in [164, 169].

In [169], an event is a Boolean-valued δ-function, i.e. a Boolean-valued
function with a value of 1 at *discrete* points. This means that an event is
an instant action, and an event takes place at a given time point iff the
Boolean-valued δ-function of the event takes the value 1 at that point. By
linking events to state transitions, this model can be used to refine from state-
based requirements, via mixed state and event specifications, to event-based
specifications of programs.

However, with integrals of functions, one cannot capture the value of a
function at a point, since the integral of a function at a point is always equal
to zero, no matter what the value of the function at that point is. In [169],
integrals of Boolean-valued functions are replaced by their *mean values*. The
mean value of a Boolean-valued function P, designated $\overline{P}$, is a function from
intervals to $[0, 1]$, i.e.

$$\overline{P} \; : \; \mathbb{Intv} \; \to \; [0, 1],$$

and is defined in real analysis as follows:

$$\overline{P}([b,e]) = \begin{cases} \int_b^e P(t)\,dt/(e-b) & \text{if } e > b \\ P(e) & \text{if } e = b \end{cases},$$

for any interval $[b, e]$.

Therefore, one can describe point properties of Boolean-valued functions by using their mean values in point intervals, and at the same time one can also define the integral of a Boolean-valued function P:

$$\int P \; \hat{=} \; \overline{P} \cdot \ell.$$

Additional axioms and rules for reasoning about δ-functions and state transitions were developed in [169].

The approach in [164] is to continue using the basic calculus for the integral of a Boolean-valued function, but atomic formulas to stand for events are added to the basic calculus. This book will follow the approach of [164] to introduce state transitions and events into the Boolean state model.

Real State Model

A real state model consists of a set of real-valued functions which describe the behavior of physical components of a software-embedded system. By using a real state model, we introduce structures into Boolean states, and a Boolean state becomes a characteristic function of a property of real states of the model. Therefore, specifications and reasoning at the level of the state may have to employ real analysis.

In [170], it was investigated how DC can be combined with real analysis, so that real state models can be specified within the framework of DC. In [165], this research was further developed by the formalization of some parts of real analysis using the left and right neighborhood modalities.

Dependability

The dependability of an implementation with regard to a given requirement can be quantitatively measured by a satisfaction probability of the requirement for this implementation.

In the context of the Boolean state model and a discrete time domain, the work presented in [86, 87, 89, 90] provides designers with a set of rules to reason about and calculate the satisfaction probability of a given requirement, formalized using DC, with respect to an implementation represented as a finite automaton with history-independent transition probabilities.

In [22], this work was generalized to a continuous time domain.

Finite-Divergence Model

The assumption of finite variability of states and events stipulates that within a finite time period, state transitions and events can happen only finitely many times. The finite-variability assumption is always adopted in the case of software systems where time progresses discretely.

The notion opposite to finite variability is called *finite divergence* (also called the *Zeno phenomenon*). Continuous mathematics does not reject finite divergence, and introduces the notion of a limit in order to study finite divergence. In [48], the finite-divergence model was formalized by introducing into DC some rules to calculate a state duration in a finite-divergence model as a limit of its approximations in a finite-variability model.

Superdense Computation

A *superdense computation* is a sequence of operations which is assumed to be timeless. This is an abstraction of a real-time computation within a context with a grand time granularity. This assumption is known as the *synchrony* hypothesis and has been adopted in the case of digital control systems, where the cycle time of an embedded computer may be nanoseconds, while the sampling period of a controller may be seconds. Therefore, the computation time of the embedded software of the digital control system is negligible, and computational operations can be abstracted as timeless actions.

To accommodate timeless operations, [164] adapts the chop modality and renames it the *superdense chop*. This can chop a time point in a grand time space into multiple points in a finer space, and hence the superdense chop introduces structure into a time point.

By generalizing the projection operator [97] of interval temporal logic, [42] introduced into DC the *visible* and *invisible* states, and computed non-negligible time through projection onto the visible state.

Thus, the properties of superdense computation can also be specified and verified in DC. In [107, 114], other approaches are considered for treating the synchrony hypothesis within the framework of DC.

Expanding Modalities

With contracting modalities such as $\frown$ and $\Diamond$, one can specify only *safety* properties of real-time systems.

In order to specify *unbounded liveness* and *fairness* properties of real-time systems within the framework of DC, [31, 103, 139, 165] introduced expanding modalities. In [165], it was proved that the left and right neighborhood modalities $\Diamond_l$ and $\Diamond_r$ are adequate, in the sense that the other contracting and expanding modalities suggested in [1, 43, 147] can be derived from them in a first-order logic with an interval length ℓ. The completeness of the first-order calculus for $\Diamond_l$ and $\Diamond_r$ given in [165] was proved in [9], and, in [8], the completeness was proved for a combination of a first-order temporal logic and an interval logic with neighborhood modalities.

In [31], an interval logic where intervals have a direction was suggested. This logic is based on the chop modality, but the "chop point" is allowed to be outside the interval under consideration, and in this way the chop modality becomes expanding. This logic, called *signed interval logic* (SIL), was further developed in [120, 123].

Infinite Intervals

The behavior of a real-time system, such as the deadline-driven scheduler or the gas burner considered here, is often assumed to be *infinite*. However, DC is a logic of finite intervals. An infinite behavior is therefore specified in DC as the set of all finite prefixes of the behavior. To specify liveness and fairness properties of the behavior of a system in terms of its finite prefixes, expanding modalities have been introduced.

An alternative to expanding modalities is to introduce infinite intervals into DC. Extensions of DC which allow infinite intervals were established in [117, 162]. These extensions include both finite and infinite intervals, and can straightforwardly express and reason about both *terminating* and *infinite* behaviors of real-time systems. References [117, 118, 119] also compare the expressive power of these extensions with the expressive power of monadic logic of order.

Higher-Order and Iteration Operators

When DC is applied to real-time programming, it becomes inevitable that one introduces advanced operators into DC corresponding to the programming notions of local variables and channels, and of the loop.

In [39, 41, 60, 108, 110, 163], the semantics and proof rules of the (higher-order) quantifiers over states and the μ operator were investigated. It is interesting to discover that, because of the finite variability of states, the quantifiers over states can be reduced to first-order quantifiers over global variables, and also that the superdense chop can be derived from the higher-order quantifiers.

1.3.2 Applications

The applications of DC focus on the formal design of real-time systems.

Case Studies of Software-Embedded Systems

DC has been applied to case studies of many software-embedded systems, such as an autopilot [126], a railway crossing [141] and interlock [127], a water level monitor [30, 64], a gas burner [127], a steam boiler [31, 83, 135], an air traffic controller [68], a production cell [113], a motor-load control system [157], an inverted pendulum [151], a chemical concentration control system [153], a heating control system [155], a redundant control system [36] and a hydraulic actuator system [125]. A case study for formalizing and synthesizing an optimal design of a double-tank control system was conducted in [62].

On the basis of these case studies, a methodology and notation for designing software-embedded systems were studied and developed in [16, 21, 149, 171].

Real-Time Semantics, Specification and Verification

In order to apply DC to the specification and verification of real-time systems, techniques for integrating DC with other formalisms such as CSP, phase transition systems, Verilog and RAISE have been developed in [37, 57, 59, 61, 78, 152], where DC has been used to define the underlying semantics. In [88], a uniform framework for DC and timed linear temporal logic was presented.

In [63], CSP, Object-Z and DC were combined into a uniform framework for the specification of processes, data and time, based on a smooth integration of the underlying semantic models.

In [58, 133, 134, 164, 166], DC was used to define the real-time semantics for OCCAM-like languages. In [164], it was assumed, in the semantics of an OCCAM-like language, that assignments and message passings take no time, and can form a superdense computation. In [171], a semantics was given to a CSP language with continuous variables which was proposed in [55] and can be used to describe software-embedded systems.

In [98], DC was used to define a real-time semantics for SDL, while [95] embedded a subset of DC into a first-order logic of *timed frames* and hence into SDL. Reference [109] defined a DC semantics for Esterel. Reference [71] proposed a DC semantics for a graphical language called Constraint Diagrams. Reference [46] gives, in terms of DC, a formal meaning of fault trees. References [37, 78] define a DC semantics for a timed RAISE Specification Language and [136, 173] define a DC semantics for Verilog. In [24, 146], a DC semantics was given to programmable logic controller (PLC) automata and, furthermore, a tool was developed for designing PLC automata from DC specifications.

In [52], DC was used to specify and reason about real-time properties of circuits. Reference [128] applied DC to prove the correctness of Fischer's mutual-exclusion protocol. References [17, 20, 25] specified and verified the correctness of the biphase mark protocol through DC. Reference [160] applied DC to specify and verify the deadline-driven scheduler, and [14, 26] presented formal specifications of several well-known real-time schedulers for processes with shared resources. In [112], DC was used to specify and verify properties of real-time database systems, and, in [49], DC was used to specify and analyze availability properties of security protocols.

Refinement of DC Specifications

In [94], there was a first attempt to define refinement laws for a restricted set of formulas of DC toward formulas called DC *implementables*, which describe properties such as timed progress and stability. A full exposition of these ideas is given in the monograph [124]. In this monograph, there is also a study of how to ensure that a set of implementables is *feasible*, i.e. that it is consistent and extendable in time. Techniques to refine a feasible set of DC implementables via a mixed specification and programming language into an executable program were developed in [100, 133, 134].

References [21, 74, 75, 132] represent work on refining DC formulas into automata. References [153, 154]proposed approaches to refining DC specifications into programs following the paradigms of the Hoare logic and the assumption-commitment logic.

1.3.3 Tools

Interesting results about the *completeness* of the calculi for interval modalities and state durations and about *decision* procedures and *model-checking* algorithms for DC subsets have been published.

In [27], the completeness of the interval logic described in Chap. 2 was proved for an *abstract* domain. A similar result was proved in [9] for the neighborhood logic described in Chap. 11. The duration calculus described in Chap. 3 has been proved to be *relatively* complete [50]. It can also be complete for an abstract domain if we use ω-rules as in [38].

Decidable subsets of DC and the complexity of decision algorithms were discovered and analyzed in [2, 18, 32, 35, 47, 79, 102, 115, 116, 131, 167]. In order to check whether state transition sequences of a subset of timed (even hybrid) automata satisfy a linear inequality of the state durations, [12, 70, 80, 81, 82, 84, 158, 159, 172] developed algorithms which employ techniques from linear and integer programming.

On the basis of the above results, a proof assistant for DC was developed in [93, 140, 144] as an extension of PVS [101], and a decision procedure [167] for DC was incorporated into this proof assistant. For example, the soundness proof in [50] of the induction rules for DC was checked by this proof assistant. Furthermore, several proofs used in case studies were checked in [140] using the DC extension of PVS, e.g. the studies of the simple gas burner system proposed in [168] and of the railway crossing proposed in [141]. In these applications of the proof assistant, errors in the original proofs were spotted. In [23], there is an analysis and comparison of the use of model-checking and logical-reasoning techniques.

In [142], a tool to check the validity of a subclass of DC was presented. Furthermore, [105] developed a tool (DCVALID) to check the validity of a subclass of discrete-time higher-order DC. In [150], DCVALID was used to verify the correctness of a multimedia communication protocol. In [34], a bounded model construction for discrete-time DC was presented, which was shown to be NP-complete.

The proof theory for signed interval logic was developed and investigated in [121, 122, 123], and SIL is encoded in the generic theorem prover Isabelle [111].

1.4 Book Structure

Chapter 2 (Interval Logic) develops the syntax, semantics, axioms and rules of a first-order interval logic. It is the logical foundation of the axiomatizations of DC models presented in this book. This first-order interval logic includes *chop* as its only modality, and it is complete for an *abstract* time domain. An abstract time domain is not necessarily the set of real numbers, but an arbitrary set which satisfies certain axioms.

Chapter 3 (Duration Calculus) presents the calculus for durations for the Boolean states. It is based on the interval logic described in Chap. 2, and the assumption of finite variability of states. The gas burner example is used in this chapter to explain the syntax, semantics, axioms and rules of DC.

Chapter 4 (Deadline-Driven Scheduler) specifies and verifies the deadline-driven scheduling algorithm in DC. This demonstrates an application of DC to a rather complicated software system.

Chapter 5 (Relative Completeness) proves the *relative* completeness of DC with respect to a continuous time domain represented by the set of real numbers. By relative completeness, we mean that, in the context of this continuous time domain, any valid formula of DC is provable in DC, provided any valid formula of interval logic can be taken as a theorem of DC.

Chapter 6 and 7 (Decidability and Undecidability) describe decidable and undecidable subsets of DC formulas in discrete and continuous time domains. The decidability of a subset of DC is proved by reducing the validity of a formula in the subset to the decidable emptiness problem of regular languages. The undecidability of a subset of DC is obtained by reducing the undecidable halting problem for two-counter machines to satisfiability of formulas in the subset.

Chapter 8 (Model Checking: Linear Duration Invariants) presents an algorithm to decide whether an implementation of a real-time system satisfies a requirement written in DC as a finite number of linear inequalities of state durations, where the implementation is taken to be a real-time automaton having an upper time bound and a lower time bound for each transition. The satisfaction problem is reduced by the algorithm to finitely many simple linear programming problems.

Chapter 9 (State Transitions and Events) introduces extra atomic formulas and axioms to express and to reason about state transitions and events. With this extension, one can refine state-based requirements into state and event mixed (or event-based) implementations. In this chapter, an implementation as a real-time automaton is verified for the gas burner example against the two design decisions.

Chapter 10 (Superdense State Transitions) treats the synchrony hypothesis, and introduces the superdense chop modality. With the superdense chop, this chapter presents a real-time semantics for an OCCAM-like language. In the semantics, it is assumed that assignments and message passings take no time.

Chapter 11 (Neighborhood Logic) introduces the left and right neighborhood modalities. It proves the adequacy of these two modalities, and applies them to specify unbounded liveness and fairness.

Chapter 12 (Probabilistic Duration Calculus) assumes that an implementation of a real-time system is represented by a *probabilistic* automaton having a probability distribution over discrete time for each transition. Axioms and rules are developed to calculate and reason about the satisfaction probability of a requirement, formalized using DC, for a probabilistic automaton over a specified time interval. The gas burner is used as an example to explain the notions and techniques involved.

2. Interval Logic

In this chapter we give the syntax, semantics and proof system for interval logic (IL). This part is based mainly on [27, 28]. Furthermore, we develop theorems and rules of IL which are useful when constructing proofs.

2.1 Syntax

The formulas of IL are constructed from the following sets of symbols:

GVar: An infinite set of *global variables* $x, y, z, \ldots$. These variables are called "global" since their meaning is independent of time and time intervals.

TVar: An infinite set of *temporal variables* $v, v', \ldots$. The meaning of a temporal variable is a real-valued interval function. We assume the existence of a special temporal variable $\ell \in TVar$. The symbol ℓ stands for the interval function which gives the length of the interval as its value.

FSymb: An infinite set of *global function symbols* $f^n, g^m, \ldots$ equipped with arities $n, m \geq 0$. If f^n has arity $n = 0$ then f is called a *constant*. The meaning of a global function symbol f^n, $n > 0$, is an n-ary function on real numbers, which is be independent of time and time intervals.

RSymb: An infinite set of *global relation symbols* G^n, H^m equipped with arities $n, m \geq 0$. The meaning of a global relation symbol G^n, $n > 0$, is an n-ary truth-valued ($\{tt, ff\}$) function on real numbers, which is independent of time and time intervals. The truth constants true and false are the only two global relation symbols with arity 0.

PLetter: An infinite set of *temporal propositional letters* $X, Y, \ldots$. The meaning of each temporal propositional letter is a truth-valued interval function.

The set of *terms* $\theta, \theta_i \in Term$ is defined by the following abstract syntax:

$$\theta ::= x \mid v \mid f^n(\theta_1, \ldots, \theta_n).$$

The set of *formulas* $\phi, \psi \in Formula$ is defined by the following abstract syntax:

$$\phi ::= X \mid G^n(\theta_1, \ldots, \theta_n) \mid \neg\phi \mid \phi \vee \psi \mid \phi^\frown\psi \mid (\exists x)\phi,$$

where $\frown$ is a binary modality for "chopping" an interval into two consecutive subintervals. We also use φ, ϕ_i, ψ_i and φ_i to denote formulas.

We shall use standard notation for constants, e.g. 0, 1, true and false, and for function and relation symbols of real arithmetic, e.g. $+$ and $\geq$.

Abbreviations and Conventions

The following abbreviations will be used:

$$\Diamond\phi \;\hat{=}\; \text{true} \frown (\phi \frown \text{true}) \qquad \text{reads: "for some subinterval: } \phi\text{"}$$
$$\Box\phi \;\hat{=}\; \neg\Diamond(\neg\phi) \qquad\qquad\quad \text{reads: "for all subintervals: } \phi\text{"} .$$

The standard abbreviations from predicate logic will be used, e.g.

$$\phi \wedge \psi \;\hat{=}\; \neg((\neg\phi) \vee (\neg\psi))$$
$$\phi \Rightarrow \psi \;\hat{=}\; ((\neg\phi) \vee \psi)$$
$$\phi \Leftrightarrow \psi \;\hat{=}\; (\phi \Rightarrow \psi) \wedge (\psi \Rightarrow \phi)$$
$$(\forall x)\phi \;\hat{=}\; \neg((\exists x)\neg\phi) .$$

When $\neg, (\exists x), (\forall x), \Box$ and $\Diamond$ occur in formulas they have higher *precedence* than the binary connectives and the modality $\frown$, e.g.

$$(\Box\phi) \Rightarrow (((\forall x)(\neg\psi)) \frown \varphi)$$

can be written as

$$\Box\phi \Rightarrow ((\forall x)\neg\psi \frown \varphi) .$$

The following conventions for quantifiers will be used:

$$\exists x > \theta.\phi \qquad\quad \hat{=}\; (\exists x)(x > \theta \wedge \phi) \quad \text{and similarly for } \geq, \leq, \ldots$$
$$\forall x > \theta.\phi \qquad\quad \hat{=}\; (\forall x)(x > \theta \Rightarrow \phi) \quad \text{and similarly for } \geq, \leq, \ldots$$
$$\forall x_1, x_2, \ldots, x_n.\phi \;\hat{=}\; (\forall x_1)(\forall x_2)\cdots(\forall x_n)\phi$$
$$\exists x_1, x_2, \ldots, x_n.\phi \;\hat{=}\; (\exists x_1)(\exists x_2)\cdots(\exists x_n)\phi .$$

2.2 Semantics

The meanings of terms and formulas are explained in this section. To do so we must first define the meaning of global and temporal variables, (global) function and relation symbols, and (temporal) propositional letters.

We are interested only in the functions and relations of real arithmetic. Let $\mathbb{R}$ stand for the set of real numbers.

We assume that a total function

$$\underline{f}^n \in \mathbb{R}^n \to \mathbb{R}$$

is associated with each n-ary function symbol f^n, and a total function

$$\underline{G}^n \in \mathbb{R}^n \to \{\text{tt,ff}\}$$

is associated with each n-ary relation symbol G^n.

Function symbols, e.g. $+$ and $-$, and relation symbols, e.g. $\geq$ and $=$, are assumed to have their standard meanings. In particular, tt and ff are associated with "true" and "false", respectively, i.e. $\underline{\text{true}} = \text{tt}$ and $\underline{\text{false}} = \text{ff}$.

The meanings of global variables are given by a *value assignment* $\mathcal{V}$, which is a function associating a real number with each global variable:

$$\mathcal{V} \in GVar \to \mathbb{R}.$$

Let *Val* stand for the set of all value assignments:

$$Val \mathrel{\hat{=}} GVar \to \mathbb{R}.$$

Two value assignments $\mathcal{V}, \mathcal{V}' \in Val$ are called *x-equivalent* if $\mathcal{V}(y) = \mathcal{V}'(y)$ for every global variable y which is different from x.

Remember that $\mathbb{I}$ntv stands for the set of all bounded and closed intervals of real numbers:

$$\mathbb{I}\text{ntv} \mathrel{\hat{=}} \{\, [b, e] \mid b, e \in \mathbb{R} \ \wedge \ b \leq e \,\}.$$

The meanings of temporal variables and propositional letters, i.e. the "interval-dependent symbols", are given by an interpretation:

$$\mathcal{J} \in \begin{pmatrix} TVar \\ \cup \\ PLetters \end{pmatrix} \to \begin{pmatrix} \mathbb{I}\text{ntv} \to \mathbb{R} \\ \cup \\ \mathbb{I}\text{ntv} \to \{\text{tt,ff}\} \end{pmatrix},$$

where $\quad \begin{cases} \mathcal{J}(v)([b, e]) \in \mathbb{R}, \ \text{for all } v \in TVar, \\ \mathcal{J}(\ell)([b, e]) = e - b, \ \text{and} \\ \mathcal{J}(X)([b, e]) \in \{\text{tt,ff}\}, \ \text{for all } X \in PLetter. \end{cases}$

Thus, an interpretation $\mathcal{J}$ associates a real-valued interval function with each temporal variable and a truth-valued interval function with each temporal propositional letter. In particular, the special temporal variable ℓ denotes the interval length.

We shall use the following abbreviations:

$$v_{\mathcal{J}} \mathrel{\hat{=}} \mathcal{J}(v) \quad \text{and} \quad X_{\mathcal{J}} \mathrel{\hat{=}} \mathcal{J}(X).$$

The *semantics of a term* θ in an interpretation $\mathcal{J}$ is a function

$$\mathcal{J}[\![\theta]\!] \in (Val \times \mathbb{I}\text{ntv}) \to \mathbb{R},$$

defined inductively on the structure of terms by

$$\mathcal{J}[\![x]\!](\mathcal{V}, [b, e]) \qquad\qquad = \mathcal{V}(x)$$
$$\mathcal{J}[\![v]\!](\mathcal{V}, [b, e]) \qquad\qquad = v_{\mathcal{J}}([b, e])$$
$$\mathcal{J}[\![f^n(\theta_1, \ldots, \theta_n)]\!] \,(\mathcal{V}, [b, e]) = \underline{f}^n(c_1, \ldots, c_n),$$

where $c_i = \mathcal{J}[\![\theta_i]\!] \,(\mathcal{V}, [b, e])$, for $1 \leq i \leq n$.

The *semantics of a formula* ϕ in an interpretation $\mathcal{J}$ is a function

$$\mathcal{J}[\![\phi]\!] \in (Val \times \mathbb{I}\text{ntv}) \to \{\text{tt}, \text{ff}\},$$

defined inductively on the structure of formulas below, where the following abbreviations will be used:

$$\mathcal{J}, \mathcal{V}, [b, e] \models \phi \;\hat{=}\; \mathcal{J}[\![\phi]\!] \,(\mathcal{V}, [b, e]) = \text{tt}$$
$$\mathcal{J}, \mathcal{V}, [b, e] \not\models \phi \;\hat{=}\; \mathcal{J}[\![\phi]\!] \,(\mathcal{V}, [b, e]) = \text{ff}.$$

The definition of $\mathcal{J}[\![\phi]\!]$ is

1. $\mathcal{J}, \mathcal{V}, [b, e] \models X$
   iff $X_{\mathcal{J}}([b, e]) = \text{tt}$

2. $\mathcal{J}, \mathcal{V}, [b, e] \models G^n(\theta_1, \ldots, \theta_n)$
   iff $\underline{G}^n(c_1, \ldots, c_n) = \text{tt}$, where $c_i = \mathcal{J}[\![\theta_i]\!](\mathcal{V}, [b, e])$ for $1 \leq i \leq n$

3. $\mathcal{J}, \mathcal{V}, [b, e] \models \neg\phi$
   iff $\mathcal{J}, \mathcal{V}, [b, e] \not\models \phi$

4. $\mathcal{J}, \mathcal{V}, [b, e] \models \phi \vee \psi$
   iff $\mathcal{J}, \mathcal{V}, [b, e] \models \phi$ or $\mathcal{J}, \mathcal{V}, [b, e] \models \psi$

5. $\mathcal{J}, \mathcal{V}, [b, e] \models \phi \frown \psi$
   iff $\mathcal{J}, \mathcal{V}, [b, m] \models \phi$ and $\mathcal{J}, \mathcal{V}, [m, e] \models \psi$ for some $m \in [b, e]$

6. $\mathcal{J}, \mathcal{V}, [b, e] \models (\exists x)\phi$
   iff $\mathcal{J}, \mathcal{V}', [b, e] \models \phi$ $\left(\begin{array}{l}\text{for some value assignment } \mathcal{V}' \\ \text{which is } x\text{-equivalent to } \mathcal{V}\end{array}\right)$.

A formula ϕ is *valid*, written

$$\models \phi,$$

iff $\mathcal{J}, \mathcal{V}, [b, e] \models \phi$ for every interpretation $\mathcal{J}$, value assignment $\mathcal{V}$, and interval $[b, e]$. Furthermore, a formula ψ is *satisfiable* iff $\mathcal{J}, \mathcal{V}, [b, e] \models \psi$ for some interpretation $\mathcal{J}$, value assignment $\mathcal{V}$ and interval $[b, e]$.

2.3 Proof System

The proof system of IL that we adopt here is called S' in [28].

To formulate the axioms and inference rules, we need the standard notions of free (global) variables. A term or formula is called *flexible* if a temporal variable including the symbol ℓ or a propositional letter occurs in the term or formula. A term or formula which is not flexible is called *rigid*.

Note that a rigid formula may include the chop modality. For example, the formula $((x \geq y)\,{}^\frown\text{true})$ is rigid.

The axioms of IL are:

A0 $\ell \geq 0$.

A1 $\begin{aligned} &((\phi\,{}^\frown\psi) \wedge \neg(\phi\,{}^\frown\varphi)) \;\Rightarrow\; (\phi\,{}^\frown(\psi \wedge \neg\varphi)). \\ &((\phi\,{}^\frown\psi) \wedge \neg(\varphi\,{}^\frown\psi)) \;\Rightarrow\; ((\phi \wedge \neg\varphi)\,{}^\frown\psi). \end{aligned}$

A2 $((\phi\,{}^\frown\psi)\,{}^\frown\varphi) \;\Leftrightarrow\; (\phi\,{}^\frown(\psi\,{}^\frown\varphi))$.

R $\begin{aligned} &(\phi\,{}^\frown\psi) \Rightarrow \phi \text{ if } \phi \text{ is a rigid formula.} \\ &(\phi\,{}^\frown\psi) \Rightarrow \psi \text{ if } \psi \text{ is a rigid formula.} \end{aligned}$

E $\begin{aligned} &(\exists x.\phi\,{}^\frown\psi) \Rightarrow \exists x.(\phi\,{}^\frown\psi) \text{ if } x \text{ is not free in } \psi. \\ &(\phi\,{}^\frown\exists x.\psi) \Rightarrow \exists x.(\phi\,{}^\frown\psi) \text{ if } x \text{ is not free in } \phi. \end{aligned}$

L1 $\begin{aligned} &((\ell = x)\,{}^\frown\phi) \Rightarrow \neg((\ell = x)\,{}^\frown\neg\phi). \\ &(\phi\,{}^\frown(\ell = x)) \Rightarrow \neg(\neg\phi\,{}^\frown(\ell = x)). \end{aligned}$

L2 $(x \geq 0 \wedge y \geq 0) \Rightarrow ((\ell = x + y) \Leftrightarrow ((\ell = x)\,{}^\frown(\ell = y)))$.

L3 $\begin{aligned} &\phi \Rightarrow (\phi\,{}^\frown(\ell = 0)). \\ &\phi \Rightarrow ((\ell = 0)\,{}^\frown\phi). \end{aligned}$

The inference rules of IL are:

MP if ϕ and $\phi \Rightarrow \psi$ then ψ.

G if ϕ then $(\forall x)\phi$.

N $\begin{aligned} &\text{if } \phi \text{ then } \neg(\neg\phi\,{}^\frown\psi). \\ &\text{if } \phi \text{ then } \neg(\psi\,{}^\frown\neg\phi). \end{aligned}$

M $\begin{aligned} &\text{if } \phi \Rightarrow \psi \text{ then } (\phi\,{}^\frown\varphi) \Rightarrow (\psi\,{}^\frown\varphi). \\ &\text{if } \phi \Rightarrow \psi \text{ then } (\varphi\,{}^\frown\phi) \Rightarrow (\varphi\,{}^\frown\psi). \end{aligned}$

The inference rule MP is called "modus ponens". The inference rule G is the standard generalization rule from first-order logic, and G is called generalization. The inference rule N is called the rule of necessity, and the inference rule M is the monotonicity rules for chop.

Predicate Logic

The proof system also contains axioms of first-order predicate logic with equality. Any axiomatic basis can be chosen. Special care must, however, be taken when universally quantified formulas are instantiated and when an existential quantifier is introduced.

A term θ is called *free for x* in ϕ if x does not occur freely in ϕ within the scope of $\exists y$ or $\forall y$, where y is any variable occurring in θ.

Furthermore, a formula is called *chop free* if $\frown$ does not occur in the formula.

We first illustrate by simple examples why side-conditions are needed in the axiom schemas for the quantifiers.

For example, the term y is free for x in $(\exists z)(z > x)$, whereas y is not free for x in $(\exists y)(y > x)$. These two formulas are both valid. Instantiation of x with y in the first formula yields $(\exists z)(z > y)$, which is a valid formula. However, instantiation of x with y in the second formula yields $(\exists y)(y > y)$, which is not valid.

Furthermore, consider the following universally quantified and valid formula:

$$(\forall x)(((\ell = x) \frown (\ell = x)) \Rightarrow (\ell = 2x)).$$

This formula is not chop free and instantiating it with the term ℓ, which is flexible, yields the formula

$$((\ell = \ell) \frown (\ell = \ell)) \Rightarrow (\ell = 2\ell),$$

which is not valid.

Therefore, side-conditions occur in the following two axiom schemas:

Q1 $\forall x.\phi(x) \Rightarrow \phi(\theta)$ $\qquad \left(\begin{array}{l} \text{if } \theta \text{ is free for } x \text{ in } \phi(x), \text{ and} \\ \text{either } \theta \text{ is rigid or } \phi(x) \text{ is chop free.} \end{array} \right)$
Q2 $\phi(\theta) \Rightarrow \exists x.\phi(x)$

The proof system has to contain axioms of a first-order logic for the value and time domain of IL, namely a first-order logic of real arithmetic. In this book, we shall avoid the issue of formalization of real arithmetic, but apply informal understanding of it in proofs.

Proof and Deduction

Formally, a *proof* of ϕ is a finite sequence of formulas $\phi_1 \cdots \phi_n$, where ϕ_n is ϕ, and each ϕ_i is either an instance of one of the above axiom schemas or obtained by applying one of the above inference rules to previous members of the sequence. We write

$$\vdash \phi$$

to denote that there exists a proof of ϕ in IL, and we call ϕ a *theorem* of IL in this case.

A *deduction of ϕ in IL from a set of formulas Γ* is a sequence of formulas $\phi_1 \cdots \phi_n$, where ϕ_n is ϕ, and each ϕ_i is either a member of Γ, an instance of one of the above axiom schemas or obtained by applying one of the above inference rules to previous members of the sequence. We write

$$\Gamma \vdash \phi$$

to denote that there exists a deduction of ϕ from Γ in IL, and we write

$$\Gamma, \phi \vdash \psi$$

for $(\Gamma \cup \{\phi\}) \vdash \psi$.

The following theorem about the soundness of the IL proof system is an example of a metatheorem which expresses a property of IL.

Theorem 2.1 *(Soundness)*

$$\vdash \phi \ \textit{implies} \ \models \phi.$$

Proof. It in not difficult to show that each axiom is a valid formula, and that each rule preserves validity in the sense that it gives a valid formula when applied to valid formulas. $\square$

Theorems and derived rules of IL will be denoted IL1, IL2, ..., to distinguish them from the metatheorems. Henceforth, in proofs of IL theorems and metatheorems, we shall use "PL" when we refer to predicate-logic theorems or real-arithmetic theorems.

The logic IL is an extension of the modal logic S4 (e.g. [66]) since the following three theorems and one derived rule can be proved in IL (remember that $\Box \phi$ is an abbreviation of $\neg \Diamond \neg \phi$ and that $\Diamond \psi$ is an abbreviation of $(\text{true} \frown (\psi \frown \text{true}))$:

IL1 $\Box(\phi \Rightarrow \psi) \Rightarrow (\Box\phi \Rightarrow \Box\psi)$.

IL2 $\Box\phi \Rightarrow \phi$.

IL3 $\Box\phi \Leftrightarrow \Box\Box\phi$.

IL4 $\phi \vdash \Box\phi$.

We give proofs of IL1 and IL4 only.

Proof. A proof of IL1:

   1. $(\neg(\text{true}^\frown(\neg\phi^\frown\text{true})) \wedge (\text{true}^\frown(\neg\psi^\frown\text{true})))$
      $\Rightarrow (\text{true}^\frown((\neg\psi^\frown\text{true}) \wedge \neg(\neg\phi^\frown\text{true})))$ A1
   2. $((\neg\psi^\frown\text{true}) \wedge \neg(\neg\phi^\frown\text{true}))$
      $\Rightarrow ((\neg\psi \wedge \neg\neg\phi)^\frown\text{true})$ A1
   3. $(\neg(\text{true}^\frown(\neg\phi^\frown\text{true})) \wedge (\text{true}^\frown(\neg\psi^\frown\text{true})))$
      $\Rightarrow (\text{true}^\frown((\phi \wedge \neg\psi)^\frown\text{true}))$ 1., 2., M, PL
   4. $(\Box\phi \wedge \neg\Box\psi) \Rightarrow \neg\Box(\phi \Rightarrow \psi)$ 3., Def($\Box$)
   5. $\Box(\phi \Rightarrow \psi) \Rightarrow (\Box\phi \Rightarrow \Box\psi)$ 4., PL.

$\square$

Proof. A proof of IL4:

   1. ϕ assumption
   2. $\neg(\neg\phi^\frown\text{true})$ 1., N
   3. $\neg(\text{true}^\frown\neg(\neg(\neg\phi^\frown\text{true})))$ 2., N
   4. $(\neg\phi^\frown\text{true}) \Rightarrow \neg(\neg(\neg\phi^\frown\text{true}))$ PL
   5. $(\text{true}^\frown(\neg\phi^\frown\text{true})) \Rightarrow (\text{true}^\frown\neg(\neg(\neg\phi^\frown\text{true})))$ 4., M
   6. $\neg(\text{true}^\frown\neg(\neg(\neg\phi^\frown\text{true}))) \Rightarrow \neg(\text{true}^\frown(\neg\phi^\frown\text{true}))$ 5., PL
   7. $\neg(\text{true}^\frown(\neg\phi^\frown\text{true}))$ 3., 6., MP.

$\square$

The following theorems and derived rule about $\Box$ will be used later in the proof of the deduction theorem:

IL5 $\Box\phi \Rightarrow \neg(\neg\phi^\frown\psi)$.
           $\Box\phi \Rightarrow \neg(\psi^\frown\neg\phi)$.

IL6 $\Box\phi \Rightarrow \psi \vdash \Box\phi \Rightarrow \Box\psi$.

IL7 $\Box(\phi \Rightarrow \varphi) \Rightarrow ((\phi^\frown\psi) \Rightarrow (\varphi^\frown\psi))$.
           $\Box(\phi \Rightarrow \varphi) \Rightarrow ((\psi^\frown\phi) \Rightarrow (\psi^\frown\varphi))$.

Proof. The two parts of IL5 are similar, so we consider only the first. We prove $(\neg\phi^\frown\psi) \Rightarrow \neg\Box\phi$, i.e. $(\neg\phi^\frown\psi) \Rightarrow (\text{true}^\frown(\neg\phi^\frown\text{true}))$, to prove IL5:

   1. $\psi \Rightarrow \text{true}$ PL
   2. $(\neg\phi^\frown\psi) \Rightarrow (\neg\phi^\frown\text{true})$ 1., M
   3. $\ell = 0 \Rightarrow \text{true}$ PL
   4. $(\ell = 0^\frown(\neg\phi^\frown\psi)) \Rightarrow (\text{true}^\frown(\neg\phi^\frown\psi))$ 3., M
   5. $(\text{true}^\frown(\neg\phi^\frown\psi)) \Rightarrow (\text{true}^\frown(\neg\phi^\frown\text{true}))$ 2., M
   6. $(\ell = 0^\frown(\neg\phi^\frown\psi)) \Rightarrow (\text{true}^\frown(\neg\phi^\frown\text{true}))$ 4., 5., PL
   7. $(\neg\phi^\frown\psi) \Rightarrow (\ell = 0^\frown(\neg\phi^\frown\psi))$ L3
   8. $(\neg\phi^\frown\psi) \Rightarrow (\text{true}^\frown(\neg\phi^\frown\text{true}))$ 7., 6., PL.

The following is a proof of IL6:

1. $\Box\phi \Rightarrow \psi$ assumption
2. $\Box(\Box\phi \Rightarrow \psi)$ 1., IL4
3. $\Box(\Box\phi \Rightarrow \psi) \Rightarrow (\Box\Box\phi \Rightarrow \Box\psi)$ IL1
4. $\Box\Box\phi \Rightarrow \Box\psi$ 2., 3., MP
5. $\Box\phi \Rightarrow \Box\Box\phi$ IL3
6. $\Box\phi \Rightarrow \Box\psi$ 5., 4., PL.

The proof of IL7 is left for the reader.   □

2.3.1 Deduction

In order to simplify proofs, we establish a deduction theorem for IL here.

Theorem 2.2 *(Deduction) If a deduction*

$$\Gamma, \phi \vdash \psi$$

involves no application of the generalization rule G in which the quantified variable is free in ϕ, then

$$\Gamma \vdash \Box\phi \Rightarrow \psi.$$

Proof. The proof is by induction on the length n of the deduction $\Gamma, \phi \vdash \psi$.

Base step: $n = 1$. Then ψ must be either ϕ, a member of Γ or an axiom.

Case where ψ is ϕ: This case is simple, since $\vdash \Box\phi \Rightarrow \phi$ by IL2 and thus, trivially, $\Gamma \vdash \Box\phi \Rightarrow \psi$.

Case where ψ is an axiom or a member of Γ: In this case the following deduction establishes $\Gamma \vdash \Box\phi \Rightarrow \psi$:

1. ψ
2. $\psi \Rightarrow (\Box\phi \Rightarrow \psi)$ PL
3. $\Box\phi \Rightarrow \psi$ 1., 2., MP.

Inductive step: Suppose $n > 0$. The induction hypothesis is: If $\Gamma, \phi \vdash \varphi$, by a deduction of length shorter than n which does not contain an application of the generalization rule G in which the quantified variable is free in ϕ, then $\Gamma \vdash \Box\phi \Rightarrow \varphi$.

The case where ψ is either ϕ, a member of Γ or an axiom is as above. Otherwise, an inference rule is applied in the last step in the deduction:

Case MP: The deduction from $\Gamma \cup \{\phi\}$ has the form

$$\vdots$$
$$\psi_1$$
$$\vdots$$
$$\psi_1 \Rightarrow \psi$$
$$\vdots$$
$$\psi .$$

There are deductions of $\Box\phi \Rightarrow \psi_1$ and $\Box\phi \Rightarrow (\psi_1 \Rightarrow \psi)$ from Γ, by the induction hypothesis. A deduction of $\Box\phi \Rightarrow \psi$ from Γ can be given as follows:

$$\left. \begin{array}{l} \vdots \\ k.\ \Box\phi \Rightarrow \psi_1 \end{array} \right\} \text{deduction of } \Box\phi \Rightarrow \psi_1 \text{ from } \Gamma$$

$$\left. \begin{array}{l} \vdots \\ l.\ \Box\phi \Rightarrow (\psi_1 \Rightarrow \psi) \end{array} \right\} \text{deduction of } \Box\phi \Rightarrow (\psi_1 \Rightarrow \psi) \text{ from } \Gamma$$

$l + 1.\ (\Box\phi \Rightarrow (\psi_1 \Rightarrow \psi)) \Rightarrow ((\Box\phi \Rightarrow \psi_1) \Rightarrow (\Box\phi \Rightarrow \psi))$ PL
$l + 2.\ (\Box\phi \Rightarrow \psi_1) \Rightarrow (\Box\phi \Rightarrow \psi)$ $l., l+1., \text{MP}$
$l + 3.\ \Box\phi \Rightarrow \psi$ $k., l+2., \text{MP}.$

Case G: ψ has the form $(\forall x)\psi_1$, and the deduction from $\Gamma \cup \{\phi\}$ has the form

$$\vdots$$
$$\psi_1$$
$$\vdots$$
$$(\forall x)\psi_1 .$$

Note that x does not occur freely in ϕ and hence in $\Box\phi$. Thus, we have, from PL,

$$\vdash (\forall x)(\Box\phi \Rightarrow \psi_1) \Rightarrow (\Box\phi \Rightarrow (\forall x)\psi_1) .$$

By the induction hypothesis, there is a deduction of $\Box\phi \Rightarrow \psi_1$ from Γ. A deduction of $\Box\phi \Rightarrow (\forall x)\psi_1$ from Γ can be given as follows:

$$\left. \begin{array}{l} \vdots \\ k.\ \Box\phi \Rightarrow \psi_1 \end{array} \right\} \text{deduction of } \Box\phi \Rightarrow \psi_1 \text{ from } \Gamma$$

$k + 1.\ (\forall x)(\Box\phi \Rightarrow \psi_1)$ $k., \text{G}$
$k + 2.\ (\forall x)(\Box\phi \Rightarrow \psi_1) \Rightarrow (\Box\phi \Rightarrow (\forall x)\psi_1)$ PL
$k + 3.\ \Box\phi \Rightarrow (\forall x)\psi_1$ $k+1., k+2., \text{MP}.$

Case N: We give only a proof of the first rule of N. The second rule can be proved similarly. Let ψ have the form $\neg(\neg\psi_1 {}^\frown \varphi)$, and the deduction from $\Gamma \cup \{\phi\}$ have the form

$$\vdots$$
$$\psi_1$$
$$\vdots$$
$$\neg(\neg\psi_1 {}^\frown \varphi)\,.$$

By the induction hypothesis, there is a deduction of $\Box\phi \Rightarrow \psi_1$ from Γ. A deduction of $\Box\phi \Rightarrow \neg(\neg\psi_1 {}^\frown \varphi)$ from Γ can be given as follows:

$$\left.\begin{array}{l} \vdots \\ k.\ \Box\phi \Rightarrow \psi_1 \end{array}\right\} \text{deduction of } \Box\phi \Rightarrow \psi_1 \text{ from } \Gamma$$

$k + 1.\ \Box\phi \Rightarrow \Box\psi_1$ $k., \text{IL6}$
$k + 2.\ \Box\psi_1 \Rightarrow \neg(\neg\psi_1 {}^\frown \varphi)$ IL5
$k + 3.\ \Box\phi \Rightarrow \neg(\neg\psi_1 {}^\frown \varphi)$ $k + 1., k + 2., \text{PL.}$

Case M: We give only a proof of the first rule of M. The second rule can be proved similarly. Let ψ have the form $(\psi_1 {}^\frown \varphi) \Rightarrow (\psi_2 {}^\frown \varphi)$, and the deduction from $\Gamma \cup \{\phi\}$ have the form

$$\vdots$$
$$\psi_1 \Rightarrow \psi_2$$
$$\vdots$$
$$(\psi_1 {}^\frown \varphi) \Rightarrow (\psi_2 {}^\frown \varphi)\,.$$

By the induction hypothesis, there is a deduction of $\Box\phi \Rightarrow (\psi_1 \Rightarrow \psi_2)$ from Γ. A deduction of $\Box\phi \Rightarrow ((\psi_1 {}^\frown \varphi) \Rightarrow (\psi_2 {}^\frown \varphi))$ from Γ can be given as follows:

$$\left.\begin{array}{l} \vdots \\ k.\ \Box\phi \Rightarrow (\psi_1 \Rightarrow \psi_2) \end{array}\right\} \text{deduction of } \Box\phi \Rightarrow (\psi_1 \Rightarrow \psi_2) \text{ from } \Gamma$$

$k + 1.\ \Box\phi \Rightarrow \Box(\psi_1 \Rightarrow \psi_2)$ $k., \text{IL6}$
$k + 2.\ \Box(\psi_1 \Rightarrow \psi_2) \Rightarrow ((\psi_1 {}^\frown \varphi) \Rightarrow (\psi_2 {}^\frown \varphi))$ IL7
$k + 3.\ \Box\phi \Rightarrow ((\psi_1 {}^\frown \varphi) \Rightarrow (\psi_2 {}^\frown \varphi))$ $k + 1., k + 2., \text{PL.}$

This ends the proof of the deduction theorem.   □

Proofs can sometimes be obtained more easily by using the deduction theorem. We can, for example, prove

IL8 $\Box(\phi \Rightarrow \psi) \Rightarrow \Box(\Box\phi \Rightarrow \Box\psi)$

from a deduction of $\Box(\Box\phi \Rightarrow \Box\psi)$ from $\{(\phi \Rightarrow \psi)\}$ using Theorem 2.2:

1. $\phi \Rightarrow \psi$
2. $\Box(\phi \Rightarrow \psi)$ 1., IL4
3. $\Box\phi \Rightarrow \Box\psi$ 2., IL1, MP
4. $\Box(\Box\phi \Rightarrow \Box\psi)$ 3., IL4.

Remark. Although we shall avoid the issue of formalizing real arithmetic, it is still interesting to mention a result in [28], where it is proved that, given any first-order logic for the value and time domain of IL which includes at least axioms for defining totally ordered commutative groups, the proof system is complete with respect to abstract domains of the given logic. $\Box$

2.4 Theorems

In this section, we shall present a collection of theorems and derived rules of IL which can help one to understand the logic and to conduct proofs. Some of the theorems are proved. Others are left as exercises.

Sometimes we shall use the following convention for presenting a proof:

$$
\begin{array}{l}
\phi_1 \\
\Rightarrow \phi_2 \\
\Rightarrow \phi_3
\end{array}
\quad \text{is an abbreviation for} \quad
\begin{array}{l}
1.\ \phi_1 \Rightarrow \phi_2 \\
2.\ (\phi_1 \wedge \phi_2) \Rightarrow \phi_3 \\
3.\ \phi_1 \Rightarrow \phi_3
\end{array}
$$

and

$$
\begin{array}{l}
\phi_1 \\
\Leftrightarrow \phi_2 \\
\Leftrightarrow \phi_3
\end{array}
\quad \text{is an abbreviation for} \quad
\begin{array}{l}
1.\ \phi_1 \Leftrightarrow \phi_2 \\
2.\ \phi_2 \Leftrightarrow \phi_3 \\
3.\ \phi_1 \Leftrightarrow \phi_3\ .
\end{array}
$$

This generalizes to longer chains: $\phi_1 \Rightarrow \cdots \Rightarrow \phi_n$ and $\phi_1 \Leftrightarrow \cdots \Leftrightarrow \phi_n$.

Quantifications

Some of the theorems and rules about quantification which will be used later are

$$
\left.
\begin{array}{l}
\forall x.(\phi \Rightarrow \psi) \Rightarrow (\exists x.\phi \Rightarrow \psi) \\
\forall x.(\psi \Rightarrow \phi) \Rightarrow (\psi \Rightarrow \forall x.\phi) \\
(\phi \Rightarrow \psi), \exists x.\phi \vdash \psi
\end{array}
\right\}
\quad \text{if } x \text{ does not occur free in } \psi.
$$

Predicate Logic and Temporal Variables

Throughout the book we shall introduce length, and other temporal variables, into "pure" theorems of predicate logic. For example

$$
\forall x.\exists y.(x = y)
$$

is a "pure" theorem of predicate logic. This formula is chop free and the term ℓ is free for x in $\exists y.(x = y)$. Hence, by Q1, the following formula is a theorem of IL:

$$\exists y.(\ell = y).$$

Many other theorems can be proved in a similar way, e.g.

$$(\ell \geq y) \Rightarrow \exists z \geq 0.(\ell = y + z).$$

In the following, we shall simply refer to PL when we introduce theorems such as the two above.

Rigid Formulas

Using the axiom schema R, one can derive many useful theorems for rigid formulas. For example

IL9 $\phi \Leftrightarrow \Box\phi$ if ϕ is a rigid formula.

IL10
$$\forall x.(\phi \Rightarrow (\varphi \frown \psi)) \vdash \forall x.(\phi \Rightarrow \varphi) \quad \text{if } \varphi \text{ is a rigid formula.}$$
$$\forall x.(\phi \Rightarrow (\varphi \frown \psi)) \vdash \forall x.(\phi \Rightarrow \psi) \quad \text{if } \psi \text{ is a rigid formula.}$$

The proofs are left as exercises.

Existence of Length

IL11 $(\ell = x) \Rightarrow \phi \vdash \phi$ if x is not free in ϕ.

Proof.

1. $(\ell = x) \Rightarrow \phi$		assumption
2. $\forall x.((\ell = x) \Rightarrow \phi)$		1., G
3. $\forall x.((\ell = x) \Rightarrow \phi) \Rightarrow (\exists x.(\ell = x) \Rightarrow \phi)$		PL (x not free in ϕ)
4. $\exists x.(\ell = x) \Rightarrow \phi$		2., 3., MP
5. $\exists x.(\ell = x)$		PL
6. ϕ		4., 5., MP.

$\square$

Existential Quantification and Chop

IL12 $\exists x.(\phi \frown \psi) \Rightarrow (\exists x.\phi \frown \exists x.\psi).$

Proof.

1. $\phi \Rightarrow \exists x.\phi$	PL
2. $\psi \Rightarrow \exists x.\psi$	PL
3. $(\phi \frown \psi) \Rightarrow (\exists x.\phi \frown \exists x.\psi)$	1., 2., M
4. $\forall x.((\phi \frown \psi) \Rightarrow (\exists x.\phi \frown \exists x.\psi))$	3., G
5. $\exists x.(\phi \frown \psi) \Rightarrow (\exists x.\phi \frown \exists x.\psi)$	4., PL.

$\square$

Chop and False

IL13 $(\psi \,{}^\frown\text{false}) \Leftrightarrow \text{false}.$
$(\text{false} \,{}^\frown\psi) \Leftrightarrow \text{false}.$

Proof. The direction $\Rightarrow$ follows from R, since false is a rigid formula. The other direction follows from PL. $\qquad\square$

Chop and Disjunction

IL14 $((\phi \vee \psi) \,{}^\frown\varphi) \Leftrightarrow ((\phi \,{}^\frown\varphi) \vee (\psi \,{}^\frown\varphi)).$
$(\phi \,{}^\frown(\psi \vee \varphi)) \Leftrightarrow ((\phi \,{}^\frown\psi) \vee (\phi \,{}^\frown\varphi)).$

Proof. The directions $\Leftarrow$ follow straightforwardly from M. We prove the other direction of the first theorem by the method of reductio ad absurdum:

$$((\phi \vee \psi) \,{}^\frown\varphi) \,\wedge\, \neg((\phi \,{}^\frown\varphi) \vee (\psi \,{}^\frown\varphi))$$
$$\Rightarrow ((\phi \vee \psi) \,{}^\frown\varphi) \,\wedge\, \neg(\phi \,{}^\frown\varphi) \,\wedge\, \neg(\psi \,{}^\frown\varphi) \quad \text{PL}$$
$$\Rightarrow ((\phi \vee \psi) \wedge \neg\phi \wedge \neg\psi) \,{}^\frown\varphi \quad \text{A1}$$
$$\Rightarrow \text{false} \,{}^\frown\varphi \quad \text{PL, M}$$
$$\Rightarrow \text{false} \quad \text{IL13}.$$

$\qquad\square$

Chop and Negation

IL15 $((\ell = x \wedge \phi) \,{}^\frown\psi) \Rightarrow \neg((\ell = x \wedge \neg\phi) \,{}^\frown\varphi).$
$(\phi \,{}^\frown(\ell = x \wedge \psi)) \Rightarrow \neg(\varphi \,{}^\frown(\ell = x \wedge \neg\psi)).$

IL16 $(\ell \geq x \wedge \neg(\ell = x \,{}^\frown\neg\phi)) \Leftrightarrow (\ell = x \,{}^\frown\phi).$
$(\ell \geq x \wedge \neg(\neg\phi \,{}^\frown\ell = x)) \Leftrightarrow (\phi \,{}^\frown\ell = x).$

Proof. We prove only the direction $\Rightarrow$ of the first theorem of IL16.

$$(\ell \geq x) \,\wedge\, \neg((\ell = x) \,{}^\frown\neg\phi)$$
$$\Rightarrow (\exists y \geq 0.(\ell = x + y)) \,\wedge\, \neg((\ell = x) \,{}^\frown\neg\phi) \quad \text{PL}$$
$$\Rightarrow ((\ell = x) \,{}^\frown\exists y \geq 0.(\ell = y)) \,\wedge\, \neg((\ell = x) \,{}^\frown\neg\phi) \quad \text{L2, IL12, M, PL}$$
$$\Rightarrow ((\ell = x) \,{}^\frown\text{true}) \,\wedge\, \neg((\ell = x) \,{}^\frown\neg\phi) \quad \text{PL, M}$$
$$\Rightarrow (\ell = x) \,{}^\frown(\text{true} \wedge \neg\neg\phi) \quad \text{A1}$$
$$\Rightarrow (\ell = x) \,{}^\frown\phi \quad \text{PL, M}.$$

$\qquad\square$

Chop and Conjunction

IL17

$$\left(\begin{array}{l}((\phi_1 \wedge \ell = x) \,^\frown \psi_1) \\ \wedge ((\phi_2 \wedge \ell = x) \,^\frown \psi_2)\end{array}\right) \Leftrightarrow ((\phi_1 \wedge \phi_2 \wedge \ell = x) \,^\frown (\psi_1 \wedge \psi_2)).$$

$$\left(\begin{array}{l}(\phi_1 \,^\frown (\psi_1 \wedge \ell = x)) \\ \wedge (\phi_2 \,^\frown (\psi_2 \wedge \ell = x))\end{array}\right) \Leftrightarrow ((\phi_1 \wedge \phi_2) \,^\frown (\psi_1 \wedge \psi_2 \wedge \ell = x)).$$

Proof. The proof of IL17 is quite tedious. We sketch here a proof of the $\Rightarrow$ part of the first theorem, and leave the rest for readers. This proof involves two lemmas. The first lemma is

$$(((\ell = x) \,^\frown \psi_1) \wedge ((\ell = x) \,^\frown \psi_2)) \Rightarrow ((\ell = x) \,^\frown (\psi_1 \wedge \psi_2)).$$

By L1, L2 and IL14, we can derive

$$(((\ell = x) \,^\frown \psi_1) \wedge ((\ell = x) \,^\frown \psi_2)) \Rightarrow ((\ell \geq x) \wedge \neg((\ell = x) \,^\frown \neg(\psi_1 \wedge \psi_2))).$$

Hence, from IL16, we can obtain the first lemma. The second lemma is

$$((((\ell = x) \wedge \phi_1) \,^\frown \text{true}) \wedge (((\ell = x) \wedge \phi_2) \,^\frown \text{true}))$$
$$\Rightarrow (((\ell = x) \wedge \phi_1 \wedge \phi_2) \,^\frown \text{true}).$$

The proof is similar to that of the first lemma but through IL11. By assuming y to be the length of the interval concerned, from L2 we can conclude that the length of the second subinterval is $(y - x)$. Therefore, we can follow the proof of the first lemma to prove

$$((\phi_1 \,^\frown (\ell = y - x)) \wedge (\phi_2 \,^\frown (\ell = y - x))) \Rightarrow ((\phi_1 \wedge \phi_2) \,^\frown (\ell = y - x))$$

and hence the lemma. On the basis of the above lemmas, we can conclude the theorem through

$$((\phi_1 \wedge \phi_2 \wedge (\ell = x)) \,^\frown \text{true}) \wedge \neg((\phi_1 \wedge \phi_2 \wedge (\ell = x)) \,^\frown (\psi_1 \wedge \psi_2))$$
$$\Rightarrow (\phi_1 \wedge \phi_2 \wedge (\ell = x)) \,^\frown \neg(\psi_1 \wedge \psi_2) \qquad\qquad \text{A1}$$
$$\Rightarrow (\ell = x) \,^\frown \neg(\psi_1 \wedge \psi_2) \qquad\qquad\qquad\qquad \text{M}$$
$$\Rightarrow \neg((\ell = x) \,^\frown (\psi_1 \wedge \psi_2)) \qquad\qquad\qquad\quad \text{L1.}$$

$\square$

Chop and Point

IL18

$$(\phi \,^\frown \ell = 0) \Leftrightarrow \phi.$$

$$(\ell = 0 \,^\frown \phi) \Leftrightarrow \phi.$$

Proof. The direction $\Leftarrow$ follows from L3. The other direction is proved as follows:

$$(\phi \,^\frown \ell = 0) \wedge \neg\phi$$
$$\Rightarrow (\phi \,^\frown \ell = 0) \wedge (\neg\phi \,^\frown \ell = 0) \quad \text{L3}$$
$$\Rightarrow (\phi \wedge \neg\phi) \,^\frown \ell = 0 \qquad\qquad \text{IL17}$$
$$\Rightarrow \text{false} \,^\frown \ell = 0 \qquad\qquad\quad\; \text{M}$$
$$\Rightarrow \text{false} \qquad\qquad\qquad\qquad\; \text{IL13.}$$

$\square$

Chop and Box

IL19
$$(\Box\phi \land (\psi \,\widehat{}\, \varphi)) \Rightarrow ((\phi \land \psi)\,\widehat{}\,\varphi)\,.$$
$$(\Box\phi \land (\psi \,\widehat{}\, \varphi)) \Rightarrow (\psi\,\widehat{}\,(\phi \land \varphi))\,.$$

Proof. The following is a proof of $(\Box\phi \land (\psi\,\widehat{}\,\varphi)) \Rightarrow ((\phi \land \psi)\,\widehat{}\,\varphi)$:

1. $(\Box\phi \land (\psi\,\widehat{}\,\varphi)) \Rightarrow (\neg(\neg\phi\,\widehat{}\,\varphi) \land (\psi\,\widehat{}\,\varphi))$ IL5, PL
2. $(\neg(\neg\phi\,\widehat{}\,\varphi) \land (\psi\,\widehat{}\,\varphi)) \Rightarrow ((\neg\neg\phi \land \psi)\,\widehat{}\,\varphi)$ A1
3. $(\Box\phi \land (\psi\,\widehat{}\,\varphi)) \Rightarrow ((\neg\neg\phi \land \psi)\,\widehat{}\,\varphi)$ 1., 2., PL
4. $((\neg\neg\phi \land \psi)\,\widehat{}\,\varphi) \Rightarrow ((\phi \land \psi)\,\widehat{}\,\varphi)$ M
5. $(\Box\phi \land (\psi\,\widehat{}\,\varphi)) \Rightarrow ((\phi \land \psi)\,\widehat{}\,\varphi)$ 3., 4., PL.

The other proof is similar.   □

Chop and Length

IL20
$$((\ell > 0)\,\widehat{}\,(\ell > 0)) \;\Leftrightarrow\; (\ell > 0)\,.$$
$$((\ell \geq 0)\,\widehat{}\,(\ell > 0)) \;\Leftrightarrow\; (\ell > 0)\,.$$
$$((\ell > 0)\,\widehat{}\,(\ell \geq 0)) \;\Leftrightarrow\; (\ell > 0)\,.$$

Proof. We first give a proof of $((\ell > 0)\,\widehat{}\,(\ell > 0)) \;\Rightarrow \ell > 0$:

1. $(\ell > 0)\,\widehat{}\,(\ell > 0)$
   $\Rightarrow \exists x > 0.(\ell = x)\,\widehat{}\,\exists y > 0.(\ell = y)$ PL, M
   $\Rightarrow \exists x > 0.\exists y > 0.((\ell = x)\,\widehat{}\,(\ell = y))$ E
2. $(x > 0 \land y > 0 \land ((\ell = x)\,\widehat{}\,(\ell = y))) \Rightarrow (\ell > 0)$ PL, L2
3. $((\ell > 0)\,\widehat{}\,(\ell > 0)) \;\Rightarrow\; (\ell > 0)$ 1., 2., PL.

The following is a proof of $(\ell > 0) \;\Rightarrow\; ((\ell > 0)\,\widehat{}\,(\ell > 0))$:

$\ell > 0$
$\Rightarrow \exists x > 0.(\ell = x)$ PL
$\Rightarrow \exists x > 0.(\ell = x/2 + x/2)$ PL
$\Rightarrow \exists x > 0.((\ell = x/2)\,\widehat{}\,(\ell = x/2))$ PL, L2
$\Rightarrow (\exists x > 0.(\ell = x/2))\,\widehat{}\,(\exists x > 0.(\ell = x/2))$ IL12
$\Rightarrow (\ell > 0)\,\widehat{}\,(\ell > 0)$ PL, M.

The other proofs are similar.   □

Box and Length

The following theorem illustrates that the □ modality can be expressed in terms of length and chop without using negation. The theorem can be proved using techniques similar to those used above in the proof of IL20.

IL21 $\Box\phi \Leftrightarrow \forall x, y \geq 0.(x + y \leq \ell) \Rightarrow ((\ell = x)\,\widehat{}\,\phi\,\widehat{}\,(\ell = y))$
provided x, y do not occur free in ϕ.

Box and Conjunction

IL22 $\Box(\phi \wedge \psi) \Leftrightarrow (\Box\phi \wedge \Box\psi)$.

Box and Disjunction

IL23 $(\Box\phi \vee \Box\psi) \Rightarrow \Box(\phi \vee \psi)$.

Prefix Intervals

It is often convenient to specify properties of *prefix intervals,* i.e. intervals starting a given interval. For example, in Chap. 4, to formulate the deadline-driven scheduler, we specify the behavior of the processes on intervals starting at time 0.

Below we give some definitions and theorems for the properties of prefix intervals:

$\Diamond_p\phi \;\hat{=}\; \phi^\frown\text{true}$ reads: "for some prefix interval: ϕ".

$\Box_p\psi \;\hat{=}\; \neg\Diamond_p\neg\psi$ reads: "for all prefix intervals: ψ".

IL24 $\Box\phi \Rightarrow \Box_p\phi$.

IL25 $\Box\phi \Leftrightarrow \Box_p\Box\phi$.
$\Box\phi \Leftrightarrow \Box\Box_p\phi$.

Many properties of $\Box_p$ resembles properties of $\Box$, e.g.

IL26 $\Box_p(\phi \Rightarrow \psi) \Rightarrow (\Box_p\phi \Rightarrow \Box_p\psi)$.

IL27 $\Box_p\phi \Rightarrow \phi$.

IL28 $\Box_p\phi \Leftrightarrow \Box_p\Box_p\phi$.

IL29 $\phi \vdash \Box_p\phi$.

IL30 $(\Box_p\phi) \Leftrightarrow \forall x \geq 0.((x \leq \ell) \Rightarrow (\phi^\frown(\ell = x)))$.

IL31 $\Box_p\phi \Rightarrow \neg(\neg\phi^\frown\psi)$.

IL32 $\Box_p\phi \Rightarrow \psi \vdash \Box_p\phi \Rightarrow \Box_p\psi$.

IL33 $\Box_p(\phi \Rightarrow \varphi) \Rightarrow ((\phi^\frown\psi) \Rightarrow (\varphi^\frown\psi))$.

IL34 $\phi \Leftrightarrow \Box_p\phi$ if ϕ is a rigid formula.

IL35 $(\Box_p\phi \wedge (\psi^\frown\varphi)) \Rightarrow ((\phi \wedge \psi)^\frown\varphi)$.

IL36 $\Box_p(\phi \wedge \psi) \Leftrightarrow (\Box_p\phi \wedge \Box_p\psi)$.

IL37 $(\Box_p\phi \vee \Box_p\psi) \Rightarrow \Box_p(\phi \vee \psi)$.

The proofs are left as exercises.

3. Duration Calculus

In this chapter we present the syntax, semantics and proof system of duration calculus. In addition, we present some theorems and rules of DC which are useful when conducting proofs.

3.1 Syntax

We establish DC as an extension of IL in the sense that temporal variables $v \in TVar$ other than ℓ have a structure

$$\int S,$$

where $\int S$ is called a *state duration* and S is called a *state expression*.

The set of state expressions is generated from a set $SVar$ of *state variables* $P, Q, R, \dots$, according to the following abstract syntax:

$$S ::= 0 \mid 1 \mid P \mid \neg S_1 \mid S_1 \vee S_2.$$

We shall use the same abbreviations for propositional connectives in state expressions as those used in Chap. 2 in IL formulas.

Remark. The propositional connectives $\neg$ and $\vee$ occur both in state expressions and in formulas but, as we shall see below, with different semantics. This does not cause problems, as state expressions always occur in the context of $\int$.

□

3.2 Semantics

When we generate temporal variables from state variables, the semantics of the temporal variables must be derived from the semantics of the state variables. The semantics of a state variable is a function from time to Boolean values $\{0,1\}$, where the function is integrable in every time interval.

Remember that we use real numbers to model time:

Time $\widehat{=}$ $\mathbb{R}$.

An *interpretation* for state variables, the symbol ℓ and propositional letters is a function

$$\mathcal{I} : \begin{pmatrix} SVar \\ \cup \\ \{\ell\} \\ \cup \\ PLetters \end{pmatrix} \rightarrow \begin{pmatrix} \text{Time} \rightarrow \{0,1\} \\ \cup \\ \text{Intv} \rightarrow \mathbb{R} \\ \cup \\ \text{Intv} \rightarrow \{tt,ff\} \end{pmatrix},$$

where

- $\mathcal{I}(P)$: Time $\rightarrow \{0,1\}$, for every state variable P; furthermore, $\mathcal{I}(P)$ has at most a finite number of discontinuity points in every interval;
- $\mathcal{I}(\ell)$: Intv $\rightarrow \mathbb{R}$ and $\mathcal{I}(\ell)[b,e] = e - b$; and
- $\mathcal{I}(X)$: Intv $\rightarrow \{tt,ff\}$, for every propositional letter X.

Thus, each function $\mathcal{I}(P)$ has the property of *finite variability*, and, hence, $\mathcal{I}(P)$ is integrable in every interval.

The *semantics of a state expression* S, given an interpretation $\mathcal{I}$, is a function

$$\mathcal{I}[\![S]\!] : \text{Time} \rightarrow \{0,1\},$$

defined inductively on the structure of state expressions by

$$\begin{aligned}
\mathcal{I}[\![0]\!](t) &= 0 \\
\mathcal{I}[\![1]\!](t) &= 1 \\
\mathcal{I}[\![P]\!](t) &= \mathcal{I}(P)(t) \\
\mathcal{I}[\![(\neg S)]\!](t) &= 1 - \mathcal{I}[\![S]\!](t) \\
\mathcal{I}[\![(S_1 \vee S_2)]\!](t) &= \begin{cases} 0 \text{ if } \mathcal{I}[\![S_1]\!](t) = 0 \text{ and } \mathcal{I}[\![S_2]\!](t) = 0 \\ 1 \text{ otherwise} \end{cases}
\end{aligned}$$

We shall use the abbreviation $S_{\mathcal{I}} \widehat{=} \mathcal{I}[\![S]\!]$.

We see from this semantics that each function $S_{\mathcal{I}}$ has at most a finite number of discontinuity points in any interval and is thus integrable in every interval.

The *semantics of temporal variables*, which now have the form $\int S$ and are called *state durations*, is given by a function

$$\mathcal{I}[\![\int S]\!] : \text{Intv} \rightarrow \mathbb{R},$$

defined by

$$\mathcal{I}[\![\int S]\!][b,e] = \int_b^e S_{\mathcal{I}}(t)\, dt.$$

This function can be used to induce an interpretation $\mathcal{J}_\mathcal{I}$ for temporal variables and propositional letters from $\mathcal{I}$:

$$\begin{aligned}
\mathcal{J}_\mathcal{I}(X) &= \mathcal{I}(X), && \text{for every propositional letter } X, \\
\mathcal{J}_\mathcal{I}(\textstyle\int S) &= \mathcal{I}[\![\textstyle\int S]\!], && \text{for every state expression } S, \\
\mathcal{J}_\mathcal{I}(\ell) &= \mathcal{I}(\ell).
\end{aligned}$$

The *semantics of a duration calculus formula* ϕ, given an interpretation $\mathcal{I}$ to state variables, is a function

$$\mathcal{I}[\![\phi]\!] \ : \ (Val \times \mathbb{Intv}) \to \{\text{tt},\text{ff}\},$$

for which we use the abbreviations

$$\begin{aligned}
\mathcal{I}, \mathcal{V}, [b, e] &\models \phi && \mathrel{\widehat{=}} && \mathcal{I}[\![\phi]\!]\,(\mathcal{V}, [b, e]) = \text{tt} \\
\mathcal{I}, \mathcal{V}, [b, e] &\not\models \phi && \mathrel{\widehat{=}} && \mathcal{I}[\![\phi]\!]\,(\mathcal{V}, [b, e]) = \text{ff}.
\end{aligned}$$

We can define the semantics of DC formulas in terms of the semantics of IL formulas, using the interpretation $\mathcal{J}_\mathcal{I}$ induced from an interpretation $\mathcal{I}$.

The *semantics of a DC formula* ϕ, for an arbitrary interpretation $\mathcal{I}$, value assignment $\mathcal{V}$ and interval $[b, e]$, is defined by

$$\mathcal{I}, \mathcal{V}, [b, e] \models \phi \text{ iff } \mathcal{J}_\mathcal{I}, \mathcal{V}, [b, e] \models \phi \quad \text{in IL.}$$

Remark. For two given interpretations $\mathcal{I}$ and $\mathcal{I}'$ whose values for any state variable P disagree in at most a finite number of points in any interval we have

$$\mathcal{I}[\![\textstyle\int P]\!]\,[b, e] \ = \ \mathcal{I}'[\![\textstyle\int P]\!]\,[b, e],$$

for any $[b, e]$.

No DC formula can distinguish between $\mathcal{I}$ and $\mathcal{I}'$, since state expressions occur only within the context of $\int$. We can therefore define $\mathcal{I}$ and $\mathcal{I}'$ to be equivalent, and build equivalence classes of interpretations if necessary. $\square$

The notions of *satisfiability* and *validity* of DC formulas are defined as for IL formulas.

In fact, the definitions of satisfiability and validity for DC formulas can be simplified as shown in Theorem 3.1 below, which gives an alternative characterization of validity and satisfiability using only *prefix* intervals, which are intervals of the form $[0, e]$, for nonnegative real numbers e.

The theorem is easy to prove using the following definition and lemma.

For a given formula ϕ, interval $[b, e]$ and interpretation $\mathcal{I}$, let $\mathcal{I}_b$ be an interpretation such that for any P occurring in ϕ and $t \in [0, e - b]$,

$$P_{\mathcal{I}_b}(t) = P_{\mathcal{I}}(b + t).$$

We have the following lemma.

Lemma 3.1

$$\mathcal{I}, \mathcal{V}, [b,e] \models \phi \quad \textit{iff} \quad \mathcal{I}_b, \mathcal{V}, [0, e-b] \models \phi .$$

Proof. A proof can be given by showing

$$\mathcal{I}[\![\int P]\!]\,[c,d] \;=\; \mathcal{I}_b[\![\int P]\!]\,[c-b, d-b]\,,$$

for any $[c,d] \subseteq [b,e]$. This follows since

$$P_{\mathcal{I}}(t+b) = P_{\mathcal{I}_b}(t)\,,$$

for any $t \in [c-b, d-b]$. $\qquad\square$

We can then easily prove the following theorem.

Theorem 3.1

1. *A formula ϕ of DC is valid iff $\mathcal{I}, \mathcal{V}, [0,e] \models \phi$ for every interpretation $\mathcal{I}$, value assignment $\mathcal{V}$ and nonnegative real number e.*
2. *A formula ϕ of DC is satisfiable iff $\mathcal{I}, \mathcal{V}, [0,e] \models \phi$ for some interpretation $\mathcal{I}$, value assignment $\mathcal{V}$ and nonnegative real number e.*

The following abbreviations will be used frequently:

$$\begin{aligned}
\lceil\,\rceil &\;\widehat{=}\; \ell = 0 \\
\lceil S \rceil &\;\widehat{=}\; \int S = \ell \,\wedge\, \ell > 0\,.
\end{aligned}$$

The formula $\lceil S \rceil$ holds in an interval $[b,e]$ iff $b < e$ and S is 1 (almost) everywhere in $[b,e]$. In fact, because of the finite variability of S, S can be 0 at at most a finite number of time points in $[b,e]$.

Gas Burner

The requirement of the gas burner can be formalized in DC by

$$GbReq \;\widehat{=}\; \ell \geq 60 \;\Rightarrow\; 20\int\text{Leak} \leq \ell\,,$$

and the two design decisions can be formalized in DC by

$$Des_1 \;\widehat{=}\; \square(\lceil\text{Leak}\rceil \;\Rightarrow\; \ell \leq 1)$$

and

$$Des_2 \;\widehat{=}\; \square((\lceil\text{Leak}\rceil \,^\frown \lceil\neg\text{Leak}\rceil \,^\frown \lceil\text{Leak}\rceil) \;\Rightarrow\; \ell \geq 30)\,.$$

$\qquad\square$

3.3 Proof System

Since DC is an extension of IL, we adopt all axioms and inference rules of IL given in the previous chapter as axioms and inference rules for DC. We add axioms reflecting the structure which DC adds to temporal variables:

DCA1 $\int 0 = 0$.

DCA2 $\int 1 = \ell$.

DCA3 $\int S \geq 0$.

DCA4 $\int S_1 + \int S_2 = \int (S_1 \vee S_2) + \int (S_1 \wedge S_2)$.

DCA5 $((\int S = x) ^\frown (\int S = y)) \Rightarrow (\int S = x + y)$.

DCA6 $\int S_1 = \int S_2$, provided $S_1 \Leftrightarrow S_2$ holds in propositional logic.

In order to formalize the finite variability of state expressions, we add two *induction rules*.

Let $H(X)$ be a formula containing the propositional letter X and let $S_1, S_2, \ldots, S_n$ be any finite collection of state expressions which is *complete* in the sense that

$$(\bigvee_{i=1}^{n} S_i) \Leftrightarrow 1.$$

For a complete collection of state expressions $S_1, S_2, \ldots, S_n$, there are two induction rules:

IR1 If $\quad H(\lceil\,\rceil)$ and $H(X) \Rightarrow H(X \vee \bigvee_{i=1}^{n}(X ^\frown \lceil S_i \rceil))$
then $H(\text{true})$

and

IR2 If $\quad H(\lceil\,\rceil)$ and $H(X) \Rightarrow H(X \vee \bigvee_{i=1}^{n}(\lceil S_i \rceil ^\frown X))$
then $H(\text{true})$.

In these rules $H(\phi)$ denotes the formula obtained from $H(X)$ by replacing every occurrence of X in H with ϕ.

$H(\lceil\,\rceil)$ is called the *base case*, $H(X)$ is called the *induction hypothesis* and X is called the *induction letter*.

Remark.

1. The soundness of these two induction rules relies on the finite-variability property of functions $S_{\mathcal{I}}$ (see below). Furthermore, in the proof of relative completeness (Lemma 5.2), we shall see that the induction rules have a major role in the formalization of the finite-variability property.

2. Although we have presented the induction rules above in their most general form, we shall often use them by choosing a state expression S and its negation $\neg S$ as the complete state set, and choosing $\Box(X \Rightarrow \phi)$ as $H(X)$, where X does not occur in ϕ.
3. In the following proofs of the soundness theorem and deduction theorems, we shall deal only with the induction rules where a state expression and its negation $\neg S$ are taken as the complete set of states. For the general case, the proofs can be derived similarly. □

A *proof* of ϕ in DC is a finite sequence of formulas $\phi_1 \cdots \phi_n$, where ϕ_n is ϕ, and each ϕ_i is either an instance of one of the above axiom schemas or an axiom schema of DC, or obtained by applying one of the induction rules or the inference rules of DC to previous members of the sequence. We write $\vdash \phi$ to denote that there exists a proof of ϕ in DC, and we call ϕ a *theorem* of DC.

A *deduction* in DC is defined similarly to a deduction in IL, and we write $\Gamma \vdash \phi$ to denote that there exists a deduction of ϕ in DC from Γ, where ϕ is a DC formula and Γ is a set of DC formulas.

3.3.1 Soundness

We want to establish the soundness of the proof system. The following definitions and lemmas are convenient for this purpose.

Definition *(Equivalence) Given an interval $[b, e]$ and an interpretation $\mathcal{I}$, we call two formulas ϕ and ψ equivalent in $[b, e]$ of $\mathcal{I}$ if*

$$\mathcal{I}, \mathcal{V}, [c, d] \models \phi \text{ iff } \mathcal{I}, \mathcal{V}, [c, d] \models \psi,$$

for any value assignment $\mathcal{V}$ and any interval $[c, d]$ where $[c, d] \subseteq [b, e]$.

Definition *(Finite alternation) Given a state expression S, the formula $FA^i(S)$, for $i \geq 0$, describes fewer than i alternations of S:*

$$\begin{aligned} FA^0(S) &\;\widehat{=}\; \lceil\rceil \\ FA^{i+1}(S) &\;\widehat{=}\; FA^i(S) \vee (\lceil S \rceil \frown FA^i(S)) \vee (\lceil \neg S \rceil \frown FA^i(S)). \end{aligned}$$

Lemma 3.2 *For a given state expression S, interval $[b, e]$ and interpretation $\mathcal{I}$, there is a natural number k such that*

true and $FA^k(S)$

are equivalent in $[b, e]$ of $\mathcal{I}$.

Proof. This follows since $S_\mathcal{I}$ has at most a finite number of alternations in $[b, e]$, and this number can be taken as k, which is an upper bound on the alternation numbers of $S_\mathcal{I}$ in any subinterval of $[b, e]$. □

Lemma 3.3 *Let $\varphi(X)$ be a formula in which the propositional letter X may occur, let $[b, e]$ be an interval and let $\mathcal{I}$ be an interpretation. Then for any two formulas ϕ_1 and ϕ_2,*

> *If ϕ_1 and ϕ_2 are equivalent in $[b, e]$ of $\mathcal{I}$*
> *then $\varphi(\phi_1)$ and $\varphi(\phi_2)$ are equivalent in $[b, e]$ of $\mathcal{I}$.*

Proof. By structural induction on $\varphi(X)$.   □

Lemma 3.4

$$\models \phi(X) \ \textit{implies} \ \models \phi(\psi) \,,$$

provided ψ is free for X in $\phi(X)$, i.e. X does not occur in $\phi(X)$ within a scope of $\exists x$ or $\forall x$, where x is a free variable of ψ.

Proof. We can apply induction on the structure of $\phi(X)$ to prove that given $\mathcal{I}$,

$$\mathcal{I}, \mathcal{V}, [c, d] \models \phi(\psi) \ \text{iff} \ \mathcal{I}', \mathcal{V}, [c, d] \models \phi(X) \,,$$

for any $\mathcal{V}$ and $[c, d] \subseteq [b, e]$, where $\mathcal{I}'$ is defined so that

$$\mathcal{I}'(X)[c, d] = \mathcal{I}[\![\psi]\!](\mathcal{V}, [c, d]) \,,$$

for any $[c, d] \subseteq [b, e]$.

The details of the proof will not be presented.   □

Theorem 3.2 *(Soundness) The proof system of DC is sound, i.e.*

$$\vdash \phi \ \textit{implies} \ \models \phi \,.$$

Proof. The proof of soundness is by induction on the structure of proofs, i.e. the soundness of each axiom and inference rule of DC must be proved. The axioms and inference rules of IL are treated in [28]. The axioms of DC are simple and left for the reader. We prove here the soundness of IR2, where S and $\neg S$ are used as the complete set of states. The soundness of IR1 can be proved similarly.

By the induction hypothesis of the soundness proof, we have

$$\models H([\![\,]\!]) \,, \ \text{i.e.} \ \models H(FA^0(S)) \,, \tag{3.1}$$

and

$$\models H(X) \Rightarrow H(X \vee ([\![S]\!] \frown X) \vee ([\![\neg S]\!] \frown X)) \,. \tag{3.2}$$

We must establish $\models H(\text{true})$.

We first prove

$$\models H(FA^n(S)),$$

for any natural number n, by induction on n.

The case for $n = 0$ is established by (3.1).

Inductive step: From Lemma 3.4 and (3.2), we obtain

$$\models H(FA^n(S)) \Rightarrow H(FA^{n+1}(S)).$$

Combining this with the induction hypothesis $\models H(FA^n(S))$ we obtain

$$\models H(FA^{n+1}(S)).$$

To show $\models H(\text{true})$, we must show that $\mathcal{I}, \mathcal{V}, [b, e] \models H(\text{true})$ for any interpretation $\mathcal{I}$, value assignment $\mathcal{V}$ and interval $[b, e]$. But, by Lemma 3.2, there is a natural number k such that true and $FA^k(S)$ are equivalent in $[b, e]$ of $\mathcal{I}$, and, by Lemma 3.3, we have the result that $H(\text{true})$ and $H(FA^k(S))$ are equivalent in $[b, e]$ of $\mathcal{I}$ also.

Thus, from

$$\mathcal{I}, \mathcal{V}, [b, e] \models H(FA^k(S)),$$

we have

$$\mathcal{I}, \mathcal{V}, [b, e] \models H(\text{true}).$$

$\square$

3.3.2 Deduction

In order to simplify proofs in DC, we establish the following deduction theorem.

Theorem 3.3 *(Deduction)*

$$\Gamma, \phi \vdash \psi \quad implies \quad \Gamma \vdash \Box\phi \Rightarrow \psi,$$

provided a deduction $\Gamma, \phi \vdash \psi$ involves no application of the generalization rule G for which the quantified variable is free in ϕ and every application of the induction rules in this deduction satisfies the condition that its induction letter does not occur in ϕ.

Proof. We must add to the proof of the deduction theorem for IL the cases where the induction rules are applied as the last step of the deduction. All other cases remain the same.

Case IR1: We consider only the simple case where S and $\neg S$ constitute the complete state set, ψ has the form $H(\text{true})$, and the deduction from $\Gamma \cup \{\phi\}$ has the form

$$\vdots$$
$$H(\lceil\!\lceil\,\rceil\!\rceil)$$
$$\vdots$$
$$H(X) \Rightarrow H(X \vee (X^\frown\lceil\!\lceil S \rceil\!\rceil) \vee (X^\frown\lceil\!\lceil\neg S \rceil\!\rceil))$$
$$\vdots$$
$$H(\text{true}).$$

By the induction hypothesis there are deductions from Γ of $\Box\phi \Rightarrow H(\lceil\!\lceil\,\rceil\!\rceil)$ and $\Box\phi \Rightarrow (H(X) \Rightarrow H(X \vee (X^\frown\lceil\!\lceil S \rceil\!\rceil) \vee (X^\frown\lceil\!\lceil\neg S \rceil\!\rceil)))$. In the following, we abbreviate $X \vee (X^\frown\lceil\!\lceil S \rceil\!\rceil) \vee (X^\frown\lceil\!\lceil\neg S \rceil\!\rceil)$ to $next(X, S)$:

$$\left.\begin{array}{l} \vdots \\ k.\ \Box\phi \Rightarrow H(\lceil\!\lceil\,\rceil\!\rceil) \end{array}\right\} \text{ deduction from } \Gamma$$

$$\left.\begin{array}{l} \vdots \\ l.\ \Box\phi \Rightarrow (H(X) \Rightarrow H(next(X, S))) \end{array}\right\} \text{ deduction from } \Gamma$$

$l + 1.\ \Box\phi \Rightarrow (H(X) \Rightarrow H(next(X, S)))$
$\qquad \Rightarrow ((\Box\phi \Rightarrow H(X)) \Rightarrow (\Box\phi \Rightarrow H(next(X, S))))$ PL
$l + 2.\ (\Box\phi \Rightarrow H(X)) \Rightarrow (\Box\phi \Rightarrow H(next(X, S)))$ $l., l + 1., \text{MP}$
$l + 3.\ \Box\phi \Rightarrow H(\text{true})$ $k., l + 2., \text{IR1}.$

Note that we have taken into account the fact that the induction letter X does not occur in ϕ in the application of IR1 with $\Box\phi \Rightarrow H(X)$ as the induction hypothesis.

Case IR2 is similar to IR1. $\qquad\qquad\qquad\qquad\qquad\qquad\qquad\qquad$ $\square$

The deduction theorem can often be used to simplify a proof. In connection with the application of the induction rules, the following theorem is convenient.

Theorem 3.4

$\Gamma \vdash H(\lceil\!\lceil\,\rceil\!\rceil)$ *and* $\Gamma, H(X) \vdash H(X \vee \bigvee_{i=1}^{n}(X^\frown\lceil\!\lceil S_i \rceil\!\rceil))$
implies $\Gamma \vdash H(\text{true})$,
where $\{S_1, S_2, \ldots, S_n\}$ *is complete*,

provided a deduction $\Gamma, H(X) \vdash H(X \vee \bigvee_{i=1}^{n}(X^\frown\lceil\!\lceil S_i \rceil\!\rceil))$ *has the property that every application of the induction rules in this deduction satisfies the condition that its induction letter does not occur in* $H(X)$.

Proof. We consider only the case where $\{S, \neg S\}$ is used as the complete set. Let $y_1, y_2, \ldots, y_n$ be all the variables occurring free in $H(X)$ and let $H_c(X)$ denote the formula $(\forall y_1)(\forall y_2) \cdots (\forall y_n) H(X)$.

Since $\Gamma \vdash H(\lceil\!\rceil)$ and $\Gamma, H(X) \vdash H(X \vee (X ^\frown \lceil S \rceil) \vee (X ^\frown \lceil \neg S \rceil))$, we also have $\Gamma \vdash H_c(\lceil\!\rceil)$ and $\Gamma, H_c(X) \vdash H_c(X \vee (X ^\frown \lceil S \rceil) \vee (X ^\frown \lceil \neg S \rceil))$ (using G and Q1).

In the following deduction, we use the deduction theorem and also the abbreviation $next(X, S)$:

$$
\left.
\begin{array}{l}
\vdots \\
k. \ \Box H_c(X) \Rightarrow H_c(next(X, S)) \\
\vdots
\end{array}
\right\} \text{deductions from } \Gamma
$$

$l.\ H_c(\lceil\!\rceil)$	
$l+1.\ \Box H_c(\lceil\!\rceil)$	$l.,$ IL4
$l+2.\ \Box H_c(X) \Rightarrow \Box H_c(next(X, S))$	$k.,$ IL6
$l+3.\ \Box H_c(\text{true})$	$l+1., l+2.,$ IR1
$l+4.\ \Box H_c(\text{true}) \Rightarrow H_c(\text{true})$	IL2
$l+5.\ H_c(\text{true})$	$l+3., l+4.,$ MP
$l+6.\ H(\text{true})$	$l+5.,$ PL,

where the application of IR1 uses $\Box H_c(X)$ as the induction hypothesis. $\Box$

The following theorem is proved in a similar way:

Theorem 3.5

> $\Gamma \vdash H(\lceil\!\rceil)$ and $\Gamma, H(X) \vdash H(X \vee \bigvee_{i=1}^{n} (\lceil S_i \rceil ^\frown X))$
> implies $\Gamma \vdash H(\text{true})$,
> where $\{S_1, S_2, \ldots, S_n\}$ is complete,

provided a deduction $\Gamma, H(X) \vdash H(X \vee \bigvee_{i=1}^{n} (\lceil S_i \rceil ^\frown X))$ has the property that every application of the induction rules in this deduction satisfies the condition that its induction letter does not occur in $H(X)$.

The two induction rules can be used to prove some properties of the finite variability of states. The properties DC1 and DC2 reject infinite oscillation of the state S at a point.

DC1 $\lceil\!\rceil \vee (\text{true} ^\frown \lceil S \rceil) \vee (\text{true} ^\frown \lceil \neg S \rceil)$.

DC2 $\lceil\!\rceil \vee (\lceil S \rceil ^\frown \text{true}) \vee (\lceil \neg S \rceil ^\frown \text{true})$.

Proof. The proof of DC1 is easy using Theorem 3.4 with

$$H(X) \ \hat{=}\ X \Rightarrow \text{DC1}.$$

By PL, we have

$$H(\lceil 1 \rceil).$$

We now establish

$$(X \Rightarrow DC1) \vdash (X \vee (X \cap \lceil S \rceil) \vee (X \cap \lceil \neg S \rceil)) \Rightarrow DC1$$

by establishing the three deductions

(a) $(X \Rightarrow DC1) \vdash X \Rightarrow DC1$

(b) $(X \Rightarrow DC1) \vdash (X \cap \lceil S \rceil) \Rightarrow DC1$

(c) $(X \Rightarrow DC1) \vdash (X \cap \lceil \neg S \rceil) \Rightarrow DC1.$

The first case, i.e. (a), is trivial. The cases (b) and (c) are similar, so we shall establish only one of them. The following constitutes a deduction for case (b):

1. $X \Rightarrow true$ PL
2. $(X \cap \lceil S \rceil) \Rightarrow (true \cap \lceil S \rceil)$ 1., M
3. $(true \cap \lceil S \rceil) \Rightarrow DC1$ PL
4. $(X \cap \lceil S \rceil) \Rightarrow DC1$ 2., 3., PL.

Having established (a), (b) and (c), we have, by PL,

$$(X \Rightarrow DC1) \vdash (X \vee (X \cap \lceil S \rceil) \vee (X \cap \lceil \neg S \rceil)) \Rightarrow DC1.$$

Thus, we obtain $(true \Rightarrow DC1)$ using Theorem 3.4, and then DC1 by PL. $\square$

Similarly, we can establish that for a complete set of states $\{S_1, S_2, \ldots, S_n\}$,

DC3 $\lceil 1 \rceil \vee \bigvee_{i=1}^{n}(true \cap \lceil S_i \rceil)$

DC4 $\lceil 1 \rceil \vee \bigvee_{i=1}^{n}(\lceil S_i \rceil \cap true).$

3.4 Theorems

In this section we present theorems and derived proof rules which can help one to understand the calculus and to conduct proofs. Some proofs are presented, while others are left as exercises.

Theorems About $\int S$

DC5 $\int S + \int \neg S = \ell.$

DC6 $\int S \leq \ell.$

DC7 $\int S_1 \geq \int S_2$, if $S_2 \Rightarrow S_1$.

Proof. The following is a proof of DC5:

  1. $\int S + \int \neg S = \int (S \wedge \neg S) + \int (S \vee \neg S)$ DCA4
  2. $\int S + \int \neg S = \ell$ 1., DCA1, DCA2, DCA6, PL.

A proof of DC6 can be derived from DC5 by use of $(\int \neg S \geq 0)$ (DCA3). In the following proof of DC7, we exploit the fact that $S_1 \Leftrightarrow (S_2 \vee (\neg S_2 \wedge S_1))$ when $S_2 \Rightarrow S_1$:

  1. $\int S_1 = (\int S_2 + \int (\neg S_2 \wedge S_1) - \int (S_2 \wedge (\neg S_2 \wedge S_1)))$ DCA6, DCA4
  2. $\int S_1 = (\int S_2 + \int (\neg S_2 \wedge S_1))$ 1., DCA1, DCA6
  3. $\int (\neg S_2 \wedge S_1) \geq 0$ DCA3
  4. $\int S_1 \geq \int S_2$ 2., 3., PL.

$\square$

DC8
$$((\int S \geq x) ^\frown (\int S \geq y)) \Rightarrow (\int S \geq x + y).$$
$$((\int S \leq x) ^\frown (\int S \leq y)) \Rightarrow (\int S \leq x + y).$$

Proof. We give a proof of the first theorem only. The proof of the second theorem is similar.

$(\int S \geq x) ^\frown (\int S \geq y)$
$\Rightarrow \exists z_1 \geq 0.(\int S = x + z_1) ^\frown \exists z_2 \geq 0.(\int S = y + z_2)$ PL, M
$\Rightarrow \exists z_1, z_2 \geq 0.((\int S = x + z_1) ^\frown (\int S = y + z_2))$ E, PL
$\Rightarrow \exists z_1, z_2 \geq 0.(\int S = x + z_1 + y + z_2)$ DCA5, PL
$\Rightarrow \int S \geq x + y$ PL.

$\square$

DC9 $((\sum_{i=1}^{m} \int S_i \leq \ell) ^\frown (\sum_{i=1}^{m} \int S_i \leq \ell)) \Rightarrow (\sum_{i=1}^{m} \int S_i \leq \ell).$

Proof. In the proof of this theorem, the following fact about arithmetic will be used:

$$(\sum_{i=1}^{m} x_i \leq z_1 \wedge \sum_{i=1}^{m} y_i \leq z_2) \Rightarrow \sum_{i=1}^{m} (x_i + y_i) \leq z_1 + z_2. \tag{3.3}$$

Having introduced the variables (x_i, y_i, z_1, z_2) for durations and lengths, we can write the main part of the proof as

$$\left(\begin{array}{c} \bigwedge_{i=1}^{m} (\int S_i = x_i) \\ \wedge (\ell = z_1) \\ \wedge \sum_{i=1}^{m} \int S_i \leq \ell \end{array} \right) ^\frown \left(\begin{array}{c} \bigwedge_{i=1}^{m} (\int S_i = y_i) \\ \wedge (\ell = z_2) \\ \wedge \sum_{i=1}^{m} \int S_i \leq \ell \end{array} \right)$$

$$\Rightarrow \left(\begin{array}{c} \bigwedge_{i=1}^{m} (\int S_i = x_i + y_i) \wedge (\ell = z_1 + z_2) \\ \wedge \sum_{i=1}^{m} x_i \leq z_1 \wedge \sum_{i=1}^{m} y_i \leq z_2 \end{array} \right)$$ A0, L2, DCA5, PL

$$\Rightarrow \left(\begin{array}{c} \bigwedge_{i=1}^{m} (\int S_i = x_i + y_i) \wedge (\ell = z_1 + z_2) \\ \wedge \sum_{i=1}^{m} (x_i + y_i) \leq z_1 + z_2 \end{array} \right)$$ PL, (3.3)

$$\Rightarrow \sum_{i=1}^{m} \int S_i \leq \ell$$ PL.

A full proof of the theorem also has to deal with the introduction and elimination of variables:

1. $\bigwedge_{i=1}^{m} \exists x_i.(\int S_i = x_i) \wedge \exists z_1.(\ell = z_1)$ PL

2. $\bigwedge_{i=1}^{m} \exists y_i.(\int S_i = y_i) \wedge \exists z_2.(\ell = z_2)$ PL

3. $(\sum_{i=1}^{m} \int S_i \leq \ell) \frown (\sum_{i=1}^{m} \int S_i \leq \ell)$

$\Rightarrow \begin{pmatrix} \bigwedge_{i=1}^{m} \exists x_i.(\int S_i = x_i) \\ \wedge \exists z_1.(\ell = z_1) \\ \wedge \sum_{i=1}^{m} \int S_i \leq \ell \end{pmatrix} \frown \begin{pmatrix} \bigwedge_{i=1}^{m} \exists y_i.(\int S_i = y_i) \\ \wedge \exists z_2.(\ell = z_2) \\ \wedge \sum_{i=1}^{m} \int S_i \leq \ell \end{pmatrix}$ 1., 2., M

$\Rightarrow \exists x_1, \ldots, x_m, y_1, \ldots, y_m, z_1, z_2.$

$\begin{pmatrix} \bigwedge_{i=1}^{m} (\int S_i = x_i) \\ \wedge (\ell = z_1) \\ \wedge \sum_{i=1}^{m} \int S_i \leq \ell \end{pmatrix} \frown \begin{pmatrix} \bigwedge_{i=1}^{m} (\int S_i = y_i) \\ \wedge (\ell = z_2) \\ \wedge \sum_{i=1}^{m} \int S_i \leq \ell \end{pmatrix}$ E

4. $\begin{pmatrix} \bigwedge_{i=1}^{m} (\int S_i = x_i) \\ \wedge (\ell = z_1) \\ \wedge \sum_{i=1}^{m} \int S_i \leq \ell \end{pmatrix} \frown \begin{pmatrix} \bigwedge_{i=1}^{m} (\int S_i = y_i) \\ \wedge (\ell = z_2) \\ \wedge \sum_{i=1}^{m} \int S_i \leq \ell \end{pmatrix}$

$\Rightarrow \sum_{i=1}^{m} \int S_i \leq \ell$ proof above

$\exists x_1, \ldots, x_m, y_1, \ldots, y_m, z_1, z_2.$

5. $\left(\begin{pmatrix} \bigwedge_{i=1}^{m} (\int S_i = x_i) \\ \wedge (\ell = z_1) \\ \wedge \sum_{i=1}^{m} \int S_i \leq \ell \end{pmatrix} \frown \begin{pmatrix} \bigwedge_{i=1}^{m} (\int S_i = y_i) \\ \wedge (\ell = z_2) \\ \wedge \sum_{i=1}^{m} \int S_i \leq \ell \end{pmatrix} \right)$ 4., PL

$\Rightarrow \sum_{i=1}^{m} \int S_i \leq \ell$

6. $((\sum_{i=1}^{m} \int S_i \leq \ell) \frown (\sum_{i=1}^{m} \int S_i \leq \ell)) \Rightarrow (\sum_{i=1}^{m} \int S_i \leq \ell)$ 3., 5., PL.

The introduction and elimination of variables, as done in the steps 1., 2., 3. and 5. above, have an archetypical form. Usually, we shall omit these steps in proofs and thereby just focus on the main part.   □

DC10 $\int S \leq x \Leftrightarrow \Box(\int S \leq x).$
         $\int S < x \Leftrightarrow \Box(\int S < x).$

Proof. The $\Leftarrow$ part of these theorems follows from IL2. The other direction ($\Rightarrow$) of the first theorem can be proved by establishing

$$\neg\Box(\int S \leq x) \Rightarrow \int S > x$$

or, equivalently,

$$(\text{true} \frown (\int S > x) \frown \text{true}) \Rightarrow \int S > x.$$

This formula can be proved using the same technique as in the proof of the previous theorem, where we introduce variables for the duration of S on the various intervals. The main part of this proof is

$$y_1 \geq 0 \wedge y_2 \geq 0 \wedge z > 0 \wedge ((\int S = y_1)^\frown (\int S = z + x)^\frown (\int S = y_2))$$
$$\Rightarrow y_1 \geq 0 \wedge y_2 \geq 0 \wedge z > 0 \wedge \int S = y_1 + y_2 + z + x$$
$$\Rightarrow \int S > x.$$

The second part of DC10 is proved similarly.   □

Theorems About $\lceil S \rceil$

DC11 $\lceil 0 \rceil \Rightarrow$ false.

Proof.

$$\lceil 0 \rceil$$
$$\Rightarrow (\int 0 = \ell) \wedge (\ell > 0) \quad \text{Def}(\lceil 0 \rceil)$$
$$\Rightarrow (0 = \ell) \wedge (\ell > 0) \quad \text{DCA1}$$
$$\Rightarrow \text{false} \qquad\qquad\quad \text{PL.}$$

□

DC12 $\lceil \neg S \rceil \Rightarrow (\int S = 0).$

Proof. This can be proved by use of DC5.   □

DC13 $(\bigwedge_{i=1}^{n-1} \lceil \neg (S_i \wedge (\bigvee_{j>i} S_j)) \rceil) \Rightarrow (\int (\bigvee_{i=1}^{n} S_i) = \sum_{i=1}^{n} \int S_i).$

Proof. We present a proof for the case of $n = 3$. Applying DCA4, we obtain

$$\int (S_1 \vee S_2 \vee S_3) = \int S_1 + \int (S_2 \vee S_3) - \int (S_1 \wedge (S_2 \vee S_3)).$$

From the antecedent $\lceil \neg (S_1 \wedge (S_2 \vee S_3)) \rceil$ and DC12, we can prove

$$\int (S_1 \vee S_2 \vee S_3) = \int S_1 + \int (S_2 \vee S_3).$$

Applying DCA4 again, we obtain

$$\int (S_1 \vee S_2 \vee S_3) = \int S_1 + \int S_2 + \int S_3 - \int (S_2 \wedge S_3).$$

From the antecedent $\lceil \neg (S_2 \wedge S_3) \rceil$ and DC12, we prove the conclusion.   □

DC14 $\lceil \bigvee_{i=1}^{k} S_i \rceil \Rightarrow (\sum_{i=1}^{k} \int S_i) \geq \ell.$

Proof. From DCA4 and DCA3, we derive

$$(\sum_{i=1}^{k} \int S_i) \geq \int (\bigvee_{i=1}^{k} S_i).$$

Hence, by use of the definition of $\lceil \_ \rceil$, we can conclude the theorem.   □

DC15 $(\int S > 0) \Leftrightarrow ((\int S = 0) \frown \lceil S \rceil \frown \text{true})$.

Proof. The direction $\Leftarrow$ can easily be proved by use of DCA5. In order to prove the other direction, we apply Theorem 3.5. Let

$$H(X) \mathrel{\hat{=}} (X \Rightarrow ((\int S > 0) \Rightarrow ((\int S = 0) \frown \lceil S \rceil \frown \text{true}))).$$

The proof of $H(\lceil\ \rceil)$ is easy, since $\lceil\ \rceil$ contradicts $(\int S > 0)$.
  We prove

$$\vdash ((\lceil S \rceil \frown X) \Rightarrow (\ell = 0) \frown \lceil S \rceil \frown \text{true})$$

by use of IL18 and M, and then establish

$$\vdash H(\lceil S \rceil \frown X)$$

by PL. Hence, $H(X) \vdash H(\lceil S \rceil \frown X)$.
  To prove $H(X) \vdash H(\lceil \neg S \rceil \frown X)$, we establish the following deduction from $H(X)$:

1. $X \Rightarrow (\neg(\int S > 0) \vee ((\int S = 0) \frown \lceil S \rceil \frown \text{true}))$ $H(X), \text{PL}$
2. $(\lceil \neg S \rceil \frown X)$
  $\Rightarrow ((\int S = 0) \frown \neg(\int S > 0))$
  $\vee((\int S = 0) \frown ((\int S = 0) \frown \lceil S \rceil \frown \text{true}))$ $1., \text{IL14}, \text{DC12}, \text{M}$
  $\Rightarrow (\int S = 0) \vee ((\int S = 0) \frown \lceil S \rceil \frown \text{true}))$ $\text{DCA3}, \text{DCA5}, \text{M}, \text{PL}$
  $\Rightarrow ((\int S > 0) \Rightarrow ((\int S = 0) \frown \lceil S \rceil \frown \text{true}))$ $\text{DCA3}, \text{PL}.$

$\square$

DC16 $\begin{aligned} &x > 0 \wedge y > 0 \\ &\Rightarrow \\ &((\ell = x + y) \wedge \lceil S \rceil) \Leftrightarrow (((\ell = x) \wedge \lceil S \rceil) \frown ((\ell = y) \wedge \lceil S \rceil)). \end{aligned}$

Proof. The direction $\Leftarrow$ can easily be proved by use of DCA5 and L2. To prove the other direction, using L2 we can chop the interval into $(\ell = x) \frown (\ell = y)$. Assuming arbitrary values for $\int S$ over the two subintervals

$$((\ell = x) \wedge (\int S = z_1)) \frown ((\ell = y) \wedge (\int S = z_2)),$$

we can apply DCA5 and DC6 to conclude that $(z_1 = x)$ and $(z_2 = y)$. Therefore we complete the proof. $\square$

As a corollary of DC16, we can establish

DC17 $\lceil S \rceil \Leftrightarrow (\lceil S \rceil \frown \lceil S \rceil)$.

DC18 $\lceil S_1 \rceil \Rightarrow \lceil S_2 \rceil$ if $S_1 \Rightarrow S_2$.

Proof. This can be derived from DC7.   □

DC19 $(\lceil S_1 \rceil \wedge \lceil S_2 \rceil) \Leftrightarrow \lceil S_1 \wedge S_2 \rceil$.

Proof. The $\Leftarrow$ part is a special case of DC18. The $\Rightarrow$ part can be proved as follows:

$$\int S_1 = \ell \wedge \int S_2 = \ell \wedge \ell > 0$$
$$\Rightarrow \int S_1 + \int S_2 - \int (S_1 \vee S_2) \geq \ell \wedge \ell > 0 \quad \text{PL}, \text{DC6}$$
$$\Rightarrow \int (S_1 \wedge S_2) = \ell \wedge \ell > 0 \qquad\qquad \text{DCA4}, \text{DC6}$$
$$\Rightarrow \lceil S_1 \wedge S_2 \rceil \qquad\qquad\qquad\qquad \text{def. } \lceil \_ \rceil.$$

□

DC20 $((\text{true}^\frown \lceil S_1 \rceil) \wedge (\text{true}^\frown \lceil S_2 \rceil)) \Leftrightarrow (\text{true}^\frown \lceil S_1 \wedge S_2 \rceil)$.
$((\lceil S_1 \rceil^\frown \text{true}) \wedge (\lceil S_2 \rceil^\frown \text{true})) \Leftrightarrow (\lceil S_1 \wedge S_2 \rceil^\frown \text{true})$.

Proof. The $\Leftarrow$ parts can be proved by use of DC18 and M. The $\Rightarrow$ parts can be proved by introducing length values of the prefix and suffix intervals, respectively. For example, assuming $x \geq y$ in the following proof, we have

$$((\ell = x)^\frown \lceil S_1 \rceil) \wedge ((\ell = y)^\frown \lceil S_2 \rceil)$$
$$\Rightarrow ((\ell = x)^\frown \lceil S_1 \rceil) \wedge ((\ell = x)^\frown \lceil S_2 \rceil) \quad \text{DC16}, \text{M}$$
$$\Rightarrow (\ell = x)^\frown (\lceil S_1 \rceil \wedge \lceil S_2 \rceil) \qquad\qquad \text{IL17}$$
$$\Rightarrow (\ell = x)^\frown \lceil S_1 \wedge S_2 \rceil \qquad\qquad\qquad \text{M}, \text{DC19}.$$

Then, by introducing and moving quantification of x by use of G and E and replacing $\exists x.\ell = x$ by true, we can complete the proof, as we have seen in earlier proofs.   □

Although $(\lceil S_1 \vee S_2 \rceil \Rightarrow (\lceil S_1 \rceil \vee \lceil S_2 \rceil))$ is not a theorem, the following is still true.

DC21 $(\text{true}^\frown \lceil S_1 \vee S_2 \rceil) \Leftrightarrow ((\text{true}^\frown \lceil S_1 \rceil) \vee (\text{true}^\frown \lceil S_2 \rceil))$.
$(\lceil S_1 \vee S_2 \rceil^\frown \text{true}) \Leftrightarrow ((\lceil S_1 \rceil^\frown \text{true}) \vee (\lceil S_2 \rceil^\frown \text{true}))$.

Proof. We prove the $\Rightarrow$ part of the first theorem.

$$\text{true}^\frown \lceil S_1 \vee S_2 \rceil$$
$$\Rightarrow \bigwedge_{i=1}^{2}((\text{true}^\frown \lceil S_i \rceil) \vee (\text{true}^\frown \lceil \neg S_i \rceil)) \quad (\ell > 0), \text{DC1}$$
$$\Rightarrow (\text{true}^\frown \lceil S_1 \rceil) \vee (\text{true}^\frown \lceil S_2 \rceil)$$
$$\qquad \vee ((\text{true}^\frown \lceil \neg S_1 \rceil) \wedge (\text{true}^\frown \lceil \neg S_2 \rceil)) \quad \text{PL}$$
$$\Rightarrow (\text{true}^\frown \lceil S_1 \rceil) \vee (\text{true}^\frown \lceil S_2 \rceil) \qquad \text{DC20}, \text{DC11}, \text{IL13}, \text{PL}.$$

□

DC22 $\neg(\text{true}^\frown \lceil S \rceil) \Leftrightarrow (\lceil\ \rceil \vee (\text{true}^\frown \lceil \neg S \rceil))$.
$\neg(\lceil S \rceil^\frown \text{true}) \Leftrightarrow (\lceil\ \rceil \vee (\lceil \neg S \rceil^\frown \text{true}))$.

Proof. This can be proved by use of DC1 and DC2. For example,

1. $\lceil\ \rceil \vee (\text{true}^\frown \lceil S \rceil) \vee (\text{true}^\frown \lceil \neg S \rceil)$ DC1
2. $(\lceil\ \rceil \wedge (\text{true}^\frown \lceil S \rceil)) \Rightarrow \text{false}$ IL20, PL
3. $((\text{true}^\frown \lceil S \rceil) \wedge (\text{true}^\frown \lceil \neg S \rceil)) \Rightarrow \text{false}$ DC20, DC11, IL13
4. $\neg(\text{true}^\frown \lceil S \rceil) \Leftrightarrow (\lceil\ \rceil \vee (\text{true}^\frown \lceil \neg S \rceil))$ 1., 2., 3., PL.

$\square$

DC23 $(\text{true}^\frown \lceil S \rceil) \Leftrightarrow (\lceil S \rceil \vee (\text{true}^\frown \lceil \neg S \rceil^\frown \lceil S \rceil))$.
$(\lceil S \rceil^\frown \text{true}) \Leftrightarrow (\lceil S \rceil \vee (\lceil S \rceil^\frown \lceil \neg S \rceil^\frown \text{true}))$.

Proof. We prove only the first theorem. Let

$$H(X) \stackrel{\frown}{=} (X \Rightarrow (\lceil\ \rceil \vee (\text{true}^\frown \lceil \neg S \rceil) \vee \lceil S \rceil \vee (\text{true}^\frown \lceil \neg S \rceil^\frown \lceil S \rceil))).$$

By applying Theorem 3.4, we can prove

$$\lceil\ \rceil \vee (\text{true}^\frown \lceil \neg S \rceil) \vee \lceil S \rceil \vee (\text{true}^\frown \lceil \neg S \rceil^\frown \lceil S \rceil).$$

Furthermore, it can be proved that any two of the above disjuncts are exclusive to each other. Thus, by use of PL and DC22, we can establish

$$(\text{true}^\frown \lceil S \rceil) \Leftrightarrow (\lceil S \rceil \vee (\text{true}^\frown \lceil \neg S \rceil^\frown \lceil S \rceil)).$$

$\square$

DC24
$$(\text{true}^\frown \lceil S_1 \rceil) \Leftrightarrow \begin{pmatrix} \lceil S_1 \rceil \vee (\text{true}^\frown \lceil \neg S_1 \wedge \neg S_2 \rceil^\frown \lceil S_1 \rceil) \\ \vee \\ (\text{true}^\frown \lceil \neg S_1 \wedge S_2 \rceil^\frown \lceil S_1 \rceil) \end{pmatrix}.$$

$$(\lceil S_1 \rceil^\frown \text{true}) \Leftrightarrow \begin{pmatrix} \lceil S_1 \rceil \vee (\lceil S_1 \rceil^\frown \lceil \neg S_1 \wedge \neg S_2 \rceil^\frown \text{true}) \\ \vee \\ (\lceil S_1 \rceil^\frown \lceil \neg S_1 \wedge S_2 \rceil^\frown \text{true}) \end{pmatrix}.$$

Proof. We prove only the first part. By DC23, $(\text{true}^\frown \lceil S_1 \rceil)$ is equivalent to

$$\lceil S_1 \rceil \vee (\text{true}^\frown \lceil \neg S_1 \rceil^\frown \lceil S_1 \rceil).$$

Furthermore, we have

$\text{true}^\frown \lceil \neg S_1 \rceil^\frown \lceil S_1 \rceil$
$\Leftrightarrow \text{true}^\frown \lceil \neg S_1 \wedge (S_2 \vee \neg S_2) \rceil^\frown \lceil S_1 \rceil$ DCA6
$\Leftrightarrow (\text{true}^\frown \lceil \neg S_1 \wedge \neg S_2 \rceil^\frown \lceil S_1 \rceil) \vee (\text{true}^\frown \lceil \neg S_1 \wedge S_2 \rceil^\frown \lceil S_1 \rceil)$ DC21, M.

$\square$

DC25 $(\lceil S\rceil \,^\frown true\,^\frown\lceil\neg S\rceil) \Rightarrow (\lceil S\rceil\,^\frown\lceil\neg S\rceil\,^\frown true)$.

Proof.

$$
\begin{aligned}
&\lceil S\rceil\,^\frown true\,^\frown\lceil\neg S\rceil\\
&\Rightarrow (\lceil S\rceil \vee (\lceil S\rceil\,^\frown\lceil\neg S\rceil\,^\frown true))\,^\frown\lceil\neg S\rceil && \text{DC23, M}\\
&\Rightarrow (\lceil S\rceil\,^\frown\lceil\neg S\rceil) \vee (\lceil S\rceil\,^\frown\lceil\neg S\rceil\,^\frown true\,^\frown\lceil\neg S\rceil) && \text{IL14}\\
&\Rightarrow (\lceil S\rceil\,^\frown\lceil\neg S\rceil\,^\frown(\ell=0)) \vee (\lceil S\rceil\,^\frown\lceil\neg S\rceil\,^\frown true\,^\frown\lceil\neg S\rceil) && \text{L3, PL}\\
&\Rightarrow \lceil S\rceil\,^\frown\lceil\neg S\rceil\,^\frown true && \text{M, PL.}
\end{aligned}
$$

$\square$

DC26 $\left(\begin{array}{c}(\lceil\neg S\rceil\,^\frown true)\\ \wedge\,(true\,^\frown\lceil S\rceil)\end{array}\right) \Leftrightarrow (\lceil\neg S\rceil\,^\frown true\,^\frown\lceil S\rceil)$.

Proof. The $\Leftarrow$ part can be derived from M, and using DC23 we can easily prove the $\Rightarrow$ part. $\square$

$$\left(\begin{array}{l}(((\Box_p\phi)\,^\frown\lceil S_1\rceil) \wedge (true\,^\frown\lceil\neg S_1\rceil\,^\frown\lceil S_2\rceil))\\ \Rightarrow (((\Box_p\phi)\,^\frown\lceil\neg S_1\rceil\,^\frown\lceil S_2\rceil) \wedge ((\Box_p\phi)\,^\frown\lceil S_2\rceil))\end{array}\right).$$

DC27 $\left(\begin{array}{l}(((\Box\phi)\,^\frown\lceil S_1\rceil) \wedge (true\,^\frown\lceil\neg S_1\rceil\,^\frown\lceil S_2\rceil))\\ \Rightarrow (((\Box\phi)\,^\frown\lceil\neg S_1\rceil\,^\frown\lceil S_2\rceil) \wedge ((\Box\phi)\,^\frown\lceil S_2\rceil))\end{array}\right).$

$$\left(\begin{array}{l}((\lceil S_1\rceil\,^\frown(\Box\phi)) \wedge (\lceil S_2\rceil\,^\frown\lceil\neg S_1\rceil\,^\frown true))\\ \Rightarrow ((\lceil S_2\rceil\,^\frown\lceil\neg S_1\rceil\,^\frown\Box\phi) \wedge (\lceil S_2\rceil\,^\frown\Box\phi))\end{array}\right).$$

Proof. We sketch a proof of the first theorem only. We first introduce interval lengths:

$$((\Box_p\phi)\,^\frown(\lceil S_1\rceil \wedge (\ell=x))) \wedge (true\,^\frown\lceil\neg S_1\rceil\,^\frown(\lceil S_2\rceil \wedge (\ell=y))).$$

When $x>y$, the above formula implies $(true\,^\frown false\,^\frown(\ell=y))$, as can be shown by applying IL17, DC20 and DC11. This is equivalent to false by IL13.

When $x\leq y$, by DC16 and IL17 the formula implies

$$((\Box_p\phi) \wedge (true\,^\frown\lceil\neg S_1\rceil\,^\frown(\lceil\,\rceil \vee \lceil S_2\rceil)))\,^\frown(\lceil S_2\rceil \wedge (\ell=x)).$$

By IL28, IL35 and DC16, the above formula implies

$$(\Box_p\phi \wedge (true\,^\frown\lceil\neg S_1\rceil))\,^\frown\lceil S_2\rceil.$$

Then, by use of IL35 and M, we can complete the proof. $\square$

$$
\begin{pmatrix}
\lceil\,\rceil \\
\vee \ (\text{true} \,^\frown \lceil \neg S_1 \wedge \neg S_2 \rceil) \\
\vee \ \lceil S_1 \rceil \\
\vee \ (\text{true} \,^\frown \lceil \neg S_1 \wedge \neg S_2 \rceil \,^\frown \lceil S_1 \rceil) \\
\vee \ (\text{true} \,^\frown \lceil \neg S_1 \wedge S_2 \rceil \,^\frown \lceil S_1 \rceil) \\
\vee \ (\text{true} \,^\frown \lceil S_2 \rceil)
\end{pmatrix} .
$$

DC28

$$
\begin{pmatrix}
\lceil\,\rceil \\
\vee \ (\lceil \neg S_1 \wedge \neg S_2 \rceil \,^\frown \text{true}) \\
\vee \ \lceil S_1 \rceil \\
\vee \ (\lceil S_1 \rceil \,^\frown \lceil \neg S_1 \wedge \neg S_2 \rceil \,^\frown \text{true}) \\
\vee \ (\lceil S_1 \rceil \,^\frown \lceil \neg S_1 \wedge S_2 \rceil \,^\frown \text{true}) \\
\vee \ (\lceil S_2 \rceil \,^\frown \text{true})
\end{pmatrix} .
$$

Proof. We prove only the first disjunction. By DC1,

$$\lceil\,\rceil \vee (\text{true}^\frown \lceil S_1 \vee S_2 \rceil) \vee (\text{true}^\frown \lceil \neg(S_1 \vee S_2)\rceil) .$$

By DC21, we have

$$(\text{true}^\frown \lceil S_1 \vee S_2 \rceil) \Rightarrow ((\text{true}^\frown \lceil S_1 \rceil) \vee (\text{true}^\frown \lceil S_2 \rceil)) .$$

By DC24,

$$
\begin{aligned}
&\text{true}^\frown \lceil S_1 \rceil \\
&\Rightarrow (\lceil S_1 \rceil \vee (\text{true}^\frown \lceil \neg S_1 \wedge \neg S_2 \rceil^\frown \lceil S_1 \rceil) \vee (\text{true}^\frown \lceil \neg S_1 \wedge S_2 \rceil^\frown \lceil S_1 \rceil)) .
\end{aligned}
$$

The first disjunction follows easily from the above properties. $\qquad\square$

With the induction rules, we can prove the reversal of DCA5.

DC29 $\forall x, y \geq 0.((\int S = x + y) \Rightarrow ((\int S = x)^\frown (\int S = y))) .$

Proof. Let

$$H(X) \mathrel{\hat=} (X \Rightarrow \text{DC29})$$

and apply Theorem 3.4. When deriving

$$(X^\frown \lceil S \rceil) \Rightarrow \text{DC29}$$

from $(X \Rightarrow \text{DC29})$, we can introduce z as the value of $\int S$ over the interval where X holds, and conclude by use of the induction hypothesis and M that

$$(X^\frown \lceil S \rceil) \Rightarrow \exists z.(\text{DC29} \wedge (\int S = z))^\frown ((\int S = \ell) \wedge (\ell > 0)) .$$

Then, we can prove

$$(X^\frown \llbracket S \rrbracket)$$
$$\Rightarrow$$
$$(((x_1 \geq 0 \wedge y_1 \geq 0) \wedge (\textstyle\int S = x_1 + y_1)) \Rightarrow ((\textstyle\int S = x_1)^\frown (\textstyle\int S = y_1)))$$

by analysis of the cases: $x_1 \leq z$ and $x_1 > z$. When $x_1 \leq z$, we can find the chopping point by using the induction hypothesis within the first subinterval where X holds. When $x_1 > z$, the chopping point can be decided using DC16 in the second subinterval where $\llbracket S \rrbracket$ holds. Similarly, we can prove

$$(X^\frown \llbracket \neg S \rrbracket) \Rightarrow \text{DC29},$$

where $x_1 \leq z$ will be the only possible case.   □

With DC29, we can establish the reversal of DC8 and then the generalization of DC15.

DC30 $((x \geq 0 \wedge y \geq 0) \wedge (\textstyle\int S \geq x + y)) \Rightarrow ((\textstyle\int S \geq x)^\frown (\textstyle\int S \geq y))$.

DC31 $((x \geq 0) \wedge (\textstyle\int S > x)) \Leftrightarrow ((\textstyle\int S = x)^\frown \llbracket S \rrbracket^\frown \text{true})$.

3.5 Example: Gas Burner

In this section, we prove the correctness of the design decisions for the gas burner. Using the same abbreviations as in Sect. 3.2,

$$
\begin{aligned}
Des_1 &\ \widehat{=}\ \Box(\llbracket \text{Leak} \rrbracket \Rightarrow \ell \leq 1) \\
Des_2 &\ \widehat{=}\ \Box((\llbracket \text{Leak} \rrbracket ^\frown \llbracket \neg \text{Leak} \rrbracket ^\frown \llbracket \text{Leak} \rrbracket) \Rightarrow \ell \geq 30) \\
GbReq &\ \widehat{=}\ \ell \geq 60 \Rightarrow 20\textstyle\int\text{Leak} \leq \ell,
\end{aligned}
$$

we must give a proof of

$$(Des_1 \wedge Des_2) \Rightarrow GbReq .$$

We first give an informal argument to introduce the main steps of the proof. Thereafter, a detailed proof is given.

3.5.1 Informal Argument

The idea behind the proof is the following.

Consider an arbitrary interval $[b, e]$ and assume that the two design decisions hold on the interval. This interval can be partitioned into a sequence of n intervals of size 30 time units followed by an interval whose size does not exceed 30 time units:

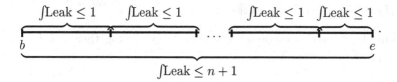

This is a consequence of the following fact of arithmetic:

$$\forall x \geq 0. \exists n \in \mathbb{N}. \exists y \geq 0. (y \leq 30 \wedge x = 30 \cdot n + y), \tag{3.4}$$

where $\mathbb{N}$ is the set of natural numbers $\{0, 1, 2, \ldots\}$.

Consider an arbitrary interval of size 30 time units (or less). For this interval, the second design decision Des_2 guarantees that there is at most one period where gas is leaking. Furthermore, Des_1 guarantees that this period is at most 1 time unit long. Therefore, gas is leaking for at most 1 time unit in any interval of size 30 or less. This property is expressed as follows:

$$(Des_1 \wedge Des_2) \Rightarrow \Box(\ell \leq 30 \Rightarrow \smallint \text{Leak} \leq 1).$$

Using this property for all the n intervals of size 30, we obtain the result that gas can be leaking for at most n time units during the first n intervals of size 30. This property is formalized as

$$\Box(\ell \leq 30 \Rightarrow \smallint \text{Leak} \leq 1) \Rightarrow \forall n \in \mathbb{N}. \Box(\ell = 30 \cdot n \Rightarrow \smallint \text{Leak} \leq n).$$

Furthermore, since the last interval does not exceed 30 time units, the duration of Leak for the full interval is at most $n+1$, i.e. we have the situation

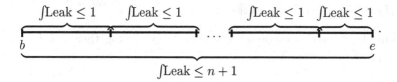

For an interval longer than 60 time units we have $n \geq 2$, and, since

$$n \geq 2 \Rightarrow 20 \cdot (n + 1) \leq 30 \cdot n, \tag{3.5}$$

we have the result that 20 times the duration of Leak does not exceed the length of the interval. Thus, the requirement holds for intervals satisfying the design decisions.

3.5.2 Proof

This informal argument will now be proved in duration calculus.

Lemma 3.5

$$(Des_1 \wedge Des_2) \;\Rightarrow\; \Box(\ell \leq 30 \Rightarrow \textstyle\int\!\text{Leak} \leq 1) \,.$$

Proof. It suffices to establish the following two deductions:

$$\left\{ \begin{array}{l} \lceil\!\lceil \text{Leak} \rceil\!\rceil \;\Rightarrow\; \ell \leq 1, \\ (\lceil\!\lceil \text{Leak} \rceil\!\rceil \,^\frown \lceil\!\lceil \neg\text{Leak} \rceil\!\rceil \,^\frown \lceil\!\lceil \text{Leak} \rceil\!\rceil) \;\Rightarrow\; \ell \geq 30 \end{array} \right\}$$

$$\vdash (\textstyle\int\!\text{Leak} = 0) \;\Rightarrow\; (\ell \leq 30 \Rightarrow \textstyle\int\!\text{Leak} \leq 1) \tag{3.6}$$

and

$$\left\{ \begin{array}{l} \lceil\!\lceil \text{Leak} \rceil\!\rceil \;\Rightarrow\; \ell \leq 1, \\ (\lceil\!\lceil \text{Leak} \rceil\!\rceil \,^\frown \lceil\!\lceil \neg\text{Leak} \rceil\!\rceil \,^\frown \lceil\!\lceil \text{Leak} \rceil\!\rceil) \;\Rightarrow\; \ell \geq 30 \end{array} \right\} \tag{3.7}$$

$$\vdash (\textstyle\int\!\text{Leak} > 0) \;\Rightarrow\; (\ell \leq 30 \Rightarrow \textstyle\int\!\text{Leak} \leq 1) \,.$$

This is because, combining the deductions using PL and DCA3, we obtain

$$\left\{ \begin{array}{l} \lceil\!\lceil \text{Leak} \rceil\!\rceil \;\Rightarrow\; \ell \leq 1, \\ (\lceil\!\lceil \text{Leak} \rceil\!\rceil \,^\frown \lceil\!\lceil \neg\text{Leak} \rceil\!\rceil \,^\frown \lceil\!\lceil \text{Leak} \rceil\!\rceil) \;\Rightarrow\; \ell \geq 30 \end{array} \right\} \vdash \ell \leq 30 \Rightarrow \textstyle\int\!\text{Leak} \leq 1 \,.$$

Then, using IL4, we have

$$\left\{ \begin{array}{l} \lceil\!\lceil \text{Leak} \rceil\!\rceil \;\Rightarrow\; \ell \leq 1, \\ (\lceil\!\lceil \text{Leak} \rceil\!\rceil \,^\frown \lceil\!\lceil \neg\text{Leak} \rceil\!\rceil \,^\frown \lceil\!\lceil \text{Leak} \rceil\!\rceil) \;\Rightarrow\; \ell \geq 30 \end{array} \right\} \vdash \Box(\ell \leq 30 \Rightarrow \textstyle\int\!\text{Leak} \leq 1) \,,$$

and, using the deduction theorem (Theorem 3.3) twice together with PL, we obtain a proof of Lemma 3.5:

$$\left(\begin{array}{l} \Box(\lceil\!\lceil \text{Leak} \rceil\!\rceil \;\Rightarrow\; \ell \leq 1) \\ \wedge \\ \Box((\lceil\!\lceil \text{Leak} \rceil\!\rceil \,^\frown \lceil\!\lceil \neg\text{Leak} \rceil\!\rceil \,^\frown \lceil\!\lceil \text{Leak} \rceil\!\rceil) \;\Rightarrow\; \ell \geq 30) \end{array} \right) \;\Rightarrow\; \Box(\ell \leq 30 \Rightarrow \textstyle\int\!\text{Leak} \leq 1) \,.$$

The deduction (3.6) is established by the argument

$$\begin{array}{ll} & \textstyle\int\!\text{Leak} = 0 \\ \Rightarrow & \textstyle\int\!\text{Leak} \leq 1 & \text{PL} \\ \Rightarrow & \ell \leq 30 \Rightarrow \textstyle\int\!\text{Leak} \leq 1 & \text{PL,} \end{array}$$

without using any assumptions.

The deduction (3.7) can be divided further into subcases according to

$$\int \text{Leak} > 0$$
$$\Leftrightarrow (\int \text{Leak} = 0) \frown \lceil \text{Leak} \rceil \frown \text{true} \qquad\qquad \text{DC15}$$
$$\Leftrightarrow (\int \text{Leak} = 0) \frown (\lceil \text{Leak} \rceil \vee (\lceil \text{Leak} \rceil \frown \lceil \neg \text{Leak} \rceil \frown \text{true})) \quad \text{DC23, M, PL}$$
$$\Leftrightarrow ((\int \text{Leak} = 0) \frown \lceil \text{Leak} \rceil)$$
$$\vee ((\int \text{Leak} = 0) \frown \lceil \text{Leak} \rceil \frown \lceil \neg \text{Leak} \rceil \frown \text{true}) \qquad \text{IL14}$$
$$\Leftrightarrow ((\int \text{Leak} = 0) \frown \lceil \text{Leak} \rceil)$$
$$\vee ((\int \text{Leak} = 0) \frown \lceil \text{Leak} \rceil \frown \lceil \neg \text{Leak} \rceil) \qquad \text{DC23, IL14,}$$
$$\vee ((\int \text{Leak} = 0) \frown \lceil \text{Leak} \rceil \frown \lceil \neg \text{Leak} \rceil \frown \lceil \text{Leak} \rceil \frown \text{true}) \quad \text{M, PL.}$$

Thus, to establish (3.7) it suffices to establish the following three deductions:

$$\left\{ \begin{array}{l} \lceil \text{Leak} \rceil \Rightarrow \ell \leq 1, \\ (\lceil \text{Leak} \rceil \frown \lceil \neg \text{Leak} \rceil \frown \lceil \text{Leak} \rceil) \Rightarrow \ell \geq 30 \end{array} \right\}$$
$$\vdash (((\int \text{Leak} = 0) \frown \lceil \text{Leak} \rceil) \Rightarrow (\ell \leq 30 \Rightarrow \int \text{Leak} \leq 1), \tag{3.8}$$

$$\left\{ \begin{array}{l} \lceil \text{Leak} \rceil \Rightarrow \ell \leq 1, \\ (\lceil \text{Leak} \rceil \frown \lceil \neg \text{Leak} \rceil \frown \lceil \text{Leak} \rceil) \Rightarrow \ell \geq 30 \end{array} \right\}$$
$$\vdash ((\int \text{Leak} = 0) \frown \lceil \text{Leak} \rceil \frown \lceil \neg \text{Leak} \rceil) \Rightarrow (\ell \leq 30 \Rightarrow \int \text{Leak} \leq 1), \tag{3.9}$$

$$\left\{ \begin{array}{l} \lceil \text{Leak} \rceil \Rightarrow \ell \leq 1, \\ (\lceil \text{Leak} \rceil \frown \lceil \neg \text{Leak} \rceil \frown \lceil \text{Leak} \rceil) \Rightarrow \ell \geq 30 \end{array} \right\}$$
$$\vdash \begin{array}{l} ((\int \text{Leak} = 0) \frown \lceil \text{Leak} \rceil \frown \lceil \neg \text{Leak} \rceil \frown \lceil \text{Leak} \rceil \frown \text{true}) \\ \Rightarrow (\ell \leq 30 \Rightarrow \int \text{Leak} \leq 1). \end{array} \tag{3.10}$$

The deductions of (3.8) and (3.9) are similar to establish, because they consider cases with only one period where gas is leaking. So we consider only (3.9):

1. $\lceil \text{Leak} \rceil \Rightarrow \ell \leq 1$
2. $\square(\lceil \text{Leak} \rceil \Rightarrow \ell \leq 1)$ IL4
3. $(\int \text{Leak} = 0) \frown \lceil \text{Leak} \rceil \frown \lceil \neg \text{Leak} \rceil$
   $\Rightarrow (\int \text{Leak} = 0) \frown \lceil \text{Leak} \rceil \frown (\int \text{Leak} = 0)$ DC12, M
   $\Rightarrow (\int \text{Leak} = 0) \frown (\ell \leq 1) \frown (\int \text{Leak} = 0)$ 2, IL19, PL
   $\Rightarrow (\int \text{Leak} = 0) \frown (\int \text{Leak} \leq 1) \frown (\int \text{Leak} = 0)$ DC6, M, PL
   $\Rightarrow (\int \text{Leak} \leq 0) \frown (\int \text{Leak} \leq 1) \frown (\int \text{Leak} \leq 0)$ M, PL
   $\Rightarrow \int \text{Leak} \leq 1$ DC8
4. $(\int \text{Leak} = 0) \frown \lceil \text{Leak} \rceil \frown \lceil \neg \text{Leak} \rceil$
   $\Rightarrow (\ell \leq 30 \Rightarrow \int \text{Leak} \leq 1)$ 3., PL.

In the last case, i.e. (3.10), we consider intervals with at least two periods where gas is leaking. The assumptions of (3.10) imply that this can happen only for intervals longer than 30 time units, and $\ell \leq 30 \Rightarrow \int \text{Leak} \leq 1$ obviously holds for such intervals. This is the main idea in the following deduction:

1. $(\lceil \text{Leak} \rceil \frown \lceil \neg \text{Leak} \rceil \frown \lceil \text{Leak} \rceil) \Rightarrow \ell \geq 30$
2. $\Box((\lceil \text{Leak} \rceil \frown \lceil \neg \text{Leak} \rceil \frown \lceil \text{Leak} \rceil) \Rightarrow \ell \geq 30)$ 1., IL4
3. $(\int \text{Leak} = 0) \frown (\lceil \text{Leak} \rceil \frown \lceil \neg \text{Leak} \rceil \frown \lceil \text{Leak} \rceil) \frown \text{true}$
    $\Rightarrow \text{true} \frown \lceil \text{Leak} \rceil \frown (\lceil \text{Leak} \rceil \frown \lceil \neg \text{Leak} \rceil \frown \lceil \text{Leak} \rceil) \frown \text{true}$ DC17, M, A2
    $\Rightarrow (\ell \geq 0) \frown (\ell > 0) \frown (\ell \geq 30) \frown (\ell \geq 0)$ 2., IL19, M
                                                      A0, PL
    $\Rightarrow \ell > 30$ DC8
4. $(\int \text{Leak} = 0) \frown (\lceil \text{Leak} \rceil \frown \lceil \neg \text{Leak} \rceil \frown \lceil \text{Leak} \rceil) \frown \text{true}$
    $\Rightarrow (\ell \leq 30 \Rightarrow \int \text{Leak} \leq 1)$ 3., PL.

$\square$

Lemma 3.6

$$\Box(\ell \leq 30 \Rightarrow \int \text{Leak} \leq 1) \Rightarrow \forall n \in \mathbb{N}.\Box(\ell = 30 \cdot n \Rightarrow \int \text{Leak} \leq n).$$

Proof. The proof follows when we apply the deduction theorem to the deduction:

1. $\ell \leq 30 \ \Rightarrow \int \text{Leak} \leq 1$
2. $\Box(\ell \leq 30 \ \Rightarrow \int \text{Leak} \leq 1)$ 1., IL4
3. $\ell = 0 \cdot 30 \ \Rightarrow \int \text{Leak} \leq 0$ DC6, PL
4. $\Box(\ell = 0 \cdot 30 \ \Rightarrow \int \text{Leak} \leq 0)$ 3., IL4
5. $\ell = (n + 1) \cdot 30$
      $\land \Box(\ell = n \cdot 30 \ \Rightarrow \int \text{Leak} \leq n)$
    $\Rightarrow \ell = n \cdot 30 + 30$ PL
    $\Rightarrow (\ell = n \cdot 30) \frown (\ell = 30)$ L2, PL
    $\Rightarrow (\int \text{Leak} \leq n) \frown (\ell = 30)$ IL19, M
    $\Rightarrow (\int \text{Leak} \leq n) \frown (\int \text{Leak} \leq 1)$ 2., IL19, M
    $\Rightarrow \int \text{Leak} \leq n + 1$ IL6
6. $\Box(\ell = n \cdot 30 \ \Rightarrow \int \text{Leak} \leq n)$
    $\Rightarrow (\ell = (n + 1) \cdot 30 \ \Rightarrow \int \text{Leak} \leq n + 1)$ 5., PL
7. $\Box(\ell = n \cdot 30 \ \Rightarrow \int \text{Leak} \leq n)$
    $\Rightarrow \Box(\ell = (n + 1) \cdot 30 \ \Rightarrow \int \text{Leak} \leq n + 1)$ 6., IL6
8. $\forall n \in \mathbb{N}.\Box(\ell = n \cdot 30 \ \Rightarrow \int \text{Leak} \leq n)$ 4., 7., PL,

where induction on natural numbers is used in the last step. $\square$

Theorem 3.6

$(Des_1 \wedge Des_2) \Rightarrow GbReq$.

Proof. The proof is established by applying the deduction theorem to the following deduction:

1. $\lceil \text{Leak} \rceil \Rightarrow \ell \leq 1$
2. Des_1 1., IL4
3. $(\lceil \text{Leak} \rceil \frown \lceil \neg \text{Leak} \rceil \frown \lceil \text{Leak} \rceil) \Rightarrow \ell \geq 30$
4. Des_2 2., IL4
5. $\ell \geq 60$
   $\Rightarrow \exists n \in \mathbb{N}. \exists y \geq 0.(n \geq 2 \wedge y \leq 30 \wedge \ell = n \cdot 30 + y)$ (3.4), PL
6. $n \geq 2 \wedge y \leq 30 \wedge (\ell = n \cdot 30 + y)$
   $\Rightarrow (\ell = n \cdot 30) \frown (\ell \leq 30)$ L2, PL
   $\Rightarrow (\int \text{Leak} \leq n) \frown (\ell \leq 30)$ 2., 4., LM3.5,
                                                        LM3.6, PL, M
   $\Rightarrow (\int \text{Leak} \leq n) \frown (\int \text{Leak} \leq 1)$ 2., 4., LM3.5, PL, M
   $\Rightarrow \int \text{Leak} \leq n + 1$ DCA5
   $\Rightarrow 20 \cdot \int \text{Leak} \leq \ell$ (3.5), PL
7. $\ell \geq 60 \Rightarrow 20 \cdot \int \text{Leak} \leq \ell$ 5., 6., PL.

(In the above deduction, the abbreviation "LM" means "Lemma".)   □

4. Deadline-Driven Scheduler

The deadline-driven scheduler of Liu and Layland [85] is considered in this chapter. The main idea of the scheduler was given in Chap. 1. The correctness proof for the deadline-driven scheduler will be carried out carefully to illustrate that the proof theory of the previous two chapters can manage a nontrivial proof. The steps of the proof wil not, however, be given in as much detail as in the previous chapters and we shall omit some simple steps and annotations that we have described earlier.

The theorem to be formalized in DC and proved is:

Theorem 4.1 (Liu and Layland) *For a given set of m processes, the deadline-driven scheduler is feasible if and only if*

$$(C_1/T_1) + (C_2/T_2) + \cdots + (C_m/T_m) \leq 1 \qquad (0 < C_i < T_i),$$

where C_i and T_i are the run time and request period, respectively, of the ith process, and $T_1, T_2, \ldots, T_m$ are integers.

In [85], there is an informal description of the algorithm and an informal proof of the theorem. The formal proof presented in this chapter is based on [160].

4.1 Formalization of the Deadline-Driven Scheduler

The deadline-driven scheduler is formalized by specifying:

- several processes running on the same processor,
- the running time, periodic requests and deadlines for each process,
- the requirements for each process, and
- the scheduling algorithm.

Suppose that m processes $p_1, \ldots, p_m$ are given. Let

$$\alpha = \{1, \ldots, m\}.$$

The behavior of the processes and the scheduler are described using three kinds of state variables:

$$\text{Run}_i : \text{Time} \rightarrow \{0,1\}$$
$$\text{Std}_i : \text{Time} \rightarrow \{0,1\}$$
$$\text{Urg}_{ij} : \text{Time} \rightarrow \{0,1\},$$

where $i,j \in \alpha$.

The intention is that

- $\text{Run}_i(t) = 1$ if p_i is running on the processor at time t, while $\text{Run}_i(t) = 0$ if p_i is not running at t.
- $\text{Std}_i(t) = 1$ means that the current request of p_i is still standing at time t, while $\text{Std}_i(t) = 0$ means that at t the current request of p_i is not standing, i.e. it has been fulfilled.
- $\text{Urg}_{ij}(t) = 1$ if p_i is more urgent than p_j at t, in the sense that the next deadline of p_i is closer than the next deadline of p_j.

4.1.1 Shared Processor

A process is only running if it has a standing request to do so:

$$A_1 \triangleq \lceil \text{Run}_i \rceil \Rightarrow \lceil \text{Std}_i \rceil .$$

Since all processes use the same processor, at most one process can run at any time:

$$A_2 \triangleq \lceil \text{Run}_i \rceil \Rightarrow \bigwedge_{j \neq i} \lceil \neg \text{Run}_j \rceil .$$

These properties must hold for every process and every interval:

$$ShP \triangleq \Box \bigwedge_{i \in \alpha} (A_1 \wedge A_2) .$$

The formula ShP implies that the sum of the running times for all processes cannot exceed the interval length:

Lemma 4.1

$$ShP \Rightarrow (\sum_{i \in \alpha} \int \text{Run}_i) \leq \ell .$$

Proof. A proof can be given as follows:

$$ShP$$
$$\Rightarrow (\sum_{i \in \alpha} \int \text{Run}_i) = \int (\bigvee_{i \in \alpha} \text{Run}_i) \quad \text{DC13}$$
$$\Rightarrow (\sum_{i \in \alpha} \int \text{Run}_i) \leq \ell \qquad\qquad \text{DC6}.$$

□

Using this lemma and DC14, we can derive the following lemma, which expresses the fact that the accumulated running time of a set of processes adds up to (and does not exceed) the interval length, on an interval throughout which they are running.

Lemma 4.2 *For any $\beta \subseteq \alpha$:*

$$(ShP \wedge \lceil \bigvee_{i \in \beta} \mathrm{Run}_i \rceil) \;\Rightarrow\; \sum_{i \in \beta} \int\!\mathrm{Run}_i = \ell.$$

4.1.2 Periodic Requests and Deadlines

Each process p_i has a periodic request for processor time. The period is $T_i > 0$ and the process requires a processor time $C_i > 0$ in each period. We assume that all processes raise their first requests simultaneously, say at time 0. Hence, all arguments are restricted to intervals starting at 0 and their subintervals. By Theorem 3.1, this restriction does not affect the validity of formulas, and it is therefore invisible.

Thus, the request periods of p_i start at times $k \cdot T_i$, for $k = 0, 1, 2, 3, \ldots$, and the time point $k \cdot T_i$ ($k \geq 1$) is the *deadline* for process p_i's kth request.

To capture the deadlines of process p_i, we define a predicate $dLine_i$ which holds for intervals whose end point is a multiple of the period T_i of p_i. This predicate is defined by

$$dLine_i \;\hat{=}\; T_i \mid \ell, \quad \text{which reads: "interval end point is a deadline of } p_i\text{",}$$

where $x \mid y$ reads: "x divides y" or "y is a multiple of x", which is true if there is a natural number k such that $k \cdot x = y$. Thus, $dLine_i$ holds for intervals which can be partitioned into a number of intervals each having length T_i.

For any real number $z \geq 0$, we can find a natural number $k \geq 0$ and a real number r, where $0 \leq r \leq T_i$ and $z = k \cdot T_i + r$.

Thus, by the definition of $dLine_i$ and L2, we have

$$(\ell = z) \;\Leftrightarrow\; (dLine_i \;{}^\frown (\ell \leq T_i))$$

and, hence, by A0,

$$dLine_i \;{}^\frown (\ell \leq T_i)$$

holds on any interval, i.e. any interval can be partitioned into a (possibly empty) sequence of periods of length T_i and a possibly not completed period.

In the proof of Liu and Layland's theorem, we must be precise about the deadlines of a process at interval end points. To this end, we use the following conventions:

- Any interval of the form $(b, e) = \{x \in \mathbb{R} \mid b < x < e\}$ is called an *open interval*.
- Any interval of the form $(b, e] = \{x \in \mathbb{R} \mid b < x \le e\}$ is called a *left open interval*.
- Any interval of the form $[b, e) = \{x \in \mathbb{R} \mid b \le x < e\}$ is called a *right open interval*.
- Any interval of the form $[b, e] = \{x \in \mathbb{R} \mid b \le x \le e\}$ is called a *closed interval* or just an interval.

For example,

- the formula $dLine_i \frown (0 < \ell < x)$ reads "p_i has a deadline in the last open interval of length x", provided that the length of the whole interval is greater than or equal to x, and
- the formula $\neg(dLine_i \frown (\ell < x))$ reads "p_i has no deadline in the last left open interval of length x".

The specification of the periodic requests of process p_i is partitioned into specifications for the last period and specifications for every period.

Specifications Concerning the Last Period of p_i

The last period must start with a standing request for processor time:

$$StartRequest_i \,\hat{=}\, dLine_i \frown \left(\begin{array}{c} \ell \le T_i \\ \wedge\, (\lceil\!\lceil\,\rceil\!\rceil \vee (\lceil\!\lceil Std_i \rceil\!\rceil \frown true)) \end{array} \right) .$$

A standing request for processor time may disappear only when the process has finished its task. This is expressed as follows: if Std_i changes to 0, then the task for p_i must be completed:

$$HoldRequest_i \,\hat{=}\, \left(\begin{array}{c} \left(dLine_i \frown \left(\begin{array}{c} \ell \le T_i \\ \wedge\, \Diamond \lceil\!\lceil \neg Std_i \rceil\!\rceil \end{array} \right) \right) \\ \Rightarrow \left(dLine_i \frown \left(\begin{array}{c} \ell \le T_i \\ \wedge\, \int Run_i = C_i \end{array} \right) \right) \end{array} \right) .$$

A standing request for processor time must disappear when the task is completed. This is expressed as follows: it is not the case that Std_i holds in a period when the task is completed for this period:

$$DisappearRequest_i \,\hat{=}\, \neg \left(dLine_i \frown \left(\begin{array}{c} \ell \le T_i \\ \wedge\, ((\int Run_i = C_i) \frown \Diamond \lceil\!\lceil Std_i \rceil\!\rceil) \end{array} \right) \right) .$$

Specifications Concerning Every Period

The three formulas above must hold for every process and for every prefix interval, i.e. the specification of the periodic requests for the running time for the m processes is

$$PrR \mathrel{\widehat{=}} \Box_p \bigwedge_{i \in \alpha} (StartRequest_i \wedge HoldRequest_i \wedge DisappearRequest_i) .$$

To formulate upper and lower bounds on the running time of processes, we use the *ceiling* ($\lceil \_ \rceil$) and *floor* ($\lfloor \_ \rfloor$) functions, where

- $\lceil x \rceil$ is the smallest integer greater than or equal to x, and
- $\lfloor x \rfloor$ is the largest integer not exceeding x.

Hence,

- $\lceil \ell / T_i \rceil$ denotes the number of periods started by process p_i in a given interval,
- $\lfloor \ell / T_i \rfloor$ denotes the number of full periods completed by process p_i, and
- $\lceil \ell / T_i \rceil \cdot C_i$ denotes the *upper bound on the running time* of p_i in an interval.

The following lemma says that ShP and PrR can guarantee that process p_i does not get too much processor time granted:

Lemma 4.3 *For any $i \in \alpha$:*

$$(ShP \wedge PrR) \;\Rightarrow\; \textstyle\int \mathrm{Run}_i \leq \lceil \ell / T_i \rceil \cdot C_i .$$

Proof. A proof of the lemma can have the following steps:

(a) $(ShP \wedge PrR) \;\Rightarrow\; (dLine_i \frown ((\ell \leq T_i) \wedge (\int \mathrm{Run}_i \leq C_i)))$.
(b) $(ShP \wedge PrR) \;\Rightarrow\; \Box_p(dLine_i \frown ((\ell \leq T_i) \wedge (\int \mathrm{Run}_i \leq C_i)))$.
(c) $(ShP \wedge PrR) \;\Rightarrow\; \int \mathrm{Run}_i \leq \lceil \ell / T_i \rceil \cdot C_i$.

It is not difficult to establish step (a). From $dLine_i \frown (\ell \leq T_i)$, PL and IL14, we have

$$(dLine_i \frown (\ell \leq T_i \wedge \textstyle\int \mathrm{Run}_i \leq C_i)) \vee (dLine_i \frown (\ell \leq T_i \wedge \textstyle\int \mathrm{Run}_i > C_i)) .$$

Furthermore, we can establish

$$
\begin{aligned}
&ShP \wedge PrR \wedge (dLine_i \frown (\ell \leq T_i \wedge \textstyle\int \mathrm{Run}_i > C_i)) \\
\Rightarrow\; &dLine_i \frown (\ell \leq T_i \wedge (\textstyle\int \mathrm{Run}_i = C_i \frown \lceil \mathrm{Run}_i \rceil \frown true)) && \text{DC31} \\
\Rightarrow\; &dLine_i \frown (\ell \leq T_i \wedge (\textstyle\int \mathrm{Run}_i = C_i \frown \Diamond \lceil \mathrm{Std}_i \rceil)) && ShP \\
\Rightarrow\; &false && DisappearRequest_i .
\end{aligned}
$$

Step (b) can be derived from step (a) by use of IL25, IL28, IL36 and IL32.

Step (c) can be derived from (b) by establishing

$$(ShP \wedge PrR \wedge ((dLine_i \wedge \ell = k \cdot T_i) ^\frown (\ell \leq T_i))) \;\Rightarrow\; \smallint Run_i \leq (k+1) \cdot C_i$$

by induction on the natural number k. $\qquad\qquad\qquad\qquad\qquad\qquad\square$

Since $T_i > C_i$, process p_i cannot occupy the processor for an entire request period. This property is implied by ShP and PrR.

Lemma 4.4

$$(ShP \wedge PrR) \;\Rightarrow\; \Box_p \bigwedge_{i \in \alpha} \neg(dLine_i ^\frown (\llbracket Run_i \rrbracket \wedge (\ell = T_i))) \,.$$

Proof. We prove $(ShP \wedge PrR) \;\Rightarrow\; \neg(dLine_i ^\frown (\llbracket Run_i \rrbracket \wedge (\ell = T_i)))$.

$$\left(dLine_i ^\frown \left(\begin{array}{c} \ell = T_i \\ \wedge \llbracket Run_i \rrbracket \end{array} \right) \right) \wedge ShP \wedge PrR$$

$$\Rightarrow dLine_i ^\frown \left(\begin{array}{c} \ell = T_i \\ \wedge (\smallint Run_i = C_i ^\frown \llbracket Run_i \rrbracket ^\frown \mathrm{true}) \end{array} \right) \quad (T_i > C_i), \mathrm{DC31}$$

$$\Rightarrow dLine_i ^\frown \left(\begin{array}{c} \ell = T_i \\ \wedge (\smallint Run_i = C_i ^\frown \Diamond \llbracket Std_i \rrbracket) \end{array} \right) \qquad ShP$$

$$\Rightarrow \mathrm{false} \qquad\qquad\qquad\qquad\qquad DisappearRequest_i.$$

The remaining part is proved as in step (b) above. $\qquad\qquad\qquad\square$

A simple consequence of this lemma is that a process can have at most one deadline in a closed interval throughout which it is running, as

$$\begin{array}{l} ShP \wedge PrR \\ \wedge \, (dLine_i ^\frown (\llbracket Run_i \rrbracket \wedge (\ell = T_i)) ^\frown \mathrm{true}) \,, \end{array}$$

by the definition of $\Box_p$, would contradict Lemma 4.4. Hence, we have the following lemma.

Lemma 4.5 *For any $i \in \alpha$:*

$$\left(\begin{array}{c} ShP \wedge PrR \\ \wedge \, (\mathrm{true} ^\frown (\llbracket Run_i \rrbracket \wedge \ell = x)) \end{array} \right) \Rightarrow \neg \exists y. \left(\begin{array}{c} 0 \leq y \wedge y + T_i \leq x \\ \wedge \, (dLine_i ^\frown (\ell = T_i + y)) \\ \wedge \, (dLine_i ^\frown (\ell = y)) \end{array} \right) \,.$$

4.1.3 Requirement

The requirement for the deadline-driven scheduler is that every process completes its task in every request period. For the process p_i, we have the condition that the length of the request period is T_i, and that it must occupy the processor for C_i to complete its task in a period. Given Lemma 4.3, which sets an upper bound on the running time, we specify here the requirement for the lower bound.

The lower bound on the running time for process p_i over an interval is given by the product of the number of full periods ($\lfloor \ell/T_i \rfloor$) and the required processor time C_i for each period:

$$req_i \mathrel{\widehat{=}} \int\!\mathrm{Run}_i \geq \lfloor \ell/T_i \rfloor \cdot C_i, \quad \text{for } i \in \alpha.$$

This must hold for every prefix interval and every process:

$$Req_i \mathrel{\widehat{=}} \Box_p req_i, \quad \text{for } i \in \alpha,$$
$$Req \mathrel{\widehat{=}} \bigwedge_{i \in \alpha} Req_i.$$

The following lemma asserts that a violation of the requirement formulated above cannot be discovered until a request period is finished.

Lemma 4.6 *For any $i \in \alpha$:*

$$\left(\begin{array}{c} Req_i \,\widehat{}\, (\ell = x) \\ \wedge \neg(dLine_i \,\widehat{}\, (\ell < x)) \end{array} \right) \Rightarrow Req_i.$$

Proof. The formula $\neg(dLine_i \,\widehat{}\, (\ell < x))$ means that p_i has no deadline in the last left open interval of length x, so consider the following situation:

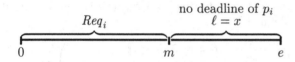

Since there is no deadline of p_i, i.e. no multiple of T_i in $(m, e]$, we have the result (from the definition of the floor operator) that the value of $\lfloor \ell/T_i \rfloor \cdot C_i$ does not change in $(m, e]$. Therefore, Req_i holds on $[0, e]$. The details of the proof will not be presented. □

When p_i does not have a standing request, its requirement is fulfilled for the current period ($HoldRequest_i$). Moreover, if p_i's requirement is also fulfilled for all the previous periods, then its running time in the entire interval reaches the upper bound:

Lemma 4.7 *For any $i \in \alpha$:*

$$\left(\begin{array}{c} ShP \wedge PrR \\ \wedge (Req_i \,\widehat{}\, \lceil\neg Std_i\rceil) \end{array} \right) \Rightarrow \left(\begin{array}{c} \int\!\mathrm{Run}_i = \lceil \ell/T_i \rceil \cdot C_i \\ \wedge Req_i \end{array} \right).$$

Proof. Notice that p_i (by $StartRequest_i$) cannot have a deadline in a right open interval where $\lceil\neg Std_i\rceil$ holds. That is, we have

$$(Req_i \,\widehat{}\, \lceil\neg Std_i\rceil) \wedge ShP \wedge PrR$$

$$\Rightarrow \left(\begin{array}{c} dLine_i \\ \wedge \int\!\mathrm{Run}_i \geq \lfloor \ell/T_i \rfloor \cdot C_i \end{array} \right) \,\widehat{}\, \left(\begin{array}{c} \ell \leq T_i \\ \wedge \, true \,\widehat{}\, \lceil\neg Std_i\rceil \end{array} \right) \qquad StartRequest_i, \text{IL35}$$

$$\Rightarrow \left(\begin{array}{c} dLine_i \\ \wedge \int\!\mathrm{Run}_i \geq (\ell/T_i) \cdot C_i \end{array} \right) \,\widehat{}\, \left(\begin{array}{c} \ell \leq T_i \\ \wedge \int\!\mathrm{Run}_i = C_i \end{array} \right) \qquad HoldRequest_i$$

$$\Rightarrow \int\!\mathrm{Run}_i = \lceil \ell/T_i \rceil \cdot C_i \qquad\qquad\qquad\qquad\qquad \text{DCA5, LM4.3.}$$

Since

$$\left(\begin{array}{c} StartRequest_i \\ \wedge \, (Req_i \frown (\lceil \neg Std_i \rceil \wedge \ell = x)) \end{array}\right) \;\Rightarrow\; \neg(dLine_i \frown (\ell < x)),$$

the remaining part of the proof follows from Lemma 4.6.   □

4.1.4 Scheduler

The role of the scheduler is to grant processes running time such that each process meets all its deadlines. The *nearest deadline* of process p_i at a given time t is the start of the next period; it can be calculated from

$$(\lfloor t/T_i \rfloor + 1) \cdot T_i \,,$$

and the distance to the nearest deadline of p_i is defined by

$$dist_i(t) = (\lfloor t/T_i \rfloor + 1) \cdot T_i - t \,.$$

A process p_i is more *urgent* than a process p_j at $t \geq 0$, if the distance to p_i's nearest deadline is smaller than p_j's distance to its nearest deadline, i.e. if $dist_i(t) < dist_j(t)$. Therefore, the state variable Urg_{ij} can be characterized by the formula $Urgent_{ij}$, defined by

$$\forall x. \left(0 < x < \ell \;\Rightarrow\; \left(\begin{array}{c} (\ell = x) \frown \lceil \mathrm{Urg}_{ij} \rceil \\ \Leftrightarrow \\ \forall z.(x < z < \ell \;\Rightarrow\; dist_i(z) < dist_j(z)) \end{array} \right) \right).$$

Notice that $\lceil \mathrm{Urg}_{ii} \rceil$ is impossible.

We introduce the abbreviation

$$Urgent \;\widehat{=}\; \Box_p \bigwedge_{i,j \in \alpha} Urgent_{ij} \,.$$

The following lemma is a direct consequence of *Urgent*.

Lemma 4.8 *For any $i, j \in \alpha$:*

$$\left(\begin{array}{c} Urgent \wedge y_1 < y_2 \\ \wedge \, (dLine_i \frown (\ell = y_1)) \\ \wedge \, (dLine_j \frown (\ell = y_2 \leq T_j)) \end{array} \right) \;\Rightarrow\; \left(true \frown \left(\begin{array}{c} \ell = y_2 - y_1 \\ \wedge \lceil \mathrm{Urg}_{ij} \rceil \end{array} \right) \frown (\ell = y_1) \right) \,.$$

Proof. The following diagram illustrates the antecedent:

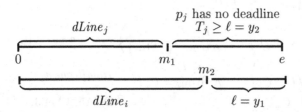

The lemma follows from the fact that p_j has no deadline in $(m_1, m_2]$ and that $dist_i(z) = m_2 - z < dist_j(z)$ for all $z \in (m_1, m_2)$. $\square$

This lemma can easily be generalized to a situation where every process p_i, for $i \in \beta$, has a deadline in the last left open interval of length y, while no process p_j, for $j \in \gamma$, has a deadline in the last closed interval of length y:

Lemma 4.9 *For any $\beta, \gamma \subseteq \alpha$:*

$$\left(\begin{array}{l} Urgent \\ \land \bigwedge_{i \in \beta}(dLine_i \,\widehat{}\,(\ell < y)) \\ \land \bigwedge_{j \in \gamma} \neg(dLine_j \,\widehat{}\,(\ell \le y)) \end{array} \right) \Rightarrow \bigwedge_{i \in \beta} \bigwedge_{j \in \gamma} (\text{true} \,\widehat{}\, \lceil Urg_{ij} \rceil \,\widehat{}\,(\ell = y)).$$

Note that a process which has no standing request may be more urgent than a process which has a standing request. The scheduler must guarantee that one of the most urgent processes with standing requests will occupy the processor at any time. This is formalized in two steps.

The formula

$$Sch_1 \,\widehat{=}\, \Box \bigwedge_{i,j \in \alpha} \neg \lceil Urg_{ij} \land Run_j \land Std_i \rceil$$

expresses the condition that a less urgent process cannot be running when a more urgent process has a standing request for processor time.

A simple consequence of Sch_1 is that if a process p_j is running throughout a left open interval where it does not have a deadline, then any other process, say p_i, can have at most one deadline in the corresponding closed interval. This is because there would otherwise be an interval where p_i was more urgent than p_j, and p_j was running despite the fact that p_i had a standing request:

Lemma 4.10 *For $i, j \in \alpha$, where $i \neq j$:*

$$\left(\begin{array}{l} PrR \land Urgent \land Sch_1 \\ \land \ (\text{true} \,\widehat{}\,(\lceil Run_j \rceil \land \ell = y)) \\ \land \ \neg(dLine_j \,\widehat{}\,(\ell < y)) \end{array} \right) \Rightarrow \neg \exists y_1, y_2. \left(\begin{array}{l} 0 \le y_1 < y_2 \le y \\ \land \ (dLine_i \,\widehat{}\, \ell = y_1) \\ \land \ (dLine_i \,\widehat{}\, \ell = y_2) \end{array} \right).$$

Proof. The following diagram shows the situation where p_i has two deadlines m_1 and m_2 in a closed interval throughout which p_j is running.

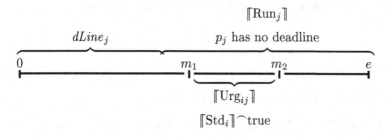

Since p_j has no deadline in the left open interval where it is running, p_i is (by *Urgent*) more urgent than p_j in the interval $[m_1, m_2]$, i.e. $\lceil \text{Urg}_{ij} \rceil$ holds on $[m_1, m_2]$. Furthermore, by *PrR*, $\lceil \text{Std}_i \rceil$ holds on a right neighborhood interval of m_1, and we have reached a contradiction with Sch_1 on this right neighborhood of m_1.   □

The formula Sch_1 is, however, true for intervals where no process is running, despite the fact that some processes have standing requests for processor time. The following formula guarantees that some process will be running when there exists a process which has a standing request for processor time:

$$Sch_2 \triangleq \bigwedge_{i \in \alpha} \Box(\lceil \text{Std}_i \rceil \Rightarrow \lceil \bigvee_{j \in \alpha} \text{Run}_j \rceil).$$

Note that Sch_2 specifies a scheduler with no *overhead*.

On an interval where no process is running we have, by Sch_2, the result that no process has a standing request. Thus, by Lemma 4.7, we obtain the result that if an interval where *Req* holds is followed by an interval where no process is running, then *Req* holds on the whole interval:

Lemma 4.11

$$\begin{pmatrix} ShP \wedge PrR \wedge Sch_2 \\ \wedge \ (Req ^\frown \lceil \bigwedge_{i \in \alpha} \neg \text{Run}_i \rceil) \end{pmatrix} \Rightarrow Req.$$

The formulas Sch_1 and Sch_2 together specify that at any time, one of the most urgent processes with a standing request must be running. Therefore, the deadline-driven scheduler can be specified as follows:

$$Sch \triangleq Urgent \wedge Sch_1 \wedge Sch_2.$$

4.2 Liu and Layland's Theorem

The theorem of Liu and Layland has two parts. One part is the necessity of the condition $(\sum_{i \in \alpha} C_i/T_i \leq 1)$ for the correctness of the scheduler. The other part is the sufficiency of this condition for the correctness.

Necessity

Consider the formula

$$(ShP \wedge PrR \wedge Sch \wedge Req) \Rightarrow (\textstyle\sum_{i \in \alpha} C_i/T_i) \leq 1.$$

The condition $(\sum_{i=1}^{m} C_i/T_i \leq 1)$ is necessary if we can find an interval such that the above formula must hold on the interval.

That is, we must find a value of x such that the following formula holds:

$$((\ell = x) \wedge ShP \wedge PrR \wedge Sch \wedge Req) \Rightarrow \left(\sum_{i \in \alpha} C_i/T_i\right) \leq 1.$$

This part is not difficult, as we can choose $x = T_1 \cdot T_2 \cdot \dots \cdot T_m$. Note that each T_i divides x (i.e. $T_i \mid x$), because the T_i ($i \in \alpha$) are integers. The necessity part is proved as follows:

$$
\begin{aligned}
&\left(\begin{matrix} \ell = T_1 \cdot T_2 \cdot \dots \cdot T_m \\ \wedge\, ShP \wedge PrR \wedge Sch \wedge Req \end{matrix}\right) \\
&\Rightarrow \bigwedge_{i \in \alpha} \int \text{Run}_i \geq \lfloor \ell/T_i \rfloor \cdot C_i && Req, \text{IL27} \\
&\Rightarrow \bigwedge_{i \in \alpha} \int \text{Run}_i \geq \ell/T_i \cdot C_i && \lfloor \ell/T_i \rfloor = \ell/T_i \\
&\Rightarrow \left(\sum_{i \in \alpha} \int \text{Run}_i\right) \geq \left(\sum_{i \in \alpha} \ell/T_i \cdot C_i\right) \\
&\Rightarrow \ell \geq \ell \cdot \left(\sum_{i \in \alpha} C_i/T_i\right) && \text{LM4.1} \\
&\Rightarrow \sum_{i \in \alpha} C_i/T_i \leq 1.
\end{aligned}
$$

Sufficiency

This part is the difficult part of the proof of Liu and Layland's theorem.

Before giving this proof, we establish some further lemmas. The first lemma expresses the fact that, for a given subset $\beta \subseteq \alpha$, if an interval can be chopped into two parts such that

1. the run time of any process p_i with $i \in \beta$ reaches $\lceil \ell/T_i \rceil \cdot C_i$ in the first interval, and
2. the accumulated run time of processes in β in the second interval equals the length of the interval,

then the sum of the accumulated run time for the processes in β will be no less than $\sum_{i \in \beta} \lfloor \ell/T_i \rfloor \cdot C_i$, provided $(\sum_{i \in \beta} C_i/T_i \leq 1)$.

Lemma 4.12 *For any $\beta \subseteq \alpha$:*

$$
\left(\sum_{i \in \beta} C_i/T_i \leq 1\right) \Rightarrow \left(\begin{matrix} ((\bigwedge_{i \in \beta} \int \text{Run}_i = \lceil \ell/T_i \rceil \cdot C_i)^\frown (\sum_{i \in \beta} \int \text{Run}_i = \ell)) \\ \Rightarrow \sum_{i \in \beta} \int \text{Run}_i \geq \sum_{i \in \beta} \lfloor \ell/T_i \rfloor \cdot C_i \end{matrix}\right).
$$

Proof. We have, from real arithmetic, the fact that

$$\lfloor z/y \rfloor \leq \lfloor (z-x)/y \rfloor + \lceil x/y \rceil, \quad \text{if } z \geq x \geq 0 \text{ and } y > 0. \tag{4.1}$$

This fact is used in the following proof:

$$\sum_{i\in\beta} C_i/T_i \le 1 \wedge$$
$$\left(\begin{array}{l}\ell = x \wedge \\ \bigwedge_{i\in\beta} \int\!\mathrm{Run}_i = \lceil \ell/T_i\rceil \cdot C_i\end{array}\right) \frown \left(\sum_{i\in\beta}\int\!\mathrm{Run}_i = \ell\right)$$

$$\Rightarrow \sum_{i\in\beta}\int\!\mathrm{Run}_i = \sum_{i\in\beta}\lceil x/T_i\rceil \cdot C_i + (\ell - x) \qquad \text{L2, DCA5}$$

$$\Rightarrow \sum_{i\in\beta}\int\!\mathrm{Run}_i \ge \left(\begin{array}{l}\sum_{i\in\beta}\lceil x/T_i\rceil \cdot C_i \\ + (\ell - x)\sum_{i\in\beta} C_i/T_i\end{array}\right) \qquad \sum_{i\in\beta} C_i/T_i \le 1$$

$$\Rightarrow \sum_{i\in\beta}\int\!\mathrm{Run}_i \ge \left(\begin{array}{l}\sum_{i\in\beta}\lceil x/T_i\rceil \cdot C_i \\ + \sum_{i\in\beta}\lfloor (\ell - x)/T_i\rfloor \cdot C_i\end{array}\right) \qquad \begin{array}{l}(\ell - x)/T_i \ge \\ \lfloor(\ell - x)/T_i\rfloor\end{array}$$

$$\Rightarrow \sum_{i\in\beta}\int\!\mathrm{Run}_i \ge \sum_{i\in\beta}(\lceil x/T_i\rceil + \lfloor(\ell - x)/T_i\rfloor)\cdot C_i \qquad \text{PL}$$

$$\Rightarrow \sum_{i\in\beta}\int\!\mathrm{Run}_i \ge \sum_{i\in\beta}\lfloor\ell/T_i\rfloor\cdot C_i \qquad (4.1).$$

□

Let

$$Spec \,\hat{=}\, \left(ShP \wedge PrR \wedge Sch \wedge \left(\sum_{i\in\alpha} C_i/T_i\right) \le 1\right).$$

In the next lemma we consider an interval and a subset $\beta \subseteq \alpha$, where every process p_i, for $i \in \beta$, does not exceed its lower bound for processor time (e.g. p_i has no processor time in its last, unfinished period in the interval):

$$\bigwedge_{i\in\beta}\int\!\mathrm{Run}_i \le \lfloor\ell/T_i\rfloor\cdot C_i.$$

If this interval can be partitioned into two parts, where

1. every process p_i, with $i \in \beta$, reaches its upper bound for processor time (e.g. p_i has processor time in all periods, possibly including a last, unfinished period in this part) in the first part, and
2. throughout the second part, processes p_i, with $i \in \beta$, are running,

then the requirement holds on this interval, for all processes in β.

Lemma 4.13 *For any $\beta \subseteq \alpha$:*

$$\left(\begin{array}{l}Spec \wedge \bigwedge_{i\in\beta}\int\!\mathrm{Run}_i \le \lfloor\ell/T_i\rfloor\cdot C_i \\ \wedge \,((\bigwedge_{i\in\beta}\int\!\mathrm{Run}_i = \lceil\ell/T_i\rceil\cdot C_i)\frown[\![\bigvee_{i\in\beta}\mathrm{Run}_i]\!])\end{array}\right) \Rightarrow \bigwedge_{i\in\beta} req_i.$$

Proof. The following fact from real arithmetic will be used in the proof of this this lemma:

$$\left(\bigwedge_{i=1}^n (x_i \le k_i) \wedge \left(\sum_{i=1}^n x_i \ge \sum_{i=1}^n k_i\right)\right) \Rightarrow \bigwedge_{i=1}^n (x_i \ge k_i). \qquad (4.2)$$

The lemma is proved as follows:

$$Spec \wedge \bigwedge_{i \in \beta} \int Run_i \leq \lfloor \ell/T_i \rfloor \cdot C_i$$
$$\wedge ((\bigwedge_{i \in \beta} \int Run_i = \lceil \ell/T_i \rceil \cdot C_i) \frown \llbracket \bigvee_{i \in \beta} Run_i \rrbracket)$$
$$\Rightarrow (\bigwedge_{i \in \beta} \int Run_i = \lceil \ell/T_i \rceil \cdot C_i) \frown (\sum_{i \in \beta} Run_i = \ell) \quad \text{LM4.2}$$
$$\Rightarrow \sum_{i \in \beta} \int Run_i \geq \sum_{i \in \beta} \lfloor \ell/T_i \rfloor \cdot C_i \quad \text{LM4.12}$$
$$\Rightarrow \bigwedge_{i \in \beta} \int Run_i \geq \lfloor \ell/T_i \rfloor \cdot C_i \quad (4.2).$$

□

The following lemma concerns the situation where the requirement holds for process p_i until an interval throughout which a process p_j is running. Furthermore, in this situation we know that p_j has no deadline in the last open interval where it is running (i.e. $\neg(dLine_j \frown (0 < \ell < x))$) holds) and that p_i's requirement is satisfied on the whole interval, but not necessarily on those prefix intervals ending in the last open interval where p_j is running.

The lemma "fills the gap" by guaranteeing that p_i's requirement in fact holds on all prefix intervals, including those ending in the open interval where p_j is running.

Lemma 4.14 *For all* $i, j \in \alpha$:

$$\left(\begin{array}{c} Spec \\ \wedge \ (Req_i \frown (\ell = x \wedge \llbracket Run_j \rrbracket)) \\ \wedge \ \neg(dLine_j \frown (0 < \ell < x)) \\ \wedge \ req_i \end{array} \right) \Rightarrow Req_i .$$

Proof. We consider the following situation:

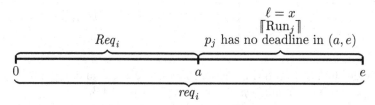

We split the proof into three cases:

1. p_i has no deadline in $(a, e]$: $\neg(dLine_i \frown (\ell < x))$.
2. p_i has e as its deadline: $dLine_i$.
3. p_i has a deadline in (a, e): $dLine_i \frown (0 < \ell < x)$.

Case 1: When p_i has no deadline in $(a, e]$, we have, by Lemma 4.6, the result that Req_i holds on $[0, e]$.

Case 2: In this case p_i has e as its deadline.

We first show that p_i cannot have a further deadline in (a, e), i.e.

$$\left(\begin{array}{l} Spec \\ \wedge \, (Req_i \frown (\ell = x \wedge \lceil Run_j \rceil)) \\ \wedge \, dLine_i \\ \wedge \, \neg(dLine_j \frown (0 < \ell < x)) \\ \wedge \, req_i \end{array} \right) \quad \Rightarrow \quad \neg(dLine_i \frown (0 < \ell < x))$$

must hold. If $i = j$ this is obvious. If $i \neq j$ and p_i has a deadline in (a, e), then we have the result that $\neg req_i$ holds on $[0, e]$:

$$\begin{array}{ll} & Spec \\ & \wedge \, (Req_i \frown (\ell = x \wedge \lceil Run_j \rceil)) \\ & \wedge \, dLine_i \frown (\ell = T_i < x) \\ \Rightarrow & (\int Run_i \leq \ell / T_i \cdot C_i) \frown (\ell = T_i \wedge \lceil Run_j \rceil) & \text{LM4.3, DC16} \\ \Rightarrow & (\int Run_i \leq \ell / T_i \cdot C_i) \frown (\ell = T_i \wedge \lceil \neg Run_i \rceil) & ShP \\ \Rightarrow & (\int Run_i \leq \ell / T_i \cdot C_i) \frown (\ell = T_i \wedge \int Run_i = 0) & \text{DC12} \\ \Rightarrow & \int Run_i < \ell / T_i \cdot C_i \,, \end{array}$$

where the last step follows from DCA5 and the following fact from real arithmetic:

$$(r_1 \leq x/T_i \cdot C_i \wedge r_2 = 0) \Rightarrow r_1 + r_2 < (x + T_i)/T_i \cdot C_i \,.$$

According to IL30, it suffices to prove

$$\left(\begin{array}{l} Spec \\ \wedge \, (Req_i \frown (\ell = x)) \\ \wedge \, dLine_i \\ \wedge \, \neg(dLine_i \frown (0 < \ell < x)) \\ \wedge \, req_i \end{array} \right) \quad \Rightarrow \quad \forall z \geq 0.((z \leq \ell) \Rightarrow (req_i \frown \ell = z)) \,.$$

We divide the proof into three cases: $z = 0$, $0 < z < x$ and $x \leq z \leq \ell$. The case $z = 0$ is trivial: $req_i \Rightarrow (req_i \frown (\ell = 0))$ by L3. The case $0 < z < x$ follows from

$$\begin{array}{ll} & \left(\begin{array}{l} (Req_i \frown (\ell = x - z)) \\ \wedge \, \neg(dLine_i \frown (\ell < x - z)) \end{array} \right) \frown (\ell = z) \\ \Rightarrow & Req_i \frown (\ell = z) & \text{LM4.6} \\ \Rightarrow & req_i \frown (\ell = z) & \text{IL27.} \end{array}$$

The case $x \leq z \leq \ell$ follows from

$$\begin{array}{ll} & Req_i \frown (\ell = x) \\ \Rightarrow & req_i \frown (\ell = z - x) \frown (\ell = x) & \text{IL30} \\ \Rightarrow & req_i \frown (\ell = z) & \text{L2.} \end{array}$$

Case 3: In this case p_i has one deadline in (a, e).

By the same argument as used in Case 2, we have the result that p_i cannot have two deadlines in (a, e), i.e.

$$\left(\begin{array}{l} Spec \\ \wedge\ (Req_i \frown (\ell = x \wedge \lceil \text{Run}_j \rceil)) \\ \wedge\ (dLine_i \frown (\ell = y < x \wedge y > 0)) \\ \wedge\ \neg(dLine_j \frown (0 < \ell < x)) \\ \wedge\ req_i \end{array}\right) \Rightarrow \neg(dLine_i \frown (\ell < y)).$$

Since p_j is running and has no deadline in (a, e), there is a right neighborhood of a where p_i is more urgent than p_j, p_j is running, and therefore p_i has no standing request. Thus, we have by Lemma 4.7 and Lemma 4.6 the result that Req_i holds on $[0, e]$:

$$
\begin{aligned}
&Spec \\
&\wedge\ (Req_i \frown (\ell = x \wedge \lceil \text{Run}_j \rceil)) \\
&\wedge\ \neg(dLine_j \frown (0 < \ell < x)) \\
&\wedge\ (dLine_i \frown (\ell = y < x)) \\
&\wedge\ \neg(dLine_i \frown (\ell < y)) \\
&\Rightarrow dLine_j \frown (\ell \geq x) && \text{since } \neg(dLine_j \frown (0 < \ell < x)) \\
&\Rightarrow Req_i \frown (\lceil \text{Urg}_{ij} \rceil \wedge (\ell = x - y)) \frown (\ell = y) && \text{LM4.8} \\
&\Rightarrow Req_i \frown \lceil \text{Urg}_{ij} \wedge \text{Run}_j \rceil \frown (\ell = y) && \text{DC16, DC19} \\
&\Rightarrow Req_i \frown \lceil \neg \text{Std}_i \rceil \frown (\ell = y) && Sch_1 \\
&\Rightarrow Req_i \frown (\ell = y) && \text{LM4.7} \\
&\Rightarrow Req_i && \text{LM4.6.}
\end{aligned}
$$

□

We shall now prove the main theorem of this chapter, i.e. the sufficiency part of Liu and Layland's theorem. The proof will rely on the lemmas proved in the previous sections.

The formal proofs needed to prove the sufficiency part are no more difficult than those we have seen so far. Therefore, the proof of the theorem will be given in a less detailed manner.

Theorem 4.2 *(Sufficiency)*

$$Spec \Rightarrow Req$$

Proof. The proof is by *induction*, using

1. $\bigwedge_{i \in \alpha} \neg \text{Run}_i$ and
2. Run_j, for $j \in \alpha$,

as the complete set of states.

We shall use Theorem 3.4, where $H(X)$ is

$$X \Rightarrow (Spec \Rightarrow Req),$$

which is the induction hypothesis. The induction hypothesis is equivalent to

$$(X \wedge Spec) \;\Rightarrow\; Req \,.$$

Note that

$$Spec \;\Rightarrow\; \Box_p Spec$$

by IL25 and IL28, i.e. when $Spec$ holds on an interval, it holds on all prefix intervals as well.

We must consider one base case and two inductive steps.

Base case: The requirement Req must hold for the point interval $\llbracket \; \rrbracket$. This is trivial, as each process obviously has its request fulfilled for that interval.

Inductive step 1: By Theorem 3.4, we must establish

$$(X \wedge Spec) \Rightarrow Req \;\vdash\; ((X \frown \llbracket \bigwedge_{i \in \alpha} \neg \mathrm{Run}_i \rrbracket) \wedge Spec) \;\Rightarrow\; Req \,.$$

The deduction

$$
\begin{aligned}
&(X \frown \llbracket \bigwedge_{i \in \alpha} \neg \mathrm{Run}_i \rrbracket) \wedge Spec \\
\Rightarrow\; & (X \wedge Spec) \frown \llbracket \bigwedge_{i \in \alpha} \neg \mathrm{Run}_i \rrbracket && \text{IL25, IL28, IL35} \\
\Rightarrow\; & Req \frown \llbracket \bigwedge_{i \in \alpha} \neg \mathrm{Run}_i \rrbracket && \text{Assumption,}
\end{aligned}
$$

shows that, for this inductive step, it suffices to prove that Req holds for an arbitrary interval of the form $Req \frown \llbracket \bigwedge_{i \in \alpha} \neg \mathrm{Run}_i \rrbracket$ under the assumption that $Spec$ holds for the interval, i.e.

$$\begin{pmatrix} Spec \\ \wedge \, (Req \frown \llbracket \bigwedge_{i \in \alpha} \neg \mathrm{Run}_i \rrbracket) \end{pmatrix} \;\Rightarrow\; Req \,.$$

Hence, the proof of this inductive step follows from Lemma 4.11.

Inductive step 2: We must establish

$$(X \wedge Spec) \Rightarrow Req \;\vdash\; ((X \frown \llbracket \mathrm{Run}_{j_0} \rrbracket) \wedge Spec) \;\Rightarrow\; Req \,,$$

for every $j_0 \in \alpha$.

By an argument similar to the one above, it suffices to prove

$$\begin{pmatrix} Spec \\ \wedge \, (Req \frown \llbracket \mathrm{Run}_{j_0} \rrbracket) \end{pmatrix} \;\Rightarrow\; Req_i \,,$$

for all $i \in \alpha$.

The proof of this inductive step is divided into two cases according to whether p_{j_0} has a deadline in the last left open interval in which it is running. The process p_{j_0} cannot have two deadlines in a closed interval throughout which it is running, since the period of a process is strictly greater than the processor time it requests in each period ($C_{j_0} < T_{j_0}$) (see Lemma 4.5).

Case 1: Process p_{j_0} has no deadline in the last left open interval in which it is running, i.e. for this case we must prove

$$\begin{pmatrix} Spec \\ \wedge \, (Req \frown (\llbracket \mathrm{Run}_{j_0} \rrbracket \wedge \ell = y)) \\ \wedge \, \neg (dLine_{j_0} \frown \ell < y) \end{pmatrix} \Rightarrow Req_i \,,$$

for all $i \in \alpha$.

Let i be an arbitrary element in α. Either p_i has a deadline in the last left open interval of length y or it has no deadline in this interval. The process p_i cannot have two or more deadlines in the closed interval in which p_{j_0} is running (see Lemma 4.10).

Suppose $\neg (dLine_i \frown (\ell < y))$, i.e. p_i has no deadline in the last left open interval of length y:

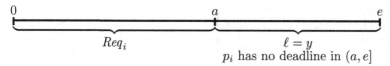

By Lemma 4.6, Req_i holds for the whole interval $[0, e]$, since $\lfloor \ell / T_i \rfloor$ does not change in the interval $(a, e]$.

Suppose $dLine_i \frown (\ell < y)$, i.e. p_i has one deadline (at time b) in the last left open interval of length y:

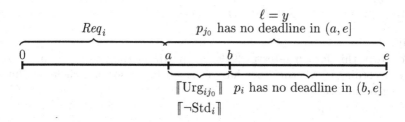

The process p_i is more urgent than the process p_{j_0} in the interval $[a, b]$, because b is a deadline for p_i and p_{j_0} has no deadline in $(a, e]$. Since p_{j_0} is running throughout $[a, b]$, p_i has no request standing in this interval. Thus Req_i holds on $[0, b]$ by Lemma 4.7 and, by Lemma 4.6, also on $[0, e]$.

The proof for Case 1 is now completed.

Case 2: Process p_{j_0} has one deadline in the last left open interval in which it is running, i.e. for this case we must prove

$$\begin{pmatrix} Spec \\ \wedge \, (Req \frown (\llbracket \mathrm{Run}_{j_0} \rrbracket \wedge \ell = y)) \\ \wedge \, (dLine_{j_0} \frown (\ell < y)) \end{pmatrix} \Rightarrow Req_i \,,$$

for all $i \in \alpha$.

Suppose p_{j_0} has one deadline (at time b) in the last left open interval of length y, i.e. we have the situation

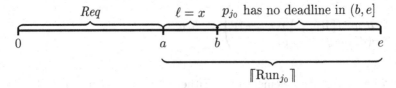

If we can prove that Req_i holds on the interval $[0, b]$ (for all $i \in \alpha$), then we have finished, because the proof of Case 1 implies that Req_i (for all $i \in \alpha$) holds on $[0, e]$ also.

Thus, to finish the proof we must establish

$$\begin{pmatrix} Spec \\ \wedge (Req \frown (\lceil \mathrm{Run}_{j_0} \rceil \wedge \ell = x)) \\ \wedge dLine_{j_0} \\ \wedge \neg(dLine_{j_0} \frown (0 < \ell < x)) \end{pmatrix} \Rightarrow Req_i \,,$$

for all $i \in \alpha$.

According to Lemma 4.14, it suffices to prove

$$\begin{pmatrix} Spec \\ \wedge (Req \frown (\lceil \mathrm{Run}_{j_0} \rceil \wedge \ell = x)) \\ \wedge dLine_{j_0} \\ \wedge \neg(dLine_{j_0} \frown (0 < \ell < x)) \end{pmatrix} \Rightarrow req_i \,,$$

for all $i \in \alpha$.

To prove this for an interval $[0, b]$, we partition the processes into two groups according to whether they have used the processor in their last unfinished period in $[0, b]$.

To express this precisely, let $\alpha_{\leq}$ and $\alpha_{>}$ be two sets such that

$$\alpha = \alpha_{\leq} \cup \alpha_{>}, \ \alpha_{\leq} \cap \alpha_{>} = \emptyset$$

and, for the interval $[0, b]$, we have the following:

1. For $j \in \alpha_{\leq}$: $\int \mathrm{Run}_j \leq \lfloor \ell/T_j \rfloor \cdot C_j$.
2. For $k \in \alpha_{>}$: $\int \mathrm{Run}_k > \lfloor \ell/T_k \rfloor \cdot C_k$.

Since

$$\int \mathrm{Run}_k > \lfloor \ell/T_k \rfloor \cdot C_k \Rightarrow req_i \,,$$

we only need to consider processes p_j, for $j \in \alpha_{\leq}$, in the following.

Since b is a deadline for p_{j_0}, we have the result that

$$\int \mathrm{Run}_{j_0} \leq \lfloor \ell/T_{j_0} \rfloor \cdot C_{j_0}$$

holds on $[0, b]$ (by Lemma 4.3 and since $\lfloor \ell/T_{j_0} \rfloor = \lceil \ell/T_{j_0} \rceil$ when $T_{j_0}|\ell$), and therefore $j_0 \in \alpha_\leq$. Hence we have the following situation:

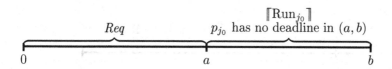

We use DC24, i.e.

$$(\text{true} ^\frown \lceil \bigvee_{j \in \alpha_\leq} \text{Run}_j \rceil) \Leftrightarrow \begin{pmatrix} \lceil \bigvee_{j \in \alpha_\leq} \text{Run}_j \rceil \\ \vee \ (\text{true} ^\frown \lceil \bigwedge_{i \in \alpha} \neg \text{Run}_i \rceil ^\frown \lceil \bigvee_{j \in \alpha_\leq} \text{Run}_j \rceil) \\ \vee \ (\text{true} ^\frown \lceil \bigvee_{k \in \alpha_>} \text{Run}_k \rceil ^\frown \lceil \bigvee_{j \in \alpha_\leq} \text{Run}_j \rceil) \end{pmatrix}$$

to split the proof into three cases.

Case 2a: The interval $[0, b]$ satisfies $\lceil \bigvee_{j \in \alpha_\leq} \text{Run}_j \rceil$.
  Since

$$\ell = 0 \ \Rightarrow \ \bigwedge_{j \in \alpha_\leq} \int \text{Run}_j = \lceil \ell/T_j \rceil \cdot C_j \, ,$$

we can establish $\bigwedge_{j \in \alpha_\leq} req_j$ by Lemma 4.13.

Case 2b: The interval satisfies $\text{true} ^\frown \lceil \bigwedge_{i \in \alpha} \neg \text{Run}_i \rceil ^\frown \lceil \bigvee_{j \in \alpha_\leq} \text{Run}_j \rceil$.
  In the diagram below, we know that c must be smaller than or equal to a and, furthermore, we have exploited the fact that if the requirement Req holds on an interval $([0, a])$, then Req holds on all prefix intervals also (i.e. for $[0, d]$ in the diagram).

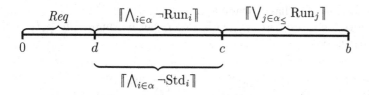

On an interval where no process is running, no process can have (by Sch) a request standing, and we can use Lemma 4.7 to show that

$$\bigwedge_{i \in \alpha} \int \text{Run}_i = \lceil \ell/T_i \rceil \cdot C_i$$

holds on $[0, c]$. We can establish $\bigwedge_{j \in \alpha_\leq} req_j$ by Lemma 4.13.

Case 2c: The interval satisfies true $\smallfrown \llbracket \bigvee_{k\in\alpha_>} \mathrm{Run}_k \rrbracket \smallfrown \llbracket \bigvee_{j\in\alpha_\le} \mathrm{Run}_j \rrbracket$.

In the diagram below, we know that c must be smaller than or equal to a and therefore *Req* holds on $[0, c]$.

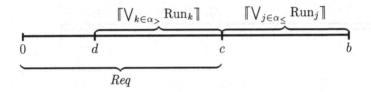

We have the following:

1. A process p_k, $k \in \alpha_>$, has no deadline in $[c, b]$, as $\int\mathrm{Run}_k > \lfloor \ell/T_k \rfloor \cdot C_k$ holds on $[0, b]$ and p_k is not running in $[c, b]$.
2. If a process p_j, for $j \in \alpha_\le$, has no deadline in $(c, b]$, then we have the situation

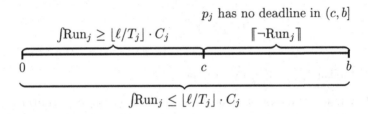

where we have exploited the fact that *Req* holds on $[0, c]$. We have that $\llbracket \neg\mathrm{Run}_j \rrbracket$ holds on $[c, b]$, because if p_j were running somewhere in $[c, b]$ then $\int\mathrm{Run}_j > \lfloor \ell/T_j \rfloor \cdot C_j$ would hold on $[0, b]$, as $\lfloor \ell/T_j \rfloor$ does not change in $(c, b]$.

Let $\beta = \{j \in \alpha_\le \mid p_j \text{ has a deadline in } (c, b]\}$.

By 2. above, only processes p_j, with $j \in \beta$, can be running in $[c, b]$, and we have the situation

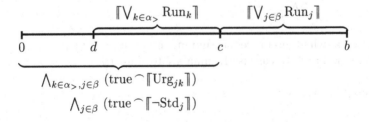

Every process p_j, $j \in \beta$, has a deadline in $(c, b]$, while no process p_k, $k \in \alpha_>$, has a deadline in $[c, b]$. Hence, by Lemma 4.9, there is a left neighborhood of

c where any p_j is more urgent than any p_k. In this neighborhood p_j has no request standing, because processes from $\alpha_>$ are running in that neighborhood.

Using Lemma 4.7, we obtain the result that

$$\bigwedge_{j\in\beta} \int \mathrm{Run}_j = \lceil \ell/T_j \rceil \cdot C_j$$

holds on $[0, c]$, and, furthermore, by Lemma 4.13, that req_j holds on $[0, b]$ for all $j \in \beta$.

A process p_i where $i \notin \beta$ has no deadline in $(c, b]$. Since Req_i holds on $[0, c]$, we have, by Lemma 4.6, the result that Req_i holds on $[0, b]$ also.

The proof is thereby completed. $\qquad\qquad\square$

5. Relative Completeness

In this chapter, we consider the question of whether there is a proof for every valid formula of DC, i.e. whether the proof system of DC is *complete*. When using DC formulas in specifications, we want $\int S$ to be the integral of a Boolean-valued function. Therefore, to show the completeness of DC, it must be shown that the axioms DCA1 – DCA6, together with the rules IR1 and IR2 and the axioms and rules of IL, are enough to ensure that temporal variables of the form $\int S$ are definable by integrals.

In so doing, functions and constants, e.g. $+$ and 0, must be interpreted as real functions and constants, and the chop modality $\frown$ occurring in the axioms must be interpreted as a modality that chops intervals of real numbers.

Since we shall avoid the issue of formalization of real arithmetic in this book, the completeness result for DC presented here is a *relative-completeness* result, where valid IL formulas (with respect to a model based on real numbers) are taken as provable formulas.

To formalize this notion, let $\mathcal{IL}$ be the set of all valid IL formulas, and we define $\mathcal{IL}_{dc}$ to be the set of all DC instances of formulas of $\mathcal{IL}$, i.e. a formula $\varphi_{dc} \in \mathcal{IL}_{dc}$ is obtained from a formula $\varphi \in \mathcal{IL}$ as follows: let $v_1, \ldots, v_n$ be the temporal variables occurring in φ; then φ_{dc} is obtained by replacing every occurrence of v_i with $\int S_i$, for some state expression S_i and for $1 \leq i \leq n$.

Each formula φ_{dc} is a valid DC formula, since φ is a valid IL formula, and we shall take $\mathcal{IL}_{dc}$ as the provable formula set of DC provided by IL.

The theorem of relative completeness is that

$$\models \phi \text{ implies } \mathcal{IL}_{dc} \vdash \phi,$$

for every formula ϕ of DC.

We first sketch the main ideas behind the proof of this theorem. The proof then follows.

5.1 Ideas Behind the Proof

For every valid DC formula ϕ, i.e. $\models \phi$, we must show the existence of a DC deduction $\mathcal{IL}_{dc} \vdash \phi$. We shall in fact give a deduction of $\mathcal{IL}_{dc} \vdash \phi$ which uses the axioms of DC together with DC1 and DC2, but not the induction rules IR1 and IR2.

This deduction of $\mathcal{IL}_{dc} \vdash \phi$ can be considered to be an IL deduction:

$$\mathcal{IL}_{dc}, DCR \vdash \phi \,,$$

where DCR denotes the infinite set of all instances of DCA1 – DCA6, DC1 and DC2, and temporal variables have the form of durations.

However, for the given ϕ, we construct an IL formula, H_ϕ, having $v_1, v_2, \ldots$ as temporal variables, with the property that a deduction

$$\mathcal{IL}_{dc}, DCR \vdash \phi$$

can be constructed from an IL deduction

$$\mathcal{IL}, H_\phi \vdash \phi_h \,,$$

where ϕ_h is obtained from ϕ by "properly" replacing durations $\int S_i$ with temporal variables v_i, and the formula H_ϕ provides a finite encoding in IL of an essential part of DCR.

Using the deduction theorem of IL, we have the result that

$$\mathcal{IL}, H_\phi \vdash \phi_h \text{ iff } \mathcal{IL} \vdash \Box H_\phi \Rightarrow \phi_h \,.$$

The main part of the proof is to show that $\Box H_\phi \Rightarrow \phi_h$ is a valid IL formula, i.e. an element of $\mathcal{IL}$, if ϕ is a valid DC formula.

Therefore, if $\models \phi$, we have the result that $(\Box H_\phi \Rightarrow \phi_h) \in \mathcal{IL}$, and that the DC formula $\Box H \Rightarrow \phi$, obtained from $\Box H_\phi \Rightarrow \phi_h$ by "properly" replacing temporal variables v_i with durations $\int S_i$, is a member of $\mathcal{IL}_{dc}$. Thus,

$$\mathcal{IL}_{dc} \vdash \Box H \Rightarrow \phi \,.$$

The formula H is a conjunction of a finite number of instances of DC axioms and DC1 and DC2, and a deduction of $\mathcal{IL}_{dc} \vdash \phi$ is then easily achieved.

5.2 Proof of Relative Completeness

Let an arbitrary duration calculus formula ϕ be given.

We now construct the IL formula H_ϕ. Let $P_1, \ldots, P_l$ be the state variables occurring in ϕ, and let $\mathcal{S}$ be the set of state expressions which can be generated from these l state variables.

We consider equivalence classes of $\mathcal{S}$ as follows:

$$[S] \triangleq \{S' \in \mathcal{S} \mid S \Leftrightarrow S' \text{ in propositional logic } \} \,,$$

for $S \in \mathcal{S}$.

Furthermore, let $\mathcal{S}_\equiv$ be the set of equivalence classes:

$$\mathcal{S}_\equiv \mathrel{\hat{=}} \{[S] \mid S \in \mathcal{S}\}\,.$$

The size k of $\mathcal{S}_\equiv$ is the number of Boolean functions in l variables, i.e. $k = 2^{2^l}$.

We select k temporal variables $v_1, \ldots, v_k$ and put them in one-to-one correspondence with the equivalence classes. We can therefore index the selected temporal variables with equivalence classes.

For the axioms DCA1 – DCA5 and for the two theorems DC1 and DC2, we construct seven finite sets of IL formulas:

$$\mathcal{H}_1 \mathrel{\hat{=}} \{v_{[0]} = 0\}\,,$$

$$\mathcal{H}_2 \mathrel{\hat{=}} \{v_{[1]} = \ell\}\,,$$

$$\mathcal{H}_3 \mathrel{\hat{=}} \{v_{[S]} \geq 0 \mid [S] \in \mathcal{S}_\equiv\}\,,$$

$$\mathcal{H}_4 \mathrel{\hat{=}} \{v_{[S_1]} + v_{[S_2]} = v_{[S_1 \vee S_2]} + v_{[S_1 \wedge S_2]} \mid [S_1], [S_2] \in \mathcal{S}_\equiv\}\,,$$

$$\mathcal{H}_5 \mathrel{\hat{=}} \{(\forall x)(\forall y)(((v_{[S]} = x) ^\frown (v_{[S]} = y)) \Rightarrow (v_{[S]} = x + y)) \mid [S] \in \mathcal{S}_\equiv\}\,,$$

$$\mathcal{H}_6 \mathrel{\hat{=}} \{\lceil\lceil\,\rceil\rceil \vee (\text{true} ^\frown \lceil\lceil v_{[S]} \rceil\rceil) \vee (\text{true} ^\frown \lceil\lceil v_{[\neg S]} \rceil\rceil) \mid [S] \in \mathcal{S}_\equiv\}\,,$$

$$\mathcal{H}_7 \mathrel{\hat{=}} \{\lceil\lceil\,\rceil\rceil \vee (\lceil\lceil v_{[S]} \rceil\rceil \,^\frown \text{true}) \vee (\lceil\lceil v_{[\neg S]} \rceil\rceil \,^\frown \text{true}) \mid [S] \in \mathcal{S}_\equiv\}\,,$$

where we define $\lceil\lceil v_{[S]} \rceil\rceil$ by $(v_{[S]} = \ell) \wedge (\ell > 0)$.

We define

- H_ϕ to be the conjunction of all the IL formulas in $\mathcal{H}_1$ to $\mathcal{H}_7$, and
- ϕ_h to be the IL formula obtained from ϕ by replacing each $\int S$ by $v_{[S]}$.

The definition and lemmas below are convenient for use in the completeness proof.

Definition. We call a triple $(\mathcal{J}, \mathcal{V}, [b, e])$ an *H-triple* if

$$\mathcal{J}, \mathcal{V}, [b, e] \models \Box H_\phi\,,$$

i.e. if for any subinterval $[c, d]$ of $[b, e]$: $\mathcal{J}, \mathcal{V}, [c, d] \models H_\phi$ according to the semantics of IL.

Notation: When an interpretation $\mathcal{J}$ to temporal variables is given in the present context, we write $\underline{v}$ for $\mathcal{J}(v)$.

Lemma 5.1 *Given an H-triple* $(\mathcal{J}, \mathcal{V}, [b, e])$, *then*

(i) $\underline{v}_{[S]}[c, d] = (d - c) - \underline{v}_{[\neg S]}[c, d]\,,$

(ii) $0 \leq \underline{v}_{[S]}[c, d] \leq d - c\,,$

(iii) $\underline{v}_{[S_1]}[c, d] \leq \underline{v}_{[S_1 \vee S_2]}[c, d]\,,$

(iv) *if* $\underline{v}_{[S]}[b, e] = (e - b)$, *then* $\underline{v}_{[S]}[c, d] = (d - c)\,,$

for any $S, S_1, S_2 \in \mathcal{S}$ *and any subinterval* $[c, d]$ *of* $[b, e]$.

Proof. (i) and (ii) are trivial, and (iv) can be proved through $\mathcal{H}_5$. We give below a proof of (iii).

Since $\neg S_1 \vee (S_1 \vee S_2)$ is a tautology, we have from $\mathcal{H}_2$ the result that

$$\underline{v}_{[1]}[c,d] = (d - c) = \underline{v}_{[\neg S_1 \vee (S_1 \vee S_2)]}[c,d] \,.$$

From $\mathcal{H}_4$, we have

$$\underline{v}_{[\neg S_1]}[c,d] + \underline{v}_{[S_1 \vee S_2]}[c,d] = \underline{v}_{[\neg S_1 \vee (S_1 \vee S_2)]}[c,d] + \underline{v}_{[\neg S_1 \wedge (S_1 \vee S_2)]}[c,d] \,.$$

Using (i) and $\mathcal{H}_2$, we obtain

$$(d - c) - \underline{v}_{[S_1]}[c,d] + \underline{v}_{[S_1 \vee S_2]}[c,d] = (d - c) + \underline{v}_{[\neg S_1 \wedge (S_1 \vee S_2)]}[c,d] \,,$$

which gives

$$\underline{v}_{[S_1]}[c,d] \le \underline{v}_{[S_1 \vee S_2]}[c,d] \,,$$

since $\underline{v}_{[\neg S_1 \wedge (S_1 \vee S_2)]}[c,d] \ge 0$ by $\mathcal{H}_3$. $\qquad\square$

Lemma 5.2 *Given an arbitrary H-triple $(\mathcal{J}, \mathcal{V}, [b,e])$, where $b < e$, then for any $S \in \mathcal{S}$, there is a finite partition $b = t_0 < t_1 < \cdots < t_n = e$ of $[b,e]$ such that*

$$\text{either} \quad \mathcal{J}, \mathcal{V}, [t_{i-1}, t_i] \models \llbracket v_{[S]} \rrbracket \quad \text{or} \quad \mathcal{J}, \mathcal{V}, [t_{i-1}, t_i] \models \llbracket v_{[\neg S]} \rrbracket \,,$$

for $i = 1, \ldots, n$.

Proof. For any $t : b < t < e$, there are (by $\mathcal{H}_6$ and $\mathcal{H}_7$) t' and t'' such that $b \le t' < t < t'' \le e$ and

$$\left\{ \begin{array}{c} \mathcal{J}, \mathcal{V}, [t', t] \models \llbracket v_{[S]} \rrbracket \quad \text{or} \quad \mathcal{J}, \mathcal{V}, [t', t] \models \llbracket v_{[\neg S]} \rrbracket \\ \text{and} \\ \mathcal{J}, \mathcal{V}, [t, t''] \models \llbracket v_{[S]} \rrbracket \quad \text{or} \quad \mathcal{J}, \mathcal{V}, [t, t''] \models \llbracket v_{[\neg S]} \rrbracket \end{array} \right\} \,. \tag{5.1}$$

Thus, there is an open interval (t', t'') covering t, and the closed interval $[t', t'']$ has the above property (5.1).

For the left end point b, there is, by $\mathcal{H}_7$, a t'' such that $b < t'' \le e$ and

$$\mathcal{J}, \mathcal{V}, [b, t''] \models \llbracket v_{[S]} \rrbracket \quad \text{or} \quad \mathcal{J}, \mathcal{V}, [b, t''] \models \llbracket v_{[\neg S]} \rrbracket \,. \tag{5.2}$$

We can select an arbitrary $t' < b$. Thus, there is an open interval (t', t'') covering b, and the closed interval $[b, t'']$ has the above property (5.2).

Similarly, for e, there is, by $\mathcal{H}_6$, a t' such that $b \le t' < e$ and

$$\mathcal{J}, \mathcal{V}, [t', e] \models \llbracket v_{[S]} \rrbracket \quad \text{or} \quad \mathcal{J}, \mathcal{V}, [t', e] \models \llbracket v_{[\neg S]} \rrbracket \,. \tag{5.3}$$

We can select an arbitrary $t'' > e$. Thus, there is an open interval (t', t'') covering e, and the closed interval $[t', e]$ has the above property (5.3).

So we have an infinite collection of open intervals covering the closed and bounded interval $[b, e]$. Then, by the Heine-Borel theorem, there is a finite sub-collection $\mathcal{C} = \{I_1, \ldots, I_m\}$ of the open intervals covering $[b, e]$, where any I_i $(1 \leq i \leq m)$ has the property $(5.1), (5.2)$ or (5.3).

We now carry out the following steps in order to find the finite partition.

Step 1: Select the open interval $I_i = (a_i, b_i)$ from $\mathcal{C}$ covering b. Then the closed interval $[b, b_i]$ satisfies (5.2):

$$\mathcal{J}, \mathcal{V}, [b, b_i] \models \lceil v_{[S]} \rceil \quad \text{or} \quad \mathcal{J}, \mathcal{V}, [b, b_i] \models \lceil v_{[\neg S]} \rceil.$$

Step 2: Stop if $b_i = e$. Otherwise, $b_i < e$. Select an open interval $I_j = (a_j, b_j)$ from $\mathcal{C}$ covering b_i. Since $b_j \leq e$, the closed interval $[b_i, b_j]$ will (by (5.1) and (iv) of Lemma 5.1) satisfy one of

1. $\mathcal{J}, \mathcal{V}, [b_i, b_j] \models \lceil v_{[S]} \rceil$,

2. $\mathcal{J}, \mathcal{V}, [b_i, b_j] \models \lceil v_{[\neg S]} \rceil$,

3. $\mathcal{J}, \mathcal{V}, [b_i, m] \models \lceil v_{[S]} \rceil$ and $\mathcal{J}, \mathcal{V}, [m, b_j] \models \lceil v_{[\neg S]} \rceil$, for some $m : b_i < m < b_j$.

4. $\mathcal{J}, \mathcal{V}, [b_i, m] \models \lceil v_{[\neg S]} \rceil$ and $\mathcal{J}, \mathcal{V}, [m, b_j] \models \lceil v_{[S]} \rceil$, for some $m : b_i < m < b_j$.

Repeat *Step 2* until a partition of $[b, e]$ is achieved. This terminates, since there is only a finite number of open intervals in $\mathcal{C}$. $\square$

Lemma 5.3 *An H-triple $(\mathcal{J}, \mathcal{V}, [b, e])$, where $b < e$, induces a DC interpretation $\mathcal{I}$ such that for every $S \in \mathcal{S}$ and $t \in [b, e)$,*

$$S_{\mathcal{I}}(t) = \begin{cases} 1, & \text{if } t \in [t_{i-1}, t_i) \text{ and } \mathcal{J}, \mathcal{V}, [t_{i-1}, t_i] \models \lceil v_{[S]} \rceil \\ 0, & \text{if } t \in [t_{i-1}, t_i) \text{ and } \mathcal{J}, \mathcal{V}, [t_{i-1}, t_i] \models \lceil v_{[\neg S]} \rceil, \end{cases}$$

where $b = t_0 < t_1 < \cdots < t_n = e$ is a partition of $[b, e]$ satisfying

$$\mathcal{J}, \mathcal{V}, [t_{i-1}, t_i] \models \lceil v_{[S]} \rceil \quad \text{or} \quad \mathcal{J}, \mathcal{V}, [t_{i-1}, t_i] \models \lceil v_{[\neg S]} \rceil,$$

for $i = 1, \ldots, n$.

Proof. Define an interpretation $\mathcal{I}$ as follows. For any state variable $Q \notin \mathcal{S}$ and $t \in \text{Time}$, let $Q_{\mathcal{I}}(t) = 0$. Furthermore, for any state variable $P \in S$, let $b = t_0 < t_1 < \cdots < t_n = e$ be a partition of $[b, e]$ for P given by Lemma 5.2.

We define

$$P_{\mathcal{I}}(t) = \begin{cases} 1, & \text{if } t_{i-1} \leq t < t_i \text{ and } \mathcal{J}, \mathcal{V}, [t_{i-1}, t_i] \models \llbracket v_{[P]} \rrbracket \text{ for } 1 \leq i \leq n \\ 0, & \text{otherwise.} \end{cases}$$

Each such function has only a finite number of discontinuity points in any interval, so $\mathcal{I}$ is indeed an interpretation in DC.

We prove the remaining parts of the lemma by structural induction on S. Assume $S \in \mathcal{S}$. The cases where S is $0, 1$ or P are trivial, so consider the following cases:

Case: S has the form $\neg S'$.

Let $b = t_0 < t_1 < \cdots < t_n = e$ be a partition of $[b, e]$ for S' given by the induction hypothesis. This can also be regarded as a partition for $\neg S'$, as $\neg\neg S' \Leftrightarrow S'$.

Consider an arbitrary t ($b \leq t < e$). By definition, $(\neg S')_{\mathcal{I}}(t) = 1 - S'_{\mathcal{I}}(t)$. Let $t_{i-1} \leq t < t_i$ for some $i \in \{1, \ldots, n\}$.

If $\mathcal{J}, \mathcal{V}, [t_{i-1}, t_i] \models \llbracket v_{[\neg\neg S']} \rrbracket$, then $(\neg S')_{\mathcal{I}}(t) = 0$, as we have $S'_{\mathcal{I}}(t) = 1$ from the induction hypothesis.

If $\mathcal{J}, \mathcal{V}, [t_{i-1}, t_i] \models \llbracket v_{[\neg S']} \rrbracket$, then $S'_{\mathcal{I}}(t) = 0$ by the induction hypothesis. But then $(\neg S')_{\mathcal{I}}(t) = 1$ as required.

Case: S has the form $S' \vee S''$.

We combine the two partitions of $[b, e]$, for S' and S'', given by the induction hypothesis to obtain a finite partition $b = t_0 < t_1 < \cdots < t_n = e$, where exactly one of the four formulas $\llbracket v_{[S']} \rrbracket \wedge \llbracket v_{[S'']} \rrbracket$, $\llbracket v_{[\neg S']} \rrbracket \wedge \llbracket v_{[\neg S'']} \rrbracket$, $\llbracket v_{[S']} \rrbracket \wedge \llbracket v_{[\neg S'']} \rrbracket$, or $\llbracket v_{[\neg S']} \rrbracket \wedge \llbracket v_{[S'']} \rrbracket$ will hold in each section $[t_{i-1}, t_i]$.

Therefore, using the induction hypotheses for S' and S'', each section $[t_{i-1}, t_i]$ of the partition will fulfill one of the following cases:

(i) $\underline{v}_{[S']} = \underline{v}_{[S'']} = t_i - t_{i-1}$ and $S'_{\mathcal{I}}(t) = S''_{\mathcal{I}}(t) = 1$, i.e. $(S' \vee S'')_{\mathcal{I}}(t) = 1$, for $t_{i-1} \leq t < t_i$.

(ii) $\underline{v}_{[\neg S']} = \underline{v}_{[\neg S'']} = t_i - t_{i-1}$ and $S'_{\mathcal{I}}(t) = S''_{\mathcal{I}}(t) = 0$, i.e. $(S' \vee S'')_{\mathcal{I}}(t) = 0$, for $t_{i-1} \leq t < t_i$.

(iii) $\underline{v}_{[S']} = t_i - t_{i-1}$, $\underline{v}_{[\neg S'']} = t_i - t_{i-1}$, $S'_{\mathcal{I}}(t) = 1$ and $S''_{\mathcal{I}}(t) = 0$, i.e. $(S' \vee S'')_{\mathcal{I}}(t) = 1$, for $t_{i-1} \leq t < t_i$.

(iv) $\underline{v}_{[\neg S']} = t_i - t_{i-1}$, $\underline{v}_{[S'']} = t_i - t_{i-1}$, $S'_{\mathcal{I}}(t) = 0$ and $S''_{\mathcal{I}}(t) = 1$, i.e. $(S' \vee S'')_{\mathcal{I}}(t) = 1$, for $t_{i-1} \leq t < t_i$.

For case (i), we must prove that $\mathcal{J}, \mathcal{V}, [t_{i-1}, t_i] \models \llbracket v_{[S' \vee S'']} \rrbracket$. From Lemma 5.1,

$$0 \leq \underline{v}_{[S' \vee S'']}[t_{i-1}, t_i] \leq t_i - t_{i-1} \quad \text{and} \quad 0 \leq v_{[S' \wedge S'']}[t_{i-1}, t_i] \leq t_i - t_{i-1},$$

so it follows from $\mathcal{H}_4$ that

$$\underline{v}_{[S' \vee S'']}[t_{i-1}, t_i] = \underline{v}_{[S' \wedge S'']}[t_{i-1}, t_i] = t_i - t_{i-1}.$$

Using the definition of $[\![v_{[S'\vee S'']}]\!]$, we have the result that

$$\mathcal{J}, \mathcal{V}, [t_{i-1}, t_i] \models [\![v_{[S'\vee S'']}]\!]\,.$$

For case (ii), we must prove that $\mathcal{J}, \mathcal{V}, [t_{i-1}, t_i] \models [\![v_{[\neg(S'\vee S'')]}]\!]$. From Lemma 5.1,

$$\underline{v}_{[S'\vee S'']}[t_{i-1}, t_i] \geq 0 \ \text{ and }\ \underline{v}_{[S'\wedge S'']}[t_{i-1}, t_i] \geq 0$$
$$\underline{v}_{[S']}[t_{i-1}, t_i] = 0 \ \text{ and }\ \underline{v}_{[S'']}[t_{i-1}, t_i] = 0\,.$$

It follows from $\mathcal{H}_4$ that $\underline{v}_{[S'\vee S'']}[t_{i-1}, t_i] = 0$. Therefore, by Lemma 5.1,

$$\underline{v}_{[\neg(S'\vee S'')]}[t_{i-1}, t_i] = t_i - t_{i-1}$$

and, hence,

$$\mathcal{J}, \mathcal{V}, [t_{i-1}, t_i] \models [\![v_{[\neg(S'\vee S'')]}]\!]\,.$$

For case (iii), we must prove that $\mathcal{J}, \mathcal{V}, [t_{i-1}, t_i] \models [\![v_{[S'\vee S'']}]\!]$. Since, by Lemma 5.1, we have

$$\underline{v}_{[S']}[t_{i-1}, t_i] \leq \underline{v}_{[S'\vee S'']}[t_{i-1}, t_i] \leq t_i - t_{i-1}\,,$$

it follows that $\underline{v}_{[S'\vee S'']}[t_{i-1}, t_i] = t_i - t_{i-1}$, i.e.

$$\mathcal{J}, \mathcal{V}, [t_{i-1}, t_i] \models [\![v_{[S'\vee S'']}]\!]\,.$$

For case (iv), the proof is similar to that for the case (iii).   □

Lemma 5.4 *For a given H-triple* $(\mathcal{J}, \mathcal{V}, [b, e])$, *let* $\mathcal{I}$ *be an interpretation given by Lemma 5.3. Then for every* $S \in \mathcal{S}$ *and interval* $[c, d] \subseteq [b, e]$,

$$\mathcal{I}[\![\int S]\!][c, d] = \underline{v}_{[S]}[c, d]\,.$$

Proof. Suppose $c = d$. Then $\mathcal{I}[\![\int S]\!][c, d] = 0$, and $\underline{v}_{[S]}[c, d] = 0$, since we have from Lemma 5.1 the result that $0 \leq \underline{v}_{[S]}[c, d] \leq d - c$.

Now suppose that $c < d$. Since $(\mathcal{J}, \mathcal{V}, [b, e])$ is an H-triple, so is $(\mathcal{J}, \mathcal{V}, [c, d])$. Let $c = t_0 < t_1 < \cdots < t_n = d$ be a finite partition of $[c, d]$ for S. The interpretation $\mathcal{I}$ given by Lemma 5.3 satisfies the condition that for $t \in [c, d)$,

$$S_{\mathcal{I}}(t) = \begin{cases} 1, & \text{if } t \in [t_{i-1}, t_i) \text{ and } \mathcal{J}, \mathcal{V}, [t_{i-1}, t_i] \models [\![v_{[S]}]\!] \\ 0, & \text{if } t \in [t_{i-1}, t_i) \text{ and } \mathcal{J}, \mathcal{V}, [t_{i-1}, t_i] \models [\![v_{[\neg S]}]\!]. \end{cases}$$

Thus,

$$\int_{t_{i-1}}^{t_i} S_{\mathcal{I}}(t)\, dt = \underline{v}_{[S]}[t_{i-1}, t_i]\,,$$

for $i = 1, \ldots, n$, and by $\mathcal{H}_5$,

$$\mathcal{I}[\![\int S]\!][c, d] = \int_c^d S_{\mathcal{I}}(t)\, dt = \sum_{i=1}^n \underline{v}_{[S]}[t_{i-1}, t_i] = \underline{v}_{[S]}[c, d]\,.$$

□

Let ϕ_h be the IL formula obtained from ϕ by replacing every occurrence of $\int S$ in ϕ with $v_{[S]}$.

Lemma 5.5

$$\models \phi \ \textit{iff} \ \models (\Box H_\phi) \Rightarrow \phi_h \,.$$

Proof. Note that $\models \phi$ means the validity of ϕ in DC, and $\models (\Box H_\phi) \Rightarrow \phi_h$ means the validity of $(\Box H_\phi) \Rightarrow \phi_h$ in IL.

We first prove that $\models \phi$ implies $\models (\Box H_\phi) \Rightarrow \phi_h$. Suppose that

$$\not\models (\Box H_\phi) \Rightarrow \phi_h \,,$$

i.e. there is an H-triple $(\mathcal{J}, \mathcal{V}, [b, e])$ such that $\mathcal{J}, \mathcal{V}, [b, e] \not\models \phi_h$. By Lemma 5.4, there is a DC interpretation $\mathcal{I}$ such that for any $S \in \mathcal{S}$ and $[c, d] \subseteq [b, e]$,

$$\mathcal{I}[\![\int S]\!][c, d] = \underline{v}_{[S]}[c, d] \,.$$

Since $\mathcal{J}, \mathcal{V}, [b, e] \not\models \phi_h$, we have the result that $\mathcal{I}, \mathcal{V}, [b, e] \not\models \phi$, and hence $\not\models \phi$.

To prove the other direction, i.e. $\models (\Box H_\phi) \Rightarrow \phi_h$ implies $\models \phi$, suppose that

$$\not\models \phi \,,$$

i.e. there are a DC interpretation $\mathcal{I}$, value assignment $\mathcal{V}$ and interval $[b, e]$ such that $\mathcal{I}, \mathcal{V}, [b, e] \not\models \phi$. Let us construct an IL interpretation $\mathcal{J}$:

$$\underline{v}_{[S]}[c, d] \cong \mathcal{I}[\![\int S]\!][c, d]$$
$$= \int_c^d S_\mathcal{I}(t) \, dt \,,$$

for all $S \in \mathcal{S}$ and any interval $[c, d]$.

By construction, we have from $\mathcal{I}, \mathcal{V}, [b, e] \not\models \phi$ the result that

$$\mathcal{J}, \mathcal{V}, [b, e] \not\models \phi_h$$

and, from Theorem 3.2 (soundness), $\mathcal{J}, \mathcal{V}, [b, e] \models \Box H_\phi$. So $\not\models (\Box H_\phi) \Rightarrow \phi_h$. □

The relative-completeness theorem can now be proved.

Theorem 5.1 *(Relative completeness) For every formula ϕ of DC,*

$$\models \phi \ \textit{implies} \ \mathcal{IL}_{dc} \vdash \phi \,.$$

Proof. Suppose $\models \phi$. By Lemma 5.5, we obtain $\models (\Box H_\phi) \Rightarrow \phi_h$. Let H be obtained from H_ϕ by replacing each $v_{[S]}$ by $\int S$. Then $(\Box H \Rightarrow \phi) \in \mathcal{IL}_{dc}$ and

$$\mathcal{IL}_{dc} \vdash \Box H \Rightarrow \phi \,.$$

We have the result that H is a conjunction of a finite number of instances of DC axioms and DC1 and DC2, and, by PL and IL4, we therefore have

$$\vdash \Box H \,.$$

A deduction of $\mathcal{IL}_{dc} \vdash \phi$ follows by applying MP. □

Remark.

1. Note that the relative-completeness result was achieved using the theorems DC1 and DC2 instead of the two induction rules IR1 and IR2. It is, however, convenient to have the two induction rules available when conducting proofs.
2. Reference [38] presents another completeness result of DC. It replaces IR1 and IR2 by an ω-rule to axiomatize the finite variability of states, and proves the completeness of the revised DC for an *abstract domain*. See Sect. 11.5 for more explanation of this completeness. □

6. Decidability

In this chapter we consider a subset of formulas of DC for which the satisfiability of a formula is decidable. Since a formula ϕ is valid iff the formula $\neg\phi$ is not satisfiable, we can decide whether a formula in the subset is valid as well. The decidability results presented here are based on [167].

We investigate now the set RDC (restricted duration calculus) of formulas generated by

1. if S is a state expression, then $\lceil S \rceil \in RDC$, and
2. if $\phi, \psi \in RDC$, then $\neg\phi, \phi \vee \psi, \phi ^\frown \psi \in RDC$.

We first present a *discrete-time* interpretation of RDC together with decidability results for the satisfiability of formulas for discrete time. It is also shown that RDC is expressive enough to formalize an interesting case study under the discrete-time interpretation. We then present a decidability result for RDC with regard to continuous time, which involves more complication.

6.1 Discrete-Time Duration Calculus

What shall we consider to be a discrete-time duration calculus?

Even when the set of natural numbers $\mathbb{N} = \{0, 1, 2, \ldots\}$ is chosen as the discrete structure of the time, questions remain concerning restrictions on interpretations, intervals, and the truth of formulas.

First of all, we require, for every interpretation

$$\mathcal{I} \; : \; SVar \to (\text{Time} \to \{0, 1\}),$$

that the set of discontinuity points of each $P_{\mathcal{I}}$ ($P \in SVar$) must be a subset of $\mathbb{N}$. An interpretation satisfying this property is called a *discrete interpretation*.

Likewise, we shall consider only *discrete intervals*

$$[b, e] \in \mathbb{Intv},$$

where $b, e \in \mathbb{N}$.

Finally, for a given RDC formula ϕ, we consider its truth value for discrete intervals and discrete interpretations only.

As a consequence of this, the definition of chop ($\phi ^\frown \psi$) is different from that given in Chap. 2 for continuous time. Assuming that $\mathcal{I}$ is a discrete interpretation and $[b, e]$ is a discrete interval, we define

$$\mathcal{I}, [b, e] \models \phi ^\frown \psi \;\; \text{iff} \;\; \left\{ \begin{array}{l} \mathcal{I}, [b, m] \models \phi \text{ and } \mathcal{I}, [m, e] \models \psi, \\ \text{for some } m \in [b, e] \text{ where } m \in \mathbb{N} \end{array} \right\}.$$

Here we leave out value assignments ($\mathcal{V}$) from the definition, since we have no global variables in formulas of RDC.

The other semantic clauses are not given, as they remain as they were in Chap. 3. However, from the semantics, we can derive

$$\mathcal{I}, [b, e] \models \lceil S \rceil$$
iff $(e - b) > 0$ and for any t, $b < t < e$ and $t \notin \mathbb{N}$: $\mathcal{I}[\![S]\!](t) = 1$.

An RDC formula ϕ is *valid for discrete time* iff $\mathcal{I}, [b, e] \models \phi$ for every discrete interpretation $\mathcal{I}$ and every discrete interval $[b, e]$, and ϕ is *satisfiable for discrete time* iff $\mathcal{I}, [b, e] \models \phi$ for some discrete interpretation $\mathcal{I}$ and some discrete interval $[b, e]$.

6.1.1 Discrete Time Versus Continuous Time

One can ask the question of what difference it makes to consider a discrete-time domain instead of a continuous-time domain.

For discrete time, we can define $\ell = 1$ in RDC as follows:

$$\ell = 1 \;\hat{=}\; \lceil 1 \rceil \wedge \neg (\lceil 1 \rceil ^\frown \lceil 1 \rceil).$$

We can do this since $\ell = 1$ is the unit of time in the discrete-time domain; it is not a time point, and cannot be divided further into smaller time periods either.

However, $\ell = 1$ cannot be defined in continuous-time RDC where ℓ is syntactically excluded, as we shall prove in Sect. 6.2 that continuous-time RDC is decidable, whereas continuous-time RDC extended with $\ell = 1$ is undecidable, as we shall see in Sect. 7.2.

There are also formulas of RDC which are valid for continuous time, but not valid for discrete time, e.g.

$$\lceil S \rceil \Rightarrow (\lceil S \rceil ^\frown \lceil S \rceil).$$

This formula is not true for a discrete interpretation over a unit interval, where S has value 1 throughout the interval.

In the following sections we shall present algorithms to identify the formulas of RDC which are valid for discrete time and the RDC formulas which are valid for continuous time, since the validities of formulas of RDC are decidable for both discrete and continuous times. However, owing to the undecidability results presented in the next chapter, there will be no algorithms to do so for DC formulas in general.

6.1.2 Expressiveness of Discrete-Time RDC

From the proof of the decidability result for discrete-time RDC given in Sect. 6.2, it is not difficult to conclude that discrete-time RDC has the same expressiveness as a formulation in terms of simple timed automata, where each transition takes place at a discrete time point and consumes one time unit. This generalizes to the case where the time consumed by a transition is within specified upper and lower bounds, including infinity and zero.

This generalization follows from the following equivalences, which imply that $0 \leq \int P \wedge \int P < k$, for example, is expressible in discrete-time RDC:

$$\ell = 0 \quad\quad \Leftrightarrow \neg\lceil 1 \rceil$$

$$\int P = 0 \quad\quad \Leftrightarrow \lceil \neg P \rceil \vee \ell = 0$$

$$\ell = 1 \quad\quad \Leftrightarrow \lceil 1 \rceil \wedge \neg(\lceil 1 \rceil ^\frown \lceil 1 \rceil)$$

$$\int P = 1 \quad\quad \Leftrightarrow (\int P = 0) ^\frown (\lceil P \rceil \wedge \ell = 1) ^\frown (\int P = 0)$$

$$\int P = k+1 \Leftrightarrow (\int P = k) ^\frown (\int P = 1)$$

$$\int P \geq k \quad\quad \Leftrightarrow (\int P = k) ^\frown \text{true}$$

$$\int P > k \quad\quad \Leftrightarrow (\int P \geq k) \wedge \neg(\int P = k)$$

$$\int P \leq k \quad\quad \Leftrightarrow \neg(\int P > k)$$

$$\int P < k \quad\quad \Leftrightarrow (\int P \leq k) \wedge \neg(\int P = k),$$

where $k \in \mathbb{N}$ and true can be defined, say, as $\lceil 1 \rceil \vee \neg\lceil 1 \rceil$.

Remark. Of the above definitions, only the first two are correct for continuous-time RDC, but the rest of them are not. The expressiveness of continuous-time RDC is, unfortunately, equivalent to that of untimed automata. See the proof in Sect. 6.3 for details. □

Regarding the gas burner example, it is obvious that the two design decisions (Des_1 and Des_2) can be expressed in discrete-time RDC. However, the requirement $GbReq$ involves inequality between state durations,

$$20 \int\text{Leak} \leq \ell.$$

In the next chapter, it is proved that after $\int S_1 = \int S_2$ is added to RDC the satisfiability problem of this extended subset becomes undecidable for both discrete and continuous time. As a corollary of the decidability of RDC and the undecidability of the extended RDC, equalities (and therefore inequalities) of state durations cannot be expressed in RDC either for continuous or for the discrete time.

Fortunately, in Sect. 3.5, it was shown that the requirement *GbReq* can be refined into

$$\Box(\ell \leq 30 \;\Rightarrow\; \textstyle\int \text{Leak} \leq 1),$$

which can be expressed in discrete-time *RDC*.

Thus, we can mechanically check the validity of

$$(Des_1 \wedge Des_2) \;\Rightarrow\; \Box(\ell \leq 30 \;\Rightarrow\; \textstyle\int \text{Leak} \leq 1),$$

for discrete time (see Lemma 3.5), following the decision algorithm developed in the next section.

6.2 Decidability for Discrete Time

We show that the satisfiability of a formula $\phi \in RDC$ for discrete time is decidable by defining a regular language $\mathcal{L}_1(\phi)$ such that

ϕ is satisfiable for discrete time iff $\mathcal{L}_1(\phi)$ is nonempty.

Let $\mathcal{S}$ be the (finite) set of all state variables occurring in ϕ. Then the *alphabet* Σ of the language $\mathcal{L}_1(\phi)$ is the set

$$\Sigma = \mathcal{P}(\mathcal{S})$$

of subsets of $\mathcal{S}$. A *letter* $a \in \Sigma$ can denote the state expression (called the *basic conjunct*) of $\mathcal{S}$

$$\bigwedge_{P \in a} P \wedge \bigwedge_{Q \in (\mathcal{S} \setminus a)} \neg Q,$$

which asserts that all state variables in a have value one, while those of $\mathcal{S}$ not in a have value zero. From now on, we shall use a to stand for both a letter of Σ and the basic conjunct of $\mathcal{S}$ denoted by that letter.

A state expression S of ϕ can be transformed into a disjunctive normal form of state variables of $\mathcal{S}$. Suppose $S \Leftrightarrow \bigvee_{i=1}^{n} a_i$, where $n \geq 0$ (when S is 0, $n = 0$). Then S can be denoted by a subset of letters of Σ, $\{a_1, \ldots, a_n\}$, abbreviated to $DNF(S)$.

With each formula ϕ we associate a regular language $\mathcal{L}_1(\phi) \subseteq \Sigma^*$, such that ϕ holds on a discrete interval $[b, e]$ for a discrete interpretation $\mathcal{I}$ iff there is a string $v \in \mathcal{L}_1(\phi)$ which corresponds to the interpretation $\mathcal{I}$ on $[b, e]$. Thus, the formula ϕ is satisfiable for discrete time iff the language $\mathcal{L}_1(\phi)$ is nonempty.

Since the emptiness of a regular language is decidable, we obtain a procedure for deciding the satisfiability of ϕ.

The definition of $\mathcal{L}_1(\phi)$ is quite straightforward. Let every letter of Σ correspond to a unit interval. Therefore, the formula $\lceil S \rceil$ is associated with the positive closure $(DNF(S))^+$, which means that the presence of state S remains for an arbitrary positive number of time units. Disjunction $\vee$ is denoted by union, negation $\neg$ by complement, and chop $\frown$ by *concatenation*, where concatenation is defined by:

$$L_1 L_2 \cong \{vu | v \in L_1 \text{ and } u \in L_2\}.$$

Since $(DNF(S))^+$ is a regular language, and the family of regular languages is closed under union, complement and concatenation [65], every formula can be denoted by a regular language. More precisely,

$$\begin{aligned}
\mathcal{L}_1(\lceil S \rceil) &= (DNF(S))^+ \\
\mathcal{L}_1(\varphi \vee \psi) &= \mathcal{L}_1(\varphi) \cup \mathcal{L}_1(\psi) \\
\mathcal{L}_1(\neg\varphi) &= \Sigma^* \setminus \mathcal{L}_1(\varphi) \\
\mathcal{L}_1(\varphi \frown \psi) &= \mathcal{L}_1(\varphi)\,\mathcal{L}_1(\psi).
\end{aligned}$$

We define the string $v = a_1 \cdots a_N \in \Sigma^*$ to *correspond* to a discrete interpretation $\mathcal{I}$ of ϕ if $\mathcal{I}[\![a_i]\!](t) = 1$ for $t \in (i-1, i), i \in \{1, \ldots, N\}$. (If $N = 0$, then v is the empty string which corresponds to any discrete interpretation on the point interval $[0, 0]$.)

Lemma 6.1 *Let a formula $\phi \in RDC$, a discrete interpretation $\mathcal{I}$ of ϕ, and its corresponding string $v = a_1 \cdots a_N$ be given. Then*

$$\mathcal{I}, [0, N] \models \phi \text{ for discrete time } \quad iff \quad v \text{ belongs to } \mathcal{L}_1(\phi).$$

Proof. By induction on the structure of ϕ. The "if" and "only if" directions must be proved jointly because of the complement ($\neg$) case.

Base case: ϕ is $\lceil S \rceil$.

1. "Only if": Suppose $\lceil S \rceil$ holds on $[0, N]$ for $\mathcal{I}$. We have $N > 0$, and for every $i \in \{1, \ldots, N\}$, $\mathcal{I}[\![S]\!](t) = 1$ for $t \in (i-1, i)$. Since $v = a_1 \cdots a_N$ corresponds to $\mathcal{I}$, for every $i \in \{1, \ldots, N\}$ and $t \in (i-1, i)$, we have the result that $\mathcal{I}[\![a_i]\!](t) = 1$. So $a_i \in DNF(S)$ by $S \Leftrightarrow \bigvee_{a \in DNF(S)} a$. Therefore $v \in DNF(S)^+$. That is, $v \in \mathcal{L}_1(\lceil S \rceil)$.

2. "If": Suppose $v \in \mathcal{L}_1(\lceil S \rceil)$. Then $v \in DNF(S)^+$, and hence $N > 0$. Since v corresponds to $\mathcal{I}$, we have $\mathcal{I}[\![a_i]\!](t) = 1$ for $i \in \{1, \ldots, N\}$ and $t \in (i-1, i)$. So $\mathcal{I}[\![S]\!](t) = 1$ for $t \in (i-1, i)$ and $i \in \{1, \ldots, N\}$, because $a_i \in DNF(S)$ for $i \in \{1, \ldots, N\}$. Thus, we can conclude $\mathcal{I}, [0, N] \models \lceil S \rceil$ from the semantic definition.

Inductive case: ϕ is $\neg\psi$.

1. "Only if": Suppose $\neg\psi$ holds on $[0, N]$ for $\mathcal{I}$. We have the result that ψ does not hold on $[0, N]$ for $\mathcal{I}$. By the induction hypothesis, $v \notin \mathcal{L}_1(\psi)$. Therefore $v \in (\Sigma^* \setminus \mathcal{L}_1(\psi))$. Hence $v \in \mathcal{L}_1(\neg\psi)$, because we have that $\mathcal{L}_1(\neg\psi) = (\Sigma^* \setminus \mathcal{L}_1(\psi))$.

2. "If": Suppose $v \in \mathcal{L}_1(\neg\psi)$, i.e. $v \notin \mathcal{L}_1(\psi)$. By the induction hypothesis, ψ does not hold on $[0, N]$ for $\mathcal{I}$. Thus $\neg\psi$ holds on $[0, N]$ for $\mathcal{I}$.

Inductive case: ϕ is $\psi \frown \varphi$.

1. "Only if": Suppose $\psi \frown \varphi$ holds on $[0, N]$ for $\mathcal{I}$. We have $M \in \{0, \ldots, N\}$ such that ψ holds on $[0, M]$ for $\mathcal{I}$, and φ holds on $[M, N]$ for $\mathcal{I}$. Since v corresponds to $\mathcal{I}$ on $[0, N]$, $v_1 = a_1 \cdots a_M$ corresponds to $\mathcal{I}$ on $[0, M]$ and $v_2 = a_{M+1} \cdots a_N$ corresponds to $\mathcal{I}_M$ on $[0, N - M]$, where the definition of $\mathcal{I}_M$ refers to Lemma 3.1, i.e.

$$\mathcal{I}_M[\![P]\!](t) \; = \; \mathcal{I}[\![P]\!](t + M),$$

   for any $P \in SVar$. By Lemma 3.1, φ holds on $[0, N - M]$ for $\mathcal{I}_M$. Therefore, by the induction hypothesis, $v_1 \in \mathcal{L}_1(\psi)$ and $v_2 \in \mathcal{L}_1(\varphi)$. Thus, $v = v_1 v_2 \in \mathcal{L}_1(\psi)\mathcal{L}_2(\varphi) = \mathcal{L}_1(\psi \frown \varphi)$.

2. "If": Suppose $v \in \mathcal{L}_1(\psi \frown \varphi)$. There must be $v_1 = a_1 \cdots a_M \in \mathcal{L}_1(\psi)$ and $v_2 = a_{M+1} \cdots a_N \in \mathcal{L}_1(\varphi)$ such that $v = v_1 v_2$. Then v_1 corresponds to $\mathcal{I}$ on $[0, M]$ and v_2 to $\mathcal{I}_M$ on $[0, N - M]$. By the induction hypothesis, ψ holds on $[0, M]$ for $\mathcal{I}$ and φ holds on $[0, N - M]$ for $\mathcal{I}_M$. By Lemma 3.1, φ also holds on $[M, N]$ for $\mathcal{I}$. Therefore we can conclude that ϕ holds on $[0, N]$ for $\mathcal{I}$.

Inductive case: ϕ is $(\psi \vee \varphi)$. This case is left for those readers who are interested in the details of the proof. $\square$

It is obvious that for every string v of length N in Σ^* there is an interpretation $\mathcal{I}$ of ϕ such that v corresponds to $\mathcal{I}$ and, conversely, for every interpretation $\mathcal{I}$ of ϕ and interval $[0, N]$ there is a string v of length N in Σ^* which corresponds to $\mathcal{I}$. By Theorem 3.1 and Lemma 6.1, we have:

Lemma 6.2 *A formula $\phi \in RDC$ is satisfiable for discrete time iff the regular language $\mathcal{L}_1(\phi)$ is nonempty.*

Theorem 6.1 *The satisfiability of RDC formulas for discrete time is decidable.*

We now show how to mechanically check the validity of RDC formulas for discrete time.

Question 1: Is the formula $(\lceil P \rceil \frown \lceil P \rceil) \Rightarrow \lceil P \rceil$ valid for discrete time?

Since P is the only state variable occurring in the formula, the alphabet $\Sigma = \{\{P\}, \{\}\}$. We have

$(\lceil P \rceil \frown \lceil P \rceil) \Rightarrow \lceil P \rceil$ is valid

iff $\neg((\lceil P \rceil \frown \lceil P \rceil) \Rightarrow \lceil P \rceil)$ is not satisfiable

iff $(\lceil P \rceil \frown \lceil P \rceil) \wedge \neg \lceil P \rceil$ is not satisfiable

iff $\mathcal{L}_1(\lceil P \rceil \frown \lceil P \rceil) \cap \mathcal{L}_1(\neg \lceil P \rceil) = \{\}$

iff $\{\{P\}^i \mid i \geq 2\} \cap (\Sigma^* \setminus \{\{P\}^i \mid i \geq 1\}) = \{\}$.

The last equality holds. Therefore, the formula $(\lceil P \rceil \frown \lceil P \rceil) \Rightarrow \lceil P \rceil$ is valid for discrete time. □

Question 2: Is the formula $\lceil P \rceil \Rightarrow (\lceil P \rceil \frown \lceil P \rceil)$ valid for discrete time?

Again, the alphabet is $\Sigma = \{\{P\}, \{\}\}$. We have

$\lceil P \rceil \Rightarrow (\lceil P \rceil \frown \lceil P \rceil)$ is valid

iff $\lceil P \rceil \wedge \neg(\lceil P \rceil \frown \lceil P \rceil)$ is not satisfiable

iff $\mathcal{L}_1(\lceil P \rceil) \cap \mathcal{L}_1(\neg(\lceil P \rceil \frown \lceil P \rceil)) = \{\}$

iff $\mathcal{L}_1(\lceil P \rceil) \cap (\Sigma^* \setminus \mathcal{L}_1(\lceil P \rceil \frown \lceil P \rceil)) = \{\}$

iff $\mathcal{L}_1(\lceil P \rceil) \subseteq \mathcal{L}_1(\lceil P \rceil \frown \lceil P \rceil)$

iff $\{\{P\}^i \mid i \geq 1\} \subseteq \{\{P\}^i \mid i \geq 2\}$.

The last inclusion is false, as the letter $\{P\}$ belongs to $\{\{P\}^i \mid i \geq 1\}$, but not to $\{\{P\}^i \mid i \geq 2\}$. Namely, for a discrete interpretation and a unit interval over which P has value 1 under the interpretation, the truth value of the formula $\lceil P \rceil \Rightarrow (\lceil P \rceil \frown \lceil P \rceil)$ is false. Thus, the formula $\lceil P \rceil \Rightarrow (\lceil P \rceil \frown \lceil P \rceil)$ is not valid for discrete time. □

Using this technique, we can decide that the formula

$$(Des_1 \wedge Des_2) \Rightarrow \Box(\ell \leq 30 \Rightarrow \int \text{Leak} \leq 1)$$

is valid.

It is, however, more interesting that the *phase automaton* of a more "realistic" gas burner specification considered in [127] can be expressed in discrete-time *RDC* as well. This phase automaton represents an implementation of a set of requirements for the gas burner which can also be expressed in discrete-time *RDC*. It was proved in [127] by the axioms and rules of DC that the phase automaton implies the requirements. In fact, the algorithm developed in this section can carry out this proof mechanically for the discrete-time domain.

6.3 Decidability for Continuous Time

Consider the formula $\lceil P \rceil \Rightarrow (\lceil P \rceil \frown \lceil P \rceil)$, which is valid for continuous time, but not for discrete time.

Recalling the answer to the question of its validity for discrete time given in Sect. 6.2, we have

$$\lceil P \rceil \Rightarrow (\lceil P \rceil \frown \lceil P \rceil) \text{ is valid iff } \mathcal{L}_1(\lceil P \rceil) \subseteq \mathcal{L}_1(\lceil P \rceil \frown \lceil P \rceil).$$

Because $\{P\} \in \mathcal{L}_1(\lceil P \rceil)$ and $\{P\} \notin \mathcal{L}_1(\lceil P \rceil \frown \lceil P \rceil)$, the inclusion property is not satisfied. In the discrete-time domain, the intuitive interpretation of $\{P\}$ is that state P lasts for one time unit.

However, a letter, say $\{P\}$, cannot be interpreted as lasting one time unit in a continuous-time domain. But with a *closure* property, it is possible to reuse ideas from the discrete-time construction to achieve a decidability result for continuous time.

A language L over the alphabet Σ is called *contraction closed* if

$$vaaw \in L \text{ implies } vaw \in L,$$

for any $v, w \in \Sigma^*$ and $a \in \Sigma$.

The language $\mathcal{L}_1(\lceil P \rceil \frown \lceil P \rceil) = \{\{P\}^i | i \geq 2\}$ is not contraction closed, since $\{P\}\{P\}$ belongs to the language and $\{P\}$ does not belong to the language.

Let $\downarrow L$ denote the contraction closure of L, i.e. the smallest contraction-closed set containing L. By a simple construction on finite automata, we can establish the following lemma.

Lemma 6.3 *If L is regular, then so is $\downarrow L$.*

Proof. Let $\mathcal{A}$ be a finite automaton accepting L. We give here the main ideas behind a construction of an automaton $\mathcal{A}'$ accepting $\downarrow L$. $\mathcal{A}'$ has the same states (including the same initial and final states) and the same alphabet as $\mathcal{A}$.

The transition relation of $\mathcal{A}'$ is defined as follows. For any states q and q' and any letter a,

there is a transition from q to q' on a in $\mathcal{A}'$,

if and only if there exist states $q_1, \ldots, q_n$ such that $q = q_1$, $q_n = q'$ and

there is a transition from q_i to q_{i+1} on a in $\mathcal{A}$, for $1 \leq i < n$.

$\square$

On the basis of Lemma 6.3, we can now construct a regular language $\mathcal{L}_2(\phi)$ for an arbitrarily given formula $\phi \in RDC$ in a way similar to the procedure used for discrete time:

$$\mathcal{L}_2(\llbracket S \rrbracket) = (DNF(S))^+$$
$$\mathcal{L}_2(\varphi \vee \psi) = \mathcal{L}_2(\varphi) \cup \mathcal{L}_2(\psi)$$
$$\mathcal{L}_2(\neg\varphi) = \Sigma^* \setminus \mathcal{L}_2(\varphi)$$
$$\mathcal{L}_2(\varphi \frown \psi) = \downarrow(\mathcal{L}_2(\varphi)\,\mathcal{L}_2(\psi)).$$

We prove in the following lemma that the above regular languages are contraction closed.

Lemma 6.4 *For any* $\phi \in RDC$, $\mathcal{L}_2(\phi)$ *is contraction closed.*

Proof. We prove the lemma by induction on the structure of ϕ. However, set subtraction does not preserve the contraction closure property. For example, $\Sigma^* \setminus \{a\}$ is not contraction closed for any a of Σ. We therefore introduce the auxiliary notions of *expansion* closed and *fully* closed. A language L is expansion closed if

$$vaw \in L \text{ implies } vaaw \in L,$$

for any $v, w \in \Sigma^*$ and $a \in \Sigma$. L is fully closed if L is both contraction and expansion closed.

It can easily be proved that $(DNF(S))^+$ is fully closed, and the operators $\cup$, $\setminus$ and $\downarrow$ preserve the full-closure property. Thus, $\mathcal{L}_2(\phi)$ is fully closed for any $\phi \in RDC$. □

Let L_1 and L_2 be contraction-closed languages over Σ and $v \in \downarrow(L_1 L_2)$. The following lemma is easily established.

Lemma 6.5 *Either there are* $v_1 \in L_1$ *and* $v_2 \in L_2$ *such that* $v = v_1 v_2$, *or there are* $v_1 \in L_1$, $v_2 \in L_2$ *and* $a \in \Sigma$ *such that* $v = v_1' a v_2'$, *where* $v_1 = v_1' a$ *and* $v_2 = a v_2'$.

In order to prove that $\phi \in RDC$ is satisfiable for continuous time iff $\mathcal{L}_2(\phi)$ is not empty, in the continuous-time domain, we introduce the correspondence between an interpretation $\mathcal{I}$ and a string v. Since a letter of v no longer represents a unit of time, the correspondence depends on a partition of the interval considered, which is derived from the finite variability of $\mathcal{I}$.

Given a formula ϕ, a *partition* of an interpretation $\mathcal{I}$ over an interval $[0, e]$ is a collection of reals $0 = b_0 < b_1 < \cdots < b_N = e$ such that $\mathcal{I}[\![P]\!](t)$ is constant on (b_{i-1}, b_i) for every state variable P of ϕ. From the assumption of the finite variability of states, it is obvious that for any ϕ, $\mathcal{I}$ and $[0, e]$ there exists a partition. (Note that in the special case of discrete time we have $b_i \in \mathbb{N}$.)

The string $v = a_1 \cdots a_N \in \Sigma^*$ corresponds to the interpretation $\mathcal{I}$ on $[0, e]$ with partition $0 = b_0 < b_1 < \cdots < b_N = e$ if $\mathcal{I}[\![a_i]\!](t) = 1$ for $t \in (b_{i-1}, b_i)$ and $i \in \{1, \ldots, N\}$. If $N = 0$, then v is the empty string and $e = 0$.

By an induction proof on the structure of ϕ, we can establish the following lemma.

Lemma 6.6 *Let a formula* $\phi \in RDC$, *an interval* $[0, e]$, *an interpretation* $\mathcal{I}$ *of* ϕ *with partition* $0 = b_0 < b_1 < \cdots < b_N = e$, *and a corresponding string* $v = a_1 \cdots a_N$ *be given. Then* $\mathcal{I}, [0, e] \models \phi$ *iff* v *belongs to* $\mathcal{L}_2(\phi)$.

Proof. We can present a proof similar to that of Lemma 6.1 by induction on the structure of ϕ. The important changes are in the inductive case: ϕ is $\psi \smallfrown \varphi$. We now present the details of the proof for this case.

Let ϕ be $\psi \smallfrown \varphi$:

"Only if": Suppose $\psi \smallfrown \varphi$ holds on $[0, e]$ for $\mathcal{I}$. There must be an $m \in [0, e]$ such that ψ holds on $[0, m]$ for $\mathcal{I}$ and φ holds on $[m, e]$ for $\mathcal{I}$.

First, the cases $m = 0$ and $m = e$ are straightforward: they can be dealt with by using the induction hypothesis for φ and ψ, respectively.

The case where $0 < m < e$ is divided into two subcases:

Subcase: there is an $M \in \{1, \ldots, N\}$ such that $m = b_M$.

By applying similar reasoning to that used in Lemma 6.1, we obtain the result that the string $a_1 \cdots a_M$ corresponds to $\mathcal{I}$ on the interval $[0, m]$ with partition $0 = b_0 < b_1 < \cdots < b_M = m$, the string $a_{M+1} \cdots a_N$ corresponds to $\mathcal{I}_m$ on the interval $[0, e - m]$ with partition $0 < b_M - m < \cdots < b_N - m$, and then $v \in \mathcal{L}_2(\psi)\mathcal{L}_2(\varphi)$. Since $\mathcal{L}_2(\psi)\mathcal{L}_2(\varphi) \subseteq \downarrow(\mathcal{L}_2(\psi)\mathcal{L}_2(\varphi))$ by the definition of $\downarrow$, we have the result that $v \in \downarrow(\mathcal{L}_2(\psi)\mathcal{L}_2(\varphi)) = \mathcal{L}_2(\psi \smallfrown \varphi)$, and thus the proof for this subcase is completed.

Subcase: there is an $M \in \{1, \ldots, N\}$ such that $b_{M-1} < m < b_M$.

Then, by the induction hypothesis, $v_1 = a_1 \cdots a_{M-1} a_M \in \mathcal{L}_2(\psi)$, because v_1 corresponds to $\mathcal{I}$ on $[0, m]$ with partition $0 = b_0 < b_1 < \cdots < b_M < m$, and $v_2 = a_M a_{M+1} \cdots a_N \in \mathcal{L}_2(\varphi)$, because v_2 corresponds to $\mathcal{I}_m$ on interval $[0, e - m]$ with partition $0 < b_M - m < \cdots < b_N - m$. Thus, we have $v_1 v_2 = a_1 \cdots a_{M-1} a_M a_M a_{M+1} \cdots a_N \in \mathcal{L}_2(\psi)\mathcal{L}_2(\varphi)$, and therefore $v = a_1 \cdots a_{M-1} a_M a_{M+1} \cdots a_N \in \downarrow(\mathcal{L}_2(\psi)\mathcal{L}_2(\varphi)) = \mathcal{L}_2(\psi \smallfrown \varphi)$.

"If": Suppose $v \in \mathcal{L}_2(\psi \smallfrown \varphi) = \downarrow(\mathcal{L}_2(\psi)\mathcal{L}_2(\varphi))$. By Lemmas 6.4 and 6.5, there are two subcases.

First, consider the subcase $v = v_1 v_2$, where

$$v_1 = a_1 \cdots a_M \in \mathcal{L}_2(\psi) \text{ and } v_2 = a_{M+1} \cdots a_N \in \mathcal{L}_2(\varphi).$$

Then, if we choose $m = b_M$, v_1 corresponds to $\mathcal{I}$ on $[0, m]$ with partition $0 < b_1 < \cdots < b_M = m$ and v_2 corresponds to $\mathcal{I}_m$ on $[0, e - m]$ with partition $0 < b_{M+1} - m < \cdots < b_N - m = e - m$. By the induction hypothesis and Lemma 3.1, ψ holds on $[0, m]$ for $\mathcal{I}$, and φ holds on $[m, e]$ for $\mathcal{I}$, so $\psi \smallfrown \varphi$ holds on $[0, e]$ for $\mathcal{I}$.

Second, consider the subcase $v = v_1' a_M v_2'$, where

$$v_1 = v_1' a_M = a_1 \cdots a_M \in \mathcal{L}_2(\psi)$$
$$\text{and } v_2 = a_M v_2' = a_M a_{M+1} \cdots a_N \in \mathcal{L}_2(\varphi).$$

If we now choose $m = (b_{M-1} + b_M)/2$, v_1 corresponds to $\mathcal{I}$ on $[0, m]$ with partition $0 < b_1 < \cdots < b_{M-1} < m$, and v_2 corresponds to $\mathcal{I}_m$ on $[0, e - m]$ with partition $0 < b_M - m < \cdots < b_N - m = e - m$. By the induction hypothesis and Lemma 3.1, ψ holds on $[0, m]$ for $\mathcal{I}$ and φ holds on $[m, e]$ for $\mathcal{I}$, so $\psi \frown \varphi$ holds on $[0, e]$ for $\mathcal{I}$.   □

It is trivial to show that for any string v of length N, given an interval $[0, e]$ and a partition of $[0, e]$ with N sections, there is an interpretation $\mathcal{I}$ such that v corresponds to $\mathcal{I}$ on $[0, e]$ with the given partition. Conversely, for any interpretation $\mathcal{I}$, given an interval $[0, e]$ and a partition of $[0, e]$, there is a unique corresponding string $v \in \Sigma^*$. Hence, by Lemma 6.6 and Theorem 3.1, we can prove:

Lemma 6.7 *A formula $\phi \in RDC$ is satisfiable for continuous time iff the language $\mathcal{L}_2(\phi)$ is not empty.*

Since $\mathcal{L}_2(\phi)$ is a regular language, we have:

Theorem 6.2 *The satisfiability of RDC formulas for continuous time is decidable.*

6.4 Complexity, Tools and Other Decidable Subclasses

The efficiency of the above decision procedure depends not only on the decision algorithm for the emptiness problem of a regular language, but also on the constructions of the regular language. Each negation occurring in the formula may cause an exponent expansion of the construction. The authors of [142] have proved that the complexity of this decision procedure is nonelementary. So the worst case is very poor indeed.

In [142], the decision procedure was implemented and used to prove the correctness of Fischer's mutual exclusion protocol. The results were not too bad. It took, for example, approximately 12 minutes to verify a formula consisting of 3775 characters on a DECStation 5000-240 with 128 MB of memory.

The proof assistant tool for DC described in [143] also supports the use of this decision procedure.

In the literature, the decidability issue of DC has been investigated further. In [105], after quantifications over states are introduced into RDC (the result is called qualified discrete-time duration calculus, QDDC, in [103]), the satisfiability of formulas is still decidable. This decision algorithm was implemented as a tool called DCVALID.

References [32, 33, 131] proved that the satisfiability of an RDC formula for a discrete interpretation but over a *continuous* interval is still decidable. References [32, 33] also extended the decidable class of RDC for continuous time by including $\int S = k$, but with a restriction on the finite variability such that the number of discontinuous points of any state in any unit interval has a fixed upper bound.

In [41], a decidability result was presented for a variant of DC where negation is removed from RDC but an iteration operator is introduced together with the inequalities $\ell \geq k$ and $\ell \leq k$, where $k \in \mathbb{N}$.

In [104], CTL* ([29]) was extended with QDDC, and it was shown how the extension could be reduced to CTL*. On the basis of this reduction, another model-checking tool, CTLDC, was implemented.

In [13, 106], the digitization of the validity problem of DC formulas and its reduction to QDDC were investigated, and results were obtained concerning how to check the validity of DC formulas (for continuous time) by using DCVALID.

7. Undecidability

All the disappointing news comes in this chapter: even for a very restricted subset of DC formulas, it is undecidable whether a formula in the subset is satisfiable.

The general technique used to show these results is to reduce the halting problem of a two-counter machine to the satisfiability of formulas belonging to the subset under consideration. The main results are taken from [167].

7.1 Extensions of RDC

Below we define three different extensions of RDC, called $RDC_1(r)$, RDC_2 and RDC_3. The extensions seem small, but in later sections we shall establish undecidability results (of satisfiability and validity problems) for each of the corresponding subsets.

Hence, each of these extensions marks a border between decidability and undecidability.

7.1.1 $RDC_1(r)$

In this extension, we add to RDC the atomic formula

$$\ell = r \,,$$

where r is a real number.

Hence, the set of formulas $RDC_1(r)$, where $r \in \mathbb{R}$ is a fixed constant, is the subset of DC generated as follows:

1. the formula $\ell = r$ belongs to $RDC_1(r)$,
2. if S is a state expression, then $\lceil S \rceil$ belongs to $RDC_1(r)$, and
3. if ϕ and ψ belong to $RDC_1(r)$, then so do $\neg\phi$, $\phi \vee \psi$, and $\phi ^\frown \psi$.

When r is a natural number, we have previously seen from Sects. 6.1.2 and 6.2 that it is decidable for discrete time whether a formula of $RDC_1(r)$ is satisfiable. Since $\ell = 0$ can be expressed by $\neg\lceil 1 \rceil$, we have the result that $RDC_1(0)$ is expressible in RDC, and thus the satisfiability question for

$RDC_1(0)$ is decidable for continuous time. If $r < 0$ then $\ell = r$ is false, which is expressible in RDC as well.

Therefore, the continuous-time domain and $r > 0$ are assumed in the undecidability proof for $RDC_1(r)$ given in Sect 7.2. This undecidability result illustrates the strength of imposing the precision $\ell = r$ on the length of an interval for continuous time.

7.1.2 RDC_2

In this extension, we allow atomic formulas of the form

$$\int S_1 = \int S_2$$

only, where S_1 and S_2 are state expressions. In the case we can still express the formulas of RDC as

$$\llbracket S \rrbracket \;\Leftrightarrow\; (\int S = \int 1) \wedge \neg (\int 1 = \int 0) \, .$$

Hence, the set of formulas RDC_2 is the subset of DC generated as follows:

1. if S_1 and S_2 are state expressions, then $\int S_1 = \int S_2$ belongs to RDC_2, and
2. if ϕ and ψ belong to RDC_2, then so do $\neg\phi$, $\phi \vee \psi$ and $\psi \frown \psi$.

The undecidability results for this case illustrate the strength of the notion of duration for both discrete and continuous time.

7.1.3 RDC_3

In this extension, we add to RDC atomic formulas of the form

$$\ell = x \, ,$$

where x is a global variable, and we allow quantification over global variables:

$$(\exists x)\phi \, .$$

Hence, the set of formulas RDC_3 is the subset of DC generated as follows:

1. if S is a state expression, then $\llbracket S \rrbracket$ belongs to RDC_3,
2. if x is a global variable, then $\ell = x$ belongs to RDC_3, and
3. if ϕ and ψ belong to RDC_3, then so do $\neg\phi$, $\phi \vee \psi$, $\phi \frown \psi$ and $(\exists x)\phi$, where x is any global variable.

The undecidability results for this case illustrate the strength of quantification in an interval logic for both discrete and continuous time.

Remark. For all of the three subsets, we shall use standard abbreviations $\wedge$, $\Rightarrow$ and $\Leftrightarrow$ from propositional logic, and $\Box$ and $\Diamond$ from IL. $\Box$

7.1.4 Two-Counter Machines

The main technique used to obtain these undecidability results is to reduce the undecidable halting problem of a counter machine the to satisfiability of formulas belonging to the subsets. In this section, we give a brief and rather informal introduction to two-counter machines. For a more careful treatment, see [11, 65, 96], for example.

A *two-counter machine* has an *initial label* q_0, two *counters* c_1 and c_2 which can hold arbitrary natural numbers from $\mathbb{N} = \{0, 1, 2, \ldots\}$, and a finite set of labeled *instructions* m_i.

The only instructions of two-counter machines are to "increase c_1 by one" (c_1^+) and "test c_1 and decrease it by one if c_1 is not zero" (c_1^-), and similarly for c_2.

For example,

$$q_i : c_1^+ \to q_j \, ,$$

is an instruction labeled q_i. It increases c_1 by one and proceeds to the instruction labeled q_j.

Another kind of instruction for c_1 is

$$q_i : c_1^- \to q_j, q_k \, ,$$

which is also an instruction labeled q_i. It tests whether the value of c_1 is zero; if so, the machine proceeds to the instruction labeled q_j; otherwise, the machine decreases c_1 by one and proceeds to the instruction labeled q_k.

A *configuration* s of a two-counter machine is a triple $s = (q, n_1, n_2)$ of the current label q and the values $n_1, n_2 \in \mathbb{N}$ of the two counters c_1 and c_2. The configuration (q, n_1, n_2) is *final* if there is no instruction labeled q in the machine.

A *computation step* of a two-counter machine, $s \implies s'$, transforms a nonfinal configuration s into a configuration s' by means of an instruction of the machine as follows (and similarly for c_2):

Instruction	s	$\implies s'$
$q : c_1^+ \to q_j$	(q, n_1, n_2)	$\implies (q_j, n_1 + 1, n_2)$
$q : c_1^- \to q_j, q_k$	$(q, 0, n_2)$	$\implies (q_j, 0, n_2)$
$q : c_1^- \to q_j, q_k$	$(q, n_1 + 1, n_2)$	$\implies (q_k, n_1, n_2)$

A *computation* of a two-counter machine is a (finite or infinite) sequence of computations

$$\sigma = s_0 \, s_1 \, s_2 \, \cdots \, ,$$

where, for any s_n and s_{n+1} in the computation, $s_n \implies s_{n+1}$ by means of an instruction of the machine. A computation terminates iff it is a finite sequence and ends up with a final configuration.

We call $s_0 = (q_0, 0, 0)$ the *initial configuration*, where q_0 is the initial label. A two-counter machine starting with the initial configuration halts if all its computations starting with $(q_0, 0, 0)$ terminate. We shall make use of the fact that the halting problem for a two-counter machine starting with the initial configuration is undecidable [11, p. 78]. This result also holds if we assume that the two-counter machine is *deterministic*. That is, every two instructions of the machine are labeled differently, and hence the computation of the machine starting with the initial configuration is determined. This result still holds even if we assume further that the two-counter machine contains precisely one final label q_{fin}, i.e. q_{fin} is the only label which no instruction has as its label.

In the following, we consider an arbitrary deterministic two-counter machine M with the initial configuration $(q_0, 0, 0)$, where

1. $q_0, \ldots, q_{fin}$ are the labels of M, where q_0 is the initial label and q_{fin} is the only final label,
2. c_1 and c_2 are the two counters, and
3. $m_1, \ldots, m_l$ are the instructions of M.

7.2 Undecidability of $RDC_1(r)$

We reduce the halting problem for M to the satisfiability of a formula in $RDC_1(r)$ (for $r > 0$). The encoding of M uses the following state variables:

- one state variable Q_i for each label q_i,
- two state variables C_1 and C_2 to represent the counter values, and
- two auxiliary state variables B and L, used as delimiters.

Let

$$Q = \{Q_0, \ldots, Q_{fin}\}$$

in the following.

The main idea is that a machine configuration (q, n_1, n_2) is encoded on an interval of length $4r$ as follows:

$$| \underbrace{Q}_{r} | \underbrace{Val_1}_{r} | \underbrace{L}_{r} | \underbrace{Val_2}_{r} |$$

where Val_j represents the value of counter c_j.

This is done so that the nth configuration of a computation occupies the interval $[4nr, 4(n+1)r], n \geq 0$.

The representation, Val_1 and Val_2, of the counter values is the following. Let the value of counter c_i be $n_i \geq 0$. Then the interval describing Val_i has the following form:

$$|B|C_i|B| \cdots |B|C_i|B|\,,$$

with n_i sections of C_i separated by B.

Since this interval is required to have a length r, and since there is no bound on the counter value, the time length of each C_i (and B) section must be arbitrary small. The denseness of the time domain makes this representation possible. This representation was inspired by [3].

The reduction must formalize the computation of M as a formula in $RDC_1(r)$. In particular, we must construct a formula representing the initial configuration and a formula expressing how the $(n+1)$th configuration relates to the nth configuration in the computation. To do so, the following abbreviations of formulas in $RDC_1(r)$ are useful:

$$
\begin{aligned}
\lceil \rceil &\;\hat{=}\; \neg\lceil 1 \rceil \\
\text{true} &\;\hat{=}\; \lceil \rceil \vee \lceil 1 \rceil \\
\ell < r &\;\hat{=}\; \neg((\ell = r)^\frown \text{true}) \\
\ell = 2r &\;\hat{=}\; (\ell = r)^\frown(\ell = r) \\
2r \leq \ell &\;\hat{=}\; (\ell = 2r)^\frown \text{true} \\
\ell < 3r &\;\hat{=}\; \neg((\ell = 2r)^\frown(\ell = r)^\frown \text{true}) \\
\ell = 4r &\;\hat{=}\; (\ell = 2r)^\frown(\ell = 2r) \\
\ell = 5r &\;\hat{=}\; (\ell = 4r)^\frown(\ell = r) \\
\lceil S \rceil^r &\;\hat{=}\; \lceil S \rceil \wedge (\ell = r) \\
\phi \rightsquigarrow \psi &\;\hat{=}\; \neg(\phi^\frown \neg(\lceil \rceil \vee \psi))\,.
\end{aligned}
$$

The formula $\lceil S \rceil^r$ reads "S has value one for a duration of r", and the formula $\phi \rightsquigarrow \psi$ reads "if the interval starts with ϕ, it must end immediately with $\lceil \rceil$ or with ψ".

The initial configuration is $(q_0, 0, 0)$, which is represented by the formula

$$Init_1 \;\hat{=}\; \lceil Q_0 \rceil^r {}^\frown \lceil B \rceil^r {}^\frown \lceil L \rceil^r {}^\frown \lceil B \rceil^r {}^\frown \text{true}\,.$$

State variables must be mutually exclusive:

$$Mutex_1 \;\hat{=}\; \bigwedge_{P_1 \neq P_2} \Box\neg\lceil P_1 \wedge P_2 \rceil\,,$$

where P_1, P_2 range over $\mathcal{Q} \cup \{C_1, C_2, B, L\}$.

Certain state expressions have a periodic appearance, since configurations are represented on intervals of length $4r$. Let

$$Per(\phi) \; \widehat{=} \; \Box((\phi \frown (\ell = 4r)) \; \Rightarrow \; ((\ell = 4r) \frown \phi)).$$

Machine labels, counter values and the separator L have a periodic appearance. Let

$$Periodic \; \widehat{=}$$
$$Per(\bigvee_{Q_i \in \mathcal{Q}} \llbracket Q_i \rrbracket^r) \wedge Per(\llbracket C_1 \vee B \rrbracket^r) \wedge Per(\llbracket L \rrbracket^r) \wedge Per(\llbracket C_2 \vee B \rrbracket^r).$$

For each instruction m of M we give a formula $F(m)$, encoding the computation steps performed by m.

Suppose the machine instruction m is $q_i : c_1^+ \rightarrow q_j$. The possible computation steps allowed by m are described by a formula

$$F(m) \; \widehat{=} \; F_1 \wedge F_2 \wedge F_3 \wedge F_4 \wedge F_5 \wedge F_6 \, ,$$

where each F_i is defined below.

From the determinism of M, q_j is the only label of the succeeding configuration that is reached when m is performed. The formula F_1 expresses this:

$$F_1 \; \widehat{=} \; (\llbracket Q_i \rrbracket^r \frown (\ell = 4r)) \; \Rightarrow \; ((\ell = 4r) \frown \llbracket Q_j \rrbracket^r).$$

The formula F_2 copies the C_1 sections to the same place in the next configuration. To encode this process, we use formulas of the form $\phi \rightsquigarrow \psi$. Here ϕ characterizes certain configurations whose label is q_i, and ψ fixes part of the next configuration. The formula is given by

$$F_2 \; \widehat{=} \; \left(\llbracket Q_i \rrbracket^r \frown (\ell < r) \frown \llbracket C_1 \rrbracket \frown \left(\begin{array}{c} \llbracket C_1 \rrbracket \frown \text{true} \\ \wedge \\ \ell = 4r \end{array} \right) \right) \; \rightsquigarrow \; (\llbracket C_1 \rrbracket \frown \text{true}).$$

We can copy the B sections before a C_1 section in Val_1 to the same place in the next configuration using the same technique:

$$F_3 \; \widehat{=} \; \left(\llbracket Q_i \rrbracket^r \frown (\ell < r) \frown \llbracket B \rrbracket \frown \left(\begin{array}{c} \llbracket B \rrbracket \frown \llbracket C_1 \rrbracket \frown \text{true} \\ \wedge \\ \ell = 4r \end{array} \right) \right) \; \rightsquigarrow \; (\llbracket B \rrbracket \frown \text{true}).$$

The formulas F_4 and F_5 increase the value of C_1 by replacing the last B section of Val_1 with $|B|C_1|B|$ in the next configuration.

The formula F_4 handles the case $n_1 = 0$:

$$F_4 \triangleq \left(\begin{array}{l} (\lceil Q_i \rceil^r \frown \lceil B \rceil^r \frown (\ell = 4r)) \\ \Rightarrow (\text{true} \frown ((\ell = r) \wedge (\lceil B \rceil \frown \lceil C_1 \rceil \frown \lceil B \rceil))) \end{array} \right).$$

The formula F_5 handles the case $n_1 > 0$:

$$F_5 \triangleq \left(\begin{array}{l} \left(\lceil Q_i \rceil^r \frown (\ell < r) \frown \lceil C_1 \rceil \frown \left(\begin{array}{c} \lceil B \rceil \frown \lceil L \rceil \frown \text{true} \\ \wedge \; (\ell = 5r) \end{array} \right) \right) \\ \Rightarrow (\text{true} \frown ((\ell = r) \wedge (\lceil B \rceil \frown \lceil C_1 \rceil \frown \lceil B \rceil \frown \lceil L \rceil))) \end{array} \right).$$

Note that the beginnings of successive L sections are exactly $4r$ apart, and therefore the length of the $\lceil B \rceil \frown \lceil C_1 \rceil \frown \lceil B \rceil$ section in the consequent in F_5 is precisely as long as the last $\lceil B \rceil$ section in the antecedent.

Thus, $F_4 \wedge F_5$ models the condition that the number of C_1 sections is increased by one, as desired.

The formula F_6 copies the value of c_2 to the next configuration using the same technique as used above:

$$F_6 \triangleq \wedge \begin{array}{l} \left(\lceil Q_i \rceil^r \frown (\ell < 3r) \frown \lceil C_2 \rceil \frown \left(\begin{array}{c} \lceil C_2 \rceil \frown \text{true} \\ \wedge \\ \ell = 4r \end{array} \right) \right) \rightsquigarrow (\lceil C_2 \rceil \frown \text{true}) \\[2em] \left(\lceil Q_i \rceil^r \frown (2r \leq \ell < 3r) \frown \lceil B \rceil \frown \left(\begin{array}{c} \lceil B \rceil \frown \text{true} \\ \wedge \\ \ell = 4r \end{array} \right) \right) \rightsquigarrow (\lceil B \rceil \frown \text{true}). \end{array}$$

The formula *Periodic* takes care of copying the L section to the next configuration.

Every instruction m_i can be encoded as formulas $F(m_i)$ by techniques similar to those used above. If this is done, the entire machine is encoded as follows:

$$Machine_1 \triangleq Mutex_1 \wedge Init_1 \wedge Periodic \wedge \bigwedge_{i=1}^{l} \Box F(m_i).$$

By the construction of the formula $Machine_1$, we know that the computation of M terminates (i.e. the computation is a finite sequence of configurations ending up with a final one) if and only if $(Machine_1 \wedge \Diamond \lceil Q_{fin} \rceil)$ is satisfiable.

Theorem 7.1 *The satisfiability problem of formulas in $RDC_1(r)$ $(r > 0)$ is undecidable for continuous time.*

Remark. This result depends on the ability to express precisely the length of intervals as $\ell = r$. One would, however, not obtain a decidable subset if the formula $\ell < r$ was used instead, since $\ell = r$ can be derived from $\ell < r$ as follows:

$$\ell = r \;\hat{=}\; \neg((\ell < r) \vee (\lceil 1 \rceil ^\frown \neg(\ell < r))) \,.$$

Thus, we cannot achieve a decidable subset by "relaxing the punctuality" from $\ell = r$ to $\ell < r$, analogously to the result discussed in [7]. We do not know whether this is possible when $\ell > r$ is considered instead of $\ell = r$. $\square$

7.3 Undecidability of RDC_2

We reduce the halting problem for M to the satisfiability of a formula in RDC_2. We give a reduction which works for both the discrete- and the continuous-time domain. The following state variables are used in this reduction:

1. two state variables C_i^+ and C_i^- for each counter $c_i, i = 1, 2$, and
2. state variables $\mathcal{Q} = \{Q_0, \dots, Q_{fin}\}$ corresponding to the labels of M.

The intension behind using the state variables for counter c_i, for $i = 1, 2$, is that the value of c_i is represented by the value of

$$\int C_i^+ - \int C_i^-$$

on a suitable interval (see below). In the reduction, it is only necessary to test whether the value of c_i is 0, and this is expressed by the formula

$$\int C_i^+ = \int C_i^- \,.$$

Hence, using C_i^+ (and C_i^-), the value of c_i can be increased (and decreased). The main idea is to encode in RDC_2 the computation

$$s_0\; s_1\; s_2\; \cdots$$

of M by a sequence of sections of the form

$$|QE_0|C_0|QE_1|C_1|QE_2|C_2|\cdots \,,$$

where QE_k is a state expression of $\mathcal{Q}$, and C_k is a state expression of $\{C_1^+, C_2^+, C_1, C_2\}$.

If $s_k = (q_k, n_{k_1}, n_{k_2})$, then QE_k is a state expression representing the label q_k, and the values n_{k_1}, n_{k_2} of the two counters in the kth configuration are represented by the values of $\int C_i^+ - \int C_i^-$, for $i = 1, 2$, over the interval covering the sections $C_0, C_1, C_2, \dots, C_k$. For this idea to work, it must be specified that all sections have the same length and that the QE_k and C_k sections are mutually exclusive.

To formalize this idea, we introduce the following abbreviations for state expressions:

$$C^\vee \; \widehat{=} \; C_1^+ \vee C_1^- \vee C_2^+ \vee C_2^-$$
$$C^\wedge \; \widehat{=} \; C_1^+ \wedge C_1^- \wedge C_2^+ \wedge C_2^-$$
$$Q^\vee \; \widehat{=} \; Q_0 \vee \cdots \vee Q_{\mathit{fin}} \,,$$

where $C^\vee$ describes a possible change of the value of c_1 and c_2, and $C^\wedge$ actually maintains the value of the counters.

Concerning counter values, we introduce the following abbreviations for formulas in RDC_2:

$$\lceil S \rceil \;\; \widehat{=} \;\; (\textstyle\int S = \int 1) \wedge \neg(\textstyle\int 0 = \int 1)$$
$$\mathit{Incr}_1 \;\; \widehat{=} \;\; \lceil C_1^+ \wedge \neg(C_1^- \vee C_2^+ \vee C_2^-) \rceil$$
$$\mathit{Decr}_1 \;\; \widehat{=} \;\; \lceil C_1^- \wedge \neg(C_1^+ \vee C_2^+ \vee C_2^-) \rceil$$
$$\mathit{Incr}_2 \;\; \widehat{=} \;\; \lceil C_2^+ \wedge \neg(C_2^- \vee C_1^+ \vee C_1^-) \rceil$$
$$\mathit{Decr}_2 \;\; \widehat{=} \;\; \lceil C_2^- \wedge \neg(C_2^+ \vee C_1^+ \vee C_1^-) \rceil$$
$$\mathit{Const} \;\; \widehat{=} \;\; \lceil C^\wedge \rceil \,.$$

The formula Incr_1 expresses the fact that the value of counter c_1 is increased by one by letting C_1^+ be one throughout one section, while the other counter state variables are zero. The formulas $\mathit{Decr}_1, \mathit{Incr}_2, \mathit{Decr}_2$ have similar explanations. Const is used to keep the counter values constant from one configuration to the next (by increasing $\int C_i^+$ as much as $\int C_i^-$).

The following abbreviations will also be used for formulas in RDC_2:

$$\textstyle\int S > 0 \;\; \widehat{=} \;\; \Diamond \lceil S \rceil$$
$$\lceil \; \rceil \;\;\;\; \widehat{=} \;\; \neg\lceil 1 \rceil$$
$$\mathrm{true} \;\;\;\; \widehat{=} \;\; \lceil \; \rceil \vee \lceil 1 \rceil$$
$$\phi \rightsquigarrow \psi \;\; \widehat{=} \;\; \neg(\phi ^\frown \neg(\lceil \; \rceil \vee \psi))$$
$$\Diamond_p \phi \;\;\;\; \widehat{=} \;\; \phi ^\frown \mathrm{true} \qquad \text{reads: ``for some prefix interval: } \phi\text{''}$$
$$\Box_p \phi \;\;\;\; \widehat{=} \;\; \neg(\Diamond_p(\neg\phi)) \qquad \text{reads: ``for all prefix intervals: } \phi\text{''.}$$

Let R and S be two exclusive and complete state expressions. Let

$$\cdots |R|S|R|S|R| \cdots$$

be a (finite or infinite) sequence of alternating R and S sections, where all sections except the first and the last (if the sequence is finite) have the same length.

Below, we construct a formula $EqSize(R, S)$ in RDC_2 which describes the above sequence.

$EqSize(R, S) \;\widehat{=}\;$

$$\Box \, (\lceil R \Leftrightarrow \neg S \rceil \vee \lceil \rceil) \tag{a}$$

$$\wedge \, \Box \left((\lceil R \rceil \frown \lceil S \rceil \frown \lceil R \rceil) \;\Rightarrow\; \left(\begin{array}{c} (\text{true} \frown (\smallint S = \smallint R > 0)) \\ \wedge \\ ((\smallint S = \smallint R > 0) \frown \text{true}) \end{array} \right) \right) \tag{b}$$

$$\wedge \, \Box \left((\lceil S \rceil \frown \lceil R \rceil \frown \lceil S \rceil) \;\Rightarrow\; \left(\begin{array}{c} (\text{true} \frown (\smallint R = \smallint S > 0)) \\ \wedge \\ ((\smallint R = \smallint S > 0) \frown \text{true}) \end{array} \right) \right), \tag{c}$$

where (a) requires that the state expressions R and S are complete and mutually exclusive, and (b) and (c) require that the length of each middle section is greater than or equal to the length of its neighboring section. Therefore all the middle sections have the same length.

The following property expresses the fact that the states corresponding to the labels of M are mutually exclusive:

$$Mutex_2 \;\widehat{=}\; \bigwedge_{P_1 \neq P_2} \Box \neg \lceil P_1 \wedge P_2 \rceil \,,$$

where P_1 and P_2 range over $\mathcal{Q}$.

The computation of M is encoded by a sequence of alternating Q and C sections defined by the formula

$$Machine_2 \;\widehat{=}\; Mutex_2 \wedge EqSize(Q^\vee, C^\vee) \wedge Init_2 \wedge \bigwedge_{i=1}^{l} \Box_p G(m_i) \,,$$

where $Init_2$ encodes the initial configuration and $G(m_i)$ encodes a transition from one configuration to the next caused by the instruction m_i. These formulas are defined below.

The initial configuration is $(q_0, 0, 0)$:

$$Init_2 \;\widehat{=}\; \lceil Q_0 \rceil \frown Const \frown \text{true} \,.$$

The formula $Init_2$ requires that the sequence will start at Q_0, and continue with $C^\wedge$. Thus, $Init_2 \wedge EqSize(Q^\vee, C^\vee)$ can guarantee that all C sections will have the same length, provided C does not appear at the end of the sequence when the sequence is finite.

The formulas $G(m_i)$ (for $i = 1, \ldots, l$), which ensure that the encoding sequence will end in $Q^\vee$ if it is finite, are defined below.

For the instruction $q_j : c_i^+ \to q_k$, we must formalize the condition that any initial segment

$$|Q_0|C_0| \cdots |Q_j|C|$$

of the sequence is expanded to

$$|Q_0|C_0| \cdots |Q_j|C|Q_k|C_i^+|Q^\vee|$$

where only one expansion is possible, owing to the determinism of M. We have

$$G(q_j : c_i^+ \to q_k) \;\widehat{=}\; \left(\left(\left(\left(\begin{matrix} \llbracket\,\rrbracket \\ \vee \\ (\text{true} \,\widehat{}\, \llbracket C^\vee \rrbracket) \end{matrix} \right) \,\widehat{}\, \left(\begin{matrix} (\llbracket Q_j \rrbracket \,\widehat{}\, \llbracket C^\vee \rrbracket) \\ \wedge \\ \smallint Q_j = \smallint C^\vee \end{matrix} \right) \right) \right) \rightsquigarrow \left(\begin{matrix} \llbracket Q_k \rrbracket \\ \vee \\ (\llbracket Q_k \rrbracket \,\widehat{}\, Incr_i) \\ \vee \\ (\llbracket Q_k \rrbracket \,\widehat{}\, Incr_i \,\widehat{}\, \llbracket Q^\vee \rrbracket \,\widehat{}\, \text{true}) \end{matrix} \right) \right).$$

The situation is slightly more complicated for the instruction $c_i^- \to q_k, q_u$, as we must take care of the question of whether the value of counter c_i is zero. We obtain

$$G(q_j : c_i^- \to q_k, q_u) \;\widehat{=}\; \left(\left(\left(\left(\left(\begin{matrix} \llbracket\,\rrbracket \\ \vee \\ (\text{true} \,\widehat{}\, \llbracket C^\vee \rrbracket) \end{matrix} \right) \,\widehat{}\, \left(\begin{matrix} (\llbracket Q_j \rrbracket \,\widehat{}\, \llbracket C^\vee \rrbracket) \\ \wedge \\ \smallint Q_j = \smallint C^\vee \end{matrix} \right) \right) \wedge \smallint C_i^+ = \smallint C_i^- \right) \rightsquigarrow \left(\begin{matrix} \llbracket Q_k \rrbracket \\ \vee \\ (\llbracket Q_k \rrbracket \,\widehat{}\, Const) \\ \vee \\ (\llbracket Q_k \rrbracket \,\widehat{}\, Const \,\widehat{}\, \llbracket Q^\vee \rrbracket \,\widehat{}\, \text{true}) \end{matrix} \right) \right) \right. \\ \wedge \\ \left. \left(\left(\left(\begin{matrix} \llbracket\,\rrbracket \\ \vee \\ (\text{true} \,\widehat{}\, \llbracket C^\vee \rrbracket) \end{matrix} \right) \,\widehat{}\, \left(\begin{matrix} (\llbracket Q_j \rrbracket \,\widehat{}\, \llbracket C^\vee \rrbracket) \\ \wedge \\ \smallint Q_j = \smallint C^\vee \end{matrix} \right) \right) \wedge \neg(\smallint C_i^+ = \smallint C_i^-) \right) \rightsquigarrow \left(\begin{matrix} \llbracket Q_u \rrbracket \\ \vee \\ (\llbracket Q_u \rrbracket \,\widehat{}\, Decr_i) \\ \vee \\ (\llbracket Q_u \rrbracket \,\widehat{}\, Decr_i \,\widehat{}\, \llbracket Q^\vee \rrbracket \,\widehat{}\, \text{true}) \end{matrix} \right) \right) \right).$$

The first conjunct of $G(q_j : c_i^- \rightarrow q_k, q_u)$ describes the case where the value of counter c_i is zero, and the second conjunct describes the case of a positive value of counter c_i.

It can be proved that if $Machine_2 \wedge \Diamond \lceil Q_{fin} \rceil$ is satisfiable, then a terminating computation of M can be constructed, and vice versa. Thus, the halting problem for a two-counter machine can be reduced to the satisfiability of formulas in RDC_2.

Theorem 7.2 *The satisfiability problem of formulas in RDC_2 is undecidable for both discrete time and continuous time.*

7.4 Undecidability of RDC_3

The halting problem for M can be reduced to the satisfiability of a formula in RDC_3. We give a reduction which works for both the discrete- and the continuous-time domain.

The encoding of M uses state variables L_1, L_2, C and $Q_0, \ldots, Q_{fin}$, where L_1 and L_2 delimit machine configurations, C is used to represent the counter values and the Qs correspond to the labels of the counter machine. All these state variables must be mutually exclusive:

$$Mutex_3 \;\;\widehat{=}\; \bigwedge_{P_1 \neq P_2} \Box \neg \lceil P_1 \wedge P_2 \rceil \,,$$

where P_1 and P_2 range over $\{Q_0, \ldots, Q_{fin}, C, L_1, L_2\}$.

A configuration of the machine is represented by a sequence of sections Q, L and C, all of the same length:

$$|Q| \underbrace{C| \cdots |C}_{n_1} |L_1| \underbrace{C| \cdots |C}_{n_2} |L_2| \,.$$

Here Q is the label of the configuration of M, n_1 is the value of the first counter c_1, and n_2 is the value of the second counter c_2. The lengths of the Q, C and L sections must be the same.

The initial configuration, $(q_0, 0, 0)$, is represented by $|Q_0|L_1|L_2|$:

$$Init_3 \;\widehat{=}\; \exists x. (\lceil Q_0 \rceil \wedge (\ell = x)) ^\frown (\lceil L_1 \rceil \wedge (\ell = x)) ^\frown (\lceil L_2 \rceil \wedge (\ell = x)) ^\frown true \,.$$

Each instruction m_i of the counter machine is encoded as a formula $H(m_i)$ in RDC_3, which relates a configuration of the machine to the next configuration.

We shall use the abbreviation $\lceil S \rceil^x$, which is a generalization of $\lceil S \rceil^r$ (for $r > 0$) used in Sect. 7.2:

$$\lceil S \rceil^x \;\widehat{=}\; (\lceil \; \rceil \vee \lceil S \rceil) \wedge (\ell = x) \,,$$

where x ranges over real numbers.

An instruction $q_j : c_1^+ \rightarrow q_k$ transforms configurations as follows:

$$|Q_j|\underbrace{C|\cdots|C}_{n_1}|L_1|\underbrace{C|\cdots|C}_{n_2}|L_2| \Longrightarrow |Q_k|\underbrace{C|C|\cdots|C}_{n_1+1}|L_1|\underbrace{C|\cdots|C}_{n_2}|L_2|\,.$$

Taking into account the determinism of M, we can encode this transformation by means of the formula

$$H(q_j : c_1^+ \rightarrow q_k) \mathrel{\hat{=}}$$

$$\forall x, y, z.$$
$$\left(\begin{array}{l}(\llbracket Q_j \rrbracket^x \frown \llbracket C \rrbracket^y \frown \llbracket L_1 \rrbracket^x \frown \llbracket C \rrbracket^z \frown \llbracket L_2 \rrbracket^x \frown (\ell = 4x + y + z)) \\ \Rightarrow ((\ell = 3x + y + z) \frown \llbracket Q_k \rrbracket^x \frown \llbracket C \rrbracket^x \frown \llbracket C \rrbracket^y \frown \llbracket L_1 \rrbracket^x \frown \llbracket C \rrbracket^z \frown \llbracket L_2 \rrbracket^x)\end{array}\right),$$

where $\forall x$ is the dual of $\exists x$ and can be expressed in RDC_3, and the formula $(\ell = 3x + y + z)$ is an abbreviation of the following formula of RDC_3: $(\ell = x) \frown (\ell = x) \frown (\ell = x) \frown (\ell = y) \frown (\ell = z)$. A similar formula of RDC_3 exists for $(\ell = 4x + y + z)$.

The formula $H(q_j : c_2^+ \rightarrow q_k)$ can be constructed similarly.

An instruction $q_j : c_1^- \rightarrow q_k, q_u$ transforms configurations as follows. When the first counter value is zero,

$$|Q_j|L_1|\underbrace{C|\cdots|C}_{n_2}|L_2| \Longrightarrow |Q_k|L_1|\underbrace{C|\cdots|C}_{n_2}|L_2|\,,$$

and when the first counter value is nonzero,

$$|Q_j|\underbrace{C|\cdots|C}_{n_1+1}|L_1|\underbrace{C|\cdots|C}_{n_2}|L_2| \Longrightarrow |Q_u|\underbrace{C|\cdots|C}_{n_1}|L_1|\underbrace{C|\cdots|C}_{n_2}|L_2|\,.$$

Because of the determinism of M, these computation steps can be encoded as the formula

$$H(q_j : c_1^- \rightarrow q_k, q_u) \mathrel{\hat{=}}$$

$$\forall x, z. \left(\begin{array}{l}(\llbracket Q_j \rrbracket^x \frown \llbracket L_1 \rrbracket^x \frown \llbracket C \rrbracket^z \frown \llbracket L_2 \rrbracket^x \frown (\ell = 3x + z)) \\ \Rightarrow ((\ell = 3x + z) \frown \llbracket Q_k \rrbracket^x \frown \llbracket L_1 \rrbracket^x \frown \llbracket C \rrbracket^z \frown \llbracket L_2 \rrbracket^x)\end{array}\right)$$

$$\wedge$$

$$\forall x, y, z.$$
$$\left(\begin{array}{l}(\llbracket Q_j \rrbracket^x \frown \llbracket C \rrbracket^x \frown \llbracket C \rrbracket^y \frown \llbracket L_1 \rrbracket^x \frown \llbracket C \rrbracket^z \frown \llbracket L_2 \rrbracket^x \frown (\ell = 3x + y + z)) \\ \Rightarrow ((\ell = 4x + y + z) \frown \llbracket Q_u \rrbracket^x \frown \llbracket C \rrbracket^y \frown \llbracket L_1 \rrbracket^x \frown \llbracket C \rrbracket^z \frown \llbracket L_2 \rrbracket^x)\end{array}\right)\,.$$

The instruction $q_j : c_2^- \rightarrow q_k, q_u$ can be encoded similarly, and the encoding of M is given by

$$Machine_3 \mathrel{\hat{=}} Mutex_3 \wedge Init_3 \wedge \bigwedge_{i=1}^{l} \Box H(m_i)\,.$$

The formula $Machine_3 \wedge \Diamond [\![Q_{fin}]\!]$ is satisfiable if and only if M terminates, and hence:

Theorem 7.3 *The satisfiability problem of formulas in RDC_3 is undecidable for both discrete time and continuous time.*

8. Model Checking: Linear Duration Invariants

In Chap. 7, it was proved that the satisfiability (and validity) of simple subclasses of DC formulas is undecidable for both the continuous- and the discrete-time domains. In Chap. 6, decidable subclasses of DC formulas were identified. Some are decidable for both the continuous- and the discrete-time domains, while others are decidable for discrete time only.

In the discrete-time domain, interpretations of DC are restricted to those Boolean-valued functions which change their values at integer points only. The research on decidability and undecidability often imposes restriction on syntax and/or on interpretation when exploring this topic.

In this chapter, we consider continuous time only, and confine ourselves to interpretations which are generated from a *real-time automaton* with upper- and lower-bound timing constraints on its transitions. Furthermore, we syntactically confine ourselves to the subclass of DC formulas which have the form

$$c_{min} \leq \ell \Rightarrow \sum_{i=1}^{n} c_i \int P_i \leq c,$$

where c_{min}, c, and c_i for $1 \leq i \leq n$ are real numbers, and P_i for $1 \leq i \leq n$ are state variables. We call a formula of this form a *linear duration invariant*.

For example, if we ignore the modality $\Box$ in *GbReq*, the *simplified requirement* of the gas burner is a linear duration invariant, since

$$60 \leq \ell \Rightarrow 20 \int \text{Leak} \leq \ell$$

can be reformulated as

$$60 \leq \ell \Rightarrow (20 \int \text{Leak} - \ell) \leq 0$$

and, by use of $\ell = (\int \text{Leak} + \int \text{NonLeak})$, it can be further reformulated as

$$60 \leq \ell \Rightarrow (19 \int \text{Leak} - \int \text{NonLeak}) \leq 0,$$

which is a linear duration invariant with state variables Leak and NonLeak. (Remember that NonLeak $\Leftrightarrow \neg$Leak.)

This chapter gives a positive answer to the question of whether we can decide that any interpretation generated by a real-time automaton with P_i

for $1 \leq i \leq n$ as its states satisfies a linear duration invariant, and describes how this can be done.

An algorithm is presented in this chapter which reduces the problem to a finite number of linear programming problems. Therefore, algorithms for solving linear programming problems can, in combination with this reduction, be used to check the truth of a linear duration invariant with respect to any interpretations generated by a real-time automaton.

It is easy to apply this algorithm to check the truth of a conjunction of linear duration invariants and to generalize the algorithm to formulas of the form

$$c_{min} \leq \ell \leq c_{max} \ \Rightarrow \ \sum_{i=1}^{l} c_i \cdot \int S_i \leq c,$$

where c_{max} is either a real number or ∞, and each S_i is constructed from the states of the real-time automaton using the Boolean connectives.

In this chapter, we first use the gas burner example to explain the main ideas of the algorithm and to explain how it can check the correctness of a gas burner design with respect to the requirement, although a formal proof through DC deduction was given in Sect. 3.5. After the example, the reduction is formalized and proved correct.

The work presented in this chapter is based on [172].

8.1 Example

The main ideas and concepts of this chapter will be introduced here using the gas burner example. Consider the formulas

$$\square (\lceil \text{Leak} \rceil \ \Rightarrow \ \ell \leq 1)$$

$$\square ((\lceil \text{Leak} \rceil \frown \lceil \text{NonLeak} \rceil \frown \lceil \text{Leak} \rceil) \ \Rightarrow \ \ell \geq 30),$$

which model a design for the gas burner.

This design can be represented by the real-time automaton in Fig. 8.1, which has two *states*, Leak and NonLeak.

The two edges of the automaton are called *transitions*, and are labeled f (for failure) and r (for recovery). The state NonLeak is called the *pre-state* of f and Leak is called the *post-state* of f, and similarly for the transition labeled r.

The transitions are also labeled with *timing constraints*. The timing constraint on transition r is a bounded and closed interval $[0, 1]$, denoting that the automaton can stay in the Leak state for at most one time unit before a transition to the NonLeak state takes place. The timing constraint on transition f is a left closed, unbounded interval $[30, \infty)$, denoting that the automaton must stay in the NonLeak state for at least 30 time units before

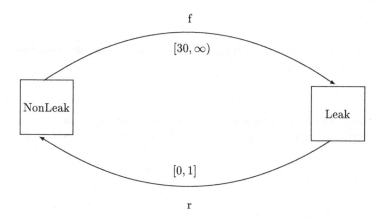

Fig. 8.1. Real-time automaton for the gas burner

a transition to the Leak state can take place, and it can even stay in the NonLeak state forever.

Suppose for the moment that NonLeak is the *initial state* of the automaton. A finite sequence of transitions represents an *untimed* behavior of the automaton, e.g. an untimed sequence of transitions

   f r f ,

which starts with an f (failure) transition since NonLeak is the initial state, and then an r (recovery) transition followed by another failure transition.

A *timed* behavior of the automaton is obtained from an untimed transition sequence by marking each transition with the number of time units the automaton spends in the pre-state of the transition, e.g.

   $(f, 31)\ (r, 0.5)\ (f, 50)$

is a timed sequence of transitions describing a timed behavior of an automaton which spends 31 time units in the NonLeak state before a failure transition to the Leak state occurs. It then stays for 0.5 time units in the Leak state before a recovery transition to the NonLeak state occurs. Finally, the automaton stays for 50 time units in the NonLeak state before a new failure transition to the Leak state occurs.

A timed behavior of the automaton must respect the timing constrains on the transitions, e.g. the timed sequence

   $(f, t_1)\ (r, t_2)\ (f, t_3)$

must satisfy

$$t_1 \geq 30,\ 0 \leq t_2 \leq 1\ \text{ and } t_3 \geq 30.$$

For this timed sequence, the total accumulated time the automaton spends in the NonLeak state is $t_1 + t_3$:

$$\int \text{NonLeak} = t_1 + t_3.$$

Similarly, the (accumulated) time spent in the Leak state is t_2 and the length of the total time period covered by this timed sequence is $t_1 + t_2 + t_3$, i.e.

$$\int \text{Leak} = t_2$$

and

$$\ell = \int \text{Leak} + \int \text{NonLeak} = t_1 + t_2 + t_3.$$

In the following, we investigate how to check the truth of the linear duration invariant representing the simplified requirement of the gas burner

$$60 \leq \ell \implies (19 \int \text{Leak} - \int \text{NonLeak}) \leq 0,$$

with respect to all timed sequences of transitions of the gas burner automaton.

First, let us fix an untimed transition sequence. Note that infinitely many timed sequences may be obtained from a given untimed sequence. An untimed sequence of transitions of a real-time automaton satisfies a linear duration invariant iff all timed sequences of the automaton obtained from the untimed sequence satisfy the invariant.

Consider the problem in Fig. 8.2.

Is the linear duration invariant

$$60 \leq \ell \implies 19 \int \text{Leak} - \int \text{NonLeak} \leq 0$$

satisfied by the untimed sequence of transitions $f\,r\,f$ of the gas burner automaton?

Fig. 8.2. Satisfaction problem for an untimed sequence

Fortunately, this problem can be formulated and solved by using linear programming (see Fig. 8.3). Therefore, the problem of whether an untimed sequence satisfies a linear duration invariant is decidable, as any algorithm solving the linear programming problem can be used to decide our problem.

It is easy to calculate that the maximum of the objective function in Fig. 8.3 under the constraints is -41, since $t_1, t_3 \geq 30$ and $t_2 \leq 1$. So the untimed sequence of $f\,r\,f$ satisfies the linear duration invariant.

Constraints:

$$t_1 \geq 30,\ 0 \leq t_2 \leq 1,\ t_3 \geq 30 \text{ and } (t_1 + t_2 + t_3) \geq 60.$$

Objective function:

$$19t_2 - (t_1 + t_3).$$

- If the maximal value of the objective function is positive, then the linear duration invariant is violated by f r f.
- If the maximal value of the objective function is less than or equal to 0, then f r f satisfies the linear duration invariant.

Fig. 8.3. Linear programming problem

Thus, if the gas burner automaton has only finitely many untimed transition sequences, then the satisfaction problem of the linear duration invariant can be transformed into a finite number of linear programming problems, and solved effectively. Unfortunately, this automaton can produce infinitely many untimed transition sequences, and they can be expressed in terms of regular language as

$$(f\,r)^* \ \cup \ (f\,r)^* f\,,$$

where $*$ stands for repetition and $\cup$ for the union (see Sect. 6.2 for more details). Remember that NonLeak is the initial state.

Therefore, the remaining part of the investigation concerns how to reduce the satisfaction problem for an infinite set of untimed transition sequences to satisfaction problems for a finite set of untimed ones.

It is obvious that the satisfaction problem for the untimed sequences defined by $((f\,r)^* \cup (f\,r)^* f)$ can be reduced to two satisfaction problems by considering $(f\,r)^*$ and $(f\,r)^* f$ individually.

Now let us consider the satisfaction problem in Fig. 8.4 for $(f\,r)^*$, which produces an infinite number of untimed transition sequences.

Is the linear duration invariant

$$60 \leq \ell \ \Rightarrow \ 19 \int \text{Leak} - \int \text{NonLeak} \leq 0$$

satisfied by every untimed transition sequence of the gas burner automaton included in $(f\,r)^*$?

Fig. 8.4. Satisfaction problem for a regular expression

Interestingly, any timed sequence obtained from a pair of transitions f r decreases the value of $(19 \int \text{Leak} - \int \text{NonLeak})$ by at least 11, since the automaton can stay in the state NonLeak for at least 30 time units and in the state Leak for at most 1 time unit.

Thus, if the timed sequences obtained from repetition of f r k times, $(\text{f r})^k$, *always* cover a time interval which is not less than 60 time units and the values of $(19 \int \text{Leak} - \int \text{NonLeak})$ given by them are not greater than 0, then repetition m times to give $(\text{f r})^m$ (for any $m \geq k$) satisfies the linear duration invariant.

The above reasoning implies that if the timed sequences obtained from $(\text{f r})^k$ always cover a time period not less than 60 time units, then the satisfaction problem for $(\text{f r})^*$ can be reduced to a similar problem for

$$\bigcup_{i=0}^{k} (\text{f r})^i ,$$

which produces only finitely many untimed transition sequences.

From the timing constraint that the automaton has to stay in NonLeak for at least 30 time units, it can be proved that the timed behavior obtained from $(\text{f r})^2$ always covers a time period not less than 60 time units. See Fig. 8.5.

If the linear duration invariant

$$60 \leq \ell \;\Rightarrow\; 19 \int \text{Leak} - \int \text{NonLeak} \leq 0$$

is satisfied by every untimed transition sequence of the gas burner automaton included in

$$\bigcup_{i=0}^{2} (\text{f r})^i$$

then it is also satisfied by every untimed transition sequence of the automaton included in

$$(\text{f r})^* .$$

Fig. 8.5. Reduction of a satisfaction problem

Similarly, any timed sequence obtained from a pair of transitions r f also decreases the value of $(19 \int \text{Leak} - \int \text{NonLeak})$ by at least 11, and the timed sequences obtained from f r f always cover a time period not less than 60 time units. Thus, the satisfaction problem for $(\text{f r})^* \text{f}$ can be reduced to a similar problem for the untimed sequences included in

$$\bigcup_{i=0}^{1} (f\,r)^i\,f\,.$$

Therefore we can reduce the satisfaction problem of the linear duration invariant for the gas burner automaton to a finite number of linear programming problems.

In fact, it can be reduced to four linear programming problems, which correspond to the untimed behaviors

f, fr, frf and frfr,

if we exclude the plain behavior for the empty sequence. Their objective functions have maximum values

$-60, -40, -41$ and -22,

respectively, and the answers are all positive. So we can prove the correctness of the design of the gas burner with respect to the simplified requirement by model checking.

The observations in the above example can be easily generalized to cover other cases. For example, if there exists a timed sequence obtained from f r which increases the value of $(19\int \text{Leak} - \int \text{NonLeak})$ by a positive amount, then the linear duration invariant will be violated eventually, since the repetition of f r will eventually cover a time period not less than 60, and increase the value of $(19\int \text{Leak} - \int \text{NonLeak})$ to go beyond any given bound.

In the following we elaborate and formalize the above observations, and develop systematically an algorithm to check linear duration invariants against real-time automata. The notion of a real-time automaton is formalized in Sect. 8.2, and Sect. 8.3 formalizes the notion of a linear duration invariant. In Sect. 8.4 an algorithm is developed to reduce the satisfaction of a linear duration invariant for a (possibly infinite) regular language of untimed sequences into a finite set of linear programming problems. Section 8.5 briefly discusses possible generalizations of the algorithm.

8.2 Real-Time Automata

The notion of real-time automata defined in this section corresponds to a subclass of the timed automata of [5], where each automaton has one clock which is reset after every transition.

A *real-time automaton* A is a tuple $(V, \mathcal{T}, low, up)$ which satisfies the following conditions:

1. V is a finite set of *states* $\{P_1, \ldots, P_n\}$, where the states are *exclusive* and *complete*.
2. $\mathcal{T} \subseteq V \times V$ is a finite set of *transitions*. If $\rho = (P_i, P_j)$ is a transition, then P_i is called the *pre-state* of ρ and P_j is called the *post-state* of ρ. We denote the indices of pre- and post-states by $\overleftarrow{\rho}$ and $\overrightarrow{\rho}$, i.e. $\overleftarrow{\rho} = i$ and $\overrightarrow{\rho} = j$.
3. The functions
$$low : \mathcal{T} \to \mathbb{R}$$
$$up : \mathcal{T} \to (\mathbb{R} \cup \{\infty\})$$

   denote the lower- and upper-bound timing constraints on the transitions, and we require, for any $\rho \in \mathcal{T}$,
$$0 \leq low(\rho) \leq up(\rho)$$
$$\text{and } low(\rho) = 0 \implies up(\rho) > 0\,,$$

   where we accept $x < \infty$ for $x \in \mathbb{R}$, and $\infty > 0$.

An *untimed sequence* of A is a finite sequence of transitions of A,
$$Seq = \rho_1 \rho_2 \cdots \rho_m\,,$$

where $m \geq 0$, $\rho_i \in \mathcal{T}$ $(1 \leq i \leq m)$ and
$$\overrightarrow{\rho_i} = \overleftarrow{\rho}_{i+1} \quad (1 \leq i < m)\,.$$

By $\overrightarrow{\rho}_i = \overleftarrow{\rho}_{i+1}$ we express the fact that ρ_i and ρ_{i+1} are two consecutive transitions, which are linked to each other at state $P_{\overrightarrow{\rho_i}}$. The empty sequence $(m = 0)$ is written as ϵ.

Let L_A denote the set of untimed sequences of A. L_A is a regular language over the alphabet $\mathcal{T}$, as it is accepted by a finite automaton (where every state is both an initial and an accepting state).

A *timed sequence* of A is a finite sequence
$$TSeq = (\rho_1, t_1)(\rho_2, t_2) \cdots (\rho_m, t_m)\,,$$

where
$$\rho_1 \rho_2 \cdots \rho_m \in L_A$$

and
$$low(\rho_i) \leq t_i \leq up(\rho_i) \quad (1 \leq i \leq m)\,.$$

From now on we assume that a real-time automaton
$$A = (V, \mathcal{T}, low, up), \text{ where } V = \{P_1, \ldots, P_n\}\,,$$

is given.

8.3 Linear Duration Invariants

A *linear duration invariant* for the real-time automaton A is a DC formula of the form

$$LDI \; \hat{=} \; c_{min} \leq \ell \; \Rightarrow \; \sum_{i=1}^{n} c_i \cdot \int P_i \leq c,$$

where

- c_{min}, c_i $(1 \leq i \leq n)$ and c are real numbers, and
- P_i $(1 \leq i \leq n)$ are states of A.

The *value* of $\int P_i$ $(1 \leq i \leq n)$ for a timed sequence of A

$$TSeq = (\rho_1, t_1)\,(\rho_2, t_2) \cdots (\rho_m, t_m)$$

is

$$TSeq(\int P_i) = \sum_{j \in \alpha_i} t_j\,,$$

where $\alpha_i = \{j \mid 1 \leq j \leq m \text{ and } \overleftarrow{\rho_j} = i\}$.

The value of ℓ for the timed sequence $TSeq$ is

$$TSeq(\ell) = \sum_{j=1}^{m} t_j\,.$$

The *linear function* in LDI is denoted by

$$LF \; \hat{=} \; \sum_{i=1}^{n} c_i \cdot \int P_i\,.$$

The value of the linear function LF for a timed sequence $TSeq$ is

$$TSeq(LF) \; = \; \sum_{i=1}^{n} c_i \cdot TSeq(\int P_i)\,.$$

Lemma 8.1 *For any timed sequences $TSeq_1$, $TSeq_2$ and a state P,*

$$(TSeq_1 \,\widehat{}\, TSeq_2)(\int P) = (TSeq_2 \,\widehat{}\, TSeq_1)(\int P)\,,$$

where $(\_\,\widehat{}\,\_)$ stands for the concatenation operator for timed sequences.

Proof. This follows from the definition of $TSeq(\int P)$ and the fact that addition is commutative. □

Remark. Careful readers may notice that a reordered timed sequence may violate the transition consecutivity of the sequence, and cannot be regarded as a timed behavior of the automaton. However, the value of $\int P$ $(P \in V)$ can be computed for any timed (or untimed) sequence, whether or not it possesses the property of consecutivity, and the satisfaction problem of a linear duration invariant remains meaningful. In the following reduction, we always take this to be understood. □

The linear duration invariant

$$c_{min} \leq \ell \;\Rightarrow\; \textstyle\sum_{i=1}^{n} c_i \cdot \int P_i \leq c$$

is *satisfied by the timed sequence TSeq of A* if

$$c_{min} \leq TSeq(\ell) \text{ implies } TSeq(LF) \leq c.$$

Otherwise, we say that the linear duration invariant is *violated* by *TSeq*.
The linear duration invariant

$$(c_{min} \leq \ell \;\Rightarrow\; \textstyle\sum_{i=1}^{n} c_i \cdot \int P_i \leq c)$$

is *satisfied by the untimed sequence* of A

$$Seq = \rho_1 \rho_2 \cdots \rho_m,$$

written as

$$Seq \models LDI,$$

if it is satisfied by every timed sequence obtained from *Seq*. Otherwise, we say that *LDI* is *violated* by *Seq*.

Theorem 8.1 *The problem*

$$Seq \models LDI$$

is solvable using linear programming.

Proof. Let $Seq = \rho_1 \rho_2 \cdots \rho_m$.
Consider the timed sequence

$$TSeq = (\rho_1, t_1)\,(\rho_2, t_2)\,\cdots\,(\rho_m, t_m),$$

and consider each t_i as a real variable.
The constraints of the linear programming problem are obtained from the timing constraints of A,

$$low(\rho_i) \leq t_i \leq up(\rho_i),$$

for $1 \leq i \leq m$, and from the left-hand side of the implication in the definition of *LDI*,

$$c_{min} \leq TSeq(\ell) \;(= \textstyle\sum_{i=1}^{m} t_i).$$

The objective function of the linear programming problem is

$$TSeq(LF) \; (= \textstyle\sum_{i=1}^{n} c_i \sum_{j\in\alpha_i} t_j)\,,$$

where $\alpha_i = \{j \mid 1 \leq j \leq m \text{ and } \overleftarrow{\rho_j} = i\}$.

If the maximal value of the objective function exceeds c, the linear duration invariant is violated by Seq. Otherwise, it is satisfied by Seq.   □

A linear duration invariant LDI is satisfied by a set $L \subseteq \mathcal{T}^*$ of untimed sequences, written $L \models LDI$, if $Seq \models LDI$ for every $Seq \in L$. Furthermore, a linear duration invariant LDI is satisfied by a real-time automaton A if it is satisfied by all untimed (and hence all timed) sequences of A, i.e. iff

$$L_A \models LDI\,.$$

8.4 Reduction

In this section we formalize the algorithm sketched in Sect. 8.1, in order to reduce

$$L_A \models LDI$$

to a finite set of linear programming problems.

In the following, we identify a regular expression with the language it denotes.

A regular expression $C(\mathcal{X})$ constructed from the transitions of $\mathcal{T}$, the empty sequence ϵ and the letter $\mathcal{X}$, using union, concatenation and repetition, is called a *regular context*. For a given regular language $L \subseteq \mathcal{T}^*$, $C(L)$ denotes the regular language obtained from $C(\mathcal{X})$ by replacing every occurrence of $\mathcal{X}$ in $C(\mathcal{X})$ with L.

Two regular languages L_1 and L_2 of $\mathcal{T}$ are called *congruently equivalent* or simply *equivalent* with respect to LDI, written

$$L_1 \equiv_{LDI} L_2\,,$$

if for any regular context $C(\mathcal{X})$,

$$C(L_1) \models LDI \quad \text{iff} \quad C(L_2) \models LDI\,.$$

Given LDI, for simplicity we shall often drop the index LDI, and simply use $\equiv$ instead of $\equiv_{LDI}$.

In the rest of this chapter, we conduct the proof of the equivalence between L_1 and L_2 by providing, for any timed sequence $TSeq_1$ in L_1, a timed sequence $TSeq_2$ in L_2 such that

$$TSeq_2(\ell) = TSeq_1(\ell) \quad \text{and} \quad TSeq_2(LF) \geq TSeq_1(LF)$$

and vice versa. In most case, we even prove $TSeq_2(LF) = TSeq_1(LF)$, by showing

$$TSeq_2(\int P) = TSeq_1(\int P), \text{ for any state } P \in V.$$

A proof of equivalence can also be conducted at the level of untimed sequences, if we can find a correspondence between untimed sequences of L_1 and L_2 which can be carried over to timed sequences.

The problem

$$L_A \models LDI$$

is reduced to a finite set of linear programming problems in two steps.

In the first step, we derive from L_A an equivalent *normal form*, and in the second step, we reduce the satisfaction problem of *LDI* for a normal form to a finite set of linear programming problems.

In order to define the normal form, we need the following concepts:

1. An untimed sequence $\rho_1\rho_2 \cdots \rho_m$ of A is called a *finite term*. Note that the empty sequence ϵ is a finite term.
2. An *infinite term* is an untimed sequence of A followed by a repetition of a single transition with zero as its lower-bound timing constraint, i.e. an infinite term has the form

$$\rho_1\rho_2 \cdots \rho_m \rho^*,$$

   where $low(\rho) = 0$.
3. A *normal form* is a regular expression over the alphabet $\mathcal{T}$ of the form

$$\bigcup_{i=1}^{k} L_i,$$

   where L_i is either a *finite term* or an *infinite term*. As a special case $\emptyset$, a regular expression for the empty language, is in normal form, as $\emptyset = \bigcup_{i=1}^{0} L_i$.

Note that it is decidable whether a finite term satisfies *LDI* (Theorem 8.1). Therefore, the main part of the second step is to solve the problem of whether an infinite term satisfies *LDI*.

8.4.1 Congruent Equivalence

Reordering the elements of a timed sequence does not change the value of $\int P$, by Lemma 8.1, where P stands for any state of A. This preservation helps us establish the following theorem.

Theorem 8.2 *For languages $L_1, L_2 \subseteq \mathcal{T}^*$:*

1. $(L_1 L_2) \equiv (L_2 L_1)$.
2. $(L_1 \cup L_2)^* \equiv (L_1^* L_2^*)$.
3. $(L_1(L_2^*))^* \equiv (\{\epsilon\} \cup (L_1(L_1^*)(L_2^*)))$.

Proof. A proof can be given by showing that each untimed sequence of an original language has a corresponding sequence in the equivalent language which contains the same letters but may have a different order among the letters, and vice versa.

For example, for the second equivalence, it is obvious that

$$(L_1 \cup L_2)^* \supseteq (L_1^* L_2^*)$$

and that by reordering the letters of an arbitrary string of $(L_1 \cup L_2)^*$ into $Seq_1 Seq_2$, where Seq_1 is a string containing only letters in L_1 and Seq_2 is a string containing only letters in L_2, we can obtain the corresponding string in $(L_1^* L_2^*)$. □

By Theorem 8.2, the distribution law for the concatenation over the union and the idempotent law for the repetition in a regular language, we can transform any regular language into an equivalent finite union of regular expressions of the form

$$\rho_1 \cdots \rho_m Seq_1^* \cdots Seq_k^*.$$

For example,

$$
\begin{aligned}
& (\rho_1 \rho_2^* \cup (\rho_3 \rho_4)^*)^* \rho_5 \\
\equiv\ & (\rho_1 \rho_2^*)^* (\rho_3 \rho_4)^{**} \rho_5 && \text{TH8.2(2)} \\
\equiv\ & (\{\epsilon\} \cup \rho_1 \rho_1^* \rho_2^*)(\rho_3 \rho_4)^* \rho_5 && \text{TH8.2(3), Idempotent} \\
\equiv\ & (\rho_3 \rho_4)^* \rho_5 \cup \rho_1 \rho_1^* \rho_2^* (\rho_3 \rho_4)^* \rho_5 && \text{Distribution} \\
\equiv\ & \rho_5 (\rho_3 \rho_4)^* \cup \rho_1 \rho_5 \rho_1^* \rho_2^* (\rho_3 \rho_4)^* && \text{TH8.2(1).}
\end{aligned}
$$

(In the above equations, "TM" means "Theorem".)

We now prove the following four theorems in order to reduce a regular expression of the form

$$\rho_1 \cdots \rho_m Seq_1^* \cdots Seq_k^*$$

to normal form. The first two theorems are concerned with the equivalence between untimed sequences having 0 as the lower bound of the timing constraints.

Theorem 8.3 *If $low(\rho_i) = 0$ $(i = 1, 2, \ldots, m)$, then*

$$(\rho_1 \rho_2 \cdots \rho_m)^* \equiv \rho_1^* \rho_2^* \cdots \rho_m^*.$$

Proof. It is obvious that the right-hand side includes the left-hand side:

$$(\rho_1\rho_2\cdots\rho_m)^* \subseteq \rho_1^*\rho_2^*\cdots\rho_m^*\,.$$

We can also prove that for any timed sequence $TSeq_1$ on the right-hand side there exists a timed sequence $TSeq_2$ on the left-hand side such that, for any state P,

$$TSeq_1(\int P) = TSeq_2(\int P)\,.$$

For example, let $m = 2$ and let

$$(\rho_1,t_1)\,(\rho_1,t_2)\,(\rho_2,t_3)$$

be a timed sequence on the right-hand side. Then

$$(\rho_1,t_1)\,(\rho_2,t_3)\,(\rho_1,t_2)\,(\rho_2,0)$$

is the corresponding timed sequence on the left-hand side. We omit further details of the proof. $\square$

Theorem 8.4 *If* $low(\rho_1) = 0$ *and* $c_{\overleftarrow{\rho}_1} \geq c_{\overleftarrow{\rho}_2}$, *then*

$$(\rho_1^*\rho_2^*) \equiv \rho_1^*\,.$$

Proof. It is trivial to show that

$$(\rho_1^*\rho_2^*) \supseteq \rho_1^*\,.$$

We shall use an example to demonstrate a proof of the other half of the equivalence. Let

$$TSeq_1 = (\rho_1,t_1),(\rho_2,t_2)$$

be a timed sequence of $\rho_1^*\rho_2^*$. According to the definition of a real-time automaton given in Sect. 8.2, $up(\rho_1) > 0$. We define

$$k = \lfloor t_2/up(\rho_1)\rfloor \quad \text{and}$$
$$\delta = t_2 - k \cdot up(\rho_1)\,,$$

i.e. we have

$$t_2 = k \cdot up(\rho_1) + \delta\,.$$

Then the following timed sequence for ρ_1^*,

$$TSeq_2 = (\rho_1,t_1)\,(\rho_1,up(\rho_1))^k\,(\rho_1,\delta)\,,$$

corresponds to $TSeq_1$, since we can prove

$$TSeq_2(\ell) \;=\; TSeq_1(\ell) \;=\; t_1 + t_2$$

and

$$\begin{aligned}
TSeq_2(LF) &= c_{\overset{\leftarrow}{\rho}_1} \cdot (t_1 + t_2)\\
&\geq c_{\overset{\leftarrow}{\rho}_1} \cdot t_1 + c_{\overset{\leftarrow}{\rho}_2} \cdot t_2 \quad (\text{as } c_{\overset{\leftarrow}{\rho}_1} \geq c_{\overset{\leftarrow}{\rho}_2})\\
&= TSeq_1(LF),
\end{aligned}$$

where we have used the proof technique discussed in the introduction to Sect. 8.4. □

By use of Theorems 8.3 and 8.4, we can directly derive the following corollary.

Corollary 8.1 *If* $low(\rho_i) = 0$ $(i = 1, 2, \ldots, m)$ *and*

$$c_{\overset{\leftarrow}{\rho}_j} = max\{c_{\overset{\leftarrow}{\rho}_i} \mid i = 1, 2, \ldots, m\},$$

then

$$(\rho_1 \rho_2 \cdots \rho_m)^* \;\equiv\; \rho_j^*.$$

The following two theorems are concerned with the equivalence of untimed sequences with a positive lower bound on the timing constraints.

Given an untimed sequence

$$Seq = \rho_1 \rho_2 \cdots \rho_m,$$

let ℓ_{min} be the shortest time period which Seq covers, i.e.

$$\ell_{min} \;=\; \sum_{i=1}^{m} low(\rho_i).$$

We can also obtain from Seq a timed sequence

$$TSeq_{max} = (\rho_1, t_1)(\rho_2, t_2) \cdots (\rho_m, t_m),$$

where

$$t_i \;=\; \begin{cases} up(\rho_i) & \text{if } c_{\overset{\leftarrow}{\rho_i}} > 0\\ low(\rho_i) & \text{otherwise} \end{cases} \quad \text{for } 1 \leq i \leq m.$$

This sequence has the maximal value of LF among all timed sequences of Seq,

$$TSeq_{max}(LF) \;=\; \sum_{i=1}^{m} c_{\overset{\leftarrow}{\rho_i}} \cdot t_i,$$

where we let $TSeq_{max}(LF) = \infty$ if some t_i is ∞.

Theorem 8.5 *If $\ell_{min} > 0$ and $TSeq_{max}(LF) > 0$, then for any regular context $C(\mathcal{X})$ containing an occurrence of $\mathcal{X}$, $C(Seq^*)$ violates LDI.*

Proof. Since $\mathcal{X}$ occurs in $C(\mathcal{X})$, there is an untimed sequence of the form

$$\rho_{j_1}\rho_{j_2} \cdots \rho_{j_n} Seq^i \rho_{l_1}\rho_{l_2} \cdots \rho_{l_n}$$

in $C(Seq^i)$, for any $i \geq 0$, with a corresponding timed sequence

$$TSeq_C(i) \,\hat{=}\, TSeq_j \; TSeq^i_{max} \, TSeq_l \,,$$

where $TSeq_j$ is a timed sequence for $\rho_{j_1}\rho_{j_2} \cdots \rho_{j_n}$ and $TSeq_l$ is a timed sequence for $\rho_{l_1}\rho_{l_2} \cdots \rho_{l_n}$.

The value of the linear function for $TSeq_C(i)$ is

$$TSeq_C(i)(LF) = TSeq_j(LF) + i \cdot TSeq_{max}(LF) + TSeq_l(LF) \,.$$

Since $TSeq_{max}(LF) > 0$ the value of $TSeq_C(i)(LF)$ is a strictly monotonically increasing function of i. Let

$$m = 1 + \lfloor (|c - TSeq_j(LF) - TSeq_l(LF)|) / TSeq_{max}(LF) \rfloor \,.$$

Then

$$TSeq_C(i)(LF) > c$$

for all $i \geq m$.

Since $\ell_{min} > 0$, by using k repetitions of Seq, where

$$k \;=\; \lceil c_{min}/\ell_{min} \rceil \,,$$

we obtain $TSeq_C(k)(\ell) \geq c_{min}$, thereby making the left-hand side of *LDI* true. Therefore, for $i_0 = max\{k, m\}$, we have the result that $TSeq_C(i_0)$ violates *LDI*, and so does $C(Seq^*)$. □

Theorem 8.6 *If $\ell_{min} > 0$ and $TSeq_{max}(LF) \leq 0$, then*

$$Seq^* \;\equiv\; Seq^k \,,$$

where $k = \lceil c_{min}/\ell_{min} \rceil$.

Proof. An argument concerning this theorem was given in Sect. 8.1 when we derived the conclusion shown in Fig. 8.5; we shall not repeat this argument here. □

8.4.2 Closure Properties of Normal Forms

We now investigate closure properties of normal forms with respect to a given linear duration invariant LDI. The proofs of the closure properties are constructive, and they constitute the main parts of the algorithm for the derivation of a normal form for a regular expression over the alphabet $\mathcal{T}$.

Theorem 8.7 *The regular expressions $\emptyset, \epsilon$ and $\rho \in \mathcal{T}$ are in normal form.*

Proof. This follows directly from the definition of a normal form.   □

Theorem 8.8 *Normal forms are closed with respect to union.*

Proof. For any normal forms, L_1 and L_2, the regular expression $L_1 \cup L_2$ is, by definition, in normal form.   □

Theorem 8.9 *If $L_1, L_2 \subseteq \mathcal{T}^*$ are in normal form, then there is a normal form equivalent to $L_1 L_2$.*

Proof. Since L_1 and L_2 are in normal form, we have

$$L_i \equiv \bigcup_{j=1}^{m_i} L_{ij} \quad (i = 1, 2),$$

where each L_{ij} is either a finite term or an infinite term.

By distributing the concatenation over the union, we can transform $L_1 L_2$ to an equivalent regular expression

$$\bigcup_{j=1}^{m_1} \bigcup_{k=1}^{m_2} L_{1j} L_{2k}.$$

We can show that for each $L_{1j} L_{2k}$ there is an equivalent normal form, by considering the following three cases:

1. L_{1j} and L_{2k} are finite terms. By definition, so is $L_{1j} L_{2k}$.
2. One of L_{1j} and L_{2k} is a finite term and the other is infinite. By Theorem 8.2(1), the necessary permutations can be applied in order to obtain an equivalent infinite term for $L_{1j} L_{2k}$.
3. Both L_{1j} and L_{2k} are infinite terms, i.e. $L_{1j} = Seq_1 \rho_1^*$, with $low(\rho_1) = 0$, and $L_{2k} = Seq_2 \rho_2^*$, with $low(\rho_2) = 0$. By Theorem 8.2(1), we obtain

   $$L_{1j} L_{2k} \equiv Seq_1 \, Seq_2 \, \rho_1^* \rho_2^*.$$

By applying Theorem 8.4 to $\rho_1^* \rho_2^*$, we can (by comparing $c_{\underset{\rho_1}{\leftarrow}}$ with $c_{\underset{\rho_2}{\leftarrow}}$) delete one of ρ_1^* and ρ_2^* and obtain an infinite term which is equivalent to $L_{1j} L_{2k}$.

□

Theorem 8.10 *If $L \subseteq \mathcal{T}^*$ is in normal form, then either there is a normal form for L^* or the linear duration invariant LDI is violated by L^*.*

Proof. Suppose $\bigcup_{i=1}^{m} L_i$ is the normal form for L. By Theorem 8.2(2),

$$L^* \equiv L_1^* L_2^* \cdots L_m^*,$$

where L_i (for $1 \le i \le m$) is either a finite or an infinite term.

We show that every L_i^* has an equivalent normal form, unless it (and also L^*) violates *LDI*. When we have done this, the proof is completed because (by Theorem 8.9) normal forms are closed with respect to concatenation.

We consider the following cases:

1. $L_i = Seq = \rho_1 \rho_2 \cdots \rho_m$ is a finite term. This part is split further into three cases:

   Case a: $\ell_{min} = 0$ (for *Seq*). By Corollary 8.1, Seq^* is equivalent to a ρ_j^* (for some j, where $1 \le j \le m$) which is an infinite term.
   Case b: $\ell_{min} > 0$ and $TSeq_{max}(LF) > 0$. By Theorem 8.5, for any regular context $C(\mathcal{X})$, $C(L_i^*)$ violates *LDI*. So does L^*.
   Case c: $\ell_{min} > 0$ and $TSeq_{max}(LF) \le 0$. By Theorem 8.6, we can transform L_i^* into an equivalent concatenation of finite terms.

2. $L_i = \rho_1 \rho_2 \cdots \rho_m \rho^*$ is an infinite term. Let $Seq = \rho_1 \rho_2 \cdots \rho_m$, which is a finite term. By Theorem 8.2(3),

   $$L_i^* \equiv (\{\epsilon\} \cup Seq\, Seq^* \rho^*).$$

   There is an equivalent normal form for Seq^*, by Case 1, unless *LDI* is violated. Since ϵ, *Seq* and ρ^* are normal forms, and normal forms are closed with respect to union and concatenation (Theorems 8.7, 8.8 and 8.9), there is a normal form equivalent to L_i^*, unless *LDI* is violated.

   $\square$

A simple consequence of the closure properties is expressed in the following theorem.

Theorem 8.11 *Any regular language over the alphabet $\mathcal{T}$ has an equivalent normal form, unless the linear duration invariant LDI is violated.*

8.4.3 An Algorithm Deriving Normal Forms

Since the proofs of the closure properties given in the previous section are all constructive, it is easy to construct a recursive algorithm which can take a regular expression over an alphabet $\mathcal{T}$ as input and produce an equivalent normal form as output, unless it detects that the linear duration invariant is violated.

8.4.4 Infinite Term

Theorem 8.1 demonstrates how to transform the satisfaction of *LDI* for a finite term into a linear programming problem. Here we show how to transform the satisfaction problem for an infinite term into a linear programming problem.

Let L be an infinite term

$$L = \rho_1 \rho_2 \cdots \rho_m \rho^*,$$

where $low(\rho) = 0$. We introduce an extra state P_{n+1} and a new transition ρ', where

$$\overleftarrow{\rho'} = n + 1, \ low(\rho') = 0 \text{ and } up(\rho') = \infty,$$

and introduce a new linear invariant LDI' derived from LDI by changing LF such that

$$LF' \ \hat{=} \ LF + c_{\overleftarrow{\rho}} \textstyle\int P_{n+1}.$$

In other words, we simulate ρ^* by ρ', and we have the result that

$$\rho_1 \rho_2 \cdots \rho_m \rho^* \models LDI \quad \text{iff} \quad \rho_1 \rho_2 \cdots \rho_m \rho' \models LDI'.$$

By transforming the satisfaction problem of LDI' for the finite term

$$\rho_1 \rho_2 \cdots \rho_m \rho'$$

into a linear programming problem, we can solve the satisfaction problem of LDI for the infinite term $\rho_1 \rho_2 \cdots \rho_m \rho^*$.

8.5 Generalization

An easy generalization is to introduce an upper bound c_{max} for ℓ in the linear duration invariant:

$$LDI = c_{min} \le \ell \le c_{max} \Rightarrow \sum_{i=1}^{n} c_i \textstyle\int P_i \le c.$$

The decision procedure for this satisfaction problem becomes simpler than for the original problem and is left to readers as an exercise.

It is also an easy generalization to introduce state expressions into the linear duration invariant. Since the states $\{P_1, P_2, \ldots, P_n\}$ are exclusive and complete, any state expression of $\{P_1, P_2, \ldots, P_n\}$ is equivalent to a disjunction of $\{P_1, P_2, \ldots, P_n\}$, e.g.

$$\neg P_1 \; \Leftrightarrow \; P_2 \vee \cdots \vee P_n \quad \text{and} \quad P_1 \wedge P_3 \; \Leftrightarrow \; 0 \,,$$

and therefore the duration of a disjunction of states (P_i) is equal to the sum of the durations of the individual states.

By Theorem 8.11, we can transform any regular language over $\mathcal{T}$ to a normal form unless the linear duration invariant is violated. Hence, the definition of a real-time automaton (in Sect. 8.2) can be generalized in any possible way, as long as the set of untimed sequences of the automaton is regular.

It is also not a difficult generalization to allow several states of the automaton to be labeled with the same DC state variable, as the algorithm presented here requires only that the DC state variables are complete and exclusive.

With these generalizations, it is possible to check whether a linear duration invariant holds for all subintervals with respect to the timed sequences generated by a real-time automaton A, as one can add extra states and transitions (with new upper and lower bounds) to A to simulate this. With this technique it can, for example, be checked whether

$$\square(60 \leq \ell \; \Rightarrow \; 20 \textstyle\int \text{Leak} \leq \ell)$$

holds for the the gas burner automaton. Details are left for the reader.

In the literature, there are other interesting algorithms to check a linear duration invariant against an automaton. For example, [70] reduces the satisfaction problem of linear duration invariants with respect to *timed automata* ([6]) to the *mixed integer programming* problem, and [12] reduces it to the linear programming problem. References [80, 81] solve this problem for a subset of *hybrid automata* ([4, 99]), restrictions on linear duration invariants to reduce the complexity of model checking are considered in [84, 159], and [158] establishes a reduction for a network of real-time automata.

9. State Transitions and Events

9.1 Introduction

A real-time system may comprise both states and events. A state of a system characterizes a *stable* aspect of the system behavior. By *stable*, we mean that once the system enters a state, it will stay in that state throughout a period. An event of a system characterizes an *instant* interaction of the system with its environment. This can drive both the system and its environment to change their behavior dramatically.

For example, in the case of the gas burner, a flame failure caused by the environment can be taken as an event sent to the gas burner from the environment, which drives the gas burner to change its behavior from the normal (NonLeak) state to an abnormal (Leak) state.

Two approaches to extending DC with instant actions have been investigated. In [169], both the state and the event are taken to be "first-class citizens", and the Boolean state model is augmented by events in the form of Boolean-valued δ-functions (i.e. Boolean-valued functions with value 1 only at isolated points). In order to express real-time properties of Boolean-valued δ-functions, *mean values* of Boolean-valued functions were introduced in [169] to replace integrals. Another approach was suggested in [164], where events are introduced as state derivatives called *state transitions*, so that the Boolean state model can be maintained. In this book, we adopt the second approach, since this approach fits better with other parts of the book.

Let S_1 and S_2 be two different Boolean states of a real-time system. They characterize two distinct aspects of the system behavior. $S_i(t) = 1$, for $i = 1, 2$, means that the system stays in S_i at t. We say that the system *satisfies* S_i at t when $S_i(t) = 1$.

A *state transition* of the system from S_1 to S_2 occurs at time t iff immediately *before* t the system is in S_1 (i.e. there exists $\delta > 0$ such that S_1 has value 1 in a period $(t - \delta, t)$), and immediately *after* t the system is in S_2 (i.e. there exists $\delta > 0$ such that S_2 has value 1 in a period $(t, t+\delta)$). Thus, a state transition from S_1 to S_2 at t represents a change of the system behavior from satisfying S_1 to satisfying S_2 at t. Hence, events can be identified by state transitions as the driving force of significant changes in the system behavior.

For example, an event of flame failure in the gas burner can be identified by a state transition from NonLeak to Leak, if flame failure is the only cause of gas leakage in the gas burner.

Let us consider the gas burner example again. A refinement of the two design decisions of the gas burner is given in [127]. A revised version of this refinement is shown as an automaton in Fig. 9.1.

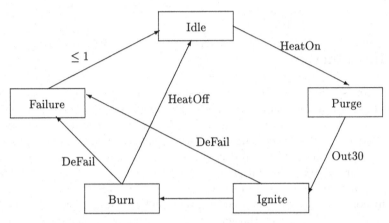

Fig. 9.1. Automaton for refined design of the gas burner

This automaton has five states: Idle, Purge, Ignite, Burn and Failure, which make up a refined Boolean state model of the gas burner. These five states characterize five *exclusive* aspects of the behavior of the gas burner, and form a *complete* characterization of the behavior of the gas burner. That is, at any time, the gas burner is in one and only one of these states.

This automaton responds to four events from its environment: HeatOn, HeatOff, DeFail and Out30. The behavior of the automaton can be explained informally as follows, and a formal specification of the automaton can be found in Sect. 9.4.

Idle: When the gas burner is in the Idle state, the gas is turned off, and the gas burner awaits a heat request. The burner will transfer to the Purge state on receiving a heat request from its environment. In the automaton, a heat request is denoted by the event HeatOn.

Purge: In this state, the gas is still turned off, and the gas burner pauses for 30 seconds by first setting a timer, and then transferring to the Ignite state on receiving a time-out signal after 30 seconds. This time-out signal is denoted by the event Out30.[1]

---

[1] Note that this automaton takes into account only events received by the automaton, such as HeatOn and Out30, and ignores events sent by the automaton, such as setting the timer.

Ignite: In the Ignite state, gas is supplied, and ignition is performed with a pilot flame. If the ignition succeeds, the gas burner transfers to the Burn state. Otherwise, it transfers to the Failure state upon receiving an ignition failure signal, which is presumably detected as soon as the gas supply reaches a leak threshold. The detected failure is denoted by the event DeFail.

Burn: When the gas burner is in the Burn state, the flame is on. The gas burner will remain in the Burn state until the heat request is cancelled (denoted by the event HeatOff) or a flame failure is detected (denoted by the event DeFail). When the heat request is cancelled, the gas is then turned off and the Idle state is entered. When a flame failure occurs, the gas burner immediately transfers to the Failure state.

Failure: In the Failure state, ignition failure and flame failure are treated urgently. The gas valve is closed within one second, and then the gas burner transfers to the Idle state. (In the automaton, by assigning to the transition from Failure to Idle a real-time constraint written as ≤ 1, we mean that the transition from Failure to Idle must take place within one second after the gas burner enters the Failure state.) In the Failure state, i.e. during the treatment of failures, it is assumed that gas is leaking.

From the above description, one can see that the automaton will not respond to the event HeatOn unless it is in Idle, and it will transfer from Idle to Purge when it responds to the event HeatOn. Hence, as far as the behavior of the automaton is concerned, HeatOn can be identified as the state transition of the automaton from Idle to Purge. Similarly, Out30 can be identified as the state transition from Purge to Ignite, and HeatOff as the state transition from Burn to Idle. However, DeFail denotes two causes of gas leakage, namely ignition failure and flame failure. When DeFail happens, the gas burner may be in either the Ignite or the Burn state, and will be driven to the Failure state by DeFail. The event DeFail can therefore be identified as a formula (i.e. a disjunction) of these two state transitions.

State transitions are instant actions. Hence, they can be expressed as formulas that are true in point intervals. A formula expressing a state transition from S_1 to S_2 must have a syntactic structure to indicate the source state S_1 and the destination state S_2 of the state transition.

However, in DC there is no such formula. Two kinds of atomic formulas constructed from states to express state transitions are introduced in Sect. 9.2. These extra formulas are called *transition formulas*.

The semantics of the transition formulas in a point interval can be determined by the properties of states in a neighborhood of the point, since a state transition from S_1 to S_2 occurs at t iff the value of S_1 is 1 throughout some *left* neighborhood of t and the value of S_2 is 1 throughout some *right* neighborhood of t. Thus, state transitions (and events treated as formulas of state transitions) can be formalized in DC without augmentation of the Boolean state model.

The syntax and semantics of transition formulas are given in Sect. 9.2, and extra axioms for transition formulas are given in Sect. 9.3. The extra axioms, together with the axioms and rules of DC, make up a calculus to describe and reason about real-time systems in terms of both states and events. This calculus is called *state transition calculus*. State transition calculus retains the result of relative completeness of DC. A formal description and verification of the refinement of the gas burner shown in Fig. 9.1 are presented in Sect. 9.4.

9.2 Transition Formulas

This section introduces transition formulas, and also demonstrates by examples how to use transition formulas to specify the behavior of real-time systems in terms of both states and events. Among the examples is a NOR circuit.

9.2.1 Formulas $\nwarrow S$, $\nearrow S$, $\diagdown S$ and $\diagup S$

To the syntax of DC, we add the following two special symbols, $\nwarrow$ and $\nearrow$, and the following rule for building formulas:

- If S is a state expression, then $\nwarrow S$ and $\nearrow S$ are formulas, also called *transition* formulas.

The semantics of $\nwarrow S$ and $\nearrow S$ are defined in terms of $\llbracket S \rrbracket$ as follows. Given an interpretation $\mathcal{I}$, a value assignment $\mathcal{V}$ and an interval $[b, e]$,

$$\mathcal{I}, \mathcal{V}, [b, e] \models \nwarrow S \quad \text{iff} \quad \mathcal{I}, \mathcal{V}, [b - \delta, b] \models \llbracket S \rrbracket, \text{ for some } \delta > 0,$$

and

$$\mathcal{I}, \mathcal{V}, [b, e] \models \nearrow S \quad \text{iff} \quad \mathcal{I}, \mathcal{V}, [e, e + \delta] \models \llbracket S \rrbracket, \text{ for some } \delta > 0,$$

where the interpretation $\mathcal{I}$ and the value assignment $\mathcal{V}$ are defined as in Chap. 3. Thus, $\nwarrow S$ or $\nearrow S$ holds for an interval iff S has a constant presence in a left or right neighborhood of the *beginning* or *ending* point, respectively, of the interval. See Fig. 9.2.

Two abbreviations are introduced here:

$$\diagdown S \; \widehat{=} \; \nwarrow S \wedge (\ell = 0)$$
$$\diagup S \; \widehat{=} \; \nearrow S \wedge (\ell = 0).$$

The formula $\diagdown S$ and $\diagup S$ define a constant presence of S in a left and a right neighborhood, respectively, of a *point*. Symbols in bold type, $\nwarrow$ and $\nearrow$, are used for transition formulas over arbitrary intervals, while symbols in ordinary type, $\diagdown$ and $\diagup$, are used for transition formulas over point intervals.

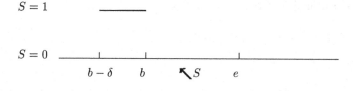

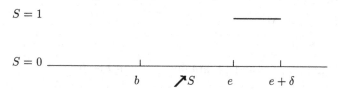

Fig. 9.2. Meaning of $\nwarrow S$ and $\nearrow S$ on the interval $[b, e]$

We can express instant state transitions in terms of $\nwarrow S$ and $\nearrow S$ with propositional connectives. Let S_1 and S_2 be states of a system. The formula

$$\nwarrow S_1 \wedge \nearrow S_2$$

means that S_1 is constantly present in a left neighborhood of a point and S_2 is constantly present in a right neighborhood of this point. Hence, when S_1 and S_2 are distinct states, $(\nwarrow S_1 \wedge \nearrow S_2)$ describes a state transition of the system from S_1 to S_2 at a point. For example,

$$\nwarrow \text{Idle} \wedge \nearrow \text{Purge}$$

describes a state transition of the automaton from Idle to Purge.

Events identified with state transitions can be expressed in terms of transition formulas. For examples, the event HeatOn can be identified with a state transition from Idle to Purge, and hence HeatOn can be expressed as

$$\nwarrow \text{Idle} \wedge \nearrow \text{Purge} .$$

The event DeFail is expressed using a state expression with more structure,

$$\nwarrow (\text{Ignite} \vee \text{Burn}) \wedge \nearrow \text{Failure} ,$$

since it can be identified with two state transitions: from either Ignite or Burn to Failure.

9.2.2 Formulas $\downarrow S$, $\uparrow S$, $\perp S$ and $\top S$

For a state S of a system, the formula

$$\nwarrow S \wedge \nearrow \neg S$$

is true at a point iff the value of S changes from 1 to 0 at a point. That is, the system leaves S at that point. Similarly, $\nwarrow \neg S \wedge \nearrow S$ is true at a point iff the value of S changes from 0 to 1 at that point. That is, the system enters state S at the point.

For these formulas, we introduce the abbreviations

$$\downarrow S \ \hat{=} \ \nwarrow S \wedge \nearrow \neg S$$
$$\uparrow S \ \hat{=} \ \nwarrow \neg S \wedge \nearrow S.$$

The meanings of $\downarrow S$ and $\uparrow S$ are illustrated in Fig. 9.3.

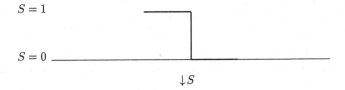

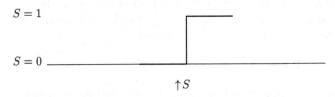

Fig. 9.3. Meanings of $\downarrow S$ and $\uparrow S$

One can also describe state transitions in terms of $\downarrow S$ and $\uparrow S$. Let S_1 and S_2 be two states of a system. Consider the formula

$$\downarrow S_1 \wedge \uparrow S_2.$$

This formula holds at a point iff the system leaves S_1 and, meanwhile, enters S_2 at that point.

When $S_1 = S_2$, the formula $\downarrow S_1 \wedge \uparrow S_2$ cannot hold, since it is a contradiction that a system leaves a state and meanwhile enters the same state. However, when $S_1 \Rightarrow \neg S_2$ (i.e. S_1 and S_2 are exclusive), the formula $\downarrow S_1 \wedge \uparrow S_2$ is meaningful, and forms another description of a state transition of the system from S_1 to S_2. In fact, we prove in the next section that

$$\downarrow S_1 \wedge \uparrow S_2$$

is equivalent to

$$\nwarrow S_1 \wedge \nearrow S_2$$

under the condition that $S_1 \Rightarrow \neg S_2$ is true.

For the case of the automaton in Fig. 9.1, the formula

$$\downarrow \text{Idle} \wedge \uparrow \text{Purge}$$

describes a state transition of the automaton from Idle to Purge. Moreover, the formula

$$\downarrow \text{Idle} \Rightarrow \uparrow \text{Purge}$$

defines Purge as the only transition destination of Idle, and can form part of a formal specification of the automaton. Similarly, the formulas

$$\downarrow \text{Purge} \Rightarrow \uparrow \text{Ignite}$$

and

$$\downarrow \text{Ignite} \Rightarrow \uparrow (\text{Burn} \vee \text{Failure}),$$

can also become a part of a formal specification for the automaton, to define the condition that from Purge, the automaton can transfer only to Ignite, and from Ignite it can transfer either to Burn or to Failure.

In circuit design, a Boolean-valued function S over time can be used to model the voltage of a wire, where $S(t) = 1$ means that the wire S is connected to a power source (i.e. it is at a high voltage) at time t, while $S(t) = 0$ means a connection of the wire S to ground (i.e. low voltage) at t.

The formula $\downarrow S$ describes a *falling edge* of the wire voltage which represents an instant fall of the wire voltage from high to low. Similarly, $\uparrow S$ describes a *rising edge* of the wire voltage, which represents an instant rise of the wire voltage from low to high.

Circuit designers also use formulas to express the stability of a voltage. For example, $\bot S$ is used to mean that the wire represented by S remains connected to ground at some time, and $\top S$ means a continuous connection of the wire to power at some time.

These two formulas can also be defined by the transition formulas

$$\bot S \ \hat{=} \ \nwarrow \neg S \wedge \nearrow \neg S$$
$$\top S \ \hat{=} \ \nwarrow S \wedge \nearrow S.$$

From the definitions, $\bot S$ and $\top S$ hold only for a point interval; $\bot S$ or $\top S$ holds at a point iff S has value 0 or 1, respectively, in both a left and a right neighborhood of the point, as illustrated in Fig. 9.4.

With $\downarrow S$, $\uparrow S$, $\bot S$ and $\top S$, we can specify and reason about the behavior of circuits.

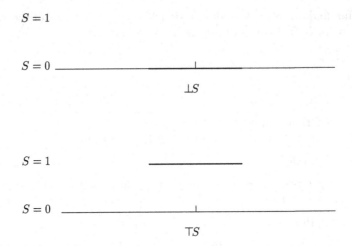

Fig. 9.4. Meanings of ⊥S and TS

9.2.3 Example: NOR Circuit

Consider a NOR circuit with one output wire and two input wires as shown in Fig. 9.5.

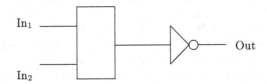

Fig. 9.5. NOR circuit

Let Out, In_1 and In_2 be three Boolean-valued functions (i.e. Boolean states), which denote the voltages of the output and input wires of the circuit. Thus, ↑Out and ↓Out represent output signals of the circuit. If we neglect the propagation delay of signals in the circuit, then the functionality of the circuit is specified by

$$↑\text{Out} ⇔ ↑¬(In_1 ∨ In_2)$$

and

$$↓\text{Out} ⇔ ↓¬(In_1 ∨ In_2).$$

Input signals which cause rising and falling of the output will be immediately propagated to the output wire. In the conventional theory of combinational circuits, it is stated that a rising signal appears at the output of a

NOR circuit iff at that time both the inputs receive a falling signal, or one of the inputs receives a falling signal while the other is at low voltage. With the transition formulas, this statement can be formally expressed as

$$\uparrow \neg(\text{In}_1 \vee \text{In}_2) \iff ((\downarrow \text{In}_1 \wedge \downarrow \text{In}_2) \vee (\downarrow \text{In}_1 \wedge \perp \text{In}_2) \vee (\perp \text{In}_1 \wedge \downarrow \text{In}_2)).$$

Symmetrically, we can express a corresponding statement for a falling signal:

$$\downarrow \neg(\text{In}_1 \vee \text{In}_2) \iff ((\uparrow \text{In}_1 \wedge \uparrow \text{In}_2) \vee (\uparrow \text{In}_1 \wedge \perp \text{In}_2) \vee (\perp \text{In}_1 \wedge \uparrow \text{In}_2)).$$

After we have established a calculus for the transition formulas in the next section, these two statements can be proved.

One can also apply DC to specify and reason about the real-time behavior of combinational and sequential circuits [52]. Although we do not elaborate on real-time issues of circuit design in this book, we indicate here how a *transmission* delay and an *inertial* delay in a rising signal Out can be expressed in DC extended with transition formulas. For example,

$$(\uparrow \neg(\text{In}_1 \vee \text{In}_2) \frown (\ell = d)) \iff ((\ell = d) \frown \uparrow \text{Out})$$

specifies a transmission delay of $d > 0$ in the output rising signal of the NOR circuit, such that the time difference between an input rising signal and its corresponding output rising signal is d, and the formula

$$(\uparrow \neg(\text{In}_1 \vee \text{In}_2) \frown (\lceil \neg(\text{In}_1 \vee \text{In}_2) \rceil \wedge (\ell = d))) \iff ((\ell = d) \frown \uparrow \text{Out})$$

specifies an inertial delay of $d > 0$ of the output rising signal of the NOR circuit. Namely, an input rising signal will not be propagated to the output wire unless the inputs are stable for d time units. Similarly, we can specify the transmission and inertial delays of the falling signals of the circuit by the formulas

$$(\downarrow \neg(\text{In}_1 \vee \text{In}_2) \frown (\ell = d)) \iff ((\ell = d) \frown \downarrow \text{Out})$$

and

$$(\downarrow \neg(\text{In}_1 \vee \text{In}_2) \frown (\lceil \text{In}_1 \vee \text{In}_2 \rceil \wedge (\ell = d))) \iff ((\ell = d) \frown \downarrow \text{Out}),$$

respecitvely.

9.3 Calculus for State Transitions

The state transition calculus described here is a conservative extension of DC. The additional axioms of state transition calculus will be presented in two groups. The first group provides propositional axioms for the transition formulas, and the second group provides axioms with respect to the chop modality. These two groups, together with DC, constitute a relatively complete state transition calculus.

9.3.1 Proof System: Part I

The first group of axioms provides a propositional calculus of the transition formulas:

ST1 $\nwarrow 1$ and $\nearrow 1$.
ST2 $\nwarrow(S_1 \vee S_2) \Leftrightarrow (\nwarrow S_1 \vee \nwarrow S_2)$ and $\nearrow(S_1 \vee S_2) \Leftrightarrow (\nearrow S_1 \vee \nearrow S_2)$.
ST3 $\nwarrow \neg S \Leftrightarrow \neg \nwarrow S$ and $\nearrow \neg S \Leftrightarrow \neg \nearrow S$.
ST4 If $S_1 \Rightarrow S_2$, then $\nwarrow S_1 \Rightarrow \nwarrow S_2$ and $\nearrow S_1 \Rightarrow \nearrow S_2$.

The axiom ST1 formalizes the constant presence of 1 in terms of the transition formulas. ST2 and ST3 certify the distributivity of $\nwarrow$ and $\nearrow$ over disjunction and negation. ST4 defines the monotonicity of $\nwarrow$ and $\nearrow$.

With this group of axioms, we can prove the following theorem.

Theorem 9.1

1. $\neg \nwarrow 0$ and $\neg \nearrow 0$.
2. $\nwarrow(S_1 \wedge S_2) \Leftrightarrow (\nwarrow S_1 \wedge \nwarrow S_2)$ and $\nearrow(S_1 \wedge S_2) \Leftrightarrow (\nearrow S_1 \wedge \nearrow S_2)$.

Proof. We present here proofs of $\neg \nwarrow 0$ and of the distributivity of $\nwarrow$ over conjunction only. A proof of the first case is

$$
\begin{aligned}
&\quad \neg \nwarrow 0 \\
&\Leftrightarrow \neg \nwarrow \neg 1 \quad \text{ST4} \\
&\Leftrightarrow \neg \neg \nwarrow 1 \quad \text{ST3} \\
&\Leftrightarrow \nwarrow 1 \qquad \text{PL} \\
&\Leftrightarrow \text{true} \qquad \text{ST1,}
\end{aligned}
$$

and a proof of the second case is

$$
\begin{aligned}
&\quad \nwarrow(S_1 \wedge S_2) \\
&\Leftrightarrow \nwarrow \neg(\neg S_1 \vee \neg S_2) \qquad \text{ST4} \\
&\Leftrightarrow \neg \nwarrow(\neg S_1 \vee \neg S_2) \qquad \text{ST3} \\
&\Leftrightarrow \neg(\nwarrow \neg S_1 \vee \nwarrow \neg S_2) \qquad \text{ST2} \\
&\Leftrightarrow \neg(\neg \nwarrow S_1 \vee \neg \nwarrow S_2) \quad \text{ST3} \\
&\Leftrightarrow \nwarrow S_1 \wedge \nwarrow S_2 \qquad\qquad \text{PL.}
\end{aligned}
$$

$\square$

A similar propositional calculus for $\nwarrow S$ and $\nearrow S$ can be derived from ST1 – ST4.

Theorem 9.2

1. $\nwarrow 1 \Leftrightarrow (\ell = 0)$ and $\nearrow 1 \Leftrightarrow (\ell = 0)$.
2. $\neg \nwarrow 0$ and $\neg \nearrow 0$.
3. $\nwarrow(S_1 \vee S_2) \Leftrightarrow (\nwarrow S_1 \vee \nwarrow S_2)$ and $\nearrow(S_1 \vee S_2) \Leftrightarrow (\nearrow S_1 \vee \nearrow S_2)$.
4. $\nwarrow \neg S \Leftrightarrow ((\ell = 0) \wedge \neg \nwarrow S)$ and $\nearrow \neg S \Leftrightarrow ((\ell = 0) \wedge \neg \nearrow S)$.
5. $\nwarrow(S_1 \wedge S_2) \Leftrightarrow (\nwarrow S_1 \wedge \nwarrow S_2)$ and $\nearrow(S_1 \wedge S_2) \Leftrightarrow (\nearrow S_1 \wedge \nearrow S_2)$.
6. If $S_1 \Rightarrow S_2$, then $\nwarrow S_1 \Rightarrow \nwarrow S_2$ and $\nearrow S_1 \Rightarrow \nearrow S_2$.

Proof. We present proofs of two of these assertions only.
  The formula $\searrow(S_1 \vee S_2) \Leftrightarrow (\searrow S_1 \vee \searrow S_2)$ is proved as follows:

$$\searrow(S_1 \vee S_2)$$
$$\Leftrightarrow (\ell = 0) \wedge \searrow(S_1 \vee S_2) \quad \text{Def}(\searrow)$$
$$\Leftrightarrow (\ell = 0) \wedge (\searrow S_1 \vee \searrow S_2) \quad \text{ST2}$$
$$\Leftrightarrow \searrow S_1 \vee \searrow S_2 \quad \text{Def}(\searrow).$$

The formula $\searrow \neg S \Leftrightarrow ((\ell = 0) \wedge \neg \searrow S)$ is proved as follows:

$$\searrow \neg S$$
$$\Leftrightarrow (\ell = 0) \wedge \searrow \neg S \quad \text{Def}(\searrow)$$
$$\Leftrightarrow (\ell = 0) \wedge \neg \searrow S \quad \text{ST3}$$
$$\Leftrightarrow (\ell = 0) \wedge (\neg(\ell = 0) \vee \neg \searrow S) \quad \text{PL}$$
$$\Leftrightarrow (\ell = 0) \wedge \neg((\ell = 0) \wedge \searrow S) \quad \text{PL}$$
$$\Leftrightarrow (\ell = 0) \wedge \neg \searrow S \quad \text{Def}(\searrow).$$

□

We can also derive a propositional calculus for $\downarrow S$, $\uparrow S$, $\bot S$ and $\top S$.

Theorem 9.3

1. *Completeness and Exclusiveness*

$$(\uparrow S \vee \downarrow S \vee \top S \vee \bot S) \Leftrightarrow (\ell = 0) \quad and$$

$$\neg(*S \wedge *'S), \ for *, *' \in \{\uparrow, \downarrow, \top, \bot\} \ and * \neq *'.$$

2. *Constant One*
   $\neg \uparrow 1, \quad \neg \downarrow 1, \quad \top 1 \Leftrightarrow (\ell = 0) \quad and \quad \neg \bot 1.$
3. *Constant Zero*
   $\neg \uparrow 0, \quad \neg \downarrow 0, \quad \neg \top 0 \quad and \quad \bot 0 \Leftrightarrow (\ell = 0).$
4. *Disjunction*
   $\uparrow(S_1 \vee S_2) \Leftrightarrow ((\uparrow S_1 \wedge \uparrow S_2) \vee (\uparrow S_1 \wedge \bot S_2) \vee (\bot S_1 \wedge \uparrow S_2)),$
   $\downarrow(S_1 \vee S_2) \Leftrightarrow ((\downarrow S_1 \wedge \downarrow S_2) \vee (\downarrow S_1 \wedge \bot S_2) \vee (\bot S_1 \wedge \downarrow S_2)),$
   $\top(S_1 \vee S_2) \Leftrightarrow (\top S_1 \vee \top S_2 \vee (\downarrow S_1 \wedge \uparrow S_2) \vee (\uparrow S_1 \wedge \downarrow S_2))$ and
   $\bot(S_1 \vee S_2) \Leftrightarrow (\bot S_1 \wedge \bot S_2).$
5. *Negation*
   $\uparrow S \Leftrightarrow \downarrow \neg S, \quad \downarrow S \Leftrightarrow \uparrow \neg S, \quad \top S \Leftrightarrow \bot \neg S \quad and \quad \bot S \Leftrightarrow \top \neg S.$
6. *Conjunction*
   $\uparrow(S_1 \wedge S_2) \Leftrightarrow ((\uparrow S_1 \wedge \uparrow S_2) \vee (\uparrow S_1 \wedge \top S_2) \vee (\top S_1 \wedge \uparrow S_2)),$
   $\downarrow(S_1 \wedge S_2) \Leftrightarrow ((\downarrow S_1 \wedge \downarrow S_2) \vee (\downarrow S_1 \wedge \top S_2) \vee (\top S_1 \wedge \downarrow S_2)),$
   $\top(S_1 \wedge S_2) \Leftrightarrow (\top S_1 \wedge \top S_2) \quad and$
   $\bot(S_1 \wedge S_2) \Leftrightarrow (\bot S_1 \vee \bot S_2 \vee (\uparrow S_1 \wedge \downarrow S_2) \vee (\downarrow S_1 \wedge \uparrow S_2)).$
7. *Congruence*
   If $S_1 \Leftrightarrow S_2$, then $*S_1 \Leftrightarrow *S_2$, where $* \in \{\uparrow, \downarrow, \top, \bot\}$.

Proof. We present only the following proofs.
Proof of $\neg(\uparrow S \wedge \downarrow S)$:

$$\uparrow S \wedge \downarrow S$$
$$\Rightarrow \nwarrow \neg S \wedge \nearrow S \wedge \nwarrow S \wedge \nearrow \neg S \quad \text{Def}(\uparrow, \downarrow)$$
$$\Rightarrow \nwarrow(\neg S \wedge S) \wedge \nearrow(S \wedge \neg S) \quad \text{TH9.2(5)}$$
$$\Rightarrow \nwarrow 0 \wedge \nearrow 0 \quad \text{TH9.2(6)}$$
$$\Rightarrow \text{false} \quad \text{TH9.2(2)}.$$

Proof of $\neg \uparrow 1$:

$$\neg \uparrow 1$$
$$\Leftrightarrow \neg(\nwarrow 0 \wedge \nearrow 1) \quad \text{Def}(\uparrow)$$
$$\Leftrightarrow \neg \nwarrow 0 \ \vee \ \neg \nearrow 1 \quad \text{PL}$$
$$\Leftrightarrow \text{true} \quad \text{TH9.2(2)}.$$

To prove $\perp 0 \Leftrightarrow (\ell = 0)$, we use the definition of $\perp$ and Theorem 9.2(1):

$$\perp 0 \ \Leftrightarrow \ (\nwarrow 1 \wedge \nearrow 1) \ \Leftrightarrow \ \ell = 0.$$

Proof of $\uparrow(S_1 \wedge S_2) \Leftrightarrow ((\uparrow S_1 \wedge \uparrow S_2) \vee (\uparrow S_1 \wedge \mathsf{T} S_2) \vee (\mathsf{T} S_1 \wedge \uparrow S_2))$:

$$\uparrow(S_1 \wedge S_2)$$
$$\Leftrightarrow \nwarrow \neg(S_1 \wedge S_2) \wedge \nearrow(S_1 \wedge S_2) \qquad \text{Def}(\uparrow)$$
$$\Leftrightarrow \nwarrow(\neg S_1 \ \vee \ \neg S_2) \wedge \nearrow(S_1 \wedge S_2) \qquad \text{TH9.2(6)}$$
$$\Leftrightarrow (\nwarrow \neg S_1 \ \vee \ \nwarrow \neg S_2) \wedge \nearrow S_1 \wedge \nearrow S_2 \qquad \text{TH9.2(3)(5)}$$
$$\Leftrightarrow (\nwarrow \neg S_1 \wedge \nearrow S_1 \wedge \nearrow S_2)$$
$$\vee(\nwarrow \neg S_2 \wedge \nearrow S_1 \wedge \nearrow S_2) \qquad \text{PL}$$
$$\Leftrightarrow (\uparrow S_1 \wedge \nearrow S_2) \vee (\uparrow S_2 \wedge \nearrow S_1) \qquad \text{Def}(\uparrow)$$
$$\Leftrightarrow (\uparrow S_1 \wedge \nearrow S_2 \wedge \nwarrow(S_2 \vee \neg S_2))$$
$$\vee(\uparrow S_2 \wedge \nearrow S_1 \wedge \nwarrow(S_1 \vee \neg S_1)) \qquad \text{TH9.2(6)(1)}$$
$$\Leftrightarrow (\uparrow S_1 \wedge \nearrow S_2 \wedge (\nwarrow S_2 \vee \nwarrow \neg S_2))$$
$$\vee(\uparrow S_2 \wedge \nearrow S_1 \wedge (\nwarrow S_1 \vee \nwarrow \neg S_1)) \qquad \text{TH9.2(3)}$$
$$\Leftrightarrow (\uparrow S_1 \wedge ((\nearrow S_2 \wedge \nwarrow S_2) \vee (\nearrow S_2 \wedge \nwarrow \neg S_2)))$$
$$\vee(\uparrow S_2 \wedge ((\nearrow S_1 \wedge \nwarrow S_1) \vee (\nearrow S_1 \wedge \nwarrow \neg S_1))) \qquad \text{PL}$$
$$\Leftrightarrow (\uparrow S_1 \wedge (\mathsf{T} S_2 \vee \uparrow S_2)) \vee (\uparrow S_2 \wedge (\mathsf{T} S_1 \vee \uparrow S_1)) \qquad \text{Def}(\uparrow, \mathsf{T})$$
$$\Leftrightarrow (\uparrow S_1 \wedge \uparrow S_2) \vee (\uparrow S_1 \wedge \mathsf{T} S_2) \vee (\mathsf{T} S_1 \wedge \uparrow S_2) \qquad \text{PL}.$$

Proof of $\uparrow S \Leftrightarrow \downarrow \neg S$:

$$\uparrow S$$
$$\Leftrightarrow \nwarrow \neg S \wedge \nearrow S \qquad \text{Def}(\uparrow)$$
$$\Leftrightarrow \nwarrow \neg S \wedge \nearrow \neg \neg S \quad \text{TH9.2(6)}$$
$$\Leftrightarrow \downarrow \neg S \qquad \text{Def}(\downarrow).$$

□

We are ready to prove three of the statements made in Sect. 9.2.

The statement

$$\text{if } S_1 \Rightarrow \neg S_2, \text{ then } (\downarrow S_1 \wedge \uparrow S_2) \Leftrightarrow (\nwarrow S_1 \wedge \nearrow S_2)$$

is proved as follows:

$$\downarrow S_1 \wedge \uparrow S_2$$
$$\Leftrightarrow \nwarrow S_1 \wedge \nearrow \neg S_1 \wedge \nwarrow \neg S_2 \wedge \nearrow S_2 \quad \text{Def}(\downarrow, \uparrow)$$
$$\Leftrightarrow \nwarrow (S_1 \wedge \neg S_2) \wedge \nearrow (\neg S_1 \wedge S_2) \quad \text{TH9.2(5)}$$
$$\Leftrightarrow \nwarrow S_1 \wedge \nearrow S_2 \quad \text{TH9.2(6), } (S_1 \Rightarrow \neg S_2).$$

The formula

$$\uparrow \neg(\text{In}_1 \vee \text{In}_2) \Leftrightarrow ((\downarrow\text{In}_1 \wedge \downarrow\text{In}_2) \vee (\downarrow\text{In}_1 \wedge \bot\text{In}_2) \vee (\bot\text{In}_1 \wedge \downarrow\text{In}_2))$$

is proved by

$$\uparrow \neg(\text{In}_1 \vee \text{In}_2)$$
$$\Leftrightarrow \downarrow(\text{In}_1 \vee \text{In}_2) \quad \text{TH9.3(5)}$$
$$\Leftrightarrow (\downarrow\text{In}_1 \wedge \downarrow\text{In}_2) \vee (\downarrow\text{In}_1 \wedge \bot\text{In}_2) \vee (\bot\text{In}_1 \wedge \downarrow\text{In}_2) \quad \text{TH9.3(4).}$$

The formula

$$\downarrow \neg(\text{In}_1 \vee \text{In}_2) \Leftrightarrow ((\uparrow\text{In}_1 \wedge \uparrow\text{In}_2) \vee (\uparrow\text{In}_1 \wedge \bot\text{In}_2) \vee (\bot\text{In}_1 \wedge \uparrow\text{In}_2))$$

is proved by

$$\downarrow \neg(\text{In}_1 \vee \text{In}_2)$$
$$\Leftrightarrow \uparrow(\text{In}_1 \vee \text{In}_2) \quad \text{TH9.3(5)}$$
$$\Leftrightarrow (\uparrow\text{In}_1 \wedge \uparrow\text{In}_2) \vee (\uparrow\text{In}_1 \wedge \bot\text{In}_2) \vee (\bot\text{In}_1 \wedge \uparrow\text{In}_2) \quad \text{TH9.3(4).}$$

9.3.2 Proof System: Part II

The second group of axioms consists of two axioms to reason about the transition formulas with respect to the chop modality:

N1 $\nwarrow S \Leftrightarrow (\nwarrow S \frown \text{true})$ and $\nearrow S \Leftrightarrow (\text{true} \frown \nearrow S)$.
N2 $((\ell > 0) \frown \nwarrow S) \Leftrightarrow (\text{true} \frown \lceil S \rceil)$ and $(\nearrow S \frown (\ell > 0)) \Leftrightarrow (\lceil S \rceil \frown \text{true})$.

The axiom N1 expresses the assertion that the truth of $\nwarrow S$ over an interval is determined by $\nwarrow S$ at the beginning point of the interval, and that the truth of $\nearrow S$ over an interval is determined by $\nearrow S$ at the ending point of the interval. N2 formalizes the assertion that $\nwarrow S$ or $\nearrow S$ holds at a point iff there exists a left or right neighborhood, respectively, of the point where S takes the value 1 constantly.

The following theorem can help us to understand these two axioms.

Theorem 9.4

1. *If $\nwarrow S$ or $\nearrow S$ holds in a prefix or suffix, respectively, of an interval, it will hold in the interval:*

$$(\nwarrow S \frown \text{true}) \Rightarrow \nwarrow S \quad \text{and} \quad (\text{true} \frown \nearrow S) \Rightarrow \nearrow S .$$

2. *If $\nwarrow S$ or $\nearrow S$ holds in an interval, it will hold in any prefix or suffix, respectively, of the interval:*

$$\nwarrow S \Rightarrow \neg(\nwarrow \neg S \frown \text{true}) \quad \text{and} \quad \nearrow S \Rightarrow \neg(\text{true} \frown \nearrow \neg S) .$$

3. *$\nwarrow S$ or $\nearrow S$ holds in an interval iff there exists a left or right neighborhood of the beginning or ending point, respectively, of the interval where S takes the value 1 constantly. That is, for any $r > 0$,*

$$((\ell = r) \frown \nwarrow S) \Leftrightarrow (((\ell = r) \wedge (\text{true} \frown \lceil\!\lceil S \rceil\!\rceil)) \frown \text{true})$$

and

$$(\nearrow S \frown (\ell = r)) \Leftrightarrow (\text{true} \frown ((\ell = r) \wedge (\lceil\!\lceil S \rceil\!\rceil \frown \text{true}))) .$$

Proof. We sketch proofs below. Proof of $(\nwarrow S \frown \text{true}) \Rightarrow \nwarrow S$:

$$
\begin{array}{lll}
& \nwarrow S \frown \text{true} & \\
\Rightarrow & \nwarrow S \frown \text{true} \frown \text{true} & \text{N1} \\
\Rightarrow & \nwarrow S \frown \text{true} & \text{M} \\
\Rightarrow & \nwarrow S & \text{N1}.
\end{array}
$$

Proof of $\nwarrow S \Rightarrow \neg(\nwarrow \neg S \frown \text{true})$:

$$
\begin{array}{lll}
& \nwarrow S \wedge (\nwarrow \neg S \frown \text{true}) & \\
\Rightarrow & (\nwarrow S \frown \text{true}) \wedge (\nwarrow \neg S \frown \text{true} \frown \text{true}) & \text{N1} \\
\Rightarrow & (\nwarrow S \wedge \nwarrow \neg S) \frown \text{true} & \text{IL17} \\
\Rightarrow & \text{false} \frown \text{true} & \text{ST3} \\
\Rightarrow & \text{false} & \text{IL13}.
\end{array}
$$

Proof of $((\ell = r) \frown \nwarrow S) \Leftrightarrow (((\ell = r) \wedge (\text{true} \frown \lceil\!\lceil S \rceil\!\rceil)) \frown \text{true})$:

$$
\begin{array}{lll}
& (\ell = r) \frown \nwarrow S & \\
\Leftrightarrow & (\ell = r) \frown \nwarrow S \frown \text{true} & \text{N1} \\
\Leftrightarrow & ((\ell = r) \wedge \text{true} \frown \lceil\!\lceil S \rceil\!\rceil) \frown \text{true} & \text{N2}.
\end{array}
$$

$\square$

From N2, we can establish a theorem expressing the relationship between a state S and the formulas $\uparrow S$, $\downarrow S$, $\mathsf{T}S$ and $\bot S$.

Theorem 9.5 *For any $r > 0$:*

1. $((\ell = r) \frown \uparrow S \frown (\ell > 0)) \Leftrightarrow (((\ell = r) \wedge (\text{true} \frown \lceil \neg S \rceil)) \frown \lceil S \rceil \frown \text{true})$.
2. $((\ell = r) \frown \downarrow S \frown (\ell > 0)) \Leftrightarrow (((\ell = r) \wedge (\text{true} \frown \lceil S \rceil)) \frown \lceil \neg S \rceil \frown \text{true})$.
3. $((\ell = r) \frown TS \frown (\ell > 0)) \Leftrightarrow (((\ell = r) \wedge (\text{true} \frown \lceil S \rceil)) \frown \lceil S \rceil \frown \text{true})$.
4. $((\ell = r) \frown \bot S \frown (\ell > 0)) \Leftrightarrow (((\ell = r) \wedge (\text{true} \frown \lceil \neg S \rceil)) \frown \lceil \neg S \rceil \frown \text{true})$.

Proof. We sketch a proof of the first assertion only, as the rest can be proved similarly.

$$(\ell = r) \frown \uparrow S \frown (\ell > 0)$$
$$\Leftrightarrow (\ell = r) \frown (\diagdown \neg S \wedge \diagup S) \frown (\ell > 0) \qquad \text{Def}(\uparrow)$$
$$\Leftrightarrow ((\ell = r) \wedge (\text{true} \frown \lceil \neg S \rceil)) \frown \lceil S \rceil \frown \text{true} \quad \text{N2}.$$

$\square$

9.3.3 Soundness and Relative Completeness

The proof system of DC, together with ST1 – ST4, N1 and N2, forms the state transition calculus considered here. We formulate here the theorems of the soundness and relative completeness of the state transition calculus, and sketch their proofs.

Theorem 9.6 *The state transition calculus is sound.*

Proof. The reasoning used in the proof of the soundness of DC (Theorem 3.2) can also be applied to the proof of this theorem, provided we can first prove that the additional axioms, ST1 – ST4, N1 and N2, are sound. The soundness of any axiom (designated ϕ) of ST1 – ST3, N1 and N2 can be formulated as the validity of ϕ. That is, for any interpretation $\mathcal{I}$, value assignment $\mathcal{V}$ and interval $[b, e]$,

$$\mathcal{I}, \mathcal{V}, [b, e] \models \phi.$$

The soundness of ST4 is formulated as follows: if $S_1 \Rightarrow S_2$ is valid in propositional logic, then for any interpretation $\mathcal{I}$, value assignment $\mathcal{V}$ and interval $[b, e]$,

$$\mathcal{I}, \mathcal{V}, [b, e] \models \diagdown S_1 \Rightarrow \diagdown S_2$$

and

$$\mathcal{I}, \mathcal{V}, [b, e] \models \diagup S_1 \Rightarrow \diagup S_2.$$

The proof of the soundness of these six axioms and rules is trivial. However, the soundness of ST2 and ST3 relies on the assumption of a finite variability of states in the interpretation $\mathcal{I}$. From the finite variability of S, we can conclude that for any point there must exist a left and a right neighborhood of the point such that in each of these neighborhoods $S_{\mathcal{I}}$ constantly has a value of either 1 or 0. We shall not present details of the proof here.

$\square$

Theorem 9.7 *The state transition calculus is relatively complete.*

Proof. We apply the same technique that was used in the proof of the relative completeness of DC (Theorem 5.1).

To transform a formula ϕ of l state variables of the state transition calculus into a formula of IL, we do the following:

- select k temporal variables, where $k = 2^{2^l}$, and
- select $2k$ temporal propositional letters $X_1, X_2, \ldots, X_k$ and $Y_1, Y_2, \ldots, Y_k$.

We index these temporal propositional letters with the k equivalence classes of the state expressions of the l state variables appearing in ϕ.

Let S be a state expression of the l state variables of ϕ. Then

- the formula $\nwarrow S$ is transformed to $X_{[S]}$, and
- the formula $\nearrow S$ is transformed to $Y_{[S]}$.

The axioms ST1 – ST4, N1 and N2 are transformed accordingly. For example, ST1 is transformed into

$$X_{[1]} \quad \text{and} \quad Y_{[1]},$$

N1 is transformed into a set of formulas of the form

$$X_{[S]} \Leftrightarrow (((\ell = 0) \land X_{[S]})^\frown \text{true}) \quad \text{and} \quad Y_{[S]} \Leftrightarrow (\text{true}^\frown((\ell = 0) \land Y_{[S]})),$$

and ST4 is transformed into a set of formulas of the form

$$X_{[S_1]} \Rightarrow X_{[S_2]} \quad \text{and} \quad Y_{[S_1]} \Rightarrow Y_{[S_2]},$$

where S_1 and S_2 range over the state expressions of the l state variables of ϕ, and $S_1 \Rightarrow S_2$ holds in propositional logic.

In order to follow the proof of Theorem 5.1, all lemmas and theorems established for Theorem 5.1 must be revised to conclude the necessary properties of not only the selected temporal variables, but also the selected propositional letters. We can therefore prove the relative completeness of the state transition calculus. However, the details of the proof are left to readers as an exercise.   □

9.4 Example: Automaton

This section presents, in the state transition calculus, a formal specification and verification of the refinement of the gas burner example shown as an automaton in Fig. 9.1.

9.4.1 Specification

A formal specification of the automaton can be given by formulating properties of its states, state transitions and events in the state transition calculus. The resulting formulas are considered nonlogical axioms to define Boolean state models of the behavior of the automaton. Let

Idle, Purge, Ignite, Burn and Failure

be the five state variables used to denote the corresponding states of the automaton. The formulas (referred to as Auto1(a), etc. in Sect. 9.4.2) are the following.

1. *State Completeness and Exclusiveness*
   (a) At any time, the automaton is in one of its five states:

   $$\lceil\ \rceil \lor \lceil\mathrm{Idle} \lor \mathrm{Purge} \lor \mathrm{Ignite} \lor \mathrm{Burn} \lor \mathrm{Failure}\rceil\,.$$

   (b) At any time, the automaton is in at most one of the five states:

   $$\lceil\ \rceil \lor \lceil \bigwedge_{S_1 \neq S_2} (S_1 \Rightarrow \neg S_2)\rceil\,,$$

   where S_1 and S_2 range over the set of the five state variables.
2. *Events and State Transitions*
   (a) Four events:

   $$
   \begin{aligned}
   \mathrm{HeatOn} &\cong (\downarrow\mathrm{Idle} \land \uparrow\mathrm{Purge}) \\
   \mathrm{Out30} &\cong (\downarrow\mathrm{Purge} \land \uparrow\mathrm{Ignite}) \\
   \mathrm{DeFail} &\cong (\downarrow(\mathrm{Ignite} \lor \mathrm{Burn}) \land \uparrow\mathrm{Failure}) \\
   \mathrm{HeatOff} &\cong (\downarrow\mathrm{Burn} \land \uparrow\mathrm{Idle})\,.
   \end{aligned}
   $$

   (b) Seven state transitions:

   $$
   \begin{aligned}
   \downarrow\mathrm{Idle} &\Rightarrow \uparrow\mathrm{Purge} \\
   \downarrow\mathrm{Purge} &\Rightarrow \uparrow\mathrm{Ignite} \\
   \downarrow\mathrm{Ignite} &\Rightarrow \uparrow(\mathrm{Burn} \lor \mathrm{Failure}) \\
   \downarrow\mathrm{Burn} &\Rightarrow \uparrow(\mathrm{Idle} \lor \mathrm{Failure}) \\
   \downarrow\mathrm{Failure} &\Rightarrow \uparrow\mathrm{Idle}\,.
   \end{aligned}
   $$

3. *Real-time Constraints*
   (a) The event Out30 appears 30 seconds after the automaton enters Purge:

   $$(\uparrow\mathrm{Purge}\,^\frown(\ell = 30)) \Leftrightarrow (\uparrow\mathrm{Purge}\,^\frown\lceil\mathrm{Purge}\rceil\,^\frown\mathrm{Out30})\,.$$

   (b) Treatment of a failure must be finished within one second:

   $$\lceil\mathrm{Failure}\rceil \Rightarrow (\ell \leq 1)\,.$$

The above three groups of formulas constitute a specification of the automaton. Let Auto denote the set of all formulas in these three groups. To verify the refinement, a deduction

$$\text{Auto} \vdash Des_1 \wedge Des_2$$

must be established in the state transition calculus. This is done in the following subsection.

9.4.2 Verification

Failure is the only state of the automaton in which gas is leaking. Thus, we can introduce Leak as corresponding to Failure:

$$\text{Leak} \;\hat=\; \text{Failure}.$$

We present a lemma first.

Lemma 9.1 *For any state expression* S,

$$(\llbracket S \rrbracket \,\hat{}\, \text{true} \,\hat{}\, \lceil \neg S \rceil) \;\Rightarrow\; (\llbracket S \rrbracket \,\hat{}\, \downarrow S \,\hat{}\, \text{true} \,\hat{}\, \lceil \neg S \rceil).$$

Proof. The proof is by induction using Theorem 3.5, and the induction hypothesis is

$$R(X) \;\hat=\; (\llbracket S \rrbracket \,\hat{}\, X \,\hat{}\, \lceil \neg S \rceil) \;\Rightarrow\; (\llbracket S \rrbracket \,\hat{}\, \downarrow S \,\hat{}\, \text{true} \,\hat{}\, \lceil \neg S \rceil).$$

The base case $\vdash R(\lceil\;\rceil)$ is established as follows:

$$
\begin{aligned}
&\llbracket S \rrbracket \,\hat{}\, \lceil\;\rceil \,\hat{}\, \lceil \neg S \rceil \\
\Rightarrow\; &\llbracket S \rrbracket \,\hat{}\, \lceil \neg S \rceil && \text{IL18} \\
\Rightarrow\; &\exists x > 0.((\ell = x) \wedge \lceil S \rceil) \,\hat{}\, \lceil \neg S \rceil && \text{Def}(\llbracket S \rrbracket) \\
\Rightarrow\; &\exists x.((\ell = x) \wedge \lceil S \rceil) \,\hat{}\, \downarrow S \,\hat{}\, \lceil \neg S \rceil && \text{TH9.5(2)} \\
\Rightarrow\; &\llbracket S \rrbracket \,\hat{}\, \downarrow S \,\hat{}\, \text{true} \,\hat{}\, \lceil \neg S \rceil && \text{L3.}
\end{aligned}
$$

The inductive step is

$$R(X) \vdash R(\lceil\;\rceil \vee (\llbracket S \rrbracket \,\hat{}\, X) \vee (\lceil \neg S \rceil \,\hat{}\, X)),$$

where the formula $R(\lceil\;\rceil \vee (\llbracket S \rrbracket \,\hat{}\, X) \vee (\lceil \neg S \rceil \,\hat{}\, X))$ is:

$$
\begin{aligned}
&\llbracket S \rrbracket \,\hat{}\, (\lceil\;\rceil \vee (\llbracket S \rrbracket \,\hat{}\, X) \vee (\lceil \neg S \rceil \,\hat{}\, X)) \,\hat{}\, \lceil \neg S \rceil \\
\Rightarrow\; &(\llbracket S \rrbracket \,\hat{}\, \downarrow S \,\hat{}\, \text{true} \,\hat{}\, \lceil \neg S \rceil).
\end{aligned}
$$

Since $\llbracket S \rrbracket \,\hat{}\, (\lceil\;\rceil \vee (\llbracket S \rrbracket \,\hat{}\, X) \vee (\lceil \neg S \rceil \,\hat{}\, X)) \,\hat{}\, \lceil \neg S \rceil$ implies, by IL14,

$$
\begin{aligned}
&\llbracket S \rrbracket \,\hat{}\, \lceil\;\rceil \,\hat{}\, \lceil \neg S \rceil \\
\vee\; &(\llbracket S \rrbracket \,\hat{}\, (\llbracket S \rrbracket \,\hat{}\, X) \,\hat{}\, \lceil \neg S \rceil) \\
\vee\; &(\llbracket S \rrbracket \,\hat{}\, (\lceil \neg S \rceil \,\hat{}\, X) \,\hat{}\, \lceil \neg S \rceil),
\end{aligned}
$$

it suffices (by PL) to prove the following three cases in order to establish the inductive step:

1. $R(X) \vdash R(\lceil\ \rceil)$: this is covered by the base case $\vdash R(\lceil\ \rceil)$.
2. $R(X) \vdash R(\lceil S \rceil ^\frown X)$:

$$\lceil S \rceil ^\frown \lceil S \rceil ^\frown X ^\frown \lceil \neg S \rceil$$
$$\Rightarrow \quad \lceil S \rceil ^\frown X ^\frown \lceil \neg S \rceil \qquad\qquad \text{DC17}$$
$$\Rightarrow \quad \lceil S \rceil ^\frown \downarrow S ^\frown \text{true} ^\frown \lceil \neg S \rceil \quad R(X).$$

3. $R(X) \vdash R(\lceil \neg S \rceil ^\frown X)$:

$$\lceil S \rceil ^\frown \lceil \neg S \rceil ^\frown X ^\frown \lceil \neg S \rceil$$
$$\Rightarrow \quad \lceil S \rceil ^\frown \downarrow S ^\frown \text{true} ^\frown \lceil \neg S \rceil ^\frown X ^\frown \lceil \neg S \rceil \quad R(\lceil\ \rceil)$$
$$\Rightarrow \quad \lceil S \rceil ^\frown \downarrow S ^\frown \text{true} ^\frown \lceil \neg S \rceil \qquad\qquad\qquad \text{M.}$$

$\square$

With this lemma, we can prove the following theorem.

Theorem 9.8

$$\text{Auto} \vdash Des_1 \wedge Des_2\,,$$

where

$$Des_1 \;\widehat{=}\; \square(\lceil\text{Leak}\rceil \Rightarrow \ell \leq 1) \quad and$$
$$Des_2 \;\widehat{=}\; \square((\lceil\text{Leak}\rceil ^\frown \lceil\neg\text{Leak}\rceil ^\frown \lceil\text{Leak}\rceil) \Rightarrow \ell \geq 30)\,.$$

Proof. The case $\text{Auto} \vdash Des_1$ is established by using Auto3(b) and IL4. We sketch a deduction of

$$\text{Auto} \vdash Des_2$$

in the following.

$$\lceil\text{Leak}\rceil ^\frown \lceil\neg\text{Leak}\rceil ^\frown \lceil\text{Leak}\rceil$$
$$\Rightarrow \quad \lceil\text{Leak}\rceil ^\frown \downarrow\text{Leak} ^\frown \lceil\neg\text{Leak}\rceil ^\frown \lceil\text{Leak}\rceil \qquad \text{TH9.5(2)}$$
$$\Rightarrow \quad \lceil\text{Leak}\rceil ^\frown \uparrow\text{Idle} ^\frown \lceil\neg\text{Leak}\rceil ^\frown \lceil\text{Leak}\rceil \qquad \text{Auto2(b)}$$
$$\Rightarrow \quad (\ell > 0) ^\frown \lceil\text{Idle}\rceil ^\frown \text{true} ^\frown \lceil\text{Leak}\rceil \qquad \text{TH9.5(1)}$$
$$\Rightarrow \quad (\ell > 0) ^\frown \lceil\text{Idle}\rceil ^\frown \text{true} ^\frown \lceil\text{Leak} \wedge \neg\text{Idle}\rceil \qquad \text{Auto1(b)}$$
$$\Rightarrow \quad (\ell > 0) ^\frown \downarrow\text{Idle} ^\frown \text{true} ^\frown \lceil\text{Leak}\rceil \qquad \text{LM9.1}$$
$$\Rightarrow \quad (\ell > 0) ^\frown \uparrow\text{Purge} ^\frown \text{true} ^\frown \lceil\text{Leak}\rceil \qquad \text{Auto2(b)}$$
$$\Rightarrow \quad \text{true} ^\frown \uparrow\text{Purge} ^\frown \lceil\text{Purge}\rceil ^\frown \text{true} ^\frown \lceil\text{Leak}\rceil \qquad \text{TH9.5(1)}$$
$$\Rightarrow \quad \text{true} ^\frown \uparrow\text{Purge} ^\frown \lceil\text{Purge}\rceil ^\frown$$
$$\qquad\qquad \text{true} ^\frown \lceil\text{Leak} \wedge \neg\text{Purge}\rceil \qquad \text{Auto1(b)}$$
$$\Rightarrow \quad \text{true} ^\frown \uparrow\text{Purge} ^\frown \lceil\text{Purge}\rceil ^\frown \downarrow\text{Purge} ^\frown \text{true} \qquad \text{LM9.1}$$
$$\Rightarrow \quad \text{true} ^\frown \uparrow\text{Purge} ^\frown \lceil\text{Purge}\rceil ^\frown$$
$$\qquad\qquad (\downarrow\text{Purge} \wedge \uparrow\text{Ignite}) ^\frown \text{true} \qquad \text{Auto2(b)}$$
$$\Rightarrow \quad \text{true} ^\frown \uparrow\text{Purge} ^\frown \lceil\text{Purge}\rceil ^\frown \text{Out30} ^\frown \text{true} \qquad \text{Auto2(a)}$$
$$\Rightarrow \quad \ell \geq 30 \qquad \text{Auto3(a).}$$

By introducing $\square$ as in IL4, we can derive Des_2 from the conclusion obtained above.

$\square$

10. Superdense State Transitions

10.1 Introduction

In the Boolean state model, we assume state *stability*. That is, whenever a system enters a state, it will stay in the state throughout some period, although the length of the period can be arbitrarily small. Therefore, a state transition is a transition of a system from one stable state to another, and two consecutive state transitions must pass through an intermediate stable state which separates these two state transitions from each other. For example, let

$$\searrow S_1 \wedge \nearrow S_2 \quad \text{and} \quad \searrow S_2 \wedge \nearrow S_3$$

be two consecutive state transitions of a system as shown in Fig. 10.1. The transition $\searrow S_1 \wedge \nearrow S_2$ occurs at time t, and $\searrow S_2 \wedge \nearrow S_3$ occurs at $(t + \delta)$. They are separated by a period of presence of the intermediate state S_2. The distance between them (i.e. the length of the presence period of S_2) is $\delta > 0$.

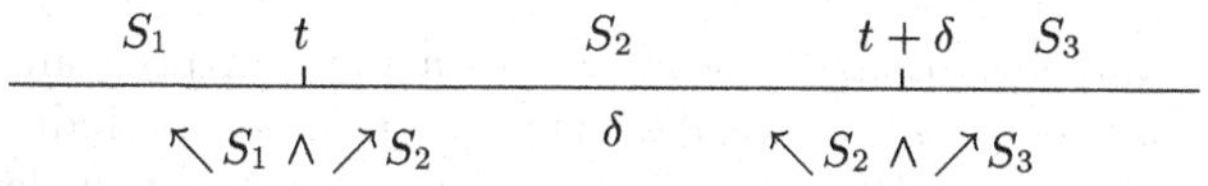

Fig. 10.1. Two transitions separated by a stable state

As δ can be arbitrarily small, one can ask the question of what could happen if δ becomes zero. That is, what could happen if the transitions $\searrow S_1 \wedge \nearrow S_2$ and $\searrow S_2 \wedge \nearrow S_3$ occur consecutively and also instantaneously.

It is clear that, by compressing the period δ of S_2 in Fig. 10.1 into a point, one can obtain the situation shown in Fig. 10.2, where $(t + \delta) = t$ (i.e. $\delta = 0$), and S_1 holds in a left neighborhood of t and S_3 holds in a right neighborhood of t. In other words, we obtain a situation with a state transition from S_1 to S_3 at time t.

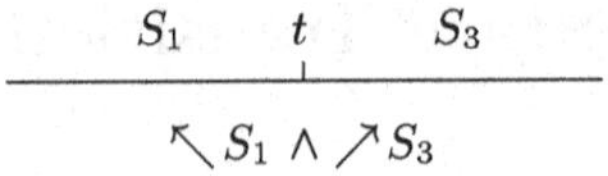

$$\frac{S_1 \quad t \quad S_3}{\nwarrow S_1 \wedge \nearrow S_3}$$

Fig. 10.2. Effect of a superdense transition

Therefore, it is interesting to allow the two consecutive state transitions

$$\nwarrow S_1 \wedge \nearrow S_2 \quad \text{and} \quad \nwarrow S_2 \wedge \nearrow S_3$$

to happen instantaneously by assuming that the intermediate state S_2 is unstable and invisible, the result beeing the state transition

$$\nwarrow S_1 \wedge \nearrow S_3 \,.$$

These two consecutive and instantaneous state transitions are called *superdense transitions*. In general, a finite sequence of state transitions which takes place instantaneously will be called a superdense state transition. By *superdense*, we mean that even a time point has a dense structure, so that it can host a series of state transitions.

The superdense state transition is not only a conceptual generalization of an ordinary state transition. It also has important applications to real-time systems. We present in the following subsection an application that motivates the introduction of superdense state transitions.

10.1.1 Superdense Computation

In a digital control system, there is always a piece of program, hosted in a computer, that acts as a controller. The program can periodically receive sampled outputs from a plant, and calculate and send control signals to the plant. The program may be written in an OCCAM-like language as a loop where the body has the form

> sensor?x; CAL(x, u); actuator!u; wait T ,

where CAL(x, u) stands for a program segment, which decides the current control signal from the current sampled data x and the previous control signal u. T is the sampling period.

Typically, the time spent in the calculation of control signals is negligible compared with the sampling period T. So control engineers can comfortably make the assumption that the calculation program (i.e. CAL(x, u)) takes no time, and hence the plant does not evolve during the calculation. Thus, CAL(x, u) becomes a sequence of statements which are executed one by one, but consume no time. The receiving and the sending (i.e. sensor?x and actuator!u) in the program are separated from CAL(x, u), and, since

CAL(x, u) consumes no time, they can also happen consecutively and instantaneously, provided the partners (i.e. sensor and actuator) are willing to communicate.

A computation of a sequence of operations which is assumed to be timeless is called a *superdense computation.*

A superdense computation is in fact an abstraction of a real-time computation within a context with a grand time granularity. For instance, in the digital control system, the cycle time of the computer may be nanoseconds, while the sampling period of the plant may be seconds. In other words, the calculation (CAL(x, u)) and the communications (sensor?x and actuator!u) may take microseconds or milliseconds, while the sampling period T may be seconds. A computation time with a fine time granularity is only negligible for computations that do not have infinite loops. Otherwise, the situation is known as the *Zeno phenomenon* or *finite divergence* [48].

Superdense computation also arises in the area of program refinement. One of the well-known algebraic laws for untimed programs is the *combine* law of assignments [129]. The combine law can allow one to conclude, for example, that the two consecutive assignments

$$x := x + 1; x := x + 2$$

are equivalent to the single assignment

$$x := x + 3 .$$

In order to retain the combine law for real-time programs, one may assume that the execution of an assignment takes no time. Otherwise, the execution time of two assignments may be twice the execution time of a single assignment, and it is hard to maintain the combine law. Under the assumption that assignments take no time, the following two consecutive assignments constitute a superdense computation:

$$x := x + 1; x := x + 2 .$$

A notion of superdense computation is adopted in Esterel [10] and statecharts [53], and semantic models of superdense computation were introduced in [67, 73, 91]. In this chapter, we express superdense computation in DC by using superdense state transitions.

A single step of a computation can be expressed as a state transition, and hence a superdense computation can be expressed as a formula of superdense state transitions. The reason is that the value of a program variable can be interpreted as a state. A real-valued variable x of a program can change its value during the execution of the program. One can interpret x as a function of time,

$$x : \text{Time} \to \mathbb{R} .$$

For $v \in \mathbb{R}$, the property

$$x = v$$

becomes a time-dependent property of x.

It is reasonable to assume that the program is *timely progressive*, and hence a program variable can only change its value finitely many times in any finite period. Thus, the property $x = v$ is *finitely variable*, and can be taken as a Boolean state of the program.

Let us use $x = v$ as an overloaded notation to designate the program state which characterizes the property $x = v$. The assignment

$$x := x + 1$$

can then be expressed as a formula of state transitions

$$\nwarrow(x = v) \wedge \nearrow(x = v + 1),$$

where we assume that the initial value of x before the assignment is v. This formula defines the condition that the assignment first inherits a value (v) of x from its predecessor in the left neighborhood, and then passes the new value $(v + 1)$ to its successor in the right neighborhood. Similarly, the assignment

$$x := x + 2$$

can be expressed as

$$\nwarrow(x = v + 1) \wedge \nearrow(x = v + 3)$$

if we assume that the initial value of x before the assignment is $(v + 1)$.

A superdense computation of the two consecutive assignments

$$x := x + 1; x := x + 2$$

assumes that the passing of a value of x from $(x := x+1)$ to $(x := x+2)$ takes no time. Thus, the intermediate state $(x = v + 1)$ of the program is unstable and invisible. The computation can then be expressed as a superdense state transition

$$\nwarrow(x = v) \wedge \nearrow(x = v + 1),$$

followed by

$$\nwarrow(x = v + 1) \wedge \nearrow(x = v + 3).$$

The result of these superdense state transitions is

$$\nwarrow(x = v) \wedge \nearrow(x = v + 3),$$

which expresses the assignment

$$x := x + 3$$

under the assumption that the initial value of x before the assignment is v.

10.1.2 Superdense Chop

The chop modality can chop a nonpoint interval into subintervals, but cannot chop a point. At a point, the chop modality degenerates into the conjunction connective. For example,

$$((\diagdown S_1 \wedge \nearrow S_2) \frown (\diagdown S_2 \wedge \nearrow S_3)) \Leftrightarrow ((\diagdown S_1 \wedge \nearrow S_2) \wedge (\diagdown S_2 \wedge \nearrow S_3)).$$

Thus, with the chop modality, one can express two simultaneous state transitions at a time point, but cannot express two consecutive state transitions at a time point.

In order to express superdense state transitions in DC, we need a new modality to introduce a dense structure into a point. The new modality is called the *superdense chop* and is denoted by •. It can map a time instant in a *grand* time space (called *macro* time in [73]) into a nonpoint interval in a *fine* time space (called *micro* time in [73]), so that an instant action (such as the value passing of x) in a grand time space can take some time in a fine time space, and hence an unstable intermediate state (such as x = v + 1) of a superdense state transition in the grand time space can become stable in the fine time space.

To explain the meaning of the superdense chop, let us consider two state transitions: $(\diagdown S_1 \wedge \nearrow S_2)$ and $(\diagdown S_2 \wedge \nearrow S_3)$. Combining them with the superdense chop, we obtain the formula

$$(\diagdown S_1 \wedge \nearrow S_2) \bullet (\diagdown S_2 \wedge \nearrow S_3).$$

Suppose that an *interpretation* of states, $\mathcal{I}$, is given. Then we define the meaning of • by stipulating that this formula is satisfied by $\mathcal{I}$ at a point t iff there exists a *refined* interpretation of states (designated $\mathcal{I}'$). In $\mathcal{I}'$, the point t of $\mathcal{I}$ is expanded into an interval $[t, t + \delta]$ of $\mathcal{I}'$ (for some $\delta > 0$), such that $\mathcal{I}'$ satisfies $(\diagdown S_1 \wedge \nearrow S_2)$ at time t and $(\diagdown S_2 \wedge \nearrow S_3)$ at time $t + \delta$, and the intermediate state S_2 holds *stably* throughout the interval $(t, t + \delta)$, which links the two transitions in $\mathcal{I}'$. This situation is sketched in Fig. 10.3.

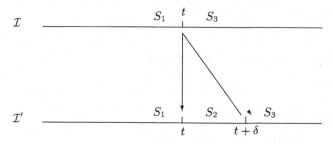

Fig. 10.3. Refined interpretation for the superdense chop

In the above explanation, both $\mathcal{I}$ and $\mathcal{I}'$ are interpretations of states, and the relation between these two interpretations is quite similar to the relation between the value assignments $\mathcal{V}$ and $\mathcal{V}'$ with which we introduce semantics for quantification over a global variable. In [60] and [163], it is indicated that the superdense chop can be defined by the original chop if we allow quantification over a state variable.

A formal calculus for superdense state transitions, called *superdense state transition calculus*, is presented in Sect. 10.2. Using this calculus, we define in Sect. 10.3 a real-time semantics for an OCCAM-like language with superdense computations.

10.2 Calculus for Superdense State Transitions

10.2.1 Syntax

The superdense state transition calculus contains durations of states, i.e. $\int S$, as *terms*, and transition formulas, i.e. $\searchpunch S$ and $\nearrow S$, as *atomic formulas*. The conventional connectives and quantifiers are also adopted. However, this calculus contains the superdense chop modality, $\bullet$, instead of the original chop modality, $\frown$. In other words, formulas of the superdense state transition calculus can be obtained from formulas of the state transition calculus presented in Chap. 9 by replacing $\frown$ with $\bullet$ and vice versa.

In this section we shall use the fact that if ϕ is a formula of the superdense state transition calculus, and $\phi[\frown/\bullet]$ is obtained from ϕ by replacing $\bullet$ with $\frown$, then $\phi[\frown/\bullet]$ is a formula of the state transition calculus. Furthermore, if ϕ does not contain any transition formulas (i.e. $\searchpunch, \nearrow \notin \phi$), then $\phi[\frown/\bullet]$ becomes a formula of DC.

10.2.2 Semantics

The calculus retains the Boolean state model. Only the semantics of $\bullet$ need to be explained, as all the other semantic definitions remain as in Chap. 9.

The semantics of $\phi \bullet \psi$ is as follows. Given an interpretation $\mathcal{I}$, a value assignment $\mathcal{V}$ and an interval $[b, e]$,

$$\mathcal{I}, \mathcal{V}, [b, e] \models \phi \bullet \psi$$

iff there exist $m \in [b, e]$, $\delta > 0$ and $\mathcal{I}'$ such that

$$\mathcal{I}', \mathcal{V}, [b, m] \models \phi \quad \text{and} \quad \mathcal{I}', \mathcal{V}, [m + \delta, e + \delta] \models \psi,$$

and for every state variable P,

$$P_{\mathcal{I}'}(t) = \begin{cases} P_{\mathcal{I}}(t) & \text{for } t \leq m \\ P_{\mathcal{I}}(t - \delta) & \text{for } t \geq (m + \delta) \\ P_{\mathcal{I}'}(m + \delta/2) & \text{for } m < t < (m + \delta). \end{cases}$$

In the semantic definition,

$$P_{\mathcal{I}'}(t) = P_{\mathcal{I}'}(m + \delta/2) \quad (m < t < (m + \delta))$$

expresses the condition that every state variable P (and hence every state) has a constant value in the inserted interval $(m, m+\delta)$. The intermediate, invisible value of P in a superdense state transition expressed by the superdense chop $\bullet$ is represented in the inserted interval $(m, m + \delta)$.

From the semantic definition of $\phi \bullet \psi$, we can prove that the formula

$$\nearrow S \bullet \nwarrow S$$

is valid for any *consistent* state S (i.e. S is not equivalent to 0).

Let $\mathcal{I}$, $\mathcal{V}$ and $[b, e]$ be an arbitrarily given interpretation, value assignment and interval. We establish

$$\mathcal{I}, \mathcal{V}, [b, e] \models \nearrow S \bullet \nwarrow S$$

by letting m be an arbitrary point in $[b, e]$, δ be an arbitrary positive real number and $\mathcal{I}'$ be an interpretation obtained from $\mathcal{I}$ by inserting an interval $(m, m + \delta)$, such that all states have constant values in $(m, m + \delta)$, and

$$S_{\mathcal{I}'}(t) = 1 \quad \text{for} \quad m < t < (m + \delta).$$

That is, state S can be taken as the intermediate state of the superdense state transition expressed by $(\nearrow S \bullet \nwarrow S)$.

However, for any state S, the formula

$$\nearrow S \bullet \nwarrow \neg S$$

is never satisfiable, since for any m and δ, one cannot find a value of S in the interval $(m, m + \delta)$ inserted to obtain $\mathcal{I}'$ such that $\nearrow S$ is satisfied in $[b, m]$ and at the same time $\nwarrow \neg S$ is satisfied in $[m + \delta, e + \delta]$. For example, if S is constant and equal to 1 in $(m, m + \delta)$ for $\mathcal{I}'$, then $\nearrow S$ is satisfied by $\mathcal{I}'$, but $\nwarrow \neg S$ is violated by $\mathcal{I}'$. In other words, $(\nearrow S \bullet \nwarrow \neg S)$ expresses an impossible superdense state transition, since no intermediate states exist for it.

10.2.3 Proof System

In this section, we present the axioms and rules of the superdense state transition calculus.

From the definition of $\bullet$, it is obvious that $\bullet$ is *associative*, *distributive* (over $\vee$ and $\exists$) and *monotone*. Hence we have the following axioms.

SDC1 $(\phi_1 \bullet (\phi_2 \bullet \phi_3)) \Leftrightarrow ((\phi_1 \bullet \phi_2) \bullet \phi_3).$

SDC2 Suppose x is not free in ψ.

$$((\phi_1 \vee \phi_2) \bullet \phi_3) \Leftrightarrow ((\phi_1 \bullet \phi_3) \vee (\phi_2 \bullet \phi_3)).$$
$$(\phi_3 \bullet (\phi_1 \vee \phi_2)) \Leftrightarrow ((\phi_3 \bullet \phi_1) \vee (\phi_3 \bullet \phi_2)).$$
$$((\exists x.\phi) \bullet \psi) \Leftrightarrow \exists x.(\phi \bullet \psi).$$
$$(\psi \bullet \exists x.\phi) \Leftrightarrow \exists x.(\psi \bullet \phi).$$

SDC3 If $(\phi_2 \Rightarrow \phi_3)$, then

$$(\phi_1 \bullet \phi_2) \Rightarrow (\phi_1 \bullet \phi_3) \quad \text{and} \quad (\phi_2 \bullet \phi_1) \Rightarrow (\phi_3 \bullet \phi_1).$$

A state S can become an intermediate state to link the two formulas $(\phi \wedge \nearrow S)$ and $(\nwarrow S \wedge \psi)$ if ϕ and ψ place no demands on the intermediate state. However, no intermediate states can link $\nearrow S$ and $\nwarrow \neg S$. Hence, we introduce the following axioms.

SDC4 If S is *consistent*, $\nearrow \not\subseteq \phi$ and $\nwarrow \not\subseteq \psi$, then

$$((\phi \wedge \nearrow S) \bullet (\nwarrow S \wedge \psi)) \Leftrightarrow (\phi \bullet \psi).$$

SDC5

$$(\nearrow S \bullet \nwarrow \neg S) \Leftrightarrow \text{false}.$$

When $\nwarrow \not\subseteq \phi$, the formula $(\nwarrow S \wedge \phi)$ merely places on a left neighborhood the requirement that S holds. The same requirement is placed by $(\nwarrow S \bullet \phi)$. Thus, we have:

SDC6 If $\nwarrow \not\subseteq \phi$, then

$$(\nwarrow S \bullet \phi) \Leftrightarrow (\nwarrow S \wedge \phi).$$

Symmetrically, if $\nearrow \not\subseteq \phi$, then

$$(\phi \bullet \nearrow S) \Leftrightarrow (\phi \wedge \nearrow S).$$

The difference between $\bullet$ and $\frown$ disappears if we are not concerned with the transition formulas.

SDC7 If $\nwarrow, \nearrow \not\subseteq \phi$, and $\phi[\frown/\bullet]$ is provable in DC, then ϕ is provable in the superdense state transition calculus.

With SDC7 we can, for example, prove

$$(\text{true} \bullet \text{true}) \Leftrightarrow \text{true},$$

$$((\smallint S = x) \bullet (\smallint S = y)) \Leftrightarrow \smallint S = (x + y) \quad (x, y \geq 0), \text{ and}$$

$$(\lceil S \rceil \bullet \lceil S \rceil) \Leftrightarrow \lceil S \rceil,$$

since the above three formulas contain no occurrences of $\nwarrow$ or $\nearrow$, and

$$(\text{true} \frown \text{true}) \Leftrightarrow \text{true},$$

$$((\textstyle\int S = x) \frown (\textstyle\int S = y)) \Leftrightarrow \textstyle\int S = (x + y) \quad (x, y \geq 0), \quad \text{and}$$

$$(\lceil S \rceil \frown \lceil S \rceil) \Leftrightarrow \lceil S \rceil$$

are provable in DC.

The semantics of the transition formulas $\nwarrow S$ and $\nearrow S$ is as given in the state transition calculus described in Chap. 9. Therefore, the axioms ST1 – ST4 can also be adopted here. However, axioms N1 and N2 cannot be used in the superdense state transition calculus, since they are expressed in terms of the original chop, $\frown$. In fact, SDC4 – SDC6 replace N1 and N2 in the context of $\bullet$.

We have the result that SDC1 – SDC7, together with ST1 – ST4, constitute the superdense state transition calculus.

10.2.4 Theorems

We prove the following theorems. In the proofs, predicate calculus is tacitly assumed.

Theorem 10.1

$$(\text{false} \bullet \phi) \Rightarrow \text{false} \quad and \quad (\phi \bullet \text{false}) \Rightarrow \text{false}.$$

Proof. We present a proof for the first case.

$$\begin{aligned}
&\text{false} \bullet \phi \\
\Rightarrow\ &\text{false} \bullet \text{true} \quad \text{SDC3} \\
\Rightarrow\ &\text{false} \qquad\qquad \text{SDC7}.
\end{aligned}$$

$\square$

Theorem 10.2

$$(\nwarrow S_1 \bullet \nearrow S_2) \Leftrightarrow (\nwarrow S_1 \wedge \nearrow S_2).$$

Proof.

$$\begin{aligned}
&\nwarrow S_1 \bullet \nearrow S_2 \\
\Leftrightarrow\ &(\nwarrow S_1 \bullet \text{true}) \bullet (\text{true} \bullet \nearrow S_2) && \text{SDC6, SDC3} \\
\Leftrightarrow\ &((\nwarrow S_1 \bullet \text{true}) \bullet \text{true}) \bullet \nearrow S_2 && \text{SDC1} \\
\Leftrightarrow\ &(\nwarrow S_1 \bullet (\text{true} \bullet \text{true})) \wedge \nearrow S_2 && \text{SDC1, SDC6, SDC3} \\
\Leftrightarrow\ &(\nwarrow S_1 \wedge (\text{true} \bullet \text{true})) \wedge \nearrow S_2 && \text{SDC6} \\
\Leftrightarrow\ &\nwarrow S_1 \wedge \nearrow S_2 && \text{SDC7}.
\end{aligned}$$

$\square$

Corollary 10.1

$$(\nwarrow S \bullet \text{true}) \;\Leftrightarrow\; \nwarrow S$$

and

$$(\text{true} \bullet \nearrow S) \;\Leftrightarrow\; \nearrow S\,.$$

Proof. The first part of the corollary can be derived by letting S_1 be S and S_2 be 1 in Theorem 10.2. The second part can be derived similarly. $\Box$

Theorem 10.3 *If $(S_1 \wedge S_2)$ is consistent, $\nearrow \not\in \phi$ and $\nwarrow \not\in \psi$, then*

$$((\phi \wedge \nearrow S_1) \bullet (\nwarrow S_2 \wedge \psi)) \;\Leftrightarrow\; (\phi \bullet \psi)\,.$$

Proof.

$$
\begin{aligned}
&(\phi \wedge \nearrow S_1) \bullet (\nwarrow S_2 \wedge \psi) \\
\Leftrightarrow\; &(\phi \wedge \nearrow((S_1 \wedge S_2) \vee (S_1 \wedge \neg S_2))) \bullet (\nwarrow S_2 \wedge \psi) && \text{ST4, SDC3} \\
\Leftrightarrow\; &(\phi \wedge \nearrow(S_1 \wedge S_2)) \bullet (\nwarrow S_2 \wedge \psi) \\
&\vee ((\phi \wedge \nearrow(S_1 \wedge \neg S_2)) \bullet (\nwarrow S_2 \wedge \psi)) && \text{ST2, SDC2} \\
\Leftrightarrow\; &(\phi \wedge \nearrow(S_1 \wedge S_2)) \bullet (\nwarrow S_2 \wedge \psi) && \text{ST4, SDC3, SDC5} \\
\Leftrightarrow\; &(\phi \wedge \nearrow(S_1 \wedge S_2)) \bullet (\nwarrow((S_2 \wedge S_1) \vee (S_2 \wedge \neg S_1)) \wedge \psi) && \text{ST4, SDC3} \\
\Leftrightarrow\; &(\phi \wedge \nearrow(S_1 \wedge S_2)) \bullet (\nwarrow(S_2 \wedge S_1) \wedge \psi) \\
&\vee ((\phi \wedge \nearrow(S_1 \wedge S_2)) \bullet (\nwarrow(S_2 \wedge \neg S_1) \wedge \psi)) && \text{ST2, SDC2} \\
\Leftrightarrow\; &(\phi \wedge \nearrow(S_1 \wedge S_2)) \bullet (\nwarrow(S_2 \wedge S_1) \wedge \psi) && \text{ST4, SDC3, SDC5} \\
\Leftrightarrow\; &\phi \bullet \psi && \text{SDC4.}
\end{aligned}
$$

$\Box$

Corollary 10.2 *If $(S_2 \wedge S_3)$ is consistent, then*

$$((\nwarrow S_1 \wedge \nearrow S_2) \bullet (\nwarrow S_3 \wedge \nearrow S_4)) \;\Leftrightarrow\; (\nwarrow S_1 \wedge \nearrow S_4)\,.$$

Proof. From Theorem 10.3, we can derive

$$((\nwarrow S_1 \wedge \nearrow S_2) \bullet (\nwarrow S_3 \wedge \nearrow S_4)) \;\Leftrightarrow\; (\nwarrow S_1 \bullet \nearrow S_4)\,.$$

Therefore, by Theorem 10.2, we can obtain the required conclusion. $\Box$

Theorem 10.4 *If $\nwarrow \not\in \phi_1, \phi_2$ and $\nearrow \not\in \psi_1, \psi_2$, then*

$$((\nwarrow S_1 \bullet \phi_1) \;\wedge\; (\nwarrow S_2 \bullet \phi_2)) \Leftrightarrow (\nwarrow(S_1 \wedge S_2) \bullet (\phi_1 \wedge \phi_2))\,.$$

$$((\psi_1 \bullet \nearrow S_1) \;\wedge\; (\psi_2 \bullet \nearrow S_2)) \Leftrightarrow ((\psi_1 \wedge \psi_2) \bullet \nearrow(S_1 \wedge S_2))\,.$$

Proof. We prove the first equivalence only.

$$
\begin{aligned}
&(\nwarrow S_1 \bullet \phi_1) \;\wedge\; (\nwarrow S_2 \bullet \phi_2) \\
\Leftrightarrow\; &(\nwarrow S_1 \wedge \phi_1) \wedge (\nwarrow S_2 \wedge \phi_2) && \text{SDC6} \\
\Leftrightarrow\; &\nwarrow(S_1 \wedge S_2) \wedge (\phi_1 \wedge \phi_2) && \text{TH9.1(2)} \\
\Leftrightarrow\; &\nwarrow(S_1 \wedge S_2) \bullet (\phi_1 \wedge \phi_2) && \text{SDC6.}
\end{aligned}
$$

$\Box$

10.3 Real-Time Semantics

In this section, an OCCAM-like notation and a real-time semantics of the notation are presented, where assignment statements and message passing of communications are assumed to be timeless actions.

10.3.1 Program Notation

Let $T \in (0, \infty)$ stand for a time delay, x, y for *program variables*, c, d for *channels*, $\langle E \rangle$ for *arithmetical expressions* of program variables, and B for *Boolean expressions* of program variables. The syntax of the notation is given by the following grammar:

$$\mathcal{S} ::= x := \langle E \rangle \mid c!\langle E \rangle \mid c?x \mid \text{wait } T \mid \mathcal{S}; \mathcal{S} \mid B \rightarrow \mathcal{S}$$
$$\mid (c?x \rightarrow \mathcal{S} [\![d?y \rightarrow \mathcal{S}) \mid (c?x \rightarrow \mathcal{S} [\![\text{wait } T \rightarrow \mathcal{S}) \mid \mu Y.\mathcal{S}$$
$$\mathcal{P} ::= \mathcal{S} \mid (\mathcal{P} \parallel \mathcal{P}),$$

where $\mathcal{S}$ stands for *sequential* processes, and $\mathcal{P}$ for *parallel* processes. The informal meanings of the statements can be given as follows.

$x := \langle E \rangle$ assigns the value of $\langle E \rangle$ to x.

$c!\langle E \rangle$ sends the value of $\langle E \rangle$ on channel c.

$c?x$ receives a message from channel c, and assigns it to x.

wait T delays the program for T ($T > 0$) time units.

$\mathcal{S}_1; \mathcal{S}_2$ is the sequential composition of $\mathcal{S}_1$ and $\mathcal{S}_2$.

$(B \rightarrow \mathcal{S})$ behaves like $\mathcal{S}$ if the values of the program variables satisfy B. Otherwise, B is false, and the process terminates immediately.

$(c?x \rightarrow \mathcal{S}_1 [\![d?y \rightarrow \mathcal{S}_2)$ is a choice. If a communication on c can be completed earlier than one on d, the first branch $\mathcal{S}_1$ is chosen; similarly, if a communication on d can be completed earlier than one on c, then the second branch $\mathcal{S}_2$ is chosen. If these two communications can be completed at the same time, the choice is random.

$(c?x \rightarrow \mathcal{S}_1 [\![\text{wait } T \rightarrow \mathcal{S}_2)$ is also a choice. If a communication on c can be completed within T time units, the first branch is chosen. Otherwise, the second branch is chosen.

$\mu Y.\mathcal{S}$ is a conventional recursion, where Y is the name of the recursion process and Y may occur in $\mathcal{S}$.[1] We exclude finite divergent behavior of processes by assuming that any occurrence of Y in $\mathcal{S}$ is guarded by a wait statement, so that a process will not be engaged in infinitely many assignments or communications in a finite period.

$\mathcal{P}$ allows a parallel system constructed from sequential processes. Shared variables are *excluded* in a parallel system. The only interactions between sequential processes in a parallel system are communications over channels. Each channel is unidirectional and owned by two sequential processes, one at each end.

---

[1] We shall not elaborate here on the details of the syntax required to build a recursion.

10.3.2 Program States

In order to model the behavior of real-time programs, program states are introduced into the superdense state transition calculus as state variables.

We consider the following set of *program* and *channel variables*:

$$\mathcal{PV} = \{x, y, z, c, d, c!, d!, c?, d?, \ldots\},$$

where

x, y and z, called *program variables*, record the values of variables of a program;

c and d, called *trace variables*,[2] record communication histories over individual channels;

c! and d! record readiness to send messages over channels; and

c? and d? record readiness to receive messages over channels.

The variables c!, d!, c? and d? are called *readiness variables*.

Let the real numbers $\mathbb{R}$ be the value domain of the program variables. The domain of the communication traces of channels is the set of the finite sequence of the real numbers

$$Trace \ \widehat{=}\ \bigcup_{n \geq 0} \mathbb{R}^n.$$

When $n = 0$, $\mathbb{R}^n \ \widehat{=}\ \{\langle\rangle\}$, where $\langle\rangle$ stands for the empty sequence. Let the truth values $\{0, 1\}$ be the domain of channel readiness.

Let us extend the set of *global variables*, $\mathcal{GV}$, so that we have

1. $v, v_1, v_2, \ldots$ as *global* variables to range over $\mathbb{R}$, and
2. $h, h_1, h_2, \ldots$ as *global* variables to range over *Trace*.

Accordingly, we extend the set of function symbols to include the *concatenation* operator

$$\widehat{\ }\ :\ Trace \times Trace\ \rightarrow\ Trace\,,$$

with the definition

$$\langle a_1, a_2, \ldots, a_m \rangle ^\frown \langle b_1, b_2, \ldots, b_n \rangle \ \widehat{=}\ \langle a_1, a_2, \ldots, a_m, b_1, b_2, \ldots, b_m \rangle\,.$$

The operator $^\frown$ is *associative*, and has the empty sequence, $\langle\rangle$, as the *left* and also the *right* unit.

---

[2] We can introduce a trace variable to record the communication histories of all channels of a process, if ordering among communications over different channels is interesting.

State variables $\mathcal{SV}$ are generated from the program and channel variables $\mathcal{PV}$ by the following rules:

1. If x is a program variable, and $\langle E \rangle$ is an arithmetical expression of global variables $v, v_1, v_2, \ldots$, then $(x = \langle E \rangle)$ is a state variable.
2. If c is a trace variable and tr is a trace expression constructed, by using $\widehat{\ }$, from global variables $h, h_1, h_2, \ldots$ and arithmetical expressions of $v, v_1, v_2, \ldots$, then $(c = tr)$ is a state variable.
3. Any readiness variable is a state variable.

State expressions (also simply called *states*) are generated from state variables by the propositional connectives $\neg$ and $\vee$, and also the quantifier $\exists$, since state expressions may contain global variables (e.g. v and h). We can say the following:

1. 0, 1 and every state variable are states.
2. If S and S' are states, so are $\neg S$, $S \vee S'$, $\exists v.S$ and $\exists h.S$.

By the definition above, a state is in fact a formula of the program and channel variables and of the global variables such as v and h, in a first-order logic with equality. In a formula, quantifiers are applied only to global variables. We shall use

$$S(x, c, c!, c?, v, h)$$

to represent a state S which contains the program and channel variables $x, c, c!$ and $c?$, and free occurrences of v and h.

An interpretation of a state is determined by an interpretation of the program and channel variables and a value assignment for those global variables which occur (freely) in the state.

We also use $\mathcal{I}$ to stand for an interpretation of the program and channel variables, and use $x_{\mathcal{I}}$, $c_{\mathcal{I}}$, $c!_{\mathcal{I}}$ and $c?_{\mathcal{I}}$ for the interpretations assigned by $\mathcal{I}$ to x, c, c! and c?. We assume that

$$\begin{aligned}
x_{\mathcal{I}} &: \text{Time} \rightarrow \mathbb{R} \\
c_{\mathcal{I}} &: \text{Time} \rightarrow \textit{Trace} \\
c!_{\mathcal{I}} &: \text{Time} \rightarrow \{0,1\} \\
c?_{\mathcal{I}} &: \text{Time} \rightarrow \{0,1\},
\end{aligned}$$

and that they are *finitely variable* for any interpretation $\mathcal{I}$. That is, they cannot change their values infinitely often in a finite period. $\mathcal{I}$ also assigns interpretations to propositional letters, as explained in Chaps. 2 and 3.

For a value assignment $\mathcal{V}$, it is assumed that

$$\mathcal{V}(v) \in \mathbb{R} \quad \text{and} \quad \mathcal{V}(h) \in \textit{Trace}.$$

Of course, $\mathcal{V}$ also assigns values to other global variables, as explained in Chaps. 2 and 3.

Given $\mathcal{I}$ and $\mathcal{V}$, the value of a state at any time is determined. Let S be a state written as $S(\mathrm{x}, \mathrm{c}, \mathrm{c!}, \mathrm{c?}, \mathrm{v}, \mathrm{h})$, and let $t \in \mathrm{Time}$. We define S to have value 1 at t under $\mathcal{I}$ and $\mathcal{V}$, iff

$$S(\mathrm{x}_{\mathcal{I}}(t), \mathrm{c}_{\mathcal{I}}(t), \mathrm{c!}_{\mathcal{I}}(t), \mathrm{c?}_{\mathcal{I}}(t), \mathcal{V}(\mathrm{v}), \mathcal{V}(\mathrm{h}))$$

is valid in a first-order logic with equality.

For example, if, for a given $\mathcal{I}$ and $\mathcal{V}$, we have $\mathrm{x}_{\mathcal{I}}(t) = 2$ and $\mathcal{V}(\mathrm{v}) = 3$, then the state $(\mathrm{x} = \mathrm{v})$ has value 0 at t under $\mathcal{I}$ and $\mathcal{V}$, since

$$\mathrm{x}_{\mathcal{I}}(t) \neq \mathcal{V}(\mathrm{v}).$$

However, the state $\exists \mathrm{v}.(\mathrm{x} = \mathrm{v})$ has value 1 at t under $\mathcal{I}$ and $\mathcal{V}$, since we can construct a value assignment $\mathcal{V}'$ which is v-equivalent to $\mathcal{V}$ and has $\mathcal{V}'(\mathrm{v}) = 2$, so that

$$\mathrm{x}_{\mathcal{I}}(t) = \mathcal{V}'(\mathrm{v}).$$

In fact, the state $\exists \mathrm{v}.(\mathrm{x} = \mathrm{v})$ has value 1 at any time under any interpretation and value assignment, since for any interpretation $\mathcal{I}$, value assignment $\mathcal{V}$ and time t one can always find a value assignment $\mathcal{V}'$ which is v-equivalent to $\mathcal{V}$ and has

$$\mathcal{V}'(\mathrm{v}) = \mathrm{x}_{\mathcal{I}}(t).$$

As we have introduced first-order quantifications in state expressions, we need an additional axiom concerning the distributivity of $\diagdown$ and $\diagup$ over the existential quantifier:

ST5

$$\diagdown \exists x.S \Leftrightarrow \exists x.\diagdown S \quad \text{and} \quad \diagup \exists x.S \Leftrightarrow \exists x.\diagup S,$$

where x stands for any global variable.

The following theorem is proved using ST5 and ST3.

Theorem 10.5

$$\diagdown \forall x.S \Leftrightarrow \forall x.\diagdown S \quad \text{and} \quad \diagup \forall x.S \Leftrightarrow \forall x.\diagup S.$$

The formula $\mathrm{Cnt}(\mathrm{x})$, defined by

$$\mathrm{Cnt}(\mathrm{x}) \mathrel{\hat=} \exists \mathrm{v}.(\diagdown (\mathrm{x} = \mathrm{v}) \wedge \diagup (\mathrm{x} = \mathrm{v})),$$

expresses the continuity of x at a point and acts as a *unit* of $\bullet$ for program states of x.

Theorem 10.6

$$(Cnt(x) \bullet (\nwarrow(x = v_1) \wedge \nearrow(x = v_2))) \Leftrightarrow (\nwarrow(x = v_1) \wedge \nearrow(x = v_2)).$$

$$((\nwarrow(x = v_1) \wedge \nearrow(x = v_2)) \bullet Cnt(x)) \Leftrightarrow (\nwarrow(x = v_1) \wedge \nearrow(x = v_2)).$$

$$(Cnt(x) \bullet \lceil x = v \rceil) \Leftrightarrow \lceil x = v \rceil.$$

$$(\lceil x = v \rceil \bullet Cnt(x)) \Leftrightarrow \lceil x = v \rceil.$$

Proof. We merely sketch the proofs here. Observe first that if $(v = v_1)$, then

$$(\nwarrow(x = v) \wedge \nearrow(x = v)) \bullet (\nwarrow(x = v_1) \wedge \nearrow(x = v_2))$$
$$\Leftrightarrow (\nwarrow(x = v) \wedge \nearrow(x = v)) \bullet (\nwarrow(x = v_1) \wedge \nearrow(x = v_2)) \quad \text{Def}(\nwarrow,\nearrow)$$
$$\Leftrightarrow \nwarrow(x = v) \bullet \nearrow(x = v_2) \qquad\qquad\qquad\qquad \text{SDC4}$$
$$\Leftrightarrow \nwarrow(x = v) \wedge \nearrow(x = v_2) \qquad\qquad\qquad\qquad \text{SDC6.}$$

Observe next that if $(v \neq v_1)$, then by SDC5, the definition of $\nearrow$ and SDC3,

$$((\nwarrow(x = v) \wedge \nearrow(x = v)) \bullet (\nwarrow(x = v_1) \wedge \nearrow(x = v_2))) \Leftrightarrow \text{false}.$$

The first two parts of Theorem 10.6 follow from the above two observations. A proof of the last two parts can be given as follows:

$$Cnt(x) \bullet \lceil x = v \rceil$$
$$\Leftrightarrow \exists v'.(\nwarrow(x = v') \wedge (\ell = 0) \wedge \nearrow(x = v'))$$
$$\qquad \bullet(\nwarrow 1 \wedge \lceil x = v \rceil) \qquad\qquad\qquad \text{Def}(\nearrow),\text{ST1}$$
$$\Leftrightarrow \exists v'.((\nwarrow(x = v') \wedge (\ell = 0) \wedge \nearrow(x = v'))$$
$$\qquad \bullet(\nwarrow 1 \wedge \lceil x = v \rceil)) \qquad\qquad\qquad \text{SDC2}$$
$$\Leftrightarrow \exists v'.((\nwarrow(x = v') \wedge (\ell = 0)) \bullet \lceil x = v \rceil) \qquad \text{TH10.3}$$
$$\Leftrightarrow \exists v.(\nwarrow(x = v) \wedge (\ell = 0)) \bullet \lceil x = v \rceil \qquad\quad \text{SDC2}$$
$$\Leftrightarrow (\nwarrow \exists v.(x = v) \wedge (\ell = 0)) \bullet \lceil x = v \rceil \qquad\quad \text{ST5}$$
$$\Leftrightarrow (\nwarrow 1 \wedge (\ell = 0)) \bullet \lceil x = v \rceil \qquad\qquad (\exists v.(x = v)) \Leftrightarrow 1$$
$$\Leftrightarrow (\ell = 0) \bullet \lceil x = v \rceil \qquad\qquad\qquad\qquad \text{ST1}$$
$$\Leftrightarrow \lceil x = v \rceil \qquad\qquad\qquad\qquad\qquad \text{SDC7.}$$

$\square$

We can define

$$Cnt(c) \,\hat{=}\, \exists h.(\nwarrow(c = h) \wedge \nearrow(c = h))$$

similarly and prove the following theorem.

Theorem 10.7

$$(Cnt(c) \bullet (\nwarrow(c = h_1) \wedge \nearrow(c = h_2))) \Leftrightarrow (\nwarrow(c = h_1) \wedge \nearrow(c = h_2)).$$

$$((\nwarrow(c = h_1) \wedge \nearrow(x = h_2)) \bullet Cnt(c)) \Leftrightarrow (\nwarrow(c = h_1) \wedge \nearrow(c = h_2)).$$

$$(Cnt(c) \bullet \lceil c = h \rceil) \Leftrightarrow \lceil c = h \rceil.$$

$$(\lceil c = h \rceil \bullet Cnt(c)) \Leftrightarrow \lceil c = h \rceil.$$

10.3.3 Program Semantics

We shall use a technique given in [56], where the semantics of each process $\mathcal{P}$ is simultaneously defined by two formulas, $[\![\mathcal{P}]\!]_{ter}$ and $[\![\mathcal{P}]\!]$. These formulas define the terminating behavior and the entire behavior, respectively, of $\mathcal{P}$. The formula $[\![\mathcal{P}]\!]$ is *prefix-closed*. By *prefix-closed*, we mean that for any interpretation $\mathcal{I}$, value assignment $\mathcal{V}$ and interval $[b, e]$, if

$$\mathcal{I}, \mathcal{V}, [b, e] \models [\![\mathcal{P}]\!],$$

then for any c, where $b \leq c < e$,

$$\mathcal{I}, \mathcal{V}, [b, c] \models [\![\mathcal{P}]\!].$$

As indicated before, our aim is to show the expressive power of the superdense state transition calculus, so we shall *not* concern ourselves with other details, for example, a proof of the *continuity* of the semantics of all program constructors, and hence the existence of a fixed point of a recursion.

Furthermore, for simplicity, we also assume that a process has only one variable, say x or y, and two channels, say c and d, over which the process may communicate. It should not be difficult to generalize the semantics to more realistic cases by introducing process alphabets.

For each process considered below, we state its semantics by defining the communications on its channels (c and d) and the evaluation of its variable (x or y).

Sequential Process: $x := \langle E \rangle$

The assignment terminates immediately. It inherits a value of x from its left neighborhood and passes the changed value to its right neighborhood. The communication histories of c and d do not change:

$$[\![x := \langle E \rangle]\!]_{ter} \;\widehat{=}\; \exists v.(\diagdown (x = v) \wedge \diagup (x = \langle E \rangle(v))) \wedge \mathrm{Cnt}(c) \wedge \mathrm{Cnt}(d)$$

$$[\![x := \langle E \rangle]\!] \;\widehat{=}\; [\![x := \langle E \rangle]\!]_{ter},$$

where $\langle E \rangle(v)$ is the expression obtained from $\langle E \rangle$ by replacing x with v.

Sequential Process: c?x

We assume that this process can input messages from d also. As soon as this process synchronizes with its partner, it will receive a message, update the communication history of channel c and assign the message to x instantly. However, it may wait forever if its partner refuses to send. The communication history of d does not change during the execution of c?x:

$$[\![c?x]\!]_{ter} \ \widehat{=}\ \exists h_1, h_2.(\text{Sync}_1(h_1, h_2) \bullet \exists v.\text{Comm}_1(h_1, h_2, v))$$

$$[\![c?x]\!] \quad \widehat{=}\ \exists h_1, h_2.\text{Sync}_1(h_1, h_2) \ \vee \ [\![c?x]\!]_{ter} ,$$

where

$$\text{Sync}_1(h_1, h_2) \ \widehat{=}\ \left(\begin{array}{l} \diagdown\!\!\!\diagup((c = h_1) \wedge (d = h_2)) \\ \wedge \ \lceil c? \wedge \neg d? \wedge \neg c! \wedge (c = h_1) \wedge (d = h_2)\rceil^* \end{array} \right)$$

and

$$\text{Comm}_1(h_1, h_2, v) \ \widehat{=}\ \diagup\!\!\!\diagup((c = h_1\widehat{\ } v) \wedge (d = h_2) \wedge (x = v)) .$$

In the formula $\text{Sync}_1(h_1, h_2)$ and henceforth, we use the abbreviation

$$\lceil S \rceil^* \ \widehat{=}\ \lceil \ \rceil \vee \lceil S \rceil .$$

The formula $\text{Sync}_1(h_1, h_2)$ therefore defines the behavior of the process while it is waiting to receive a value from channel c. The process first inherits the values (h_1 and h_2) of the histories of channels c and d, and keeps the readiness variable c? at 1 as long as its partner does not engage in communication (i.e. c! = 0). During the waiting period (if any), the process will keep the channel histories of c and d constant, so that no communications over c and d are possible. Note that Sync_1 deliberately avoids specifying the value of x in the waiting period, since it follows the assumption that only the initial and terminating values of a program variable are observable. The following definitions of Sync_2, Sync_3, Wait_1 and Wait_2 follow the same assumption.

The formula $\text{Comm}_1(h_1, h_2, v)$ describes the time instant when v is received over channel c and assigned to x. Note that the trace of c is changed, while the trace of d is kept constant.

Sequential Process: c!⟨E⟩

We assume that this process has y as its program variable and that it outputs messages over d. The semantics is described in a way similar to c?x:

$$[\![c!\langle E\rangle]\!]_{ter} \ \widehat{=}\ \exists h_1, h_2, v. (\text{Sync}_2(h_1, h_2, v) \bullet \text{Comm}_2(h_1, h_2, v))$$

$$[\![c!\langle E\rangle]\!] \quad \widehat{=}\ \exists h_1, h_2, v. \text{Sync}_2(h_1, h_2, v) \ \vee \ [\![c!\langle E\rangle]\!]_{ter} ,$$

where

$$\text{Sync}_2(h_1, h_2, v) \ \widehat{=}\ \left(\begin{array}{l} \diagdown\!\!\!\diagup((c = h_1) \wedge (d = h_2) \wedge (y = v)) \\ \wedge \ \lceil c! \wedge \neg d! \wedge \neg c? \wedge (c = h_1) \wedge (d = h_2)\rceil^* \end{array} \right)$$

and

$$\text{Comm}_2(h_1, h_2, v) \ \widehat{=}\ \diagup\!\!\!\diagup((c = h_1\widehat{\ } \langle E\rangle(v)) \wedge (d = h_2) \wedge (y = v)) .$$

Sequential Process: wait T

We assume that this process has x as its program variable and can input messages from both c and d. The process always terminates, and nothing happens to its program variable and channels until a time $T > 0$ has elapsed:

$$[\![\text{wait } T]\!]_{ter} \;\hat{=}\; \text{Wait}_1 \wedge (\ell = T)$$

$$[\![\text{wait } T]\!] \;\hat{=}\; \left(\begin{array}{l} \exists h_1, h_2, v. \left(\begin{array}{l} \nwarrow ((c = h_1) \wedge (d = h_2) \wedge (x = v)) \\ \wedge \; \lceil \neg c? \wedge \neg d? \wedge (c = h_1) \wedge (d = h_2) \rceil^* \\ \wedge \; \ell < T \end{array} \right) \\ \vee \; [\![\text{wait } T]\!]_{ter} \end{array} \right),$$

where

$$\text{Wait}_1 \;\hat{=}\; \exists h_1, h_2, v. \left(\begin{array}{l} \nwarrow ((c = h_1) \wedge (d = h_2) \wedge (x = v)) \\ \wedge \; \lceil \neg c? \wedge \neg d? \wedge (c = h_1) \wedge (d = h_2) \rceil^* \\ \wedge \; \nearrow ((c = h_1) \wedge (d = h_2) \wedge (x = v)) \end{array} \right).$$

When wait T controls y and the outputs of c and d, the semantics of wait T can be defined by Wait_2 in a similar way:

$$\text{Wait}_2 \;\hat{=}\; \exists h_1, h_2, v. \left(\begin{array}{l} \nwarrow ((c = h_1) \wedge (d = h_2) \wedge (y = v)) \\ \wedge \; \lceil \neg c! \wedge \neg d! \wedge (c = h_1) \wedge (d = h_2) \rceil^* \\ \wedge \; \nearrow ((c = h_1) \wedge (d = h_2) \wedge (y = v)) \end{array} \right).$$

Sequential Process: $S_1; S_2$

The prefix of the behavior of $S_1; S_2$ consists of the prefix of the behavior of S_1 and its terminating part, continued with S_2:

$$[\![S_1; S_2]\!]_{ter} \;\hat{=}\; [\![S_1]\!]_{ter} \bullet [\![S_2]\!]_{ter}$$

$$[\![S_1; S_2]\!] \;\hat{=}\; [\![S_1]\!] \vee ([\![S_1]\!]_{ter} \bullet [\![S_2]\!]).$$

Now we can prove the combine law introduced in Sect. 10.1.1. Consider, for example,

$$[\![x := x + 1; x := x + 2]\!] \;\Leftrightarrow\; [\![x := x + 3]\!].$$

According to the semantic definitions of assignment and sequential composition, the equivalence above can be transformed to the formula

$$\exists v.(\nwarrow (x = v) \wedge \nearrow (x = v + 1)) \bullet \exists v.(\nwarrow (x = v) \wedge \nearrow (x = v + 2))$$
$$\Leftrightarrow \exists v.(\nwarrow (x = v) \wedge \nearrow (x = v + 3)).$$

This formula can be proved by showing that if $v' = v + 1$, then

$$(\diagdown(x = v) \land \nearrow(x = v + 1)) \bullet (\diagdown(x = v') \land \nearrow(x = v' + 2))$$
$$\Leftrightarrow \diagdown(x = v) \land \nearrow(x = v' + 2)$$
$$\Leftrightarrow \diagdown(x = v) \land \nearrow(x = v + 3)$$

COR10.2
$v' = v + 1$,

and if $v' \neq v + 1$, then by $(x = v + 1) \Rightarrow \neg(x = v')$ and SDC5,

$$(\diagdown(x = v) \land \nearrow(x = v + 1)) \bullet (\diagdown(x = v') \land \nearrow(x = v' + 2)) \Leftrightarrow \text{false}.$$

(In the above equations, "COR" means "Corollary".)

Hence, by SDC2,

$$\exists v.(\diagdown(x = v) \land \nearrow(x = v + 1)) \bullet \exists v.(\diagdown(x = v) \land \nearrow(x = v + 2))$$
$$\Leftrightarrow \exists v, v'.((\diagdown(x = v) \land \nearrow(x = v + 1)) \bullet (\diagdown(x = v') \land \nearrow(x = v' + 2)))$$
$$\Leftrightarrow \exists v.(\diagdown(x = v) \land \nearrow(x = v + 3)).$$

Sequential Process: $(B \rightarrow \mathcal{S})$

We assume that this process contains x and can input from c and d.

$$[\![B \rightarrow \mathcal{S}]\!]_{ter} \,\hat{=}\, (\diagdown B \land [\![\mathcal{S}]\!]_{ter}) \lor ((\diagdown \neg B) \land \text{Cnt}(c) \land \text{Cnt}(d) \land \text{Cnt}(x))$$

$$[\![B \rightarrow \mathcal{S}]\!] \quad \hat{=}\, (\diagdown B \land [\![\mathcal{S}]\!]) \lor ((\diagdown \neg B) \land \text{Cnt}(c) \land \text{Cnt}(d) \land \text{Cnt}(x)),$$

where we assume that B can be expressed as a program state, i.e. a first-order formula of the program and channel variables.

Sequential Process: $(c?x \rightarrow \mathcal{S}_1 [\![d?x \rightarrow \mathcal{S}_2)$

We assume that this process contains x and can input from c and d.

$$[\![c?x \rightarrow \mathcal{S}_1 [\![d?x \rightarrow \mathcal{S}_2]\!]_{ter} \,\hat{=}$$
$$\exists h_1, h_2.(\text{Sync}_3(h_1, h_2) \bullet \exists v.\text{Comm}_1(h_1, h_2, v)) \bullet [\![\mathcal{S}_1]\!]_{ter}$$
$$\lor \exists h_1, h_2.(\text{Sync}_3(h_1, h_2) \bullet \exists v.\text{Comm}_3(h_1, h_2, v)) \bullet [\![\mathcal{S}_2]\!]_{ter}$$

$$[\![c?x \rightarrow \mathcal{S}_1 [\![d?x \rightarrow \mathcal{S}_2]\!] \,\hat{=}$$
$$\exists h_1, h_2, .\text{Sync}_3(h_1, h_2)$$
$$\lor \exists h_1, h_2.(\text{Sync}_3(h_1, h_2) \bullet \exists v.\text{Comm}_1(h_1, h_2, v))$$
$$\lor \exists h_1, h_2.(\text{Sync}_3(h_1, h_2) \bullet \exists v.\text{Comm}_3(h_1, h_2, v))$$
$$\lor \exists h_1, h_2.(\text{Sync}_3(h_1, h_2) \bullet \exists v.\text{Comm}_1(h_1, h_2, v)) \bullet [\![\mathcal{S}_1]\!]$$
$$\lor \exists h_1, h_2.(\text{Sync}_3(h_1, h_2) \bullet \exists v.\text{Comm}_3(h_1, h_2, v)) \bullet [\![\mathcal{S}_2]\!],$$

where

$$\text{Sync}_3(h_1, h_2) \,\hat{=}\, \left(\begin{array}{l} \diagdown((c = h_1) \land (d = h_2)) \\ \land \, \lceil c? \land d? \land \neg c! \land \neg d! \land (c = h_1) \land (d = h_2) \rceil^* \end{array} \right)$$

and

$$\text{Comm}_3(h_1, h_2, v) \,\hat{=}\, \nearrow((c = h_1) \land (d = h_2\hat{\ } v) \land (x = v)).$$

Sequential Process: $(c?x \rightarrow S_1 \| \text{wait } T \rightarrow S_2)$

We assume that this process contains x and can input from c and d.

$$[\![c?x \rightarrow S_1 \| \text{wait } T \rightarrow S_2]\!]_{ter} \quad \hat{=}$$
$$\exists h_1, h_2.((\text{Sync}_1(h_1, h_2) \wedge (\ell < T)) \bullet \exists v.\text{Comm}_1(h_1, h_2, v)) \bullet [\![S_1]\!]_{ter}$$
$$\vee \; \exists h_1, h_2.(\text{Sync}_1(h_1, h_2) \wedge (\ell = T)) \bullet [\![S_2]\!]_{ter}$$

$$[\![c?x \rightarrow S_1 \| \text{wait } T \rightarrow S_2]\!] \quad \hat{=}$$
$$\exists h_1, h_2.(\text{Sync}_1(h_1, h_2) \wedge (\ell \leq T))$$
$$\vee \; \exists h_1, h_2.((\text{Sync}_1(h_1, h_2) \wedge (\ell < T)) \bullet \exists v.\text{Comm}_1(h_1, h_2, v))$$
$$\vee \; \exists h_1, h_2.((\text{Sync}_1(h_1, h_2) \wedge (\ell < T)) \bullet \exists v.\text{Comm}_1(h_1, h_2, v)) \bullet [\![S_1]\!]$$
$$\vee \; \exists h_1, h_2.(\text{Sync}_1(h_1, h_2) \wedge (\ell = T)) \bullet [\![S_2]\!] \, .$$

Sequential Process: $\mu Y.S(Y)$

We write $S(Y)$ to denote that Y may occur in S. The terminating and complete behaviors of $\mu Y.S(Y)$ can be extracted from iterations of S. Let $S^i(Y) = S(S(\cdots S(Y) \cdots))$ denote the ith iteration of S. We also introduce an auxiliary syntactical entity, called $\mathcal{M}$, with the definition

$$[\![\mathcal{M}]\!]_{ter} \quad \hat{=} \quad \text{false}$$
$$[\![\mathcal{M}]\!] \quad \hat{=} \quad \text{false} \, .$$

$\mathcal{M}$ acts like a *miracle*, from which one can derive any conclusion.[3] The terminating and nonterminating behaviors of $\mu Y.S(Y)$ can be defined, using $\mathcal{M}$ and iterations of S, by

$$[\![\mu Y.S(Y)]\!]_{ter} \quad \hat{=} \quad \exists n > 0.[\![S^n(\mathcal{M})]\!]_{ter}$$
$$[\![\mu Y.S(Y)]\!] \quad \hat{=} \quad \exists n > 0.[\![S^n(\mathcal{M})]\!] \, ,$$

where $(\exists n > 0.\phi_n)$ means an *infinite* disjunction of $\phi_1, \phi_2, \ldots$. We shall not discuss here how to define $(\exists n > 0.\phi_n)$ in DC. References [39, 41, 60, 108, 110] have introduced an operator μ into DC for this purpose.

Parallel Process: $(S_1 \| S_2)$

We assume that S_1 contains the variable x and can input from c and d, and that S_2 contains y and can output to c and d. S_1 and S_2 synchronize the communication histories of the channels c and d first, by initializing them as $\langle \rangle$, and then run in parallel. Any terminating process maintains its status (described by Wait_1 for S_1 and by Wait_2 for S_2) until the other process also terminates.

---

[3] However, since we assume that any occurrence of Y in $\mu Y.S(Y)$ is guarded by a wait statement, the program notation can exclude $\mathcal{M}$.

The semantics of $(\mathcal{S}_1 \parallel \mathcal{S}_2)$ is

$$[\![\mathcal{S}_1 \parallel \mathcal{S}_2]\!]_{ter} \;\; \widehat{=} \;\; \left(\begin{array}{l} \diagdown\!\!\!\nwarrow ((c = \langle\rangle) \wedge (d = \langle\rangle)) \\ \wedge \left(\begin{array}{l} ([\![\mathcal{S}_1]\!]_{ter} \wedge ([\![\mathcal{S}_2]\!]_{ter} \bullet \mathrm{Wait}_2)) \\ \vee (([\![\mathcal{S}_1]\!]_{ter} \bullet \mathrm{Wait}_1) \wedge [\![\mathcal{S}_2]\!]_{ter}) \end{array} \right) \end{array} \right)$$

$$[\![\mathcal{S}_1 \parallel \mathcal{S}_2]\!] \;\; \widehat{=} \;\; \left(\begin{array}{l} \diagdown\!\!\!\nwarrow ((c = \langle\rangle) \wedge (d = \langle\rangle)) \\ \wedge \left(\begin{array}{l} ([\![\mathcal{S}_1]\!] \wedge ([\![\mathcal{S}_2]\!]_{ter} \bullet \mathrm{Wait}_2)) \\ \vee (([\![\mathcal{S}_1]\!]_{ter} \bullet \mathrm{Wait}_1) \wedge [\![\mathcal{S}_2]\!]) \\ \vee ([\![\mathcal{S}_1]\!] \wedge [\![\mathcal{S}_2]\!]) \end{array} \right) \end{array} \right) .$$

10.3.4 Program Specification

We specify here the real-time properties of program termination and liveness. As we have discussed in Chap. 1, DC with contracting modalities is not able to formulate and prove unbounded liveness including termination. Only bounded liveness is discussed here. In Chap. 11, two expanding modalities are introduced, and unbounded liveness can therefore be treated there.

Partial Correctness

The partial correctness of a program $\mathcal{P}$ with Pre as its pre-condition and Post as its post-condition can be formulated as

$$(\diagdown\!\!\!\nwarrow \mathrm{Pre} \wedge [\![\mathcal{P}]\!]_{ter}) \;\; \Rightarrow \;\; \diagup\!\!\!\nearrow \mathrm{Post} ,$$

where Pre and Post are first-order formulas of program and trace variables.

Bounded Termination

The bounded termination of $\mathcal{P}$ with the pre-condition Pre holds if there exists $r \geq 0$ such that

$$(\diagdown\!\!\!\nwarrow \mathrm{Pre} \wedge [\![\mathcal{P}]\!]) \;\; \Rightarrow \;\; (\ell \leq r) .$$

Let $\mathcal{S}_i$ $(i = 1, 2)$ be two sequential processes,

$\mathcal{S}_1$: wait $2; c?\mathrm{x}$

$\mathcal{S}_2$: wait $1; c!\mathrm{y}; \mathrm{y} := \mathrm{y} + 1 ,$

where $\mathcal{S}_1$ has the variable x and input c?, and $\mathcal{S}_2$ has the variable y and output c!. Let $\mathcal{P}_1$ be the parallel system

$\mathcal{P}_1 : \mathcal{S}_1 \parallel \mathcal{S}_2 .$

We can expect that $\mathcal{P}_1$ always terminates in two time units, and $y = x+1$ holds when $\mathcal{P}_1$ terminates:

$$(\nwarrow 1 \wedge [\![\mathcal{P}_1]\!]) \;\Rightarrow\; (\ell \le 2)$$

and

$$(\nwarrow 1 \wedge [\![\mathcal{P}_1]\!]_{ter}) \;\Rightarrow\; \nearrow(y = x + 1).$$

Since $\nwarrow 1$ is true (ST1), the termination properties can be simplified to:

$$[\![\mathcal{P}_1]\!] \;\Rightarrow\; (\ell \le 2)$$

and

$$[\![\mathcal{P}_1]\!]_{ter} \;\Rightarrow\; \nearrow(y = x + 1).$$

In order to prove the above properties of $\mathcal{P}_1$, we first simplify the semantics of $\mathcal{P}_1$:

$$[\![\mathcal{P}_1]\!]_{ter} \;\Leftrightarrow\; \exists v. \left(\begin{array}{l} \nwarrow((c = \langle\rangle) \wedge (y = v)) \\ \bullet\; (\lceil \neg c! \wedge \neg c? \wedge (c = \langle\rangle)\rceil \wedge (\ell = 1)) \\ \bullet\; (\lceil c! \wedge \neg c? \wedge (c = \langle\rangle)\rceil \wedge (\ell = 1)) \\ \bullet\; \nearrow((c = v) \wedge (x = v) \wedge (y = v + 1)) \end{array} \right)$$

$$[\![\mathcal{P}_1]\!] \;\Leftrightarrow\; \left(\begin{array}{l} \exists v. \left(\begin{array}{l} \nwarrow((c = \langle\rangle) \wedge (y = v)) \\ \bullet\; (\lceil \neg c! \wedge \neg c? \wedge (c = \langle\rangle)\rceil^* \wedge (\ell < 1)) \end{array} \right) \\ \vee\; \exists v. \left(\begin{array}{l} \nwarrow((c = \langle\rangle) \wedge (y = v)) \\ \bullet\; (\lceil \neg c! \wedge \neg c? \wedge (c = \langle\rangle)\rceil \wedge (\ell = 1)) \\ \bullet\; (\lceil c! \wedge \neg c? \wedge (c = \langle\rangle)\rceil^* \wedge (\ell < 1)) \end{array} \right) \\ \vee\; [\![\mathcal{P}_1]\!]_{ter} \end{array} \right).$$

We do not present the proof of the simplification here, since it is tedious to derive program properties directly from program semantics.

With the simplified semantics of $\mathcal{P}_1$, we can prove

$$[\![\mathcal{P}_1]\!] \;\Rightarrow\; (\ell \le 2)$$

as follows. By SDC3, we have

$$[\![\mathcal{P}_1]\!] \;\Rightarrow\; \left(\begin{array}{l} (\ell = 0) \bullet (\ell < 1) \\ \vee\; ((\ell = 0) \bullet (\ell = 1) \bullet (\ell < 1)) \\ \vee\; ((\ell = 0) \bullet (\ell = 1) \bullet (\ell = 1)) \end{array} \right).$$

Since the consequent part of the implication contains no occurrences of $\nwarrow$ and $\nearrow$, we obtain, by replacing $\bullet$ with $\frown$ in the consequent part of the implication, the following DC formula:

$$(\ell = 0) \frown (\ell < 1)$$
$$\vee \ ((\ell = 0) \frown (\ell = 1) \frown (\ell < 1))$$
$$\vee \ ((\ell = 0) \frown (\ell = 1) \frown (\ell = 1)).$$

Therefore, by use of SDC7, the conclusion

$$[\![\mathcal{P}_1]\!] \ \Rightarrow \ (\ell \leq 2)$$

is easily proved using DC.

The property

$$[\![\mathcal{P}_1]\!]_{ter} \ \Rightarrow \ \nearrow (y = x + 1),$$

can be derived easily from the simplified $[\![\mathcal{P}_1]\!]_{ter}$, since

$$\begin{array}{ll} & [\![\mathcal{P}_1]\!]_{ter} \\ \Rightarrow & \exists v. \ \nearrow ((c = \langle \rangle) \wedge (x = v) \wedge (y = v + 1)) \quad \text{SDC6} \\ \Rightarrow & \nearrow (y = x + 1) \quad\quad\quad\quad\quad\quad\quad\quad\quad \text{Def}(\nearrow). \end{array}$$

Bounded Liveness

A program is not deadlocked if the communication traces of the program are expandable. A *bounded liveness* can therefore be established by proving an upper bound on the time period in which the communication traces of the program remain constant.

Let $\mathcal{P}$ be a process which has channels c and d. $\mathcal{P}$ has $r \geq 0$ as its upper bound of liveness under the pre-condition Pre, if

$$(\nwarrow \text{Pre} \wedge [\![\mathcal{P}]\!]) \ \Rightarrow \ \Box_{sdc} \forall h_1, h_2. ([\![(c = h_1) \wedge (d = h_2)]\!] \Rightarrow (\ell \leq r)),$$

where $\Box_{sdc}$ is the counterpart of $\Box$ in the context of the superdense chop, i.e.

$$\Diamond_{sdc} \phi \ \hat{=} \ \text{true} \bullet \phi \bullet \text{true}$$
$$\Box_{sdc} \phi \ \hat{=} \ \neg \Diamond_{sdc} \neg \phi.$$

Consider, for example,

$$\mathcal{S}_3 \ \hat{=} \ \mu Y. \mathcal{S}_1 ; Y$$
$$\mathcal{S}_4 \ \hat{=} \ \mu Y. \mathcal{S}_2 ; Y$$

and

$$\mathcal{P}_2 \ \hat{=} \ \mathcal{S}_3 \parallel \mathcal{S}_4 .$$

We can prove that $\mathcal{P}_2$ always has 2 as an upper bound of liveness:

$$(\diagdown 1 \wedge \llbracket \mathcal{P}_2 \rrbracket) \;\Rightarrow\; \square_{sdc} \forall h_1, h_2. (\llbracket (c = h_1) \wedge (d = h_2) \rrbracket \Rightarrow (\ell \leq 2)).$$

The proof from the semantic definition of $\mathcal{P}_2$ is too tedious to present here. Verification techniques with DC formulas as specifications have been investigated in [93]. This book will not cover this topic.

11. Neighborhood Logic

11.1 Introduction

The chop-based interval temporal logics, such as ITL [43], IL and DC, are useful for the specification and verification of safety properties of real-time systems. In these logics, one can easily express properties such as

- "if ϕ holds for an interval, then there is a subinterval where ψ holds", and
- "if ϕ holds for an interval, then ψ holds for all subintervals".

However, these logics cannot express (unbounded) liveness properties such as

- "eventually there is an interval where ϕ holds", and
- "ϕ will hold infinitely often in the future".

Surprisingly, these logics cannot express even state transitions, and hence we had to introduce extra atomic formulas ($\nwarrow S$ and $\nearrow S$) in Chap. 9.

The reason for this limitation is that the modality *chop* $\frown$, is a *contracting* modality, in the sense that the truth of $\phi \frown \psi$ on the interval $[b, e]$ depends only on subintervals of $[b, e]$:

$\phi \frown \psi$ holds on $[b, e]$

iff there exists $m \in [b, e]$ such that ϕ holds on $[b, m]$ and ψ holds on $[m, e]$:

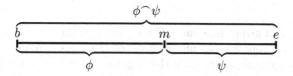

Hence, with $\frown$, one cannot access any interval outside a given reference interval. Therefore, formulas constructed from the connectives of first-order logic and the chop modality cannot express state transitions or liveness and fairness properties unless specific atomic formulas are introduced.

When logics based on $\frown$ are used to specify hybrid systems, as done in [170] for example, notions of real analysis such as limits, continuity and differentiability, which are definable through the notion of a *neighborhood*, cannot be formalized. The definition of a limit at a point must refer to neighborhood properties of the point, i.e. properties over superintervals of the point.

To cope with this, an informal mathematical theory of real analysis was assumed in [170] and also in other languages for specifying hybrid systems, e.g. in hybrid statecharts [92], hybrid automata [4] and TLA$^+$ [76]. In order to improve the expressiveness of the chop-based interval temporal logic, people have introduced *infinite* intervals [97, 162] and *expanding* modalities [31, 103, 139, 148].

For example, [148] establishes a complete propositional calculus for three binary interval modalities: $\frown$ (denoted by C in [148]), T and D. The last two are expanding in the sense that the truth value of formulas $\phi T \psi$ and $\phi D \psi$ on an interval $[b, e]$ depends on intervals "outside" $[b, e]$:

$\phi T \psi$ holds on $[b, e]$

iff there exists $c \geq e$ such that ϕ holds on $[e, c]$ and ψ holds on $[b, c]$:

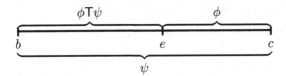

Hence, T refers to an expansion of a given interval in future time.
Symmetrically, D refers to an expansion in past time:

$\phi D \psi$ holds on $[b, e]$

iff there exists $a \leq b$ such that ϕ holds on $[a, b]$ and ψ holds on $[a, e]$:

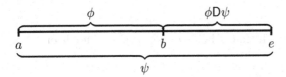

Liveness can be specified using these modalities [139], and there is a complete axiomatization of a propositional modal logic of the three modalities C, T and D. Some of the axioms and rules of this logic are, however, complicated.

Interval modalities are not necessarily binary. In [1], there is a list of thirteen possible unary interval modalities, and in [44] it was shown that six of them are basic in the sense that the remaining unary modalities can be derived from the basic ones in propositional logic. Of the basic modalities, two are contracting, and four are expanding. If one confines oneself to propositional logic, one cannot derive the chop from the thirteen unary modalities [147].

In this chapter, we present a first-order interval logic [165], which has two simple expanding modalities:

- $\Diamond_l \phi$ reads "for some left neighborhood ϕ", and
- $\Diamond_r \phi$ reads "for some right neighborhood".

They are defined as follows:

- $\Diamond_l \phi$ holds on $[b, e]$ iff there exists $\delta \geq 0$ such that ϕ holds on $[b - \delta, b]$, and
- $\Diamond_r \phi$ holds on $[b, e]$ iff there exists $\delta \geq 0$ such that ϕ holds on $[e, e + \delta]$.

With $\Diamond_l$ and $\Diamond_r$, one can reach *left* and *right* neighborhoods, respectively, of the beginning and ending points of an interval:

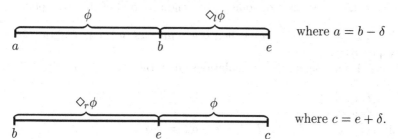

When the interval is a *point* interval (i.e. $b = e$ in the definitions), these neighborhoods can become the conventional left and right neighborhoods of a point, if we assume $\delta > 0$. We therefore call $\Diamond_l$ and $\Diamond_r$ the *left* and *right* neighborhood modalities, respectively. They are expanding modalities, and very similar to $\langle A \rangle$ and $\langle \bar{A} \rangle$ of the six basic modalities of [44].

This first-order interval logic is called *neighborhood logic* (abbreviated to NL). NL is adequate in the sense that the six basic unary modalities of [44] and the three binary modalities of [147] are expressible in NL. Similarly to the axiomatization of IL in [27], we can give a complete proof system for NL. This proof system is much more intuitive than the propositional calculus for the modalities C, T and D given in [147].

On the basis of NL, we can also establish a duration calculus which can express state transitions, and liveness and fairness properties. In [165], notions from real analysis are also expressed in an NL-based duration calculus.

11.2 Syntax and Semantics

The syntax and semantics of NL are similar to those of IL given in Chap. 2, except that the chop modality, $\frown$, is replaced by the left and right neighborhood modalities, $\Diamond_l$ and $\Diamond_r$.

The set of *formulas* of NL is defined by the following syntax:

$$\phi ::= X \mid G^n(\theta_1, \ldots, \theta_n) \mid \neg\phi \mid \phi \vee \psi \mid (\exists x)\phi \mid \Diamond_l \phi \mid \Diamond_r \phi.$$

The semantics of the formulas $\Diamond_l\phi$ and $\Diamond_r\phi$ are given below:

$$\mathcal{J}, \mathcal{V}, [b,e] \models \Diamond_l\phi \text{ iff there exists } \delta \geq 0: \mathcal{J}, \mathcal{V}, [b-\delta, b] \models \phi$$

$$\mathcal{J}, \mathcal{V}, [b,e] \models \Diamond_r\phi \text{ iff there exists } \delta \geq 0: \mathcal{J}, \mathcal{V}, [e, e+\delta] \models \phi,$$

where $\mathcal{J}$ and $\mathcal{V}$ are the interpretation and value assignment, as defined in Chap. 2 for IL.

The notions of *validity* and *satisfiability* are defined as for IL.

We introduce the following abbreviations:

$\Diamond_l^c\phi \; \hat{=} \; \Diamond_r\Diamond_l\phi$ reads "for some left neighborhood of the end point: ϕ"

$\Diamond_r^c\psi \; \hat{=} \; \Diamond_l\Diamond_r\psi$ reads "for some right neighborhood of the start point: ψ".

The modalities $\Diamond_l^c$ and $\Diamond_r^c$ are called the *converses* of the modalities $\Diamond_l$ and $\Diamond_r$, respectively.

The following semantical calculations show the meaning of $\Diamond_l^c$:

$$\mathcal{J}, \mathcal{V}, [b,e] \models \Diamond_l^c\phi$$
iff $\mathcal{J}, \mathcal{V}, [b,e] \models \Diamond_r\Diamond_l\phi$
iff there exists $\delta' \geq 0: \mathcal{J}, \mathcal{V}, [e, e+\delta'] \models \Diamond_l\phi$
iff there exists $\delta \geq 0: \mathcal{J}, \mathcal{V}, [e-\delta, e] \models \phi$.

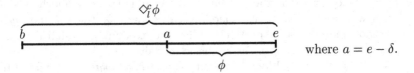

where $a = e - \delta$.

A similar calculation for $\Diamond_r^c$ establishes that

$$\mathcal{J}, \mathcal{V}, [b,e] \models \Diamond_r^c\psi \text{ iff for some } \delta \geq 0: \mathcal{J}, \mathcal{V}, [b, b+\delta] \models \psi.$$

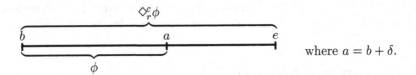

where $a = b + \delta$.

We use the same conventions for precedence of the modalities introduced in this chapter as for IL (see Sect. 2.1). Hence, the unary modalities have the same precedence as $\Box$ and $\Diamond$, and the binary modalities have the same precedence as $\frown$.

Table 11.1. The six basic modalities listed in [44]

Modality	Intervals reachable from "reference interval"
$\langle A \rangle$	Nonpoint right neighborhoods
$\langle \bar{A} \rangle$	Nonpoint left neighborhoods
$\langle B \rangle$	Strict prefix intervals
$\langle \bar{B} \rangle$	Intervals which have the reference interval as a strict prefix
$\langle E \rangle$	Strict suffix intervals
$\langle \bar{E} \rangle$	Intervals which have the reference interval as a strict suffix

11.3 Adequacy of Neighborhood Modalities

In this section, we show that the six basic unary interval modalities of [44] and the three binary interval modalities (i.e. C, T and D) of [148] can be defined in NL. The six basic modalities of [44] are denoted by the symbols listed in Table 11.1.

The meaning of these six unary modalities and the three binary modalities ⌢, T and D is given by:

1. $\mathcal{J}, \mathcal{V}, [b, e] \models \langle A \rangle \phi$ iff there exists $a > e :\ \mathcal{J}, \mathcal{V}, [e, a] \models \phi$.

2. $\mathcal{J}, \mathcal{V}, [b, e] \models \langle \bar{A} \rangle \phi$ iff there exists $a < b :\ \mathcal{J}, \mathcal{V}, [a, b] \models \phi$.

3. $\mathcal{J}, \mathcal{V}, [b, e] \models \langle B \rangle \phi$
   iff there exists a such that $b \leq a < e$ and $\mathcal{J}, \mathcal{V}, [b, a] \models \phi$.

4. $\mathcal{J}, \mathcal{V}, [b, e] \models \langle \bar{B} \rangle \phi$ iff there exists $a > e :\ \mathcal{J}, \mathcal{V}, [b, a] \models \phi$.

5. $\mathcal{J}, \mathcal{V}, [b, e] \models \langle E \rangle \phi$
   iff there exists a such that $b < a \leq e$ and $\mathcal{J}, \mathcal{V}, [a, e] \models \phi$.

6. $\mathcal{J}, \mathcal{V}, [b, e] \models \langle \bar{E} \rangle \phi$ iff there exists $a < b :\ \mathcal{J}, \mathcal{V}, [a, e] \models \phi$.

7. $\mathcal{J}, \mathcal{V}, [b, e] \models \phi \frown \psi$
   iff there exists $m \in [b, e] :\ \mathcal{J}, \mathcal{V}, [b, m] \models \phi$ and $\mathcal{J}, \mathcal{V}, [m, e] \models \psi$.

8. $\mathcal{J}, \mathcal{V}, [b, e] \models \phi T \psi$
   iff there exists $a \geq e :\ \mathcal{J}, \mathcal{V}, [e, a] \models \phi$ and $\mathcal{J}, \mathcal{V}, [b, a] \models \psi$.

9. $\mathcal{J}, \mathcal{V}, [b, e] \models \phi D \psi$
   iff there exists $a \leq b :\ \mathcal{J}, \mathcal{V}, [a, b] \models \phi$ and $\mathcal{J}, \mathcal{V}, [a, e] \models \psi$.

Theorem 11.1 *(Adequacy) The above nine modalities can be expressed in NL.*

Proof. The following equivalences establish the theorem. The validity of each of them can be easily concluded by using the semantic definitions.

1. $\langle A \rangle \phi \Leftrightarrow \Diamond_r((\ell > 0) \wedge \phi)$,
   where $(\ell > 0)$ guarantees that the right expansion is a *nonpoint* interval.

2. $\langle \bar{A} \rangle \psi \Leftrightarrow \Diamond_l((\ell > 0) \wedge \psi)$,
   where $(\ell > 0)$ guarantees that the left expansion is a *nonpoint* interval.

3. $\langle B \rangle \phi \Leftrightarrow \exists x.((\ell = x) \wedge \Diamond_r^c((\ell < x) \wedge \phi))$,
   where $\Diamond_r^c$ defines an interval that has the same beginning point as the original interval, and $(\ell < x)$ stipulates that the defined interval is a strict subinterval of the original interval.

4. $\langle \bar{B} \rangle \phi \Leftrightarrow \exists x.((\ell = x) \wedge \Diamond_r^c((\ell > x) \wedge \phi))$.
   This equivalence is similar to that for $\langle B \rangle \phi$, except that $(\ell > x)$ is used to stipulate a strict superinterval of the original interval.

5. $\langle E \rangle \phi \Leftrightarrow \exists x.((\ell = x) \wedge \Diamond_l^c((\ell < x) \wedge \phi))$.
   This equivalence is similar to that for $\langle B \rangle \phi$, except that here $\Diamond_l^c$ defines an interval that has the same ending point as the original interval.

6. $\langle \bar{E} \rangle \phi \Leftrightarrow \exists x.((\ell = x) \wedge \Diamond_l^c((\ell > x) \wedge \phi))$.
   This equivalence is similar to that for $\langle E \rangle \phi$, except that $(\ell > x)$ is used to stipulate a strict superinterval of the original interval.

7. $\phi \frown \psi \Leftrightarrow \exists x, y.((\ell = x + y) \wedge \Diamond_l^c((\ell = x) \wedge \phi \wedge \Diamond_r((\ell = y) \wedge \psi)))$,
   where $(\ell = x + y)$ stipulates that the two consecutive right expansions of lengths x and y exactly cover the original interval.

8. $\phi T \psi \Leftrightarrow \exists x, y.((\ell = x) \wedge \Diamond_r((\ell = y) \wedge \phi \wedge \Diamond_l^c((\ell = x + y) \wedge \psi)))$,
   where $(\ell = x + y)$ guarantees that the left expansion, $\Diamond_l^c$, exactly covers the original interval and its right expansion, $\Diamond_r$.

9. $\phi D \psi \Leftrightarrow \exists x, y.((\ell = x) \wedge \Diamond_l((\ell = y) \wedge \phi \wedge \Diamond_r^c((\ell = x + y) \wedge \psi)))$,
   where $(\ell = x + y)$ guarantees that the right expansion, $\Diamond_r^c$, exactly covers the original interval and its left expansion, $\Diamond_l$.

$\square$

11.4 Proof System

In this section we present the proof systems of NL and establish a set of theorems which can help us in understanding this logic.

11.4.1 Axioms and Rules

In the following axiom and rule schemas, $\diamond$ is a parameter, which can be instantiated by either $\diamond_l$ or $\diamond_r$. As is usual when a schema is instantiated, the instantiation must be consistent for all occurrences of $\diamond$ in the schema.

We adopt the abbreviations

$$\bar{\diamond} \;\hat{=}\; \begin{cases} \diamond_r, \text{ if } \diamond = \diamond_l \\ \diamond_l, \text{ if } \diamond = \diamond_r \end{cases}$$

$$\Box \;\hat{=}\; \neg\diamond\neg$$

$$\bar{\Box} \;\hat{=}\; \neg\bar{\diamond}\neg$$

$$\diamond^c \;\hat{=}\; \bar{\diamond}\,\diamond.$$

To formulate the axioms and inference rules, we need the notions of *flexible* and *rigid* terms and formulas, as introduced for IL. A term is called "flexible" if it contains temporal variables or ℓ. A formula is called "flexible" if it contains flexible terms or propositional letters. A term or formula is called "rigid" if it is not flexible.

The axiom schemas of NL are:

- Interval length is nonnegative:

  NLA1 $\ell \geq 0$.

- Rigid formulas are not connected to intervals:

  NLA2 $\diamond\phi \Rightarrow \phi$, provided ϕ is rigid.

- A neighborhood can be of arbitrary length:

  NLA3 $x \geq 0 \Rightarrow \diamond(\ell = x)$.

- Neighborhood modalities can be distributed over disjunction and the existential quantifier:

  NLA4 $\diamond(\phi \vee \psi) \Rightarrow (\diamond\phi \vee \diamond\psi)$.
  $\diamond\exists x.\phi \;\;\Rightarrow \exists x.\diamond\phi$.

- A neighborhood is determined by its length:

  NLA5 $\diamond((\ell = x) \wedge \phi) \Rightarrow \Box((\ell = x) \Rightarrow \phi)$.

- Left and right neighborhoods of an interval always end and start, respectively, at the same point:

  NLA6 $\diamond\bar{\diamond}\phi \Rightarrow \Box\bar{\diamond}\phi$.

- Left neighborhoods of the ending point of an interval must be the same interval if they have the same length, and, similarly, right neighborhoods of the beginning point of an interval must be the same interval if they have the same length:

  NLA7 $(\ell = x) \;\Rightarrow\; (\phi \Leftrightarrow \Diamond^c((\ell = x) \wedge \phi))$.

- Two consecutive left or right expansions can be replaced by a single left or right expansion, if the latter expansion has a length equal to the sum of the lengths of the two former expansions:

  NLA8 $(x \geq 0 \wedge y \geq 0) \;\Rightarrow$
  $(\Diamond((\ell = x) \wedge \Diamond((\ell = y) \wedge \Diamond\phi)) \;\Leftrightarrow\; \Diamond((\ell = x + y) \wedge \Diamond\phi))$.

The rule schemas of NL are:

NLM   If $\phi \Rightarrow \psi$ then $\Diamond\phi \Rightarrow \Diamond\psi$.   (monotonicity)

NLN   If ϕ then $\Box\phi$.   (necessity)

MP   If ϕ and $\phi \Rightarrow \psi$ then ψ.   (modus ponens)

G   If ϕ then $(\forall x)\phi$.   (generalization)

The monotonicity and necessity rules are taken from modal logic, and the modus ponens and generalization rules are taken from first-order predicate logic.

Similarly to IL, the proof system also contains axioms of first-order predicate logic with equality, including Q1 and Q2 with side-conditions:

Q1 $\forall x.\phi(x) \;\Rightarrow\; \phi(\theta)$ $\left(\begin{array}{l}\text{if } \theta \text{ is free for } x \text{ in } \phi(x), \text{ and}\\ \text{either } \theta \text{ is rigid or } \phi(x) \text{ is modality free}\end{array}\right)$,
Q2 $\phi(\theta) \;\Rightarrow\; \exists x.\phi(x)$

where a formula is called *modality free* if it contains neither $\Diamond_l$ nor $\Diamond_r$.

The proof system also has to include a first-order theory for the time and value domain, i.e. a first-order theory of real arithmetic. We shall discuss this issue in Sect. 11.5 with regard to the completeness of IL and NL.

The notions of *proof*, *theorem* and *deduction* are defined as for IL.

The soundness of the NL proof system can be established by proving the soundness of every axiom and rule. In [93], NL is encoded in PVS and the soundness of NL proved.

Theorem 11.2 *(Soundness)*

   if $\vdash \phi$ then $\models \phi$.

11.4.2 Theorems

We list and sketch proofs of a set of theorems which can help in understanding the calculus.

The first deduction to be derived is the monotonicity of $\Box$:

NL1 $\phi \Rightarrow \psi \vdash \Box\phi \Rightarrow \Box\psi$.

Proof.

> 1. $\phi \Rightarrow \psi$ assumption
> 2. $\neg\psi \Rightarrow \neg\phi$ 1., PL
> 3. $\Diamond\neg\psi \Rightarrow \Diamond\neg\phi$ 2., NLM
> 4. $\neg\Diamond\neg\phi \Rightarrow \neg\Diamond\neg\psi$ 3., PL.

$\Box$

NL2 $\Diamond\,\text{true}$.
$\Diamond\,\text{false} \Rightarrow \text{false}$.

Proof. Note that a reference interval is neither a left nor a right neighborhood of itself when its length is nonzero. That is, $\Diamond_l$ and $\Diamond_r$ are not reflexive, and $\phi \Rightarrow \Diamond\phi$ is not valid for an arbitrary formula ϕ. So the proof of the first part is a little tricky:

> 1. $(0 \geq 0) \Rightarrow \Diamond(\ell = 0)$ NLA3
> 2. $\Diamond\,(\ell = 0)$ $(0 \geq 0), 1., \text{MP}$
> 3. $\Diamond\,\text{true}$ NLM.

The second part of NL2 is an instance of NLA2. $\Box$

The following theorem proves the truth of the inverse of NLA4.

NL3 $(\Diamond\phi \vee \Diamond\psi) \Rightarrow \Diamond(\phi \vee \psi)$.
$\exists x.\Diamond\phi \Rightarrow \Diamond\exists x.\phi$.

Proof. Proof of the first part:

> 1. $\phi \Rightarrow (\phi \vee \psi)$ PL
> 2. $\Diamond\phi \Rightarrow \Diamond(\phi \vee \psi)$ 1., NLM
> 3. $\psi \Rightarrow (\phi \vee \psi)$ PL
> 4. $\Diamond\psi \Rightarrow \Diamond(\phi \vee \psi)$ 3., NLM
> 5. $(\Diamond\phi \vee \Diamond\psi) \Rightarrow \Diamond(\phi \vee \psi)$ 2., 4., PL.

Proof of the second part:

> 1. $\phi \Rightarrow \exists x.\phi$ PL
> 2. $\Diamond\phi \Rightarrow \Diamond\exists x.\phi$ 1., NLM
> 3. $\forall x.(\Diamond\phi \Rightarrow \Diamond\exists x.\phi)$ 2., G
> 4. $\forall x.(\Diamond\phi \Rightarrow \Diamond\exists x.\phi) \Rightarrow (\exists x.\Diamond\phi \Rightarrow \Diamond\exists x.\phi)$ PL, x is not free in $\Diamond\exists x.\phi$
> 5. $\exists x.\Diamond\phi \Rightarrow \Diamond\exists x.\phi$ 3., 4., MP.

$\Box$

The modalities $\Box$ and $\Diamond$ have the typical relations of modal logic.

NL4
$$\Box\phi \Rightarrow \Diamond\phi.$$
$$(\Diamond\phi \wedge \Box\psi) \Rightarrow \Diamond(\phi \wedge \psi).$$
$$(\Box\phi \wedge \Box\psi) \Leftrightarrow \Box(\phi \wedge \psi).$$

Proof. We present proofs of the first two parts only.
Proof of the first part:

$$\Box\phi$$
$$\Rightarrow \Diamond(\phi \vee \neg\phi) \quad \text{NL2, PL}$$
$$\Rightarrow \Diamond\phi \vee \Diamond\neg\phi \quad \text{NLA4}$$
$$\Rightarrow \Diamond\phi \quad\quad\quad \text{Def}(\Box), \text{PL}.$$

Proof of the second part:

$$\Diamond\phi \wedge \Box\psi$$
$$\Rightarrow \Diamond((\phi \wedge \psi) \vee (\phi \wedge \neg\psi)) \wedge \Box\psi \quad\quad \text{PL, NLM}$$
$$\Rightarrow (\Diamond(\phi \wedge \psi) \vee \Diamond(\phi \wedge \neg\psi)) \wedge \Box\psi \quad \text{NLA4}$$
$$\Rightarrow (\Diamond(\phi \wedge \psi) \wedge \Box\psi) \vee (\Diamond\neg\psi \wedge \Box\psi) \quad \text{PL}$$
$$\Rightarrow \Diamond(\phi \wedge \psi) \quad\quad\quad\quad\quad\quad\quad\quad \text{PL, Def}(\Box).$$

$\Box$

As explained above, $\Diamond$ is not reflexive when the length of the reference interval is nonzero. However, $\Diamond^c$ is reflexive, and the intervals reachable by $\Diamond_l^c$ and $\Diamond_r^c$ have the same ending and beginning points, respectively, as the reference interval. So we can prove the following theorem.

NL5
$$\phi \Rightarrow \Diamond^c\phi.$$
$$\bar{\Diamond}^c\Diamond\phi \Leftrightarrow \Diamond\phi.$$
$$(\Diamond\phi \wedge \bar{\Diamond}^c\psi) \Leftrightarrow \Diamond(\phi \wedge \bar{\Diamond}\psi).$$

Proof. Proof of the first part, where we assume that x is not free in ϕ:

1. $(\ell = x) \wedge \phi$
   $$\Rightarrow \Diamond^c((\ell = x) \wedge \phi) \quad \text{NLA7}$$
   $$\Rightarrow \Diamond^c\phi \quad\quad\quad\quad \text{PL, NLM}$$
2. $\exists x.((\ell = x) \wedge \phi)$
   $$\Rightarrow \Diamond^c\phi \quad \text{1., PL}, x \text{ not free in } \Diamond^c\phi$$
3. ϕ
   $$\Rightarrow (\exists x.(\ell = x)) \wedge \phi \quad \text{PL}$$
   $$\Rightarrow \exists x.((\ell = x) \wedge \phi) \quad \text{PL}, x \text{ not free in } \phi$$
4. $\phi \Rightarrow \Diamond^c\phi \quad\quad \text{2., 3., PL}.$

Proof of the second part:

The direction $\Leftarrow$ follows from the first part when NLM is applied. The following proof establishes the direction $\Rightarrow$:

1. $\bar{\Diamond}^c \Diamond \phi$

    $\Rightarrow \Box \bar{\Diamond} \Diamond \phi$ NLA6 $(\bar{\Diamond}^c \Diamond = \Diamond \bar{\Diamond} \Diamond)$

    $\Rightarrow \Box \bar{\Box} \Diamond \phi$ NLA6, NL1

2. $\bar{\Diamond}^c \Diamond \phi \wedge \neg \Diamond \phi$

    $\Rightarrow \Box \bar{\Box} \Diamond \phi \wedge \bar{\Diamond}^c \neg \Diamond \phi$ 1., NL5 (part 1), PL

    $\Rightarrow \Diamond (\bar{\Box} \Diamond \phi \wedge \bar{\Diamond} \neg \Diamond \phi)$ NL4 $(\bar{\Diamond}^c = \Diamond \bar{\Diamond})$

    $\Rightarrow \Diamond \bar{\Diamond} (\Diamond \phi \wedge \neg \Diamond \phi)$ NL4, NLM

    $\Rightarrow$ false   PL, NL2, NLM

3. $\bar{\Diamond}^c \Diamond \phi \Rightarrow \Diamond \phi$ 2., PL.

Proof of the third part:

The direction $\Leftarrow$ follows from PL and NLM. The following proof establishes the direction $\Rightarrow$:

$\Diamond \phi \wedge \bar{\Diamond}^c \psi$

$\Rightarrow \Diamond \phi \wedge \Box \bar{\Diamond} \psi$ NLA6, PL

$\Rightarrow \Diamond (\phi \wedge \bar{\Diamond} \psi)$ NL4.

$\qquad\qquad\qquad\qquad\qquad\qquad\qquad\qquad\qquad\qquad\qquad$ □

From NLA6 and NLA7, we can derive more properties of combinations of $\Diamond$, $\bar{\Diamond}$ and $\bar{\Box}$.

$\qquad \Diamond \bar{\Box} \phi \Rightarrow \Box \bar{\Box} \phi.$

NL6 $\qquad \bar{\Diamond}^c \Box \phi \Leftrightarrow \Box \phi.$

$\qquad (\Diamond \phi \wedge \Diamond \bar{\Box} \psi) \Leftrightarrow \Diamond (\phi \wedge \bar{\Box} \psi).$

Proof. The proofs of these theorems are similar to those for NL5, and are omitted here. $\qquad\qquad\qquad\qquad\qquad\qquad\qquad\qquad\qquad\qquad\qquad\qquad\qquad$ □

In order to understand the application of NLA8, we prove the following theorems. In the formulation of these theorems, we assume that $(x \geq 0)$ and $(y \geq 0)$.

$$1. \ (\ell = x) \ \Rightarrow \ (\Diamond((\ell = y) \wedge \Diamond\phi) \ \Leftrightarrow \ \Diamond^c((\ell = x + y) \wedge \Diamond\phi)).$$

$$2. \ (\ell = x) \ \Rightarrow \ \left(\begin{array}{l} \Diamond((\ell = y) \wedge \phi) \\ \Leftrightarrow \ \Diamond^c((\ell = x + y) \wedge \bar{\Diamond}^c((\ell = y) \wedge \phi)) \end{array} \right).$$

NL7 $$3. \ \left(\begin{array}{l} \Diamond((\ell = x) \wedge \Diamond((\ell = y) \wedge \phi)) \\ \Leftrightarrow \ \Diamond((\ell = x + y) \wedge \bar{\Diamond}^c((\ell = y) \wedge \phi)) \end{array} \right).$$

$$4. \ (y \geq x) \ \Rightarrow \ \left(\begin{array}{l} \bar{\Diamond}^c((\ell = x) \wedge \Diamond^c((\ell = y) \wedge \Diamond\phi)) \\ \Leftrightarrow \ \Diamond((\ell = y - x) \wedge \Diamond\phi) \end{array} \right).$$

$$5. \ (y \geq x) \ \Rightarrow \ \left(\begin{array}{l} \bar{\Diamond}^c((\ell = x) \wedge \Diamond^c((\ell = y) \wedge \phi)) \\ \Leftrightarrow \ \Diamond((\ell = y - x) \wedge \bar{\Diamond}^c((\ell = y) \wedge \phi)) \end{array} \right).$$

Proof. Proof of the first part:

$$\ell = x$$

$$\Rightarrow \ \left(\begin{array}{l} \Diamond((\ell = y) \wedge \Diamond\phi) \\ \Leftrightarrow \ \Diamond^c((\ell = x) \wedge \Diamond((\ell = y) \wedge \Diamond\phi)) \end{array} \right) \quad \text{NLA7}$$

$$\Rightarrow \ \left(\begin{array}{l} \Diamond((\ell = y) \wedge \Diamond\phi) \\ \Leftrightarrow \ \Diamond^c((\ell = x + y) \wedge \Diamond\phi) \end{array} \right) \quad \text{NLA8, NLM, PL.}$$

Proof of the second part:

$$\ell = x$$

$$\Rightarrow \ \left(\begin{array}{l} \Diamond((\ell = y) \wedge \phi) \\ \Leftrightarrow \ \Diamond((\ell = y) \wedge \bar{\Diamond}^c((\ell = y) \wedge \phi)) \end{array} \right) \quad \text{NLA7}$$

$$\Rightarrow \ \left(\begin{array}{l} \Diamond((\ell = y) \wedge \phi) \\ \Leftrightarrow \ \Diamond^c((\ell = x + y) \wedge \bar{\Diamond}^c((\ell = y) \wedge \phi)) \end{array} \right) \quad \text{NL7(part 1).}$$

We now give a proof of the fourth part, leaving the proofs of the third and fifth parts to the reader.

Assume $y \geq x$:

1. $\bar{\Diamond}^c((\ell = x) \wedge \Diamond^c((\ell = y) \wedge \Diamond\phi))$

   $\Leftrightarrow \bar{\Diamond}^c((\ell = x) \wedge \Diamond((\ell = y - x) \wedge \Diamond\phi))$ NL7 (part 1)

2. $\bar{\Diamond}^c((\ell = x) \wedge \Diamond((\ell = y - x) \wedge \Diamond\phi))$

   $\Rightarrow \bar{\Diamond}^c(\ell = x) \wedge \bar{\Diamond}^c\Diamond((\ell = y - x) \wedge \Diamond\phi)$ NLM, PL

   $\Rightarrow \Diamond((\ell = y - x) \wedge \Diamond\phi)$ NL5, PL

3. true $\Rightarrow \bar{\Diamond}\,(\ell = x)$ PL, NLA3

4. $\Diamond$true $\Rightarrow \Diamond\bar{\Diamond}\,(\ell = x)$ 3., NLM

5. $\bar{\Diamond}^c(\ell = x)$ 4., NL2, MP

6. $\Diamond((\ell = y - x) \wedge \Diamond\phi)$

   $\Rightarrow \bar{\Diamond}^c(\ell = x) \wedge \bar{\Diamond}^c\Diamond((\ell = y - x) \wedge \Diamond\phi)$ 5., NL5, PL

   $\Rightarrow \Diamond(\bar{\Diamond}\,(\ell = x) \wedge \Diamond^c((\ell = y - x) \wedge \Diamond\phi))$ NL5

   $\Rightarrow \Diamond\bar{\Diamond}\,((\ell = x) \wedge \Diamond((\ell = y - x) \wedge \Diamond\phi))$ NL5

7. $\bar{\Diamond}^c((\ell = x) \wedge \Diamond^c((\ell = y) \wedge \Diamond\phi)) \Leftrightarrow \Diamond((\ell = y - x) \wedge \Diamond\phi)$ 1., 2., 6., PL.

$\square$

A deduction theorem can be proved for NL which is similar to the deduction theorem for IL given in Chap. 2. The following abbreviation is useful for formulating the theorem:

$$\Box_a\psi \;\hat{=}\; \Box_r\Box_r\Box_l\Box_l\psi \quad \text{reads "for all intervals: } \psi\text{"}.$$

Theorem 11.3 *(Deduction) If a deduction $\Gamma, \phi \vdash \psi$, involves no application of the generalization rule G in which the quantified variable is free in ϕ, then*

$$\Gamma \vdash \Box_a\phi \Rightarrow \psi.$$

Proof. See [130]. $\square$

11.5 Completeness for an Abstract Domain

So far, real numbers ($\mathbb{R}$) have been used as the time and value domain for IL and NL, and we have indicated that each of the proof systems of IL and NL considered has to include a first-order theory of real arithmetic for its time and value domain. In this section, we discuss the issue of completeness of IL and NL with regard to the first-order theory chosen.

Given a first-order theory of the domain of time and value, denoted by $\mathcal{A}$, a formula is $\mathcal{A}$-*valid* if it is valid for any time and value domain satisfying $\mathcal{A}$.

To show the *completeness of IL or NL with respect to $\mathcal{A}$-validity*, one must show that any $\mathcal{A}$-valid IL or NL formula is provable in an IL or NL proof system in which $\mathcal{A}$ is chosen as the first-order theory for its time and value domain.

This completeness is called *completeness for an abstract domain*.
In this section, we assume that $\mathcal{A}$ always includes the following axioms.

D1 Axioms for =:

    1. $x = x$.
    2. $(x = y) \Rightarrow (y = x)$.
    3. $((x = y) \wedge (y = z)) \Rightarrow (x = z)$.
    4. $((x_1 = y_1) \wedge \cdots \wedge (x_n = y_n)) \Rightarrow (f^n(x_1, \ldots, x_n) = f(y_1, \ldots, y_n))$,
       where f^n is an n-ary function symbol.
    5. $((x_1 = y_1) \wedge \cdots \wedge (x_n = y_n)) \Rightarrow (G^n(x_1, \ldots, x_n) \Leftrightarrow G^n(y_1, \ldots, y_n))$,
       where G^n is an n-ary relation symbol.

D2 Axioms for +:

    1. $(x + 0) = x$.
    2. $(x + y) = (y + x)$.
    3. $x + (y + z) = (x + y) + z$.
    4. $((x + y) = (x + z)) \Rightarrow (y = z)$.

D3 Axioms for $\geq$:

    1. $0 \geq 0$.
    2. $((x \geq 0) \wedge (y \geq 0)) \Rightarrow (x + y) \geq 0$.
    3. $(x \geq y) \Leftrightarrow \exists z \geq 0.(x = (y + z))$.
    4. $\neg(x \geq y) \Leftrightarrow (y > x)$,
       where $(y > x) \; \widehat{=} \; ((y \geq x) \wedge \neg(y = x))$.

D4 Axiom for $-$:

$$(x - y) = z \; \Leftrightarrow \; x = (y + z).$$

The above axioms constitute a *minimal* first-order theory that can guarantee the completeness of IL and NL with respect to $\mathcal{A}$-validity. However, they are far away from the "best" theory to characterize real numbers. For example, a singleton of 0 will satisfy all the above axioms. One may wish to introduce *multiplication* and *division*, or to have additional axioms and rules that capture more features of real numbers, such as the *infinitude* and the *density* of the reals, as follows.

D5 Axioms for infinitude:

    1. $1 > 0$.
    2. $(x + 1) > x$.

D6 Axioms for density:

$$(x > y) \; \Rightarrow \; \exists z.((x > z) \wedge (z > y)).$$

Given $\mathcal{A}$, a set $\mathbb{D}$ is called an $\mathcal{A}$-set if the function symbols and the relation symbols of IL or NL are defined over $\mathbb{D}$ and satisfy $\mathcal{A}$. When an $\mathcal{A}$-set $\mathbb{D}$ is chosen as a time and value domain of IL or NL, we denote the set of time intervals of $\mathbb{D}$ by $\mathbb{Intv}_{\mathbb{D}}$, denote a value assignment from global variables to $\mathbb{D}$ by $\mathcal{V}_{\mathbb{D}}$, and denote an interpretation with respect to $\mathbb{D}$ by $\mathcal{J}_{\mathbb{D}}$:

- $\mathbb{Intv}_{\mathbb{D}} \; \hat{=} \; \{ [b, e] \mid b, e \in \mathbb{D} \wedge b \le e \}$,
- $\mathcal{V}_{\mathbb{D}} : GVar \rightarrow \mathbb{D}$,
- $\mathcal{J}_{\mathbb{D}}(v) : \mathbb{Intv}_{\mathbb{D}} \rightarrow \mathbb{D}$, for $v \in TVar$, and
- $\mathcal{J}_{\mathbb{D}}(X) : \mathbb{Intv}_{\mathbb{D}} \rightarrow \{tt, ff\}$, for $X \in PLetter$.

An $\mathcal{A}$-*model* $\mathcal{M}_{\mathbb{D}}$ is a pair consisting of an $\mathcal{A}$-set, i.e. $\mathbb{D}$, and an interpretation $\mathcal{J}_{\mathbb{D}}$.

The truth value of a formula ϕ of IL or NL for the $\mathcal{A}$-model $\mathcal{M}_{\mathbb{D}}$, value assignment $\mathcal{V}_{\mathbb{D}}$ and interval $[b, e] \in \mathbb{Intv}_{\mathbb{D}}$ is similar to the semantic definitions given in Sect. 2.2 for IL and Sect. 11.2 for NL. We write $\mathcal{M}_{\mathbb{D}}, \mathcal{V}_{\mathbb{D}}, [b, e] \models_{\mathbb{D}} \phi$ to denote that ϕ is true for the given $\mathcal{A}$-model, value assignment and interval.

Formula ϕ is $\mathcal{A}$-*valid* (written $\models_{\mathcal{A}} \phi$) iff ϕ is true for any $\mathcal{A}$-model $\mathcal{M}_{\mathbb{D}}$, value assignment $\mathcal{V}_{\mathbb{D}}$ and interval $[b, e] \in \mathbb{Intv}_{\mathbb{D}}$. ϕ is $\mathcal{A}$-*satisfiable* iff ϕ is true for some $\mathcal{A}$-model $\mathcal{M}_{\mathbb{D}}$, value assignment $\mathcal{V}_{\mathbb{D}}$ and interval $[b, e] \in \mathbb{Intv}_{\mathbb{D}}$.

The proof systems of IL and NL are sound and complete with respect to the $\mathcal{A}$-models. For both IL and NL, we have:

Theorem 11.4 *(Soundness)* If $\vdash \phi$ then $\models_{\mathcal{A}} \phi$.

Theorem 11.5 *(Completeness)* If $\models_{\mathcal{A}} \phi$ then $\vdash \phi$.

A proof of the soundness theorem can be given by proving that each axiom is sound and that each inference rule preserves soundness in the sense that it gives a sound formula when applied to sound formulas. A proof of the completeness theorem for IL can be found in [27]. One can first prove the completeness of the calculus with respect to a kind of Kripke model, and then map the interval models to the Kripke models. Following [27], a completeness proof for NL is given in [9].

Remark. In [38], there is a similar completeness result for DC for an abstract domain. The main ideas are the following:

1. The induction rules IR1 and IR2 are replaced by an ω-rule to axiomatize the finite variability of states. Let us use $\{S, \neg S\}$ as the set of complete state expressions to explain the ω-rule. In Sect. 3.3, we introduced the abbreviations

$$FA^0(S) \quad \hat{=} \quad \lceil \rceil$$
$$FA^{i+1}(S) \quad \hat{=} \quad FA^i(S) \vee (\lceil S \rceil ^\frown FA^i(S)) \vee (\lceil \neg S \rceil ^\frown FA^i(S)) \, .$$

The ω-rule can be formulated as

   If $\quad H(FA^i(S))$, for any i
   then $H(\text{true})$.

2. On the basis of the finite variability of states, we can calculate $\int S$ over an interval of $\mathbb{I}\mathrm{ntv}_{\mathbb{D}}$ (given an $\mathcal{A}$-set $\mathbb{D}$ and an interpretation $\mathcal{J}_{\mathbb{D}}$) by summing the lengths of the subintervals where the value of S is the constant 1 under $\mathcal{J}_{\mathbb{D}}$. Therefore, we can avoid the concept of an integral when we define the semantics of $\int S$ for an abstract domain. □

11.6 NL-Based Duration Calculus

An NL-based duration calculus can be established as an extension of NL in the same way as DC was established as an extension of IL in Chap. 3. The induction rules of DC must, however, be weakened when the DC is based on NL, as it turns out that the original induction rules for DC are not sound when the DC is an extension of NL [130]. (A counterexample is given in [130].)

The induction rules for this NL-based DC are restricted to formulas $H(X)$ having a specific form. Let X be a propositional letter and ϕ be a formula in which X does not occur. Let $H(X)$ denote the formula $\Box_a(X \Rightarrow \phi)$.

The two induction rules are still the following:

IR1 If $H(\lceil\rceil)$ and $H(X) \Rightarrow H(X \vee \bigvee_{i=1}^{n}(X^{\frown}\lceil S_i\rceil))$
then $H(\mathrm{true})$

and

IR2 If $H(\lceil\rceil)$ and $H(X) \Rightarrow H(X \vee \bigvee_{i=1}^{n}(\lceil S_i\rceil^{\frown}X))$
then $H(\mathrm{true})$,

where $S_1, S_2, \ldots, S_n$ are state expressions which are *complete*.

In the NL-based DC, the deduction theorem and relative-completeness result can also be proved [130] in a way similar to the proofs presented in Chaps. 3 and 5. Completeness for an abstract domain can also be proved if we replace the above IR1 and IR2 by the ω-rule.

As a possible application of the NL-based DC, we introduce below some ideas about how to express state transitions, liveness and fairness within this logical framework.

11.6.1 State Transitions, Liveness and Fairness

State Transitions

The atomic formulas $\nwarrow S$ and $\nearrow S$ given in Chap. 9 can be defined in the NL-based DC. The definitions are

$$\nwarrow S \;\;\hat{=}\;\; \Diamond_l\lceil S\rceil$$
$$\nearrow S \;\;\hat{=}\;\; \Diamond_r\lceil S\rceil .$$

Equal Distribution

Suppose two processes are competing for a resource and $S_i(t) = 1$ denotes that process i ($i = 1, 2$) has access to the resource at time t. Assume that S_1 and S_2 are mutually exclusive (i.e. $\neg(S_1 \wedge S_2)$).

We can use the following formula to specify an equal distribution of the resource in the sense that the two processes should eventually have the same access time to the resource:

$$\forall \epsilon > 0.\, \exists T.\, \Box_r (\ell > T \Rightarrow |\textstyle\int S_1 - \int S_2| < \epsilon)\,,$$

where ϵ and T are regarded as global variables.

Liveness

The following formula specifies that the state S occurs infinitely often:

$$inf(S) \,\hat{=}\, \Box_r \Diamond_r \Diamond_r \lceil\!\lceil S \rceil\!\rceil\,.$$

For example, an oscillator is specified for S by

$$inf(S) \wedge inf(\neg S)\,.$$

Strong Fairness

If S_1 denotes a request for a resource and S_2 denotes a response from the resource, then strong fairness requires that if requests occur infinitely often then responses must occur infinitely often. This can be formulated as

$$inf(S_1) \Rightarrow inf(S_2)\,.$$

Weak Fairness

The following formula express the condition that a state S stabilizes to $S = 1$ after some time:

$$stabilize(S) \,\hat{=}\, \Diamond_r \Box_r \lceil\!\lceil S \rceil\!\rceil^*\,,$$

where $\lceil\!\lceil S \rceil\!\rceil^* \,\hat{=}\, \lceil\rceil \vee \lceil\!\lceil S \rceil\!\rceil$ as in Sect. 10.3.3.

Weak fairness requires that if the requests for a resource stabilize, then there will be response from the resource infinitely often:

$$stabilize(S_1) \Rightarrow inf(S_2)\,.$$

11.6.2 Example: Delay-Insensitive Circuits

A delay-insensitive circuit is a circuit which can behave correctly regardless of the delays in its components. Its components may have unknown delays, which may even vary with time because of, for example, dependences on data or temperature.

In [52], there is a DC specification of a delay-insensitive circuit and a proof of its correctness. This specification contains a free (global) variable for each component, denoting a changeable delay. The introduction of these free variables makes the specification and also its correctness proof rather clumsy. However, by applying the NL-based DC, we can model delay-insensitive circuits succinctly.

Let us use an example to explain the main idea. Figure 11.1 shows a delay-insensitive oscillator, which has an input P and an output Q and consists of a C-gate and an inverter with unknown delays.

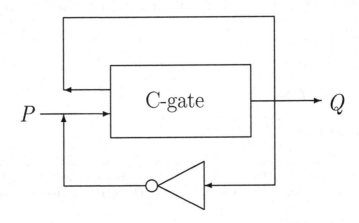

Fig. 11.1. A delay-insensitive oscillator

The input P and output Q are modeled by state variables P and Q, i.e.

$$P, Q \; : \; \text{Time} \to \{0, 1\}.$$

The behavior of the C-gate is: if $\neg(P \Leftrightarrow Q)$ then Q will take the value of P after a delay, and if $P \Leftrightarrow Q$ then Q will retain its value after a delay. This can be specified in the NL-based DC as $CG \; \widehat{=} \; CG_1 \wedge CG_2 \wedge CG_3 \wedge CG_4$, where

$$CG_1 \; \widehat{=} \; \Box_a(\lceil P \wedge \neg Q \rceil \Rightarrow \Diamond_r \Diamond_r \lceil Q \rceil)$$
$$CG_2 \; \widehat{=} \; \Box_a(\lceil \neg P \wedge Q \rceil \Rightarrow \Diamond_r \Diamond_r \lceil \neg Q \rceil)$$
$$CG_3 \; \widehat{=} \; \Box_a(\lceil P \wedge Q \rceil \Rightarrow \Diamond_r \Diamond_r \lceil Q \rceil)$$
$$CG_4 \; \widehat{=} \; \Box_a(\lceil \neg P \wedge \neg Q \rceil \Rightarrow \Diamond_r \Diamond_r \lceil \neg Q \rceil).$$

The behavior of the inverter is: P will take the complementary value of Q after a delay. This can be specified as $IG \mathrel{\widehat{=}} IG_1 \wedge IG_2$, where

$$IG_1 \mathrel{\widehat{=}} \square_a(\llbracket Q \rrbracket \Rightarrow \Diamond_r \Diamond_r \lceil \neg P \rceil)$$
$$IG_2 \mathrel{\widehat{=}} \square_a(\lceil \neg Q \rceil \Rightarrow \Diamond_r \Diamond_r \lceil P \rceil).$$

An oscillator is a circuit whose output cannot be stable:

$$OC \mathrel{\widehat{=}} \mathit{inf}(Q) \wedge \mathit{inf}(\neg Q).$$

The above circuit is an oscillator no matter what the initial values of P and Q are. That is, we can prove

$$(CG \wedge IC) \Rightarrow OC.$$

12. Probabilistic Duration Calculus

12.1 Introduction

This chapter provides a DC-based approach to the analysis of the dependability of real-time systems.

For a safe gas burner, a flame detector designed to detect failure of the flame of the burner is necessary. However, no flame detector is perfect. That is, no flame detector will always be able to detect a flame failure immediately. The dependability of a flame detector can be described by a probability function that depends on time. Therefore, undesirable behavior of a gas burner with an imperfect flame detector may not be avoidable; the dependability of the gas burner relies on the dependability of the flame detector.

In this chapter we shall use a *probabilistic automaton* to model a fault-prone implementation of a system, where transitions are attached to (history-independent) *probability functions*, following an idea presented in [45, 77]. We shall also develop a probabilistic extension of DC. Using this extension, called probabilistic duration calculus (PDC), we can calculate and reason about the system dependability of an imperfect implementation.

This chapter is based on [86, 87, 89, 90] and concentrates on discrete time. Transitions of a (discrete-time) probabilistic automaton can take place only at discrete time points. Each transition of a probabilistic automaton is labeled with a constant p ($0 \leq p \leq 1$), which is the probability of the transition occurring in one time unit. A continuous-time version is presented in [22].

In Fig. 12.1, a (discrete-time) probabilistic automaton to model an abstract implementation of the gas burner is shown.

For the gas burner automaton, we assume that the gas and the ignition are turned on at the start, and that the gas remains on throughout the time period of interest. The ignition is ideal and instant, so that the flame is established whenever ignition is applied.

However, the flame may disappear at any discrete time point, and cause a gas leakage from the burner, i.e. the automaton will transit from NonLeak to Leak. Detection of a missing flame may be delayed for any number of time units, but when it succeeds, ignition will be applied immediately and the gas leakage will be stopped, i.e. the automaton will transit from Leak to NonLeak.

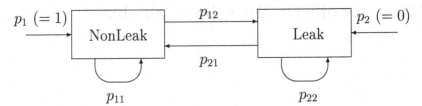

Fig. 12.1. Probabilistic automaton: abstract implementation of a gas burner

In this gas burner automaton, p_1 and p_2 are the probabilities of the gas burner starting in NonLeak and Leak, respectively. By assumption, the gas burner always starts in NonLeak, and hence $p_1 = 1$ and $p_2 = 0$. p_{11} is the probability that the flame keeps burning for another time unit, i.e. the probability for the gas burner to remain in NonLeak for another time unit. The probability that the flame fails in one time unit is p_{12}, i.e. the probability for the gas burner to transit from NonLeak to Leak in one time unit. Therefore,

$$0 \leq p_{11} \leq 1, 0 \leq p_{12} \leq 1 \text{ and } p_{11} + p_{12} = 1,$$

since in NonLeak the gas burner can, in one time unit, make either an idle transition, thereby staying in the NonLeak state, or make the other possible transition to reach Leak.

Similarly, the probability that a missing flame remains undetected for another time unit is p_{22}, and the probability that a missing flame is detected in one time unit is p_{21}, and we have

$$0 \leq p_{22} \leq 1, 0 \leq p_{21} \leq 1 \text{ and } p_{21} + p_{22} = 1.$$

Given this automaton as an implementation of the gas burner, it is interesting to know the satisfaction probability of this implementation with respect to the two design decisions $(Des_1 \wedge Des_2)$ in a given time period. With PDC, we provide axioms and rules to calculate and reason about such satisfaction probabilities.

The continuous-time probabilistic automaton described in [22] preserves the Markov property (i.e. the property of history independence), but assigns to each transition a probability of choosing this transition and a density function to determine the probability that the automaton performs the chosen transition in any time period.

In Sect. 12.2, we shall present a mathematical definition of a (discrete-time) probabilistic automaton, and introduce the satisfaction probability of a DC formula with respect to a given automaton. In Sect. 12.3, a set of axioms and rules will be established in order to calculate and reason about the satisfaction probabilities of DC formulas. In Sect. 12.4, we shall apply these axioms and rules to estimate the probability that the requirements of the gas burner ($GbReq$) will be violated by the automaton shown in Fig. 12.1.

12.2 Probabilistic Automata

A *probabilistic automaton* is a tuple $PA = (V, \tau_0, \tau)$, where

1. V is a finite but nonempty *exclusive* and *complete* set of state variables, i.e.

$$\bigvee_{P \in V} P \Leftrightarrow 1$$

and

$$P \Rightarrow \neg Q \,,$$

for any $P, Q \in V$ and $P \neq Q$.

2. $\tau_0 : V \to [0, 1]$ is called the *initial probability mass function* and must satisfy the condition

$$\Sigma_{P \in V} \tau_0(P) = 1 \,.$$

Note that $\tau_0(P)$ is the probability that the automaton starts in state P.

3. $\tau : V \times V \to [0, 1]$ is called the *single-step probability transition function* and must satisfy the condition

$$\Sigma_{Q \in V} \tau(P, Q) = 1 \,,$$

for every $P \in V$.

The gas burner automaton of Fig. 12.1 is a tuple $PA = (V, \tau_0, \tau)$, where V, τ_0 and τ are defined as follows:

1. The set V is given by

$$V = \{\text{NonLeak}, \text{Leak}\} \quad \text{and} \quad \text{NonLeak} \Leftrightarrow \neg \text{Leak} \,.$$

2. The initial probability mass function is given by

$$\tau_0(\text{NonLeak}) = p_1 = 1 \quad \text{and} \quad \tau_0(\text{Leak}) = p_2 = 0 \,.$$

3. The single-step probability transition function is given by

$$\tau(\text{NonLeak}, \text{NonLeak}) = p_{11} \,,$$
$$\tau(\text{NonLeak}, \text{Leak}) = p_{12} \,,$$
$$\tau(\text{Leak}, \text{Leak}) = p_{22} \,,$$
$$\tau(\text{Leak}, \text{NonLeak}) = p_{21} \,.$$

12.2.1 State Sequence

The behavior of a probabilistic automaton PA can be defined by its state sequences. Given a positive integer t, a sequence of states in V

$$\sigma = P_1 P_2 \cdots P_t$$

defines a possible behavior of PA for the first t time units. The automaton starts in P_1 and remains there for one time unit. Then it makes a transition from P_1 to P_2 and remains in P_2 for another one time unit, and so on. It completes $t - 1$ transitions and stays in P_t for one time unit.

For state sequences such as σ, we also use the notation

$$\langle P_1, P_2, \ldots, P_t \rangle .$$

When $t = 0$, the state sequence is empty (written $\langle \rangle$).

The probability that PA starts in P_1 is defined by the mass function as $\tau_0(P_1)$, and the probability that PA makes a transition from P_i to P_{i+1} is defined by the transition function as $\tau(P_i, P_{i+1})$. Therefore, the probability $\mu(\sigma)$ that PA follows the behavior σ is

$$\mu(\sigma) = \tau_0(P_1) \cdot \tau(P_1, P_2) \cdot \cdots \cdot \tau(P_{t-1}, P_t) .$$

For example, for the gas burner automaton shown in Fig. 12.1, we can calculate

$$\left. \begin{array}{l} \mu(\langle \text{NonLeak} \rangle) = p_1 = 1 \\ \mu(\langle \text{Leak} \rangle) = p_2 = 0 \end{array} \right\} \text{state sequences of length 1}$$

$$\left. \begin{array}{l} \mu(\langle \text{NonLeak}, \text{NonLeak} \rangle) = p_1 \cdot p_{11} = p_{11} \\ \mu(\langle \text{NonLeak}, \text{Leak} \rangle) = p_1 \cdot p_{12} = p_{12} \\ \mu(\langle \text{Leak}, \text{NonLeak} \rangle) = p_2 \cdot p_{21} = 0 \\ \mu(\langle \text{Leak}, \text{Leak} \rangle) = p_2 \cdot p_{22} = 0 \end{array} \right\} \text{state sequences of length 2.}$$

Note that the sum of the probabilities of all state sequences of length 1 is 1 and that the sum of the probabilities of all state sequences of length 2 is 1. In fact, given any length $t \geq 0$, the sum of the probabilities of all state sequences of length t is 1, as we shall prove below.

Given an arbitrary probabilistic automaton $PA = (V, \tau_0, \tau)$, the probability function

$$\mu : V^* \to [0, 1]$$

is defined as follows:

$$\mu(\sigma) = \begin{cases} 1 & \text{if } \sigma = \langle \rangle \\ \tau_0(P_1) \cdot \tau(P_1, P_2) \cdot \cdots \cdot \tau(P_{t-1}, P_t) & \text{if } \sigma = \langle P_1, P_2, \ldots, P_t \rangle. \end{cases}$$

Furthermore, let V^t be the set of all state sequences of V with length t, for $t \geq 0$. Thus V^0 is the set containing only the empty state sequence.

We can prove the following theorem expressing the fact that (V^t, μ) constitutes a *probabilistic space*, for every nonnegative integer t.

Theorem 12.1 *For any* $PA = (V, \tau_0, \tau)$ *and nonnegative integer* t,

- $0 \leq \mu(\sigma) \leq 1$, *for any* $\sigma \in V^t$, *and*
- $\Sigma_{\sigma \in V^t} \mu(\sigma) = 1$.

Proof. The first part is obvious from the definitions of μ, τ_0 and τ. The second part can be proved by induction on t using the following facts:

$$V^{t+1} = V^t V = \{\sigma_1 {}^\frown \sigma_2 \mid \sigma_1 \in V^t \wedge \sigma_2 \in V\}$$

and

$$\Sigma_{P \in V} \mu(\sigma {}^\frown P) = \mu(\sigma).$$

□

12.2.2 Satisfaction Probability

For a given probabilistic automaton $PA = (V, \tau_0, \tau)$ and DC formula ϕ, we shall define the following concepts in this section:

- The statement that the formula ϕ holds for a given state sequence $\sigma \in V^*$.
- The probability that ϕ holds for all state sequences in V^t, where t is a nonnegative integer.

To this end, we assume that PA starts at time 0 and we consider discrete interpretations over the state variables in V over discrete time intervals $[0, t]$ for the first t time units.

A state sequence $\sigma \in V^t$ of PA determines the presence and absence of the state variables in V in the first t time units, and thus defines a discrete interpretation (see Chap. 6) of the state variables in V in the interval $[0, t]$.

For example, the state sequence

⟨NonLeak, Leak⟩

defines a discrete interpretation $\mathcal{I}$ for Leak (and thus for NonLeak) in the interval $[0, 2]$, for which

$$\text{Leak}_{\mathcal{I}}(t) = \begin{cases} 0 & \text{for } 0 \leq t < 1 \\ 1 & \text{for } 1 \leq t < 2, \end{cases}$$

where the value of $\text{Leak}_{\mathcal{I}}$ at the end point of $[0, 2]$ is irrelevant and will not affect the truth of a DC formula over the interval $[0, 2]$, provided that Leak and NonLeak are the only state variables which occur in the formula.

We say that $\mathcal{I}$ is *consistent* with the above state sequence in the interval $[0, 2]$. This generalizes easily to arbitrary state sequences.

A DC formula ϕ is called a *V-formula* if ϕ contains only state variables in V, and does not contain temporal propositional letters. The truth of ϕ is therefore independent of the interpretation of temporal propositional letters and of state variables outside V.

For any V-formula ϕ, value assignment $\mathcal{V}$ and state sequence $\sigma \in V^t$, we say that ϕ *holds for σ given $\mathcal{V}$*, written $\sigma, \mathcal{V} \models \phi$, if

$$\mathcal{I}, \mathcal{V}, [0, t] \models \phi,$$

where $\mathcal{I}$ is any discrete interpretation consistent with σ for the state variables in V in the interval $[0, t]$.

In the following text we shall always refer to an arbitrarily given value assignment, but, for simplicity, we shall not mention it explicitly.

The *probability that PA satisfies a V-formula ϕ over the interval* $[0, t]$, denoted by $\mu(\phi)[t]$, can be defined as the sum of the probabilities of state sequences which are of length t and satisfy ϕ.

Let $V^t(\phi)$ be the set of state sequences in V^t which satisfy ϕ; then

$$\mu(\phi)[t] \,\,\hat{=}\,\, \Sigma_{\sigma \in V^t(\phi)} \mu(\sigma) \,.$$

Consider the probabilistic automaton *PA* defined in Fig. 12.1. The first design decision (Des_1) for the gas burner,

$$\Box(\llbracket \text{Leak} \rrbracket \,\Rightarrow\, \ell \leq 1)$$

is a V-formula, where

$$V = \{\text{NonLeak}, \text{Leak}\} \quad \text{and} \quad \text{NonLeak} \Leftrightarrow \neg \text{Leak} \,.$$

The set of state sequences of length 2 satisfying this formula is

$$V^2(Des_1) = \{\langle \text{NonLeak}, \text{NonLeak}\rangle, \langle \text{NonLeak}, \text{Leak}\rangle, \langle \text{Leak}, \text{NonLeak}\rangle\} \,,$$

and we have the result that the satisfaction probability over the interval $[0, 2]$ is

$$\mu(Des_1)[2] = p_1 \cdot p_{11} + p_1 \cdot p_{12} + p_2 \cdot p_{21} = 1 \,.$$

So the gas burner automaton shown in Fig. 12.1 represents a fully dependable implementation of the gas burner in the first two time units as far as the first design decision is concerned.

Since (V^t, μ) is a probabilistic space (Theorem 12.1), the following theorem follows from the definition of the satisfaction probability.

Theorem 12.2 *For any PA and $t \geq 0$,*

- $0 \leq \mu(\phi)[t] \leq 1$, *for any V-formula ϕ*
- $\mu(\text{true})[t] = 1$.

12.3 Probabilistic Duration Calculus: Axioms and Rules

In accordance with the definition of the satisfaction probability given in Sect. 12.2, this section proposes a set of axioms and rules to calculate and reason about $\mu(\phi)[t]$ with respect to an arbitrarily given probabilistic automaton PA and V-formula ϕ.

Since $\mu(\phi)[t]$ is a real number and t is a nonnegative integer, PDC is an extension of real arithmetic and integer arithmetic. PDC is also an extension of discrete-time DC which can derive properties of V-formulas.

The proof system for PDC presented here is not complete, but [40] provides a complete calculus for a probabilistic neighborhood logic.

12.3.1 Syntax

Syntactically, PDC extends real and integer arithmetic with $\mu(\phi)[t]$ as the additional terms, where ϕ ranges over the V-formulas of a given PA.

For example, the following formulas are well-formed formulas of PDC with respect to the gas burner automaton:

1. $\mu(GbReq)[t] = p$, which expresses the condition that p is the probability that the gas burner automaton satisfies the requirement in the first t time units.
2. $\forall t.(\mu(\neg GbReq)[t] \leq \mu(\neg Des_1)[t] + \mu(\neg Des_2)[t])$, which expresses the condition that the probability of violation of the requirement of the gas burner automaton is not greater than the sum of the probabilities of violation of the two design decisions.
3. $\forall t.(\mu(GbReq)[t] = 1 - \mu(\neg GbReq)[t])$, which expresses how to calculate the satisfaction probability of the requirement from its violation probability.

In these examples, t is regarded as a global variable ranging over nonnegative integers.

By proving the truth of the last two formulas (2 and 3) above, one can estimate the dependability of the gas burner automaton through the calculation of violation probabilities of the design decisions.

In the following, we shall use

$$R(\mu(\phi), \mu(\psi))$$

as an abbreviation of

$$\forall t.R(\mu(\phi)[t], \mu(\psi)[t]) \,,$$

where R is a relation of arithmetic.

For example, the formulas 2 and 3 above can be abbreviated as follows:

$$\mu(\neg GbReq) \leq \mu(\neg Des_1) + \mu(\neg Des_2)$$
$$\mu(GbReq) = 1 - \mu(\neg GbReq) \,.$$

The axioms and rules of real arithmetic, integer arithmetic and DC are taken as axioms and rules of PDC, as PDC extends these logics. In the following sections we list the additional axioms and rules for μ, and assume that all formulas appearing in the scope of μ are V-formulas.

The proof system is presented in two parts, where the axioms and rules in the first part are generic, and can be applied to any probabilistic automaton, while the axioms and rules in the second part are specific to a given automaton.

12.3.2 Proof System: Part I

The DC formula "true" holds for state sequences of any probabilistic automaton in any interval.

PA1 $\mu(\text{true}) = 1$.

For any interval, ϕ and $\neg\phi$ form an exclusive partition of all state sequences of any probabilistic automaton.

PA2 $\mu(\phi) + \mu(\neg\phi) = 1$.

From PA2, we can straightforwardly derive

$$\mu(GbReq) = 1 - \mu(\neg GbReq).$$

The additivity axiom of probability theory holds for PDC.

PA3 $\mu(\phi) + \mu(\psi) = \mu(\phi \vee \psi) + \mu(\phi \wedge \psi)$.

The satisfaction probability is monotone.

PA4   If $\phi \Rightarrow \psi$, then $\mu(\phi) \leq \mu(\psi)$.

The following theorem can be easily derived from the above axioms and rules.

PDC1

1. $\mu(\text{false}) = 0$.
2. $0 \leq \mu(\phi) \leq 1$.
3. $\mu(\phi \vee \psi) \leq \mu(\phi) + \mu(\psi)$.
4. If $\neg(\phi \wedge \psi)$, then $\mu(\phi \vee \psi) = \mu(\phi) + \mu(\psi)$.
5. If $\phi \Leftrightarrow \psi$, then $\mu(\phi) = \mu(\psi)$.
6. $\mu(\phi) = 1 \Rightarrow \mu(\phi \wedge \psi) = \mu(\psi)$.

Proof. The proofs of the first five cases are trivial. The last case can be proved as follows:

1. $\mu(\phi \wedge \psi) \leq \mu(\psi)$ PA4
2. $\mu(\phi) + \mu(\psi) = \mu(\phi \vee \psi) + \mu(\phi \wedge \psi)$ PA3
3. $\mu(\phi) = 1 \ \Rightarrow \ \mu(\phi \vee \psi) \leq \mu(\phi)$ PA1, PA4
4. $\mu(\phi) = 1 \ \Rightarrow \ \mu(\phi \wedge \psi) \geq \mu(\psi)$ 2., 3.
5. $\mu(\phi) = 1 \ \Rightarrow \ \mu(\phi \wedge \psi) = \mu(\psi)$ 1., 4.

□

If we consider state sequences of length t, the formulas ϕ and $(\phi \wedge \ell = t)$ hold for the same sequences.

PA5 $\mu(\phi)[t] = \mu(\phi \wedge \ell = t)[t]$.

Using this axiom, the following theorem can be proved.

PDC2 $\mu(\ell = t)[t] = 1$.
$\mu(\ell \neq t)[t] = 0$.

Proof. From PA5, PA1 and PDC1, we have

$$\mu(\text{true})[t] = \mu(\text{true} \wedge \ell = t)[t] = \mu(\ell = t)[t] = 1.$$

Furthermore, using PA2, we have

$$\mu(\ell \neq t)[t] = 1 - \mu(\ell = t)[t] = 0.$$

□

A formula ϕ holds for a state sequence of length t if and only if the formula $(\phi \frown \ell = \delta)$ holds for any extension of the sequence to a length $(t + \delta)$, where δ is a nonnegative integer.

PA6 $\mu(\phi \frown \ell = \delta)[t + \delta] = \mu(\phi)[t]$.

Using this axiom, the following theorem can be proved.

PDC3 $\mu((\phi \wedge \ell = t) \frown \psi)[t + \delta] \leq \mu(\phi)[t]$.

Proof.

$$\mu((\phi \wedge \ell = t) \frown \psi)[t + \delta]$$
$$= \mu((\phi \wedge \ell = t) \frown \psi \wedge \ell = t + \delta)[t + \delta] \quad \text{PA5}$$
$$= \mu((\phi \wedge \ell = t) \frown (\psi \wedge \ell = \delta))[t + \delta] \quad \text{PDC1}$$
$$\leq \mu((\phi \wedge \ell = t) \frown \ell = \delta)[t + \delta] \quad \text{PA4}$$
$$= \mu(\phi \wedge \ell = t)[t] \quad \text{PA6}$$
$$= \mu(\phi)[t] \quad \text{PA5.}$$

□

12.3.3 Proof System: Part II

The axioms and rules in this section refer to an arbitrarily given probabilistic automaton PA. We shall use the abbreviation

$$\lceil P \rceil^1 \;\hat{=}\; \lceil P \rceil \wedge \ell = 1 .$$

We refer to Sect. 7.2 for the definition of $\lceil P \rceil^r$.

For the initial probability mass function of PA, we have

PA7 $\mu(\lceil P \rceil^1)[1] \;=\; \tau_0(P) .$

For the transition probability function τ of PA, we have

PA8   If $\phi \Rightarrow (\text{true} ^\frown \lceil P \rceil)$
then $\mu(\phi ^\frown \lceil Q \rceil^1)[t + 1] = \tau(P, Q) \cdot \mu(\phi)[t] .$

Using these two axioms, we can prove the following theorem.

PDC4
1. $\tau_0(P) = 0 \;\Rightarrow\; \mu(\lceil P \rceil ^\frown \phi) = 0 .$
2. $\tau(P, Q) = 0 \;\Rightarrow\; \mu(\phi ^\frown \lceil P \rceil ^\frown \lceil Q \rceil^1) = 0 .$

Proof. The first part can be proved as follows. Let us assume $\tau_0(P) = 0$ and $t \geq 1$. From PA7, we can derive

$$\mu(\lceil P \rceil^1)[1] \;=\; 0 ;$$

then

$$
\begin{aligned}
&\mu(\lceil P \rceil ^\frown \phi)[t] \\
&= \mu(\lceil P \rceil^1 ^\frown (\lceil\;\rceil \vee \lceil P \rceil) ^\frown \phi)[t] \quad \text{PDC1} \\
&\leq \mu(\lceil P \rceil^1)[1] \quad\quad\quad\quad\quad\quad\quad \text{PDC3} \\
&= 0 \quad\quad\quad\quad\quad\quad\quad\quad\quad\quad\quad \text{PA7.}
\end{aligned}
$$

When $t = 0$, we have

$$
\begin{aligned}
&\mu(\lceil P \rceil ^\frown \phi)[0] \\
&= \mu((\lceil P \rceil ^\frown \phi) \wedge (\ell = 0))[0] \quad \text{PA5} \\
&= \mu(\text{false})[0] \quad\quad\quad\quad\quad\quad\quad \text{PDC1} \\
&= 0 \quad\quad\quad\quad\quad\quad\quad\quad\quad\quad \text{PDC1.}
\end{aligned}
$$

For the second part, let us assume $\tau(P, Q) = 0$. When $t \geq 1$, using PA8 we can derive

$$\mu(\phi ^\frown \lceil P \rceil ^\frown \lceil Q \rceil^1)[t] \;=\; 0 .$$

When $t = 0$, we can follow the same reasoning as for the first part to prove

$$\mu(\phi ^\frown \lceil P \rceil ^\frown \lceil Q \rceil^1)[0] \;=\; 0 .$$

$\square$

In [90], PDC is extended with classical probability matrices, and the satisfaction probabilities of many useful DC formulas, such as

$\mu(\text{true} \frown \lceil P \rceil^1)$,
$\mu(\Box \neg \lceil P \rceil)$,
$\mu(\Diamond \lceil P \rceil)$,
$\mu(\Box \neg (\lceil P \rceil \frown \lceil Q \rceil))$,
$\mu(\Diamond (\lceil P \rceil \frown \lceil Q \rceil))$,
$\mu((\phi \land (\text{true} \frown \lceil P \rceil)) \frown \lceil Q \rceil)$,
$\mu((\phi \land (\text{true} \frown \lceil P \rceil)) \frown \Diamond \lceil Q \rceil)$,

can be computed using matrix scalar products.

12.4 Example: Gas Burner

In this section, we use PDC to give an estimate of the violation probability of *GbReq* with respect to the probabilistic automaton shown in Fig. 12.1. In obtaining this estimate, we assume that the time unit is one second, and we often reason informally in order to focus on the main ideas.

Since

$$(Des_1 \land Des_2) \;\Rightarrow\; GbReq,$$

we have

$$\neg GbReq \;\Rightarrow\; (\neg Des_1 \lor \neg Des_2).$$

Then, using PA4 and PDC1, we obtain

$$\mu(\neg GbReq) \;\leq\; \mu(\neg Des_1 \lor \neg Des_2) \;\leq\; \mu(\neg Des_1) + \mu(\neg Des_2).$$

Therefore, the sum of the violation probabilities of the two design decisions is an upper bound on the violation probability of the requirement.

In the next two subsections, we use the proof system of PDC to derive recursive functions for the computation of the violation probabilities of the design decisions, i.e. we give *programs* (in terms of recursive functions) for computing $\mu(\neg Des_1)[t]$ and $\mu(\neg Des_2)[t]$ and prove the correctness of the programs.

Hence, using these programs, we can estimate the violation probability of the requirements as $\mu(\neg GbReq)[t] \;\leq\; \mu(\neg Des_1)[t] + \mu(\neg Des_2)[t]$.

The design decisions are formulated in Sect. 3.2 for the continuous-time domain as follows:

$Des_1 \;\widehat{=}\; \Box(\lceil \text{Leak} \rceil \Rightarrow \ell \leq 1)$
$Des_2 \;\widehat{=}\; \Box((\lceil \text{Leak} \rceil \frown \lceil \neg \text{Leak} \rceil \frown \lceil \text{Leak} \rceil) \Rightarrow \ell \geq 30)$.

However, for the discrete-time domain, the second design decision, i.e. that the distance between two leaks is not less than 30 seconds, must be reformulated by taking into account the fact that each leak lasts for at least one second:

$$\Box((\lceil \text{Leak} \rceil \,^\frown \lceil \neg\text{Leak} \rceil \,^\frown \lceil \text{Leak} \rceil) \;\Rightarrow\; \ell \geq 32) \,.$$

12.4.1 Calculation of $\mu(\neg Des_1)$

Here we establish a recursive function to calculate $\mu(\neg Des_1)[t]$.

In order to calculate $\mu(\neg Des_1)[t]$, we shall need an auxiliary function. Let

$$f_1(t) = \mu(\neg Des_1)[t]$$

and

$$g_1(t) = \mu(Des_1 \,^\frown \lceil \neg\text{Leak} \rceil^1)[t]$$

We show below that f_1 can be defined recursively by the program:

$$
\begin{aligned}
f_1(0) \quad &= 0 \\
f_1(1) \quad &= 0 \\
f_1(2) \quad &= 0 \\
f_1(t+1) &= f_1(t) + p_{12} \cdot p_{22} \cdot g_1(t-1), \text{ for } t \geq 2,
\end{aligned}
$$

and that the auxiliary function g_1 can be defined recursively by the program:

$$
\begin{aligned}
g_1(0) \quad &= 0 \\
g_1(1) \quad &= 1 \\
g_1(2) \quad &= p_{11} \\
g_1(t+1) &= p_{11} \cdot g_1(t) + p_{12} \cdot p_{21} \cdot g_1(t-1), \text{ for } t \geq 2.
\end{aligned}
$$

It is easy to see that f_1 and g_1 terminate for any natural number $t \geq 0$. We now use PDC to prove that they compute the correct functions.

We shall exploit the fact that

$$\neg Des_1 \;\Leftrightarrow\; \Diamond(\lceil \text{Leak} \rceil \,\wedge\, \ell > 1) \,.$$

The formula Des_1 is violated in the interval comprising the first $t+1$ time units if and only if Des_1 is violated in the first t time units or Des_1 holds for the first t time units but is violated in the full interval comprising the $t+1$ time units:

$$\neg Des_1 \wedge \ell = t+1 \;\Leftrightarrow\; \left(\begin{array}{l} ((\neg Des_1 \,^\frown \ell = 1) \wedge \ell = t+1) \\ \vee\, ((Des_1 \,^\frown \ell = 1) \wedge \neg Des_1 \wedge \ell = t+1) \end{array} \right) \,.$$

The two formulas on the right-hand side above are mutually exclusive. From PDC1 and PA5, we have

$$\mu(\neg Des_1)[t+1]$$
$$= \mu(\neg Des_1 \frown \ell = 1)[t+1] + \mu((Des_1 \frown \ell = 1) \wedge \neg Des_1)[t+1],$$

and from PA6 we have

$$\mu(\neg Des_1 \frown \ell = 1)[t+1] = \mu(\neg Des_1)[t].$$

In the rest of this subsection and in the next subsection, we shall often apply the following expansion of $\Box \phi$:

$$\Box \phi \Leftrightarrow \left(\begin{array}{l} (\lceil \rceil \wedge \phi) \\ \vee\ (((\Box \phi \frown \lceil \neg \text{Leak} \rceil^1) \vee (\Box \phi \frown \lceil \text{Leak} \rceil^1)) \wedge \Box \phi) \end{array} \right).$$

To calculate $\mu((Des_1 \frown \ell = 1) \wedge \neg Des_1)[t+1]$, we expand Des_1 and exploit the fact that

$$(Des_1 \frown \ell = 1) \wedge \neg Des_1$$
$$\Leftrightarrow (\lceil \text{Leak} \rceil^2 \vee (Des_1 \frown \lceil \neg \text{Leak} \rceil^1 \frown \lceil \text{Leak} \rceil^2)).$$

From PDC1, we obtain

$$\mu((Des_1 \frown \ell = 1) \wedge \neg Des_1)[t+1]$$
$$= \mu(\lceil \text{Leak} \rceil^2)[t+1] + \mu(Des_1 \frown \lceil \neg \text{Leak} \rceil^1 \frown \lceil \text{Leak} \rceil^2)[t+1],$$

and from PDC4 and PA8 we obtain

$$\mu((Des_1 \frown \ell = 1) \wedge \neg Des_1)[t+1]$$
$$= p_{12} \cdot p_{22} \cdot \mu(Des_1 \frown \lceil \neg \text{Leak} \rceil^1)[t-1],$$

where $t \geq 2$.

In order to calculate $\mu(Des_1 \frown \lceil \neg \text{Leak} \rceil^1)$, we establish the expansion

$$(Des_1 \frown \lceil \neg \text{Leak} \rceil^1) \Leftrightarrow \left(\begin{array}{l} \lceil \neg \text{Leak} \rceil^1 \\ \vee (Des_1 \frown \lceil \neg \text{Leak} \rceil^2) \\ \vee (\lceil \text{Leak} \rceil^1 \frown \lceil \neg \text{Leak} \rceil^1) \\ \vee (Des_1 \frown \lceil \neg \text{Leak} \rceil^1 \frown \lceil \text{Leak} \rceil^1 \frown \lceil \neg \text{Leak} \rceil^1) \end{array} \right).$$

Using PDC1, we obtain

$$\mu(Des_1 \frown \lceil \neg \text{Leak} \rceil^1)[t+1]$$
$$= \left(\begin{array}{l} \mu(\lceil \neg \text{Leak} \rceil^1)[t+1] \\ + \mu(Des_1 \frown \lceil \neg \text{Leak} \rceil^2)[t+1] \\ + \mu(\lceil \text{Leak} \rceil^1 \frown \lceil \neg \text{Leak} \rceil^1)[t+1] \\ + \mu(Des_1 \frown \lceil \neg \text{Leak} \rceil^1 \frown \lceil \text{Leak} \rceil^1 \frown \lceil \neg \text{Leak} \rceil^1)[t+1] \end{array} \right).$$

Furthermore, from PDC2, PA8 and PDC4, we have the result that

$$\mu(Des_1 \frown \lceil \neg \text{Leak} \rceil^1)[t+1]$$
$$= \left(\begin{array}{l} p_{11} \cdot \mu(Des_1 \frown \lceil \neg \text{Leak} \rceil^1)[t] \\ + p_{12} \cdot p_{21} \cdot \mu(Des_1 \frown \lceil \neg \text{Leak} \rceil^1)[t-1] \end{array} \right) ,$$

when $t \geq 2$.

We can now establish the recursive cases for f_1 and g_1, since when $t \geq 2$, we have the result that

$$\mu(\neg Des_1)[t+1]$$
$$= \left(\begin{array}{l} \mu(\neg Des_1)[t] \\ + p_{12} \cdot p_{22} \cdot \mu(Des_1 \frown \lceil \neg \text{Leak} \rceil^1)[t-1] \end{array} \right) ,$$

which establishes the recursive case for f_1, and

$$\mu(Des_1 \frown \lceil \neg \text{Leak} \rceil^1)[t+1]$$
$$= \left(\begin{array}{l} p_{11} \cdot \mu(Des_1 \frown \lceil \neg \text{Leak} \rceil^1)[t] \\ + p_{12} \cdot p_{21} \cdot \mu(Des_1 \frown \lceil \neg \text{Leak} \rceil^1)[t-1] \end{array} \right) ,$$

which establishes the recursive case for g_1.

In order to establish the base cases for f_1 and g_1, we observe first that

1. $(\neg Des_1 \wedge (\ell = 2)) \Leftrightarrow \lceil \text{Leak} \rceil^2$
2. $(\neg Des_1 \wedge (\ell \leq 1)) \Leftrightarrow \text{false}$
3. $\left(\begin{array}{l} ((Des_1 \frown \lceil \neg \text{Leak} \rceil^1) \wedge (\ell = 2)) \\ \Leftrightarrow (\lceil \text{Leak} \rceil^1 \frown \lceil \neg \text{Leak} \rceil^1 \vee \lceil \neg \text{Leak} \rceil^2) \end{array} \right)$
4. $((Des_1 \frown \lceil \neg \text{Leak} \rceil^1) \wedge (\ell = 1)) \Leftrightarrow \lceil \neg \text{Leak} \rceil^1$
5. $((Des_1 \frown \lceil \neg \text{Leak} \rceil^1) \wedge (\ell = 0)) \Leftrightarrow \text{false}.$

We can derive the following using PA5:

1. $\mu(\neg Des_1)[2] = 0$ PDC4
2. $\mu(\neg Des_1)[1] = \mu(\neg Des_1)[0] = 0$ PDC1
3. $\mu(Des_1 \frown \lceil \neg \text{Leak} \rceil^1)[2] = p_{11}$ PDC1, PDC4, PA8, PA7
4. $\mu(Des_1 \frown \lceil \neg \text{Leak} \rceil^1)[1] = 1$ PA7
5. $\mu(Des_1 \frown \lceil \neg \text{Leak} \rceil^1)[0] = 0$ PDC1.

These account for all the base cases of f_1 and g_1, and we have now shown how to calculate the violation probability of Des_1 with respect to the implementation shown in Fig. 12.1.

12.4.2 Calculation of $\mu(\neg Des_2)$

The calculation of $\mu(\neg Des_2)$ can also be done recursively.
To establish this, we show that the functions

$$f_2(t) = \mu(\neg Des_2)[t]$$
$$g_2(t) = \mu(Des_2)[t]$$
$$h_2(t) = \mu(Des_2 \wedge (Des_2 \frown \lceil \neg \text{Leak} \rceil^1))[t]$$
$$k_2(t) = \mu(Des_2 \wedge (Des_2 \frown \lceil \text{Leak} \rceil^1))[t]$$

can be defined by mutual recursion as follows:

$$f_2(t) = 1 - g_2(t)$$

$$g_2(t) = \begin{cases} 1 & \text{if } t = 0 \\ h_2(t) + k_2(t) & \text{otherwise} \end{cases}$$

$$h_2(t) = \begin{cases} 0 & \text{if } t = 0 \\ 1 & \text{if } t = 1 \\ p_{11} \cdot h_2(t-1) + p_{21} \cdot k_2(t-1) & \text{otherwise} \end{cases}$$

$$k_2(t) = \begin{cases} 0 & \text{if } t = 0 \text{ or } t = 1 \\ p_{22} \cdot k_2(t-1) + p_{11}^{t-2} \cdot p_{12} & \text{if } 2 \le t < 32 \\ p_{22} \cdot k_2(t-1) + p_{11}^{29} \cdot p_{12} \cdot h_2(t-30) & \text{if } 32 \le t. \end{cases}$$

In this case also, it is not difficult to see that these programs all terminate for any natural number $t \ge 0$. We shall now prove that they compute the correct functions.

The recursion formula for f_2 is easy to justify, since from PA2 we have

$$\mu(\neg Des_2) = 1 - \mu(Des_2).$$

In order to justify the recursion formula for g_2, we expand Des_2:

$$(Des_2 \wedge \ell > 0) \Leftrightarrow \begin{pmatrix} (Des_2 \wedge (Des_2 \frown \lceil \neg \text{Leak} \rceil^1)) \\ \vee (Des_2 \wedge (Des_2 \frown \lceil \text{Leak} \rceil^1)) \end{pmatrix}.$$

By using PDC1, we obtain

$$\mu(Des_2 \wedge \ell > 0) = \begin{pmatrix} \mu(Des_2 \wedge (Des_2 \frown \lceil \neg \text{Leak} \rceil^1)) \\ + \mu(Des_2 \wedge (Des_2 \frown \lceil \text{Leak} \rceil^1)) \end{pmatrix},$$

which establishes the recursive case for g_2.
For the base case for g_2, we must show that $\mu(Des_2)[0] = 1$.

Since

$$\mu(\ell = 0)[0] = 1$$

by PDC2, and

$$\ell = 0 \;\Rightarrow\; Des_2$$

holds in DC, the base case can be established by using PA4 and PDC1, as we have

$$1 = \mu(\ell = 0)[0] \le \mu(Des_2)[0] \le 1.$$

To establish the recursive case for h_2, we assume that the length of the interval concerned is not less than 2, i.e. $\ell \ge 2$, and expand Des_2 as follows:

$$Des_2 \wedge (Des_2 \,^\frown \lceil \neg \text{Leak} \rceil^1)$$
$$\Leftrightarrow \left(\begin{array}{l} (Des_2 \wedge (Des_2 \,^\frown \lceil \neg \text{Leak} \rceil^2)) \\ \vee\, (Des_2 \wedge (Des_2 \,^\frown \lceil \text{Leak} \rceil^1 \,^\frown \lceil \neg \text{Leak} \rceil^1)) \end{array} \right).$$

Hence, by PDC1,

$$\mu(Des_2 \wedge (Des_2 \,^\frown \lceil \neg \text{Leak} \rceil^1))$$
$$= \left(\begin{array}{l} \mu(Des_2 \wedge (Des_2 \,^\frown \lceil \neg \text{Leak} \rceil^2)) \\ +\, \mu(Des_2 \wedge (Des_2 \,^\frown \lceil \text{Leak} \rceil^1 \,^\frown \lceil \neg \text{Leak} \rceil^1)) \end{array} \right).$$

However, in DC we have the result that

$$(Des_2 \,^\frown \lceil \neg \text{Leak} \rceil^1) \;\Rightarrow\; Des_2,$$

since Des_2 is a constraint about the distance between two leaks, and the last occurrence of $\lceil \neg \text{Leak} \rceil^1$ is irrelevant to this constraint. Thus, we have

$$Des_2 \wedge (Des_2 \,^\frown \lceil \neg \text{Leak} \rceil^2)$$
$$\Leftrightarrow (Des_2 \wedge (Des_2 \,^\frown \lceil \neg \text{Leak} \rceil^1)) \,^\frown \lceil \neg \text{Leak} \rceil^1$$

and

$$Des_2 \wedge (Des_2 \,^\frown \lceil \text{Leak} \rceil^1 \,^\frown \lceil \neg \text{Leak} \rceil^1)$$
$$\Leftrightarrow (Des_2 \wedge (Des_2 \,^\frown \lceil \text{Leak} \rceil^1)) \,^\frown \lceil \neg \text{Leak} \rceil^1.$$

So, by use of PDC1 and PA8, when $t \ge 2$, we can derive

$$\mu(Des_2 \wedge (Des_2 \,^\frown \lceil \neg \text{Leak} \rceil^1))[t]$$
$$= \left(\begin{array}{l} \mu((Des_2 \wedge (Des_2 \,^\frown \lceil \neg \text{Leak} \rceil^1)) \,^\frown \lceil \neg \text{Leak} \rceil^1)[t] \\ +\, \mu((Des_2 \wedge (Des_2 \,^\frown \lceil \text{Leak} \rceil^1)) \,^\frown \lceil \neg \text{Leak} \rceil^1)[t] \end{array} \right)$$
$$= \left(\begin{array}{l} p_{11} \cdot \mu(Des_2 \wedge (Des_2 \,^\frown \lceil \neg \text{Leak} \rceil^1))[t-1] \\ +\, p_{21} \cdot \mu(Des_2 \wedge (Des_2 \,^\frown \lceil \text{Leak} \rceil^1))[t-1] \end{array} \right),$$

which establishes the recursive case for h_2. We leave the base cases for the reader.

To establish the two recursive cases for k_2, we assume that $\ell \geq 2$ and expand Des_2 as follows:

$$Des_2 \wedge (Des_2 \frown \llbracket \text{Leak} \rrbracket^1)$$
$$\Leftrightarrow \left(\begin{array}{l} (Des_2 \wedge (Des_2 \frown \llbracket \text{Leak} \rrbracket^2)) \\ \vee (Des_2 \wedge (Des_2 \frown \llbracket \neg\text{Leak} \rrbracket^1 \frown \llbracket \text{Leak} \rrbracket^1)) \end{array} \right).$$

We consider the two cases in the above disjunction:

1. If Des_2 ends with $\llbracket \text{Leak} \rrbracket^2$, then we can prove in DC that

$$Des_2 \wedge (Des_2 \frown \llbracket \text{Leak} \rrbracket^2) \Leftrightarrow (Des_2 \wedge (Des_2 \frown \llbracket \text{Leak} \rrbracket^1)) \frown \llbracket \text{Leak} \rrbracket^1 ,$$

since both $\llbracket \text{Leak} \rrbracket^2$ and $\llbracket \text{Leak} \rrbracket^1$ are regarded as a single gas leakage and have the same effect on the truth of Des_2. Hence, by PDC1 and PA8, we have, when $t \geq 2$, the result that

$$\mu(Des_2 \wedge (Des_2 \frown \llbracket \text{Leak} \rrbracket^2))[t]$$
$$= p_{22} \cdot \mu(Des_2 \wedge (Des_2 \frown \llbracket \text{Leak} \rrbracket^1))[t-1] .$$

2. If Des_2 ends with $(\llbracket \neg\text{Leak} \rrbracket^1 \frown \llbracket \text{Leak} \rrbracket^1)$, then in order to keep Des_2 (i.e. $\Box((\llbracket \text{Leak} \rrbracket \frown \llbracket \neg\text{Leak} \rrbracket \frown \llbracket \text{Leak} \rrbracket) \Rightarrow \ell \geq 32))$ true, we must consider two cases:

   Case: $2 \leq \ell < 32$. In this case we have

$$(Des_2 \wedge (Des_2 \frown \llbracket \neg\text{Leak} \rrbracket^1 \frown \llbracket \text{Leak} \rrbracket^1)) \Leftrightarrow (\llbracket \neg\text{Leak} \rrbracket \frown \llbracket \text{Leak} \rrbracket^1) .$$

   Hence, by PA5, PDC1, PA7 and PA8, we have, when $2 \leq t < 32$, the result that

$$\mu(Des_2 \wedge (Des_2 \frown \llbracket \neg\text{Leak} \rrbracket^1 \frown \llbracket \text{Leak} \rrbracket^1))[t] = p_1 \cdot p_{11}^{t-2} \cdot p_{12}$$

   and

$$\mu(Des_2 \wedge (Des_2 \frown \llbracket \text{Leak} \rrbracket^1))[t]$$
$$= p_{22} \cdot \mu(Des_2 \wedge (Des_2 \frown \llbracket \text{Leak} \rrbracket^1))[t-1] + p_{11}^{t-2} \cdot p_{12} ,$$

   as $p_1 = 1$. This establishes the first recursive case for k_2.

   Case: $\ell \geq 32$. In this case we have

$$Des_2 \wedge (Des_2 \frown \llbracket \neg\text{Leak} \rrbracket^1 \frown \llbracket \text{Leak} \rrbracket^1)$$
$$\Leftrightarrow ((Des_2 \wedge (Des_2 \frown \llbracket \neg\text{Leak} \rrbracket^1)) \frown \llbracket \neg\text{Leak} \rrbracket^{29} \frown \llbracket \text{Leak} \rrbracket^1)$$

   and, therefore, also

$$\mu(Des_2 \wedge (Des_2 \frown \llbracket \neg\text{Leak} \rrbracket^1 \frown \llbracket \text{Leak} \rrbracket^1))[t]$$
$$= p_{11}^{29} \cdot p_{12} \cdot \mu(Des_2 \wedge (Des_2 \frown \llbracket \neg\text{Leak} \rrbracket^1))[t-30]$$

and

$$\mu(Des_2 \wedge (Des_2 \frown \llbracket \text{Leak} \rrbracket^1))[t]$$

$$= \left(\begin{array}{l} p_{22} \cdot \mu(Des_2 \wedge (Des_2 \frown \llbracket \text{Leak} \rrbracket^1))[t-1] \\ + p_{11}^{29} \cdot p_{12} \cdot \mu(Des_2 \wedge (Des_2 \frown \llbracket \neg \text{Leak} \rrbracket^1))[t-30] \end{array} \right),$$

which establishes the second recursive case for k_2.

We leave the base cases for k_2 for the reader.

In [90], the recursions required to calculate $\mu(\neg Des_1)$ and $\mu(\neg Des_2)$ were derived in a more direct way by using probability matrices and the satisfaction probabilities of a set of useful DC formulas. The dependability of a communication protocol over an unreliable medium [45] was also calculated in [90].

References

1. Allen J.F. (1984) Towards a General Theory of Action and Time. Artificial Intelligence 23:123–154
2. Chetcuti-Serandio N., L.F. del Cerro L.F. (2000) A Mixed Decision Method for Duration Calculus. Journal of Logic and Computation, 10(6):877–895
3. Alur R., Courcoubetis C., Dill D. (1990) Model-Checking for Real-Time Systems. In: Fifth Annual IEEE Symposium on Logic in Computer Science. IEEE Press, Piscataway, NJ, 414–425
4. Alur R., Courcoubetis C., Henzinger T.A., Ho P-H. (1993) Hybrid automata: An Algorithmic Approach to the Specification and Verification of Hybrid Systems. In: Grossman R.L., Nerode A., Ravn A.P., Rischel H. (Eds.) Hybrid Systems, Lecture Notes in Computer Science 736. Springer, Berlin, Heidelberg, 209–229
5. Alur R., Dill D. (1992) The Theory of Timed Automata. In: de Bakker J.W., Huizing C., de Roever W.P., Rozenberg G. (Eds.) Real-Time: Theory in Practice. Lecture Notes in Computer Science 600. Springer, Berlin, Heidelberg, 45–73
6. Alur R., Dill D. (1994) A Theory of Timed Automata. Theoretical Computer Science 126:45–73
7. Alur R., Feder T., Henzinger T.A. (1991) The Benefits of Relaxing Punctuality. In: Tenth Annual ACM Symposium on Principles of Distributed Computing. ACM Press, New York, 139–152
8. Barua R. (2003) Completeness of a Combination of Neighbourhood Logic and Temporal Logic. Formal Aspects of Computing. To appear
9. Barua R., Roy S., Zhou C.C. (2000) Completeness of Neighbourhood Logic. Journal of Logic and Computation 10(2):271–295
10. Berry G., Gonthier G. (1992) The Esterel Synchronous Programming Language: Design, Semantics, Implementation. Science of Computer Programming 19:87–152
11. Bird R. (1976) Programs and Machines. Wiley, London
12. Braberman V.A., Dang V.H. (1998) On Checking Timed Automata for Linear Duration Invariants. In: Proceedings of the 19th IEEE Real-Time Systems Symposium. IEEE Press, Piscataway, NJ, 264–273
13. Chakravorty G.,Pandya P.K. (2003) Digitizing Interval Duration Logic. In: Hunt Jr., Warren A., Somenzi F. (Eds.) Computer Aided Verification (CAV 2003), Lecture Notes in Computer Science 2725. Springer, Berlin, Heidelberg, 167–179
14. Chan P., Dang V.H. (1995) Duration Calculus Specification of Scheduling for Tasks with Shared Resources. In: Kanchanasut K., Levy J.-J. (Eds.) Asian Computing Science Conference 1995, Lecture Notes in Computer Science 1023. Springer, Berlin, Heidelberg, 365–380

15. Chellas B.F. (1980) Modal Logic: An Introduction. Cambridge University Press, Cambridge

16. Chen Z.J., Wang J., Zhou C.C. (1995) An Abstraction of Hybrid Control Systems. In: IEEE Singapore International Conference on Intelligent Control and Instrumentation. IEEE Press, Piscataway, NJ, 1–6

17. Dang V.H. (1998) Modelling and Verification of Biphase Mark Protocols in Duration Calculus using PVS/DC$^-$. In: Application of Concurrency to System Design (CSD'98). IEEE Press, Piscataway, NJ, 88–98

18. Dang V.H., Guelev D.P. (1999) Completeness and Decidability of a Fragment of Duration Calculus with Iteration. In: Thiagarajan P.S., Yap R. (Eds.) Advances in Computing Science, Lecture Notes in Computer Science 1742. Springer, Berlin, Heidelberg, 139–150

19. Dang V.H., Ko K.I. (1996) Verification via Digitized Model of Real-Time Systems. In: Proceedings of Asia–Pacific Software Engineering Conference. IEEE Press, Piscataway, NJ, 4–15

20. Dang V.H., Phan H.G. (1996) A Sampling Semantics of Duration Calculus. In: Jonsson B., Parrow J. (Eds.) Formal Techniques in Real-Time and Fault Tolerant Systems, Lecture Notes in Computer Science 1135. Springer, Berlin, Heidelberg, 188–207

21. Dang V.H., Wang J. (1996) On Design of Hybrid Control Systems using I/O Automata Models. In: Chandru V., Vinay V. (Eds.) Foundations of Software Technology and Theoretical Computer Science, Lecture Notes in Computer Science 1180. Springer, Berlin, Heidelberg, 156–167

22. Dang V.H., Zhou C.C. (1999) Probabilistic Suration Calculus for Continuous Time. Formal Aspects of Computing 11(1):21–44

23. Dierks H. (2003) Comparing Model-Checking and Logical Reasoning for Real-Time Systems. Formal Aspects of Computing. To appear

24. Dierks H., Fehnker A., Mader A., Vaandrager F.W. (1998) Operational and Logical Semantics for Polling Real-Time Systems. In: Ravn A.P., Rischel H. (Eds.) Formal Techniques in Real-Time and Fault-Tolerant Systems, Lecture Notes in Computer Science 1486. Springer, Berlin, Heidelberg, 29–40

25. Do V.N., Dang V.H. (2001) A Systematic Design of Real-Time Systems using Duration Calculus. In: Proceedings of SCI 2001. IEEE Press, Piscataway, NJ, 241–246

26. Dong S.Z., Xu Q.W., Zhan N.J. (1999) A Formal Proof of the Rate Monotonic Scheduler. In: Proceedings of the Sixth International Conference on Real-Time Computing Systems and Applications. IEEE Press, Piscataway, NJ, 500–507.

27. Dutertre B. (1995) Complete Proof Systems for First Order Interval Temporal Logic. In: Tenth Annual IEEE Symposium on Logic in Computer Science. IEEE Press, Piscataway, NJ, 36–43

28. Dutertre B. (1995) On First Order Interval Temporal Logic. Technical report, Report No. CSD-TR-94-3, Department of Computer Science, Royal Holloway College, University of London

29. Emerson E.A., Lei C.-L.(1985) Modalities for Model Checking: Branching Time Strikes Back. In: 12th Symposium on Principles of Programming Languages. ACM Press, New York, 84–96

30. Engel M., Kubica M., Madey J., Parnas D.L., Ravn A.P., van Schouwen A.J. (1993) A Formal Approach to Computer Systems Requirements Documentation. In: Grossman R.L., Nerode A., Ravn A.P., Rischel H. (Eds.) Hybrid Systems, Lecture Notes in Computer Science 736. Springer, Berlin, Heidelberg, 452–474

31. Engel M., Rischel H. (1994) Dagstuhl-Seminar Specification Problem – a Duration Calculus Solution. Technical report, Department of Computer Science, Technical University of Denmark, Lyngby

32. Fränzle M. (1996) Synthesizing Controllers from Duration Calculus. In: Jonsson B., Parrow J. (Eds.) Formal Techniques in Real-Time and Fault-Tolerant Systems, Lecture Notes in Computer Science 1135. Springer, Berlin, Heidelberg, 168–187

33. Fränzle M. (1997) Controller Design from Temporal Logic: Undecidability Need Not Matter. PhD thesis, Institut für Informatik und Praktische Mathematik der Christian-Albrechts-Universität Kiel, Germany

34. Fränzle M. (2002) Take it NP-Easy: Bounded Model Construction for Duration Calculus. In: Damm W., Olderog E.-R. (Eds.) Formal Techniques in Real-Time and Fault-Tolerant Systems, Lecture Notes in Computer Science 2469. Springer, Berlin, Heidelberg, 245–264

35. Fränzle M. (2003) Model-Checking Dense-Time Duration Calculus. Formal Aspects of Computing. To appear

36. Gao J.P., Xu Q.W. (1999) Rigorous Design of a Fault Diagnosis and Isolation Algorithm. In: Antsaklis P.J., Kohn W., Lemmon M., Nerode A., Sastry S. (Eds.) Hybrid Systems V, Lecture Notes in Computer Science 1567. Springer, Berlin, Heidelberg, 100–121

37. George C., Xia Y. (1999) An Operational Semantics for Timed RAISE. In: Wing J., Woodcock J., Davies J. (Eds.) World Congress on Formal Methods (FM '99), Lecture Notes in Computer Science 1709. Springer, Berlin, Heidelberg, 1008–1027

38. Guelev D.P. (1998) A Calculus of Durations on Abstract Domains: Completeness and Extensions. UNU/IIST Report No. 139, International Institute for Software Technology, Macau

39. Guelev D.P. (2000) A Complete Fragment of Higher-Order Duration μ-Calculus. In: Kapoor S., Prasad S. (Eds.) Foundations of Software Technology and Theoretical Computer Science, Lecture Notes in Computer Science 1974. Springer, Berlin, Heidelberg, 264–276

40. Guelev D.P. (2000) Probabilistic Neighbourhood Logic. In: Joseph M. (Ed.) Formal Techniques in Real-Time and Fault-Tolerant Systems, Lecture Notes in Computer Science 1926. Springer, Berlin, Heidelberg, 264–275

41. Guelev D.P., Dang V.H. (1999) On the Completeness and Decidability of Duration Calculus with Iteration. In: Thiagarajan S., Yap R. (Eds.) Advances in Computing Science, Lecture Notes in Computer Science 1742. Springer, Berlin, Heidelberg, 139–150

42. Guelev D.P., Dang V.H. (2002) Prefix and Projection onto State in Duration Calculus. In: Asarin E., Maler O., Yovine S. (Eds.) Electronic Notes in Theoretical Computer Science 65:6. Elsevier, Amsterdam

43. Halpern J., Moszkowski B., Manna Z. (1983) A Hardware Semantics based on Temporal Intervals. In: Diaz J. (Ed.) ICALP'83, Lecture Notes in Computer Science 154. Springer, Berlin, Heidelberg, 278–291

44. Halpern J.Y., Shoham Y. (1986) A Propositional Modal Logic of Time Intervals. In: Proceedings of the First IEEE Symposium on Logic in Computer Science. IEEE Press, Piscataway, NJ, 279–292

45. Hansen H., Jonsson B. (1994) A Logic for Reasoning about Time and Reliability. Formal Aspects of Computing 6(5):512–535

46. Hansen K.M., Ravn A.P., Stavridou V. (1996) From Safety Analysis to Formal Specification. Technical report, Department of Information Technology, Technical University of Denmark, Lyngby

47. Hansen M.R. (1994) Model-Checking Discrete Duration Calculus. Formal Aspects of Computing 6A:826–845
48. Hansen M.R., Pandya P.K., Zhou C.C. (1995) Finite Divergence. Theoretical Computer Science 138:113–139
49. Hansen M.R., Sharp R. (2003) Using Interval Logics for Temporal Analysis of Security Protocols. In First ACM Workshop on Formal Methods in Security Engineering (FMSE'03). ACM Press, New York, 24–31
50. Hansen M.R., Zhou C.C. (1992) Semantics and Completeness of Duration Calculus. In: de Bakker J. W, Huizing C., de Roever W.-P., Rozenberg G. (Eds) Real-Time: Theory in Practice, Lecture Notes in Computer Science 600. Springer, Berlin, Heidelberg, 209–225
51. Hansen M.R., Zhou C.C. (1997) Duration Calculus: Logical Foundations. Formal Aspects of Computing 9:283–330
52. Hansen M.R., Zhou C.C., Staunstrup J. (1992) A Real-Time Duration Semantics for Circuits. In: TAU'92: 1992 Workshop on Timing Issues in the Specification and Synthesis of Digital Systems, Princeton University, Princeton, NJ
53. Harel D. (1987) StateSharts: A Visual Formalism for Complex Systems. Science of Computer Programming 8:231–274
54. Harel E., Lichtenstein O., Pnueli A. (1990) Explicit Clock Temporal Logic. In: 5th IEEE Symposium on Logic in Computer Science. IEEE Press, Piscataway, NJ, 402–413
55. He J.F. (1994) From CSP to Hybrid Systems. In: Roscoe A.W. (Ed.) A Classical Mind: Essays in Honour of C.A.R. Hoare. Prentice Hall International, London, 171–190
56. He J.F. (1995) Provably Correct Systems: Modelling of Communication Languages and Design of Optimized Compilers. McGraw-Hill, New York
57. He J.F. (2000) An Integrated Approach to Hardware/Software Co-design. In: Yulin Feng, Notkin D., Gaudel M.-C. (Eds.) ICS 2000, 16th IFIP World Computer Congress 2000. Publishing House of Electronics Industry, Beijing, 5–16
58. He J.F., Bowen J. (1992) Time Interval Semantics and Implementation of a Real-Time Programming Language. In: 1992 Euromicro Workshop on Real-Time Systems. IEEE Press, Piscataway, NJ, 110–115
59. He J.F., Verbovsky V. (2002) Integrating CSP and DC. In: Proceedings of the 8th IEEE International Conference on Engineering of Complex Computer Systems. IEEE Press, Piscataway, NJ, 47–54
60. He J.F., Xu Q.W. (2000) Advanced Features of the Duration Calculus. In: Davies J., Roscoe B., Woodcock J. (Eds.) Millennial Perspectives in Computer Science. Palgrave Macmillan, Houndmills, Hampshire, 133–146
61. He J.F., Xu Q.W. (2000) An Operational Semantics of a Simulator Algorithm. In: Arabnia H.R. (Ed.) Prococeedings of the International Conference on Parallel and Distributed Processing Techniques and Applications. CSREA Press, Las Vegas, 203–208
62. He W.D., Zhou C.C. (1995) A Case Study of Optimization. The Computer Journal 38(9):734–746
63. Hoenicke J., Olderog E.-R. (2002) CSP-OZ-DC: A Combination of Specification Techniques for Processes, Data and Time. Nordic Journal of Computing 9(4):301–334
64. Hong K.T., Dang V.H. (2001) Formal Design of Hybrid Control Systems: Duration Calculus Approach. In: Proceedings of the 25th Annual International Computer Software and Applications Conference. IEEE Press, Piscataway, NJ, 423–428

65. Hopcroft J.E., Ullman J.D. (1979) Introduction to Automata Theory, Languages, and Computation. Addison-Wesley, Reading, Massachusetts
66. Hughes G.E., Crestwell M.J. (1968) An Introduction to Modal Logic. Routledge, London
67. Huizing C., Gerth R., de Roever W.P. (1988) Modelling StateCharts Behaviour in a Fully-Abstract way. In: Dauchet M., Nivat M. (Eds.) CAAP'88, Lecture Notes in Computer Science 299. Springer, Berlin, Heidelberg, 271–294
68. Inal R. (1994) Modular Specification of Real-Time Systems. In: 1994 Euromicro Workshop on Real-Time Systems. IEEE Press, Piscataway, NJ, 16–21
69. Jahanian F., Mok. A.K.-L. (1986) Safety Analysis of Timing Properties in Real-Time Systems. IEEE Transactions on Software Engineering 12(9):890–904
70. Kesten Y., Pnueli A., Sifakis J., Yovine S. (1993) Integration Graphs: A Class of Decidable Hybrid Systems. In: Grossman R.L., Nerode A., Ravn A.P., Rischel H. (Eds.) Hybrid Systems, Lecture Notes in Computer Science 736. Springer, Berlin, Heidelberg, 179–208
71. Kleuker C. (2000) Constraint Diagrams. PhD thesis, Oldenburg University, Germany
72. Koymans R. (1990) Specifying Real-Time Properties with Metric Temporal Logic. Real-Time Systems 2(4):255–299
73. Koymans R. (1992) Specifying Message Passing and Time-Critical Systems with Temporal Logic, Lecture Notes in Computer Science 651. Springer, Berlin, Heidelberg
74. Kääramees M. (1995) Transformation of Duration Calculus Specifications to DISCO Language. Master's thesis, Tallinn Technical University, Estonia
75. Kääramees M. (1995) Transforming Designs Towards Implementations. In: 1995 Euromicro Workshop on Real-Time Systems. IEEE Press, Piscataway, NJ, 197–204
76. Lamport L. (1993) Hybrid Systems in TLA$^+$. In: Grossman R.L., Nerode A., Ravn A.P., Rischel H. (Eds.) Hybrid Systems, Lecture Notes in Computer Science 736. Springer, Berlin, Heidelberg, 77–102
77. Larsen K.G., Skou A. (1991) Bisimulation Through Probabilistic Testing. Information and Computation 94(1):1–28
78. Li L., He J.F. (1999) A Denotational Semantics of Timed RSL using Duration Calculus. In: Proceedings of the Sixth International Conference on Real-Time Computing Systems and Applications. IEEE Press, Piscataway, NJ, 492–503
79. Li X.S. (1993) A Mean Value Calculus. PhD thesis, Software Institute, Academia Sinica
80. Li X.D., Dang V.H. (1996) Checking Linear Duration Invariants by Linear Programming. In: Jaffar J., Roland H., Yap C. (Eds.) Concurrency and Parallelism, Programming, Networking, and Security, Lecture Notes in Computer Science 1179. Springer, Berlin, Heidelberg, 321–332
81. Li X.D., Dang V.H., Zheng T. (1997) Checking Hybrid Automata for Linear Duration Invariants. In: Shyamasundar R.K., Ueda K. (Eds.) Advances in Computing Science, ASIAN '97, Lecture Notes in Computer Science 1345. Springer, Berlin, Heidelberg, 166–180
82. Li ., Li ., Zhao J., Zheng G. (2003) Duration-Constrained Regular Expressions. Formal Aspects of Computing. To appear
83. Li X.S., Wang J.A. (1996) Specifying Optimal Design of a Steam-Boiler System. In: Abrial J.-R., Börger E., Langmaack H. (Eds.) Formal Methods for Industrial Applications, Lecture Notes in Computer Science 1165. Springer, Berlin, Heidelberg, 359–378

84. Li Y., Dang V.H. (2002) Checking Temporal Duration Properties of Timed Automata. Journal of Computer Science and Technology 17(6):689–698

85. Liu C.L., Layland. J.W. (1973) Scheduling Algorithm for Multiprogramming in a Hard Real-Time Environment. Journal of the ACM 20(1):46–61

86. Liu Z. (1996) Specification and Verification in DC. In: Joseph M. (Ed.) Mathematics of Dependable Systems, International Series in Computer Science. Prentice Hall, London, 182–228

87. Liu Z., Nordahl J., Sørensen E.V. (1995) Composition and Refinement of Probabilistic Real-Time Systems. In: Mitchell C., Stavridou V. (Eds.) Mathematics of Dependable Systems. Oxford University Press, Oxford, 149–163

88. Liu Z., Ravn A.P., Li X.S. (2003) Unifying Proof Methodologies of Duration Calculus and Timed Linear Temporal Logic. Formal Aspects of Computing. To appear

89. Liu Z., Ravn A.P., Sørensen E.V., Zhou C.C. (1993) A Probabilistic Duration Calculus. In: Kopetz H., Kakuda Y. (Eds.) Dependable Computing and Fault-Tolerant Systems Vol. 7: Responsive Computer Systems. Springer, Berlin, Heidelberg, 30–52

90. Liu Z., Ravn A.P., Sørensen E.V., Zhou C.C. (1994) Towards a Calculus of Systems Dependability. High Integrity Systems 1(1):49–75

91. Maler O., Manna Z., Pnueli A. (1992) From Timed to Hybrid Systems. In: de Bakker J.W., Huizing C., de Roever W.P., Rozenberg G. (Eds.) Real-Time: Theory in Practice, Lecture Notes in Computer Science 600. Springer, Berlin, Heidelberg, 447–484

92. Manna Z., Pnueli A. (1993) Verifying Hybrid Systems. In: Grossman R.L., Nerode A., Ravn A.P., Rischel H. (Eds.) Hybrid Systems, Lecture Notes in Computer Science 736. Springer, Berlin, Heidelberg, 4–35

93. Mao X.G., Xu Q.W., Dang V.H., Wang J. (1996) Towards a Proof Assistant for Interval Logics. UNU/IIST Report No. 77, International Institute for Software Technology, Macau

94. P.C. Masiero, A.P. Ravn, and H. Rischel. (1993) Refinement of real-time specifications. ProCoS Technical Report ID/DTH PCM 1/1, Department of Computer Science, Technical University of Denmark, Lyngby

95. Middelburg C.A. (1998) Truth of Duration Calculus Formulae in Timed Frames. Fundamenta Informaticae Journal 36(2/3):235–263

96. Minsky M.L. (1967) Computation: Finite and Infinite Machines. Prentice Hall, Englewood Cliffs, NJ

97. Moszkowski B. (1995) Compositional Reasoning about Projected and Infinite Time. In: First International Conference on Engineering of Complex Computer Systems. IEEE Press, Piscataway, NJ, 238–245

98. Mørk S., Godskesen J.C., Hansen M.R., Sharp R. (1996) A Timed Semantics for SDL. In: Gotzhein R., Bredereke J. (Eds.) Formal Description Techniques IX: Theory, Application and Tools. Chapman & Hall, London, 295–309

99. Nicollin X., Olivero A., Sifakis J., Yovine S. (1993) An Approach to the Description and Analysis of Hybrid Systems. In: Grossman R.L., Nerode A., Ravn A.P., Rischel H. (Eds.) Hybrid Systems, Lecture Notes in Computer Science 736. Springer, Berlin, Heidelberg, 149–178

100. Olderog E.-R., Ravn A.P., Skakkebæk J.U. (1996) Refining System Requirements to Program Specifications. In: Heitmeyer C., Mandrioli D. (Eds.) Formal Methods in Real-Time Systems, Trends in Software-Engineering. Wiley, London, 107–134

101. Owre S., Shankar N., Rushby J. (1993) Users Guide for the PVS Specification and Verification System, Language, and Proof Checker (beta release) (three

volumes). Technical report, Computer Science Laboratory, SRI International, Menlo Park, CA

102. Pandya P.K. (1996) Some Extensions to Propositional Mean Value Calculus: Expressiveness and Decidability. In: Kleine Buening H. (Ed.) CSL'95, Lecture Notes in Computer Science 1092. Springer, Berlin, Heidelberg, 434–451

103. Pandya P.K. (1996) Weak Chop Inverses and Liveness in Duration Calculus. In: Jonsson B., Parrow J. (Eds.) Formal Techniques in Real-Time and Fault-Tolerant Systems, Lecture Notes in Computer Science 1135. Springer, Berlin, Heidelberg, 148–167

104. Pandya P.K. (2001) Model Checking CTL*[DC]. In: Margaria T., Wang Yi (Eds.) Tools and Algorithms for the Construction and Analysis of Systems, Lecture Notes in Computer Science 2031. Springer, Berlin, Heidelberg, 559–573

105. Pandya P.K. (2001) Specifying and Deciding Quantified Discrete-Time Duration Calculus Formulae using DCVALID: An automata theoretical approach. In: Workshop on Real-Time Tools (RTTOOLS'2001), Aalborg

106. Pandya P.K. (2002) Interval Duration Calculus: Expressiveness and Decidability. In: Asarin E., Maler O., Yovine S. (Eds.) Electronic Notes in Theoretical Computer Science 65:6. Elsevier, Amsterdam

107. Pandya P.K., Dang V.H. (1998) Duration Calculus with Weakly Monotonic Time. In: Ravn A.P., Rischel H. (Eds.) Formal Techniques in Real-Time and Fault-Tolerant Systems, Lecture Notes in Computer Science 1486. Springer, Berlin, Heidelberg, 55–64

108. Pandya P.K., Ramakrishna Y.S. (1998) A Recursive Mean Value Calculus. In: Arvind V., Ramanujam R. (Eds.) FSTTCS 1998, Lecture Notes in Computer Science 1530. Springer, Berlin, Heidelberg, 257–268

109. Pandya P.K., Ramakrishna Y.S., Shyamasundar R.K. (1995) A Compositional Semantics of Esterel in Duration Calculus. Technical report, Computer Science Group, TIFR, Bombay

110. Pandya P.K., Wang H.P., Xu Q.W. (1998) Towards a Theory of Sequential Hybrid Systems. In: Gries D., de Roever W.-P. (Eds.) PROCOMET'98. Chapman & Hall, London, 366–384

111. Paulson L.C. (1994) Isabelle, A Generic Theorem Prover, Lecture Notes in Computer Science 828. Springer, Berlin, Heidelberg

112. Pavlova E., Dang V.H. (1999) A Formal Specification of the Concurrency Control in Real-Time Databases. In: Proceedings of the 6th Asia–Pacific Software Engineering Conference. IEEE Press, Piscataway, NJ, 94–101

113. Petersen J.L., Rischel H. (1994) Formalizing Requirements and Design for a Production Cell System. In: Symposium ADPM '94: Automatisation des Processus Mixtes: Les Systemes Dynamiques Hybrides. Belgian Institute of Automatic Control, BIRA, Antwerpen, 37–46

114. Qiu Z.Y., Zhou C.C. (1998) A Combination of Interval Logic and Linear Temporal Logic. In: Gries D., de Roever W.-P. (Eds.) Programming Concepts and Methods. Chapman & Hall, London, 444–461

115. Rabinovich A. (1998) Nonelementary Lower Bound for Propositional Duration Calculus. Information Processing Letters 66:7–11

116. Rabinovich A. (1998) On the Decidability of Continuous Time Specification Formalisms. Journal of Logic and Computation 8(5):669-678

117. Rabinovich A. (2000) Expressive Completeness of Duration Calculus. Information and Computation, 156(1-2):320–344

118. Rabinovich A. (2000) Succinctness Gap between Monadic Logic and Duration Calculus. Fundamenta Informaticae, 44:1–10

119. Rabinovich A. (2002) Finite Variability Interpretation of Monadic Logic of Order. Theoretical Computer Science, 275(1-2):111–125

120. Rasmussen T.M. (1999) Signed Interval Logic. In: Flum J., Rodriguez-Artalejo M. (Eds.) Computer Science Logic, CSL'99, Lecture Notes in Computer Science 1683. Springer, Berlin, Heidelberg, 157–171

121. Rasmussen T.M. (2001) Automated Proof Support for Interval Logics. In: Nieuwenhuis R., Voronkov A. (Eds.) LPAR 2001, Lecture Notes in Artificial Intelligence 2250. Springer, Berlin, Heidelberg, 317–326

122. Rasmussen T.M. (2001) Labelled Natural Deduction for Interval Logics. In: Fribourg L. (Ed.) Computer Science Logic, CSL'01, Lecture Notes in Computer Science 2142. Springer, Berlin, Heidelberg, 308–323

123. Rasmussen T.M. (2002) Interval Logic: Proof Theory and Theorem Proving. PhD thesis, Technical University of Denmark, Lyngby

124. Ravn A.P. (1995) Design of Embedded Real-Time Computing Systems. Doctoral dissertation, Technical University of Denmark, Lyngby

125. Ravn A.P., Eriksen T.J., Holdgaard M., Rischel H. (1998) Engineering of Real-Time Systems with an Experiment in Hybrid Control. In: Rozenberg G., Vaandrager F.W. (Eds.) Embedded Systems, Lecture Notes in Computer Science 1494. Springer, Berlin, Heidelberg, 316–352

126. Ravn A.P., Rischel H. (1991) Requirements Capture for Embedded Real-Time Systems. In: Proceedings of IMACS-MCTS'91 Symposium on Modelling and Control of Technological Systems, Villeneuve d'Ascq, France, volume 2. IMACS, Paris, 147–152

127. Ravn A.P., Rischel H., Hansen K.M. (1993) Specifying and Verifying Requirements of Real-Time Systems. IEEE Transactions on Software Engineering 19(1):41–55

128. Rischel H. (1992) A Duration Calculus Proof of Fischer's Mutual Exclusion Protocol. ProCoS II, ESPRIT BRA 7071, Report No. DTH HR 4/1, Department of Computer Science, Technical University of Denmark, Lyngby

129. Roscoe A.W., Hoare C.A.R. (1988) The Laws of OCCAM Programming. Theoretical Computer Science 60:177–229

130. Roy S., Zhou C.C. (1997) Notes on Neighbourhood Logic. UNU/IIST Report No. 97, International Institute for Software Technology, Macau

131. Satpathy M., Dang V.H., Pandya P.K. (1998) Some Results on the Decidability of Duration Calculus under Synchronous Interpretation. In: Ravn A.P., Rischel H. (Eds.) Formal Techniques in Real-Time and Fault-Tolerant Systems, Lecture Notes in Computer Science 1486. Springer, Berlin, Heidelberg, 186–197

132. Schenke M. (1994) Specification and Transformation of Reactive Systems with Time Restrictions and Concurrency. In: Langmack H., de Roever W.-P., Vytopil J. (Eds.) Formal Techniques in Real-Time and Fault-Tolerant Systems, Lecture Notes in Computer Science 863. Springer, Berlin, Heidelberg, 605–620

133. Schenke M. (1995) Requirements to Programs: A Development Methodology for Real Time Systems, Part 2. Technical report, Fachbereich Informatik, Universität Oldenburg, Germany

134. Schenke M., Olderog E.-R. (1995) Requirements to Programs: A Development Methodology for Real Time Systems, Part 1. Technical report, Fachbereich Informatik, Universität Oldenburg, Germany

135. Schenke M., Ravn A.P. (1996) Refinement from a Control Problem to Programs. In: Abrial J.-R., Börger E., Langmaack H. (Eds.) Formal Methods for Industrial Applications, Lecture Notes in Computer Science 1165. Springer, Berlin, Heidelberg, 403–427

136. Schneider G., Xu Q.W. (1998) Towards a Formal Semantics of Verilog using Duration Calculus. In: Ravn A.P., Rischel H. (Eds.) Formal Techniques in Real-Time and Fault-Tolerant Systems, Lecture Notes in Computer Science 1486. Springer, Berlin, Heidelberg, 282–293

137. Siewe F., Dang V.H. (2000) From Continuous Specification to Discrete Design. In: Notkin D., Yulin Feng, Gaudel M.-C. (Eds.) Proceedings of the International Conference on Software: Theory and Practice. Publishing House of Electronics Industry, Beijing, 407–414.

138. Siewe F., Dang V.H. (2001) Deriving Real-Time Programs from Duration Calculus Specification. In: Margaria T., Melham T. (Eds.) Correct Hardware Design and Verification Methods, Lecture Notes in Computer Science 2144. Springer, Berlin, Heidelberg, 92–97

139. Skakkebæk J.U. (1994) Liveness and Fairness in Duration Calculus. In: Jonsson B., Parrow J. (Eds.) CONCUR'94: Concurrency Theory, Lecture Notes in Computer Science 836. Springer Verlag, 283–298

140. Skakkebæk J.U. (1994) A Verification Assistant for a Real-Time Logic. PhD thesis, Technical University of Denmark, Lyngby

141. Skakkebæk J.U., Ravn A.P., Rischel H., Zhou C.C. (1992) Specification of Embedded, Real-Time Systems. In: Proceedings of 1992 Euromicro Workshop on Real-Time Systems. IEEE Press, Piscataway, NJ, 116-121

142. Skakkebæk J.U., Sestoft P. (1994) Checking Validity of Duration Calculus Formulas. ProCoS II, ESPRIT BRA 7071, Report No. ID/DTH JUS 3/1, Department of Computer Science, Technical University of Denmark

143. Skakkebæk J.U., Shankar N. (1993) A Duration Calculus Proof Checker: Using PVS as a Semantic Framework. Report No. SRI-CSL-93-10, Computer Science Laboratory, SRI International, Menlo Park, CA

144. Skakkebæk J.U., Shankar N. (1994) Towards a Duration Calculus Proof Assistant in PVS. In: Langmack H., de Roever W.-P., Vytopil J. (Eds.) Formal Techniques in Real-Time and Fault-Tolerant Systems, Lecture Notes in Computer Science 863. Springer, Berlin, Heidelberg, 660–679

145. Sørensen E.V., Ravn A.P., Rischel H. (1990) Control Program for a Gas Burner: Part 1: Informal Requirements, ProCoS Case Study 1. ProCoS I, ESPRIT BRA 3104, Report No. ID/DTH EVS2, Department of Computer Science, Technical University of Denmark, Lyngby

146. Tapken J., Dierks H. (1998) Moby/PLC – Graphical Development of PLC-Automata. In: Ravn A.P., Rischel H. (Eds.) Formal Techniques in Real-Time and Fault-Tolerant Systems, Lecture Notes in Computer Science 1486. Springer, Berlin, Heidelberg, 311–314

147. Venema Y. (1990) Expressiveness and Completeness of an Interval Tense Logic. Notre Dame Journal of Formal Logic 31(4):529–547

148. Venema Y. (1991) A Modal Logic for Chopping Intervals. Journal of Logic and Computation 1(4):453–476

149. Wang J., He W.D. (1996) Formal Specification of Stability in Hybrid Control Systems. In: Alur R., Henzinger T.A., Sontag E.D. (Eds.) Hybrid Systems III, Lecture Notes in Computer Science 1066. Springer, Berlin, Heidelberg, 294–303

150. Wang J.Z., Xu Q.W., Ma H.D. (2000) Modelling and Verification of Network Player System with DCVALID. In: Tse T.H., Chen T.Y. (Eds.) First Asia–Pacific Conference on Quality Software. IEEE Press, Piscataway, NJ, 44–49

151. Widjaja B.H., He W.D., Chen Z.J., Zhou C.C. (1996) A Cooperative Design for Hybrid Control Systems. In: Pnueli A., Lin H. (Eds.) Proceedings of Logic and Software Engineering International Workshop in Honor of Chih-Sung Tang. World Scientific Press, Singapore, 127–150

152. Xu Q.W. (1997) Semantics and Verification of the Extended Phase Transition Systems in the Duration Calculus. In: Maler O. (Ed.) Proceedings of International Workshop on Hybrid and Real-Time Systems, Lecture Notes in Computer Science 1201. Springer, Berlin, Heidelberg, 301–315

153. Xu Q.W., He W.D. (1996) Hierarchical Design of a Chemical Concentration Control System. In: Alur R., Henzinger T.A., Sontag D.E. (Eds.) Hybrid Systems III: Verification and Control, Lecture Notes in Computer Science 1066. Springer, Berlin, Heidelberg, 270–281

154. Xu Q.W., Swarup M. (1998) Compositional Reasoning using Assumption-Commitment Paradigm. In: Langmaack H., Pnueli A., de Roever W.-P. (Eds.) Compositionality – The Significant Difference, Lecture Notes in Computer Science 1536. Springer, Berlin, Heidelberg, 565–583

155. Xu Q.W., Yang Z.Y. (1996) Derivation of Control Programs: a Heating System. UNU/IIST Report No. 73, International Institute for Software Technology, Macau

156. Yu H.Q., Pandya P.K., Sun Y.Q. (1994) A Calculus for Hybrid Sampled Data Systems. In Langmack H., de Roever W.-P., Vytopil J. (Eds.) Formal Techniques in Real-Time and Fault-Tolerant Systems, Lecture Notes in Computer Science 863. Springer, Berlin, Heidelberg, 716–737

157. Yu X.Y., Wang J., Zhou C.C., Pandya P.K. (1994) Formal Design of Hybrid Systems. In: Langmack H., de Roever W.-P., Vytopil J. (Eds) Formal Techniques in Real-Time and Fault-Tolerant Systems, Lecture Notes in Computer Science 863. Springer, Berlin, Heidelberg, 738–755

158. Zhao J.H., Dang V.H. (1998) On Checking Real-Time Parallel Systems for Linear Duration Properties. In: Ravn A.P., Rischel H. (Eds.) Formal Techniques in Real-Time and Fault-Tolerant Systems, Lecture Notes in Computer Science 1486. Springer, Berlin, Heidelberg, 241–250

159. Zhao J.H., Dang V.H. (2000) Checking Timed Automata for some Discretisable Duration Properties. Journal of Computer Science and Technology, 15(5):423–429

160. Zheng Y.H., Zhou C.C. (1994) A Formal Proof of the Deadline Driven Scheduler. In: Langmack H., de Roever W.-P., Vytopil J.(Eds.) Formal Techniques in Real-Time and Fault-Tolerant Systems, Lecture Notes in Computer Science 863. Springer, Berlin, Heidelberg, 756–775

161. Zhou C.C. (1993) Duration Calculi: An Overview. In: Bjørner D., Broy M., Pottosin I.V. (Eds.) Proceedings of Formal Methods in Programming and Their Applications, Lecture Notes in Computer Science 735. Springer, Berlin, Heidelberg, 256–266

162. Zhou C.C., Dang V.H., Li X.S. (1995) A Duration Calculus with Infinite Intervals. In: Reichel H. (Ed.) Fundamentals of Computation Theory, Lecture Notes in Computer Science 965. Springer, Berlin, Heidelberg, 16–41

163. Zhou C.C., Guelev D.P., Zhan N. (2000) A Higher-Order Duration Calculus. In: Davies J., Roscoe B., Woodcock J. (Eds.) Millennial Perspectives in Computer Science. Palgrave Macmillan, Houndmills, Hampshire, 407–416

164. Zhou C.C., Hansen M.R. (1996) Chopping a Point. In: Cooke J., He Jifeng, Wallis, P. (Eds.) BCS–FACS 7th Refinement Workshop, Electronic Workshops in Computing. Springer, Berlin, Heidelberg

165. Zhou C.C., Hansen M.R. (1998) An Adequate First Order Logic of Intervals. In: Langmaack H., de Roever W.-P., Pnueli A. (Eds.) Compositionality: The Significant Difference, Lecture Notes in Computer Science 1536. Springer, Berlin, Heidelberg, 584–608

166. Zhou C.C., Hansen M.R., Ravn A.P., Rischel H. (1991) Duration Specifications for Shared Processors. In: Vytopil J. (Ed.) Symposium on Formal Techniques

in Real-Time and Fault Tolerant Systems, Lecture Notes in Computer Science 571. Springer, Berlin, Heidelberg, 21–32

167. Zhou C.C., Hansen M.R., Sestoft P. (1993) Decidability and Undecidability Results for Duration Calculus. In: Enjalbert P., Finkel A., Wagner K.W. (Eds.) STACS'93, Lecture Notes in Computer Science 665. Springer, Berlin, Heidelberg, 58–68

168. Zhou C.C., Hoare C.A.R., Ravn A.P. (1991) A Calculus of Durations. Information Processing Letters 40(5):269–276

169. Zhou C.C., Li X.S. (1994) A Mean Value Calculus of Durations. In: Roscoe A.W. (Ed.) A Classical Mind: Essays in Honour of C.A.R. Hoare. Prentice Hall International, London, 431–451

170. Zhou C.C., Ravn A.P., Hansen M.R. (1993) An Extended Duration Calculus for Hybrid Systems. In: Grossman R.L., Nerode A., Ravn A.P., Rischel H. (Eds.) Hybrid Systems. Lecture Notes in Computer Science 736. Springer, Berlin, Heidelberg, 36–59

171. Zhou C.C., Wang J., Ravn A.P. (1996) A Formal Description of Hybrid Systems. In: Alur R., Henzinger T.A., Sontag E.D. (Eds.) Hybrid Systems III, Lecture Notes in Computer Science 1066. Springer, Berlin, Heidelberg, 511–530

172. Zhou C.C., Zhang J.Z., Yang L., Li X.S. (1994) Linear Duration Invariants. In: Langmack H., de Roever W.-P., Vytopil J. (Eds.) Formal Techniques in Real-Time and Fault-Tolerant Systems, Lecture Notes in Computer Science 863. Springer, Berlin, Heidelberg, 86–109

173. Zhu H.B., He J.F. (2000) A DC-based Semantics for Verilog. In: Notkin D., Yulin Feng, Gaudel M.-C. (Eds.) Proceedings of International Conference on Software: Theory and Practice. Publishing House of Electronics Industry, Beijing, 421–432

Abbreviations

Symbol Index

Index

Monographs in Theoretical Computer Science · An EATCS Series

K. Jensen
Coloured Petri Nets
Basic Concepts, Analysis Methods
and Practical Use, Vol. 1
2nd ed.

K. Jensen
Coloured Petri Nets
Basic Concepts, *Analysis Methods*
and Practical Use, Vol. 2

K. Jensen
Coloured Petri Nets
Basic Concepts, Analysis Methods
and *Practical Use,* Vol. 3

A. Nait Abdallah
The Logic of Partial Information

Z. Fülöp, H. Vogler
Syntax-Directed Semantics
Formal Models Based on Tree Transducers

A. de Luca, S. Varricchio
Finiteness and Regularity
in Semigroups and Formal Languages

E. Best, R. Devillers, M. Koutny
Petri Net Algebra

S.P. Demri, E. S. Orłowska
Incomplete Information:
Structure, Inference, Complexity

J.C.M. Baeten, C.A. Middelburg
Process Algebra with Timing

L. A. Hemaspaandra, L. Torenvliet
Theory of Semi-Feasible Algorithms

E. Fink, D. Wood
Restricted-Orientation Convexity

Zhou Chaochen, M. R. Hansen
Duration Calculus

M. Große-Rhode
Semantic Integration of Heterogeneous
Software Specifications

Texts in Theoretical Computer Science · An EATCS Series

J. L. Balcázar, J. Díaz, J. Gabarró
Structural Complexity I
2nd ed. (see also overleaf, Vol. 22)

M. Garzon
Models of Massive Parallelism
Analysis of Cellular Automata
and Neural Networks

J. Hromkovič
Communication Complexity
and Parallel Computing

A. Leitsch
The Resolution Calculus

G. Păun, G. Rozenberg, A. Salomaa
DNA Computing
New Computing Paradigms

A. Salomaa
Public-Key Cryptography
2nd ed.

K. Sikkel
Parsing Schemata
A Framework for Specification
and Analysis of Parsing Algorithms

H. Vollmer
Introduction to Circuit Complexity
A Uniform Approach

W. Fokkink
Introduction to Process Algebra

K. Weihrauch
Computable Analysis
An Introduction

J. Hromkovič
Algorithmics for Hard Problems
Introduction to Combinatorial Optimization,
Randomization, Approximation, and Heuristics
2nd ed.

S. Jukna
Extremal Combinatorics
With Applications in Computer Science

P. Clote, E. Kranakis
Boolean Functions and Computation
Models

L. A. Hemaspaandra, M. Ogihara
The Complexity Theory Companion

C.S. Calude
Information and Randomness.
An Algorithmic Perspective
2nd ed.

J. Hromkovič
Theoretical Computer Science
Introduction to Automata, Computability,
Complexity, Algorithmics, Randomization,
Communication and Cryptography

A. Schneider
Verification of Reactive Systems
Formal Methods and Algorithms

Former volumes appeared as
EATCS Monographs on Theoretical Computer Science